D0174238

PRAISE FOR GARY HAMEL'S *LEADING THE REVOLUTION*

"Hamel is no armchair revolutionary ... [He] makes a strong case that bringing fresh thinking to the job can produce wealth as well as satisfaction—and rekindle passion for the work, regardless of what it is."
—*BusinessWeek*

"Gary Hamel captures the moment with a no-holds-barred assessment of the issues facing companies all around the world as they struggle to catch up with the new economy."
–Sir Richard Branson, Chairman, Virgin Group

"In *Leading the Revolution*, Hamel provides a blueprint for shaking things up."
—*Newsday*

"Gary Hamel is a sophisticated business thinker."
—*The New York Times*

"Gary Hamel captures the new competitive business environment, one in which dreams and reality merge. *Leading the Revolution* will inspire innovation at all levels and provide insight into opportunities for rewarding revolutionary thinking in new and bigger ways."
–Arthur M. Blank, President & CEO,
The Home Depot, Inc.

GARY HAMEL is a founder and chairman of Strategos, and Visiting Professor of Strategic and International Management at the London Business School. He is the coauthor of the international bestseller *Competing for the Future*. He lives in Woodside, California.

Contact Gary Hamel via e-mail at hamel@leadingtherevolution.com or visit www.leadingtherevolution.com

"Hamel says tomorrow's [business] winners will produce torrents of innovations, of which a few of the most radical will be successes. Out of the torrents of business books published these days, Hamel's is one of those good, if radical, ideas."
—*Entrepreneur*

"As venture capitalists, we like to finance swarms of start-ups that kick the stuffing out of the established companies. So please put this book down. Now slowly back away from the counter ... Because if you and your company put Hamel's revolutionary principles to work, it's going to be a lot harder for our start-ups to take your company by surprise."
–Steve T. Jurvetson, Managing Director,
Draper Fisher Jurvetson

"Gary Hamel conveys his cutting-edge ideas with clearly crafted sentences, using creative and often picturesque wording."
—*Fort Worth Star-Telegram*

"A clarion call for the gray battalions of corporate America to rise up from their trenches and break out of the constraints of conventional management thinking."
—*Strategy + Business*

Gary Hamel
LEADING THE
REVOLUTION

How to Thrive in Turbulent Times
by Making Innovation a Way of Life

A PLUME BOOK

PLUME
Published by the Penguin Group
Penguin Putnam Inc., 375 Hudson Street, New York, New York 10014, U.S.A.
Penguin Books Ltd, 80 Strand, London WC2R 0RL, England
Penguin Books Australia Ltd, Ringwood, Victoria, Australia
Penguin Books Canada Ltd, 10 Alcorn Avenue, Toronto, Ontario, Canada M4V 3B2
Penguin Books (N.Z.) Ltd, 182–190 Wairau Road, Auckland 10, New Zealand

Penguin Books Ltd, Registered Offices: Harmondsworth, Middlesex, England

Published by Plume, a member of Penguin Putnam Inc. This revised and updated
edition is published by arrangement with Harvard Business School Press.
For information address Harvard Business School Press, Boston, Massachusetts 02163.

First Plume Printing, August 2002
10 9 8 7 6 5 4 3 2 1

Copyright © Gary Hamel, 2000, 2002
All rights reserved

 REGISTERED TRADEMARK—MARCA REGISTRADA

The Library of Congress has catalogued the Harvard Business School Press edition as
follows:

Hamel, Gary
    Leading the revolution/Gary Hamel.
    p.   cm.
    Includes bibliographical references and index.
    ISBN 1-57851-189-5 (hc.)
    ISBN 0-452-28324-8 (pbk.)
    1. Creative ability in business. 2. Strategic planning. I. Title.
    HD53.H353 2000
    658.4'012—dc21   00-038920

Printed in the United States of America

Without limiting the rights under copyright reserved above, no part of this publication
may be reproduced, stored in or introduced into a retrieval system, or transmitted, in
any form, or by any means (electronic, mechanical, photocopying, recording, or
otherwise), without the prior written permission of both the copyright owner and the
above publisher of this book.

BOOKS ARE AVAILABLE AT QUANTITY DISCOUNTS WHEN USED TO PROMOTE PRODUCTS OR
SERVICES. FOR INFORMATION PLEASE WRITE TO PREMIUM MARKETING DIVISION, PENGUIN
PUTNAM INC., 375 HUDSON STREET, NEW YORK, NEW YORK 10014.

○ CONTENTS

○ INTRODUCTION TO THE PLUME EDITION

In our newly sober, post–bubble economy, one thing should be clear—there's a difference between helium and oxygen. Dot–com fever was helium. Instant messaging, to take one example, is oxygen—real innovation, not hyperbole. There's a difference between creative accounting and creative business models. Creative accounting brought down Enron, gutting a genuinely creative business model in the process—Enron's online market for energy—which was ultimately sold to UBS AG, Switzerland's largest bank. There's a difference between stupid crazy and smart crazy. Selling pet food on the Web was stupid crazy. Selling PCs online, à la Dell, is smart crazy. There's a difference between an illusory "slash–and–burn" turnaround (remember Chainsaw Al Dunlap) and a wholehearted attempt at renewal (what Steve Ballmer is hoping to bring about with Microsoft.Net). There's a difference between deal makers (Tyco's Dennis Kozlowski, to name just one), and visionaries who build new business (like Sony's Ken Kutaragi, who turned the PlayStation into a knockout success). There's a difference between self–serving executives (Enron's Andrew Fastow springs to mind) and those who labor tirelessly to advance a world–changing idea (Steve Jobs and the original Macintosh). There's a difference between a compelling "story" and a rock–solid profit model. "Broadband" à la Global Crossing, Williams Companies, et al. was a story; satellite TV is a profit model. There's a difference between doing your job (you'd rather be anywhere else) and having a cause (there's nothing you'd rather be doing). Most of all, there's a difference between bland incrementalism and rock–the–industry innovation. Cup holders are nice. One hundred channels of mostly commercial–free radio in your car is to die for. (Thanks, XM Radio!)

This book is all about these differences—it's about distinguishing rule–busting, profit–producing innovation from more–of–the–same improvement programs dressed up in revolutionary rhetoric. It's about understanding the difference between getting better and getting different—and then learning how to get different in ways that will stun competitors and thrill customers. It's about differentiating between catching up and breaking out, and then moving beyond best practice to invent new practice. It's about distinguishing between innovation as a buzzword and innovation as a deeply embedded, corporation-wide capability. It's about the difference between being a corporate serf and being a corporate citizen, between accepting your lot and changing your world. The ability to recognize and act on these differences will be, I believe, the distinguishing characteristic of companies that thrive in the turbulent times ahead.

In the wake of the dot-com fizzle, various accounting scandals and a suddenly unforgiving business environment, it's easy to be cynical. This is a book about innovation, about the quest to escape the old and embrace the new. But, you may ask, is that really what the world needs right now? Is innovation what *my* company needs? Didn't the new economy falter because there was *too much* innovation? What about Enron—it was named America's most innovative company for five years running by *Fortune* magazine—what kind of an advertisement for innovation is *that*? In tough times, retrenchment seems like a safer bet than bold forays into untested market territory. And, you might add, this isn't exactly the best time to be raising one's head above the corporate parapet. OK, fair enough, but remember—overhyped, over-funded dot-com business models were to real innovation what phone sex is to true love—a shallow surrogate for something deep and lasting. Enron's mistake wasn't that it innovated, but that it tried to be as inventive with its balance sheet as it had been in its core business—that, and the fact that it rushed pell-mell over the line that separates ambition from hubris. And as for retrenchment—it's a perfectly understandable response to an unexpectedly severe downturn of the sort that recently wreaked havoc in the semiconductor industry—but retrenchment is completely inadequate if your goal is to flourish in a world of disorderly, never-ending change. Retrenchment buys you time, but it won't buy you opportunity. It won't buy you growth and it won't buy you a future.

So what is the case for innovation upon which this book rests? Why, given all the above, should you devote a good chunk of your time to mastering the disciplines of radical innovation? Because, quite simply, you have no alternative. Yes, the dot-com bubble burst, as anyone who understands the principles of competitive advantage knew it would. Yes, chastened CFOs have sworn an oath to tell the truth, the whole truth and nothing but the truth. Yes, all those venture funds and corporate incubators were a sideshow—a junk-food substitute for the meat-and-potatoes work of building solid new businesses while simultaneously renewing the core. And yes, "back to basics" is once again in fashion. But it would be a profound mistake to believe that nothing has changed—that the new millennium is distinguished from the old by nothing more than a few numbers on the calendar.

Something *has* changed. Something *is* different. The signs are all around you. CEOs have been losing their jobs at a record pace. Newcomers have been capturing a growing share of the market value in a host of industries. Customers have been growing more restless, demanding and fickle. Web-enabled connectivity has been reshaping value chains. New technologies have been undermining old business models—from publishing to radio to pharmaceuticals. Traditional strategies for pumping up profits and the share price—incremental cost cutting, megamergers, share buybacks, outsourcing and financial engineering—have been losing their punch. Something *is* going on here.

Yes, the "long boom" of the 1990s was an aberration, not to be repeated anytime soon. But the 1990s and all that "new economy" blather were more than some kind of weird anomaly in the otherwise steady course of economic history. The 1990s were a time when investors, companies and consumers struggled to make sense of a world in which change no longer ambled, nor even ran, but lurched spasmodically in new directions. What *is* different and what will remain different is change itself. We have reached a tipping point, a point where the cumulative impact of social, geopolitical, technological, organizational and biological discontinuities has changed change itself. We are about to find out which organizations are truly resilient and which are not.

In recent years, many companies got a boost from the "irrational exuberance" of investors, a polite term for the temporary insanity that decoupled share prices from earnings. Investors may be less exuberant, but they're still demanding and more impatient than ever. In this environment, any company that hopes to do better than its dull-as-dishwater peers will need to be capable of innovating in ways its competitors can't or won't. This is the challenge of *industry revolution*. Innovation is the only cure for the debilitating hypercompetition that drives margins ever downward. Yet it is not enough to innovate with respect to one's industry, one must be capable of innovating with respect to one's past, as well. There are dozens, maybe hundreds, of industry revolutionaries who've never led a second revolution. Yesterday's insurgents are today's incumbents. Hence a second challenge—that of *corporate renewal*. Renewal is the capacity to reinvent not only processes and systems but purpose and mission as well. Revolution and renewal—these are the twin themes of this book, and they are imperatives for any organization and any individual who hope to stay relevant in a tough and testing world where more-of-the-same is a sure route to ir-relevance.

Change is the mother of both opportunity and calamity—opportunity for those who are as fleet of foot as change itself and calamity for those with an inappropriate affection for the past. This is not a book about how to *cope* with change. We're aiming higher than that. This is a book about how to ride the winds of change, a book about what it takes to change the course of change to one's own advantage. So enough with the apprehension already. We're in danger of throwing the baby out with the bathwater. Let's jettison the irrationality, but let's keep the exuberance. For never before in history have human beings lived in an age so pregnant with possibility.

To meet the twin challenges of revolution and renewal, you and your colleagues are going to have to throw out many of the industrial-age beliefs you are carrying around in your heads right now. While there are a clutch of industrial-age virtues that will survive the turbulent times ahead, there is a great swath of managerial and organizational orthodoxy that will not. A few examples ...

> ... Senior executives set corporate direction.
> ... Resources get *allocated*—from the top.
> ... Our core business will always be our core business.
> ... Predictability is better than serendipity.
> ... Radical equals risky.
> ... Experience is more valuable than curiosity.
> ... Entrepreneurship is something that happens on the fringes of the organization.
> ... Alignment is better than dissension.

Expunging these superannuated beliefs won't be easy. Like veins of mold in a richly marbled wedge of Stilton, the vestiges of industrial-age dogma are found everywhere—in start-ups, in savvy e-businesses and in industry stalwarts. For this reason, we must address the challenge of innovation from many angles. We must:

○ Build a case as to why innovation belongs atop the corporate transformation agenda.

○ Understand how business concept innovation is different from R&D and new product development.

○ Learn how to tell the difference between smart innovation and dumb innovation.

○ Help individuals see beyond the familiar in order to discover truly unconventional—and truly profitable—opportunities.

○ Teach individuals how to prevail against "the system," with its built-in bias toward perpetuation rather than innovation.

○ Plant the seeds of perpetual renewal deeply within companies, helping even industry veterans become "gray-haired revolutionaries."

○ Make innovation a systemic capability rather than an exceptional and singular act.

It is to this challenging agenda that I and my colleagues at Strategos have devoted ourselves over the past many years. This book is a distillation of what we have learned about helping companies *lead the revolution*.

This is a book for those who want to make a difference—in their world and in their organization. It is a manifesto and a manual. It is a book for those who refuse to surrender to cynicism. It is a book for those who believe the future is something you create, not something that happens to you. It is a book for those who believe passion is just as important as profits. It is a book for those who refuse to believe that large companies can't innovate or that small companies can't escape their first business model.

This is a book for those who are unwilling to play it safe. It is a book for those who are unwilling to sacrifice their dreams on the altar of conventional wisdom. It is a book for those who care so much about their customers, their colleagues and their own legacy that they simply can't imagine not leading the revolution.

ACKNOWLEDGMENTS

Whatever the shortcomings of this book, they are mine; whatever its strengths, they owe much to the generous contributions of others. In large part, this book is the product of what I and my colleagues at Strategos have learned from the thousands of individuals we have had the privilege of working with in our worldwide innovation practice.

Peter Skarzynski, Strategos's CEO, shouldered a disproportionate share of executive burdens as I took time off to write this book. For this, I thank him. I also thank him and his colleagues for demonstrating so conclusively that the principles laid out in this book really *can* ignite revolutionary passions and spawn rule-breaking strategies in companies of every size and shape.

Professor Peter Williamson of INSEAD, founder of the Strategos Institute, played an important role in helping to develop several of the key conceptual themes of this book. Mark Bonchek and Robert Chapman Wood, part of the original Institute research team, deserve credit for helping to crystallize the idea of "innovation styles," and for illuminating many of the impediments to innovation that exist in large companies. Pierre Loewe and David Crosswhite also made a significant contribution to the development of the Institute's point of view on innovation and, thereby, my own understanding. Peter Birkeland spent a year as my personal research associate, navigating through an ocean of financial data in order to better document the diminishing returns achieved by cost–cutting, reengineering and other incremental improvement programs. Michael Hickcox, an extraordinarily capable researcher, worked to develop much of the anecdotal evidence used throughout the book.

Liisa Valikangas and Amy Muller, also of the Strategos Institute, informed and challenged me in countless ways. Their success in developing tools and methods for "strategy activists" further strengthened my belief that so–called ordinary employees can indeed re–vector even the largest and most hidebound of companies. Anthony Campbell, a consultant at Strategos, also provided valuable research support. Ellen Pruyne, a researcher at the Harvard Business School, helped me identify the important parallels between political and corporate activism.

Erick Schonfeld took a six–month leave of absence from his responsibilities as a writer at *Fortune* to help me prepare key sections of the manuscript. As research partner, sounding board and writer, he played a critical role in documenting the successes of real–world corporate activists and in describing the practices of companies that seem to have found the secret of perpetual innovation. His enthusiasm, diligence and professionalism were a blessing.

There are many who let me interrupt their busy lives so that I might better understand the challenge of building revolutionary strategies. Faith Popcorn, Jim Barksdale, Andy Bechtolsheim, Jim Clark, John Seely Brown, Marc Andreessen, Bill Gross, Alan Kay, John Naisbitt, Nick Negroponte and Jim Taylor helped me better understand what it takes to be a seer, a heretic and a serial revolutionary. Courageous activists like John Patrick, David Grossman, Ken Kutaragi and Georges Dupont-Roc took the time to teach me about what it takes to change large, complicated organizations when you're *not* the CEO. And executives at GE Capital, Charles Schwab, Cemex, UPS, Disney, Virgin and Shell helped me uncover some of the secrets of perpetual innovation.

Marjorie Williams, of the Harvard Business School Press, exercised an extraordinarily deft hand in her role as editor. She strengthened the manuscript in countless ways. At the beginning of this project, I asked the HBS Press team to help me produce a book that wouldn't look like a typical, turgid business tome. To the extent we have succeeded in this, much of the credit must go to the superb design and art program created by Mike Fender and Anton Marc. Thanks also to Carol Franco, Director of the HBS Press, who committed the Press so enthusiastically and completely to the success of this book. Suffice to say, I count it as an enormous privilege to have worked with the remarkable HBSP team, including Chuck Dresner, Genoveva Llosa, Katie Mascaro, Sarah McConville, Greg Mroczek, Barbara Roth, Gayle Treadwell and Leslie Zheutlin. I am also most grateful to the fantastic team at Penguin/Putnam, Sara Bixler, Trena Keating and Kathryn Court, for their commitment to the book and all they did to make it accessible to a wider audience through this paperback edition.

More than anyone else, it is Grace Reim who made this book possible. In addition to her substantial duties within the Strategos Institute, she voluntarily took on the task of project manager for what turned out to be a two-year, globe-spanning enterprise. Her spectacular competence and unflagging dedication made this book possible.

Writing entails long periods of solitude when family responsibilities are all too easily neglected. I am deeply grateful to my wife, Eldona, and my children, Paul and Jessica, for their forbearance, solicitude and support.

1

THE END OF PROGRESS

THE AGE OF PROGRESS IS OVER. IT WAS
born in the Renaissance, achieved its exuberant
adolescence during the Enlightenment, reached
a robust maturity in the industrial age, and
died with the dawn of the twenty-first century. For countless millennia there was no progress, only cycles. Seasons turned. Generations came
and went. Life didn't get better, it simply repeated
itself in an endlessly familiar pattern. There was no
future, for the future was indistinguishable from
the past.

Then came the unshakable belief that progress
was not only possible, it was inevitable. Life spans
would increase. Material comforts would multiply.
Knowledge would grow. There was nothing that
could not be improved upon. The discipline of
reason and the deductive routines of science could
be applied to every problem, from designing a
more perfect political union to unpacking the
atom to producing semiconductors of mind-
boggling complexity and unerring quality.

Yet the age of progress has been a stern taskmaster—and never more so than in recent times. Employees around the world have been run through a never-ending gauntlet of efficiency programs—from downsizing to reengineering to postmerger cost-cutting to enterprise resource planning to supply chain rationalization and more. With eyes glazed, they have repeated the mantra: faster, better, cheaper. **All too often, employees have found themselves working harder and harder to achieve less and less.** That's the reward for surviving the downsizing, outsourcing, and restructuring that have so dramatically thinned the ranks of industrial-age companies.

The late-twentieth-century version of progress made us cynical. We were promised relief from tedium; we got the white-collar factory. We were promised a degree of autonomy; we got binders full of corporate policy. We were promised a sense of true purpose; we got the tyranny of quarterly returns. We were promised the chance to contribute, we got endless meetings where form regularly beat substance to a pulp. We were called "associates" but were no less expendable than worn-out machines. Our backs were straighter—the age of progress lightened the physical load—but our minds were numb and all too often our spirits were anywhere but at work.

The so-called "new economy" was supposed to bring us a respite from the mind-numbing incrementalism of the age of progress. Thousands of bored-to-tears employees left their "big, dumb companies" for the chance to join start-ups. Hundreds of e-business incubators were created in hopes of spawning "killer app" business models. Otherwise sated customers looked forward to a dazzling array of new economy services and diversions. Yet in the end—and the end came pretty damn fast—the new economy turned out to have been a ruse to sell dumb-as-dirt business models to naive investors and loads of IT gear to panicked CEOs. All the e-biz pundits, investment banks and tyro entrepreneurs had to admit that the Internet wasn't a business model after all, it was merely a technology—one that was best suited to the mundane tasks of cutting procurement costs, whittling down inventories and slashing customer service staffing levels. Far from "changing life as we know it," the Internet turned out to be, in its first iteration, little more than reengineering on steroids. Though the long-term impact of the Net may still be underestimated, short-term competitive impact was vastly overstated.

Yet the demise of dot-com mania is not a vindication for steady-as-she-goes incrementalism. What confronts every company, large or small, today and in the years ahead, is not merely the challenge of harnessing the power of "e" but of learning to thrive in a world where change is discontinuous, unrelenting and pitiless. What distinguishes the future from the past is not "e"—not electronic commerce, but "t"— profound and inescapable environmental turbulence.

Many industrial-age paragons—from AT&T to Motorola to Coca-Cola to British Telecom to DaimlerChrysler to Merrill Lynch—are right now struggling to adapt to a world where change jumps and spins, tumbles and careens. Along with virtually every other company born before yesterday, these companies are much better at optimization than they are at rule-breaking, game-changing innovation. Incrementalism is wired into their metrics, woven into their management processes and baked into their compensation criteria. They were built for progress, not for perpetual radical innovation—and yet, that is exactly what is required in turbulent times.

THE AGE OF REVOLUTION

We are now standing on the threshold of a new age—an age of revolution. Change has changed. No longer is it additive. No longer does it move in a straight line. In the twenty-first century, change is discontinuous, abrupt, seditious. In a single generation, the cost of decoding a human gene has dropped from millions to less than a hundred bucks. The cost of storing a megabyte of data has dropped from hundreds of dollars to essentially nothing. Bandwidth has become a cheaper-than-cheap commodity. Global capital flows have become a raging torrent, eroding national economic sovereignty. Family structures have been pulled asunder. Bare-knuckled capitalism has vanquished all competing ideologies, and a tsunami of deregulation and privatization has swept the globe. Religiously inspired terrorism has created ripples of anxiety and fear throughout the world economy. And despite the dot-com debacle, the Internet is still proving itself to be a profoundly destabilizing force.

The Web is rapidly becoming a dense global matrix of connections between people, their ideas and their resources—and it has always been the number and quality of such connections that determine the pace of economic change. Just as the number of neurons and neurotransmitters determines cognitive ability, the number of individuals and the interconnections between them drives the pace of innovation. Before the nineteenth century, when individuals and their communities were mostly isolated, innovation proceeded at an imperceptible pace. The village baker, banker and blacksmith might swap pipe dreams down at the pub, but the narrow range of their experience and their meager resources severely limited the number of things they could collectively invent. Then came the steamship, the railroad, the telegraph, the telephone, the car and the airplane. Ideas and capital began to circulate, mingle and fuse in ways never before possible. Innovation started to trot.

And now, with the Internet set to connect virtually everyone and everything, the number of combinational possibilities is set to soar. The Web is fast becoming humanity's collective brain. And there's no telling what it is likely to create. The forces of change and innovation are no longer loping along. They are now a breathless, rampaging horde, trampling underfoot all who would pause for a backward glance. Put simply, we are on the verge of a phase shift where economic evolution becomes perpetual revolution.

It's not that things didn't change back there in the age of progress; they did. Old companies faded away—remember American Motors and Eastern Airlines?—and new companies emerged. But to use a metaphor from the theory of biological evolution, it was a world of *punctuated equilibrium*, where change was episodic. Today we live in a world that is all punctuation and no equilibrium. To thrive in this new age, every company and every individual will have to become as nimble as change itself.

THE NEW INDUSTRIAL ORDER

Out of the age of progress came a world of industrial giants: Mitsubishi, ABB, Citigroup, General Electric, Ford, Du Pont and their peers. These companies harnessed the disciplines of progress: rigorous planning, continuous improvement, statistical process control, six sigma, reengineering and enterprise resource planning. Decade after decade they focused single-mindedly on getting better. If they happened to miss something that was changing in the environment, there was plenty of time to catch up. The advantages of incumbency—global distribution, respected brands, a deep pool of talent, cash flow—granted them the luxury of time. For instance, although Apple Computer got an early start in the microcomputer business, IBM quickly reversed Apple's lead when it threw its worldwide distribution might behind the PC. But in a world of discontinuous change, a company that misses a critical bend in the road may never catch up. Consider these examples:

○ Between 1994 and 2000, the number of mobile phones sold each year exploded from 26 million to more than 400 million. At the same time, the technology changed from analog to digital. Motorola, the world leader in the cellular telephone business until

1997, missed the shift to digital wireless technology by just a year or two. In that sliver of time, Nokia, a hitherto unknown company, perched on the edge of the Arctic circle, became the world's new number one. A decade earlier Nokia had been making snow tires and rubber boots; suddenly it was one of Europe's fastest growing high-tech companies. For Motorola, regaining its top spot will be a Herculean task.

○ Want to build a world-beating Internet portal site? Sorry, too late. If you're a traditional entertainment or media company like Disney, Bertelsmann or Viacom and you want to grab a few million online eyeballs, you've probably already missed the boat. AOL and Microsoft, both media newcomers, built commanding positions in the online world while most of the old line media companies were otherwise occupied.

○ You might be surprised to learn that the fastest growing sector of the commercial aircraft market, regional jets, is dominated by two comparative newcomers: Canada's Bombardier and Brazil's Embraer. Airbus and Boeing have been virtually foreclosed from this booming market. And should they commit themselves to recovering the ground they've lost, they can expect a brutal fight with their new rivals.

Yes, incumbency still matters. This is a lesson that more than a few dot-com start-ups learned to their sorrow. But it is also true that incumbency matters less than ever before. Schumpeter's gale of "creative destruction" has become a hurricane. New winds are battering down the fortifications that once protected the status quo. Economic integration has blown open protected markets. Deregulation has destroyed comfortable monopolies. *Easily bored customers have become ever more promiscuous in their loyalties.* Online search tools have created a class of almost perfectly informed customers.

Compaq, Novell, Westinghouse, Kodak, Kmart, Philips—these and a hundred other incumbents have found themselves struggling to stay relevant in this new topsy-turvy world. Just as the Age of Reason undermined the authority of organized religion in matters secular, this age of revolution is undermining the authority of the world's industrial incumbents in matters commercial.

Consider some evidence. If you're an American over the age of 40, you may remember Main Street—that humble row of shops operated by neighborly souls who knew your kids by name and catered to your every need. All that is gone now, replaced decades ago by look-alike shopping malls with Sears at one end, JCPenney at the other, and a row of specialty shops such as B. Dalton and KB Toys in between. Then, when you weren't looking, those suburban malls started down the long road toward retail irrelevance. Category killers like Toys "R" Us, The Home Depot and Staples slowly crushed many of the specialty retailers that once made the malls work, and Wal-Mart displaced Sears as America's biggest retailer. But what's the chance that the retailing revolution stops with Wal-Mart and Toys "R" Us? None. Consumers aren't going to spend the rest of their lives wandering the soulless canyons of Wal-Mart to save a couple of bucks on a hammer. Woolworth's never escaped Main Street. Sears got stuck in the mall. And all those "big box" retailers afloat in a sea of asphalt may one day find themselves on the wrong side of yet another retailing revolution.

Or consider one of America's most venerable brands—Coca-Cola. A Morgan Stanley survey of 25,000 consumers in 2001 found that the Coke brand was weaker among young people than at any time in recent memory.[1] The culprits? A slew of hip, new beverage brands from Red Bull to Starbucks to SoBe. With their increasingly eclectic and hair-trigger tastes, young consumers are less and less likely to be satisfied with the same-old same-old. In the age of revolution, great companies are as vulnerable as they are venerable.

If you have any doubts about the waning power of incumbency, consider for a moment all the goods and services you buy from companies that are no more than a generation old—airline tickets from Southwest Airlines, furniture from IKEA, mutual funds from Charles Schwab, computers from Dell, collectibles via eBay, video games from Nintendo, coffee from Starbucks, books from Amazon.com and so on. Never has the world been a more hospitable place for unorthodox newcomers.

Of course, industry newcomers are just as vulnerable as the firms they displace. During the 1990s, Gap Inc. was one of retailing's hottest stories. The company had transformed itself from a pile-them-high purveyor of Levi's and T-shirts into a trendy retailer of Gap-branded fashion basics. Yet as the century turned, The Gap's clothing and its store format were no longer fresh and hip. A slew of competitors— some new, some old—had copied many of The Gap's retailing ideas, and the company seemed incapable of refreshing its image and strategy. In recent years, CNN, the pioneer of 24-hour television news, has seen a significant number of its viewers jump to Fox News Channel, MSNBC, CNBC and other newbie news channels. Incumbency may be worth less than ever, but the wet cement of orthodoxy and dogma sets fast in even the most revolutionary of newcomers. In an age of revolution, the trip from insurgent to incumbent is often a short one.

Just as the collapse of communism gave us a new world order, the decline of incumbency is giving us a new industrial order. In the new industrial order, the battle lines don't run between regions and countries. It's no longer Japan versus the United States versus the European Union versus the developing world. Today it's the insurgents versus the incumbents, the revolutionaries versus the landed gentry.

Royal Dutch/Shell is one of the world's premier oil companies, with a history as old as the industry. Yet one day Shell awoke to find that a supermarket, Tesco, had become the largest retailer of "petrol" in Britain, one of Shell's home markets. How do you handle that? You've spent hundreds of millions of pounds over several decades trying to convince consumers that your brand of petrol is better than the next guy's, and suddenly it's being sold as a loss leader along with milk and eggs.

Starbucks has become America's premier coffee brand with the most loyal clientele of any retailer in the United States—the average Starbucks customer visits a store 18 times a month! (You'll have to find your own legal drug to sell—caffeine's already taken.) So picture all the brand managers sitting at Nestlé headquarters in Vevey, Switzerland, running Nescafé, the best-selling coffee in the world. Do you think they ever wondered how they could entice bus drivers and schoolteachers to line up five deep to pay three bucks for a latte? No? What were they worrying about? What color cans to put on supermarket shelves? How to beat Procter & Gamble? The result? In mid 2000, Starbucks had a stock market value of $9 billion—11 percent of Nestlé's market value, yet Starbucks' revenues were a scant 4 percent of Nestlé's. All too often, industry incumbents mistake historical rivals for the enemy—a potentially catastrophic mistake in the age of revolution.

Industry revolutionaries will exploit any protective urge, any hesitancy on the part of the oligarchy. Any attempt to hunker down, to fall back and regroup, or to disengage will be seized as an opportunity to claim more ground. **First the revolutionaries will take your markets and your customers.** Southwest Airlines might have started in Texas, but it's not just serving the Southwest anymore. It now serves virtually every major city in the United States. **Next they'll take your best employees.** Think about it: if you're a bright young executive eager to make your mark, who would you rather work for—Hewlett-Packard or Dell, United Airlines or NetJets (the pioneer in fractional jet ownership)? Sooner or later, bold thinking and growth attract the best talent. Finally, they'll take your assets. How unexpected that eBay acquired the third largest auction house in the United States, Butterfield & Butterfield. How surprising that Vodafone, still in its teens, bought Mannesmann, one of Germany's oldest and proudest companies. How weird that AOL's leadership team would end up in control of a postmerger AOL Time Warner. The barbarians are banging on the gate—and if you're not careful, they'll be eating off your best china. This is the old guard versus the vanguard. The power of incumbency versus the power of imagination.

While the battle is always between new thinking and old, it is not always between newbies and veterans, much less between the "new economy" and the "old." As it turns out, many industry revolutionaries are large, well-established companies—they are newcomers insofar as the incumbents are concerned, but they aren't new companies. Bombardier had a long history as a snowmobile manufacturer before it acquired Canadair, a near-bankrupt manufacturer of executive jets. It was this acquisition that established the platform for Bombardier's expansion into regional jets. Likewise, Hughes Electronics had a history as a manufacturer of military and commercial satellites before it challenged the monopoly of America's cable television companies with its DirecTV service. These companies were newcomers to aerospace and television, respectively, but they weren't start-ups. Though the odds don't always favor it, new thinking can be found in old companies. When "gray-haired revolutionaries" combine their substantial resources with a revolutionary spirit, they are often able to surprise the incumbents *and* squash the start-ups. The future belongs to the unorthodox and the agile—be they start-ups or giants.

LIMITED ONLY BY IMAGINATION

Every age brings its own blend of promise and peril, and the age of revolution has plenty of both. But there is reason to be more hopeful than fearful, for the age of revolution is presenting us with an opportunity never before available to humankind: For the first time in history we can work backward from our imagination rather than forward from our past. For all of history, human beings have longed to explore other worlds, to reverse the ravages of aging, to transcend distance, to shape their environment, to conquer their destructive moods, to share any bit of knowledge that might exist on the planet. With the International Space Station, genetic engineering, videoconferencing, virtual reality, mood-altering drugs and global search engines, we've begun to turn each of these timeless dreams into reality. *Indeed, the gap between*

*what can be imagined and what can be accomplished has
never been smaller.*

We have not so much reached the end of history (as Francis
Fukuyama claimed) as we have developed the capacity to interrupt
history—to escape the linear extrapolation of what was. Our heritage is
no longer our destiny.

Today we are limited not by our tools, but by our imagination. Those
who can imagine a new reality have always been outnumbered by
those who cannot. For every Leonardo da Vinci, Jonas Salk or Charles
Babbage, there are tens of thousands whose imagination cannot escape
the greased grooves of history. For though there is nothing that cannot
be imagined, there are few who seem able to wriggle free from the
strictures of a linear world. Like a long-captive elephant that stands in
place out of habit, even when untethered, most minds have not
grasped the possibilities inherent in our escape from the treadmill of
progress. Yet individuals and organizations that are incapable of escaping the gravitational pull of the past will be foreclosed from the future.

To fully realize the promise of our new age, each of us must become
a dreamer, as well as a doer. In the age of progress, dreams were often
little more than fantasies. Today, as never before, they are doorways to
new realities. Our collective selves—our organizations—must also learn
to dream. In many organizations there has been a massive failure of
collective imagination. How else can one account for the fact that so
many organizations have been caught flat-footed by the future?

THRIVING IN THE AGE OF REVOLUTION

Somewhere out there is a bullet with your company's name on it.
That bullet may be a company that's eager to exploit a disruptive technology, it may be an impending shift in customer preferences, a demo-
graphic change, a lifestyle trend or a regulatory upheaval that will
render your strategy obsolete. You can't dodge these bullets—you're
going to have to shoot first. You're going to have to out-innovate the
innovators.

When Bill Gates says, "Microsoft is always two years away from failure," he's not defending himself yet again from the charge of being a
monopolist. Gates understands the competitive reality of the new age.
He knows that it's not only product life cycles that are shrinking; strategy life cycles are getting shorter, too. An almost stupefying pace of
change ensures that any business concept, no matter how brilliant, will,
over time, lose its economic efficiency. The difference between being a
leader and a laggard is no longer measured in decades, but in years,

and sometimes months. Today, a company must be capable of reinventing its strategy, not just once a decade or once a generation in the midst of a crisis when it trades out one CEO for another, but continuously, year after year.

The fact that few companies are capable of making right–angle turns is evidenced by the increasing number of CEOs who lose their jobs every year. Apparently, investors and boards have concluded that the only way to revector a large company is to jettison its CEO and bring in a new leader. While this is sometimes effective, it doesn't address the deeper problem—the inability of companies and leaders to renew themselves in the absence of a crisis. Indeed, too many companies are like Third World governments—banana republics where the only way to effect a change in policy is to depose the despot. Changing the CEO is an expensive and wrenching process—and too often happens only *after* a company has missed an important turn on the road to the future. **WHAT WE NEED ARE COMPANIES THAT ARE CAPABLE OF SELF–RENEWAL, ORGANIZATIONS THAT ARE CAPABLE OF CONTINUALLY REINVENTING THEMSELVES AND THE INDUSTRIES IN WHICH THEY COMPETE.** We need fewer stories about heroic and belated turnarounds, and more stories about perpetual revolutionaries.

Microsoft is unlikely to oust its chairman anytime soon. Instead, the company is dealing with the threat of unconventional competitors and new business models by launching a blizzard of new services and products—including Passport, Hailstorm, the X–box and a host of others. Microsoft's ".Net" strategy—the label for a cluster bomb of innovation initiatives—is aimed at nothing less than remaking the company. Bill Gates and his team at Microsoft understand that in the age of revolution, there is no defense, there's only offense. Those who live by the sword will be shot by those who don't.

Gates isn't the only corporate leader who understands the dynamics of the new industrial order. In a Gallup survey I authored,[2] approximately 500 CEOs were asked, "Who took best advantage of change in your industry over the past ten years—newcomers, traditional competitors or your own company?" The number one answer was newcomers. They were then asked whether those newcomers had won by "executing better" or "changing the rules of the game." Fully 62 percent of the CEOs said the newcomers had won by changing the rules. Despite this, how many times have you heard a CEO or divisional vice president say, "Our real problem is execution"? Or worse, tell people that "strategy is the easy part, implementation is the hard part." What rubbish! These worthless aphorisms are favored by executives afraid to admit that their strategies are seriously out of date, executives who'd prefer their people stop asking awkward questions and get back to work. Strategy is easy only if you're content to have a strategy that is a derivative of someone else's strategy. Strategy is anything but easy if your goal is to be the author of industry transformation—again and again. It is, however, immensely rewarding. What could be more gratifying than putting one's fingerprints all over the future?

One CEO put it to me this way: "I used to spend most of my time worrying about the *how*—how we did things, how we operated, how efficient we were. Now I spend much of my time worrying about the *what*—what opportunities to pursue, what partnerships to form, what technologies to back, what experiments to start." The point is simple. By the time an organization has wrung the last 5 percent of efficiency out of the how, someone else will have invented a new what. Inventing new whats—that's the key to thriving in the age of revolution.

RADICAL INNOVATION

The signal accomplishment of the industrial age was the notion of incremental, continuous improvement. It remains the secular religion of most managers. Its first incarnation came in Frederick Winslow Taylor's scientific management. Its many descendants include the Japanese concept of *kaizen* and the oh-so-'90s notions of reengineering and enterprise resource planning. Taylor is the spiritual godfather of every manager or consultant who has ever sought to describe, measure and streamline a business process.

Organizational learning and knowledge management are first cousins to continuous improvement. They are more about getting better than getting different. The final accomplishment of the age of progress was to turn knowledge into a commodity. Today you can buy knowledge by the pound—from consultants hawking best practice, from the staff you've just hired from your competitor, and from all those companies that hope you'll outsource everything. Yet in the age of revolution it is not knowledge that produces new wealth, but insight—insight into opportunities for discontinuous innovation. Discovery is the journey; insight is the destination. You must become your own seer.

In a nonlinear world, only nonlinear ideas will create new wealth. Most companies have reached the point of diminishing returns in their incremental improvement programs. Continuous improvement is an industrial-age concept, and while it is better than no improvement at all, it is insufficient in the age of revolution.

Radical, nonlinear innovation is the only way to escape the ruthless hypercompetition that has been hammering down margins in industry after industry. Nonlinear innovation requires a company to escape the shackles of precedent and imagine entirely novel solutions to customer needs and dramatically more cost-effective ways of meeting those needs.

In tough economic times, there are always those who urge top management to get "back to basics." I agree with this sentiment. I have long argued that the foundation for radical innovation must be a company's core competencies (what it knows) and its strategic assets (what it owns)—you can't get any more basic than that. Unrelated acquisitions, new venture divisions and corporate incubators seldom if ever bring genuine renewal. They are tangential to the core and typically leverage little of what a company already knows and owns. Yet to argue that a company must leverage its core is not to argue for inch-by-inch incrementalism. Nor is leveraging the core simply a matter of finding obvious "adjacencies"—nearby channels and customers (à la "Baby Gap," "Cherry Diet Coke" and "Double Stuf Oreos"). Instead, leveraging the core is a matter of reinterpreting the very essence of a company in ways that allow it to create completely new market space. This is what UPS did when it built a billion-dollar-a-year logistics and supply chain management business. Who would have guessed that a package delivery company could win a contract to deliver Ford cars to dealers across the United States or mend Compaq and HP computers in a huge UPS-owned repair facility?

And what about the core business? Here the goal is pretty simple: to grow revenues, pump up prices and reduce costs. Other things being equal, this will yield real earnings growth. Having discovered, to their chagrin, that earnings actually matter, investors are once again in search of companies that can deliver sustained profitable growth. They are demanding that companies get back to basics. In recent years, CFOs regularly tested the outer limits of investor credulity and generally accepted accounting principles in hopes of somehow disguising faltering growth rates and shrinking margins. In the wake of Enron's collapse—engineered by a swashbuckling finance function that was, to use the British expression, "too clever by half"—investors have said "enough is enough" to the "extraordinary" charges, off-balance sheet financing and pro forma accounting that have so often been used to divert attention from a slowly atrophying or nonexistent business model.

But here's where back to basics runs straight into a brick wall. Growing the top line, raising prices and cutting costs are hard and getting harder. In fact, without radical innovation, they're near impossible. In the summer of 1999, Procter & Gamble announced 15,000 layoffs around the world and warned investors of a potential $1.9 billion charge against earnings. This despite the fact that in 1995 P&G set itself the ambitious goal of doubling its revenues to $70 billion by 2005. This would have required a 10-percent annual growth rate. In 1999 P&G was a long way off that pace.[3] For the last several years, McDonald's growth engine in the United States has been sputtering. In a heavily touted move, the company introduced a new cooking system that promised made-for-you hamburgers even quicker off the grill. Will this solve McDonald's growth problem? It might, but maybe McDonald's should ask itself if Americans are already eating as many hamburgers as they're ever going to. Maybe Americans have reached their cholesterol limit. In a recent survey across 20 industries, I found that only 11 percent of companies had been able to grow revenues twice as fast as their industry over a decade, and only 7 percent had been able to grow shareholder returns at twice the industry average.

In 1999, DoCoMo, a division of NTT, Japan's largest telecom company, gave the world its first large-scale packet-switched mobile phone network, iMode. With their always-on, data-enabled phones, DoCoMo's customers could get instant news updates, automatic downloads of cartoons and horoscopes, weather reports and much more. By the end of 2001, the service had attracted 30 million customers—probably the fastest growth for any new consumer service in history. The message is clear: If you're an established company in a "mature" industry, it's impossible to significantly grow the top line in the absence of radical innovation.

What about raising prices? In a world of ever more powerful customers, and relentless competition at home and abroad, few companies have the luxury of raising their prices. In the good old days, when inflation moved along at a double-digit clip, it was easy for companies to hide their price increases in the upward spiral of inflation. But with inflation now at less than 2 percent per annum in most of the world's developed economies, there is little scope for hidden price increases. The only way to raise prices is to find a truly novel way of differentiating your product or service. In Britain, you can buy lunch at Burger King for a pound or two less than you can at Pret A Manger (prêt-à-manger is French for "ready-to-eat"), a chain of trendy fast-food outlets where every sandwich is made fresh on the premises each morning. Pret's hundred-plus stores are testament to the fact that many customers are willing to pay a premium for gourmet fare like a Thai Chicken Miracle-Mayo sandwich. Despite its decentralized production system, Pret's cost structure is low enough to give it margins that match those of its most efficient fast-food competitors. Accountants and imagination-challenged executives often forget that productivity has two components—the efficiency with which you use your inputs (labor and capital) and the value that customers place on your outputs. Too many managers know everything about cost and next to nothing about perceived value. Pret willingly adds cost to its sandwiches—fresh, additive-free and sometimes exotic ingredients—because the quality and flavor of those sandwiches commands a price advantage (over a typical fast-food "value meal"). Pret's example suggests that it's possible to charge a price premium—but not unless you have a unique value proposition—and you're not going to get one of those without radical innovation.

Another response to razor-thin margins is to whack away at the cost structure. Yet with virtually every company on the planet thoroughly committed to cost cutting, what is required is not another incrementalist margin-improvement program, but a radical reinvention of the cost structure. Wal-Mart's superstores and its pioneering use of information technology have allowed it to reap unmatched economies of scale and scope. Southwest Airline's point-to-point route system, its 737-only fleet and its multitasking employees produce a level of capital efficiency unmatched by any traditional rival. IKEA's flat-packed furniture, manufactured at global scale and sold in warehouse-style stores, offers frugal customers "affordable solutions for better living." Indeed, IKEA claims that in its never-ending attempts to drive down costs, "the only thing it doesn't skimp on is ideas." Finally, Dell's lack of vertical integration and its direct, Internet-based distribution model allow it to make hundreds of millions each quarter while its competitors are losing a similar amount. Each of these companies brought radical innovation to the cost side of the equation, and each views every market downturn as an opportunity to acquire market share from less efficient competitors who have no choice but to retrench when demand goes slack.

So while the basics never change, "more of the same" is no longer enough if the goal is sustainable, profitable growth. If you're trying to grow revenues or slice costs with a straight line approach, you're going to find yourself facing an "innovation gap" with competitors who have managed to break conventions and achieve step-function changes. Soon the world will be divided into two kinds of organizations: those that can get no further than continuous improvement and those that have made the jump to radical innovation.

Now, let me be clear: there is nothing wrong with incrementalism. Gillette used to make razors with a single blade. Later, one of its diligent students of stubble asked, Wouldn't two blades be better than one? Thus was born the Trac II. Next came—guess what?—a razor with three blades—the Mach III. I love Gillette razors—use one every morning—but they are examples of incremental innovation. Incremental innovation is desirable, indispensable and, in a discontinuous world, insufficient—that is, if your goal is to create *new* wealth, year after year.

Tough economic times can make timidity seem like a virtue. A CEO or business leader struggling to "make the quarter" may view radical innovation as—well, too *radical*. The unstated assumption is that incrementalism is low-risk and radical innovation high-risk. Yet in a fast-changing world with few second chances, more of the same often represents the biggest risk of all, as the recent histories of Xerox, TWA, Kmart and dozens of other incumbents so clearly show.

Without doubt, innovation can be risky—think of Motorola's multibillion-dollar bet on satellite telephony, Iridium, which ultimately went bust. Innovation risk is determined by four things: first, the size of the irreversible and nonrecoverable financial commitment that must be made to get a project off the ground; second, the degree to which the new opportunity departs from the company's existing base of technical and market understanding; third, the amount of irreducible uncertainty surrounding critical project assumptions (particularly with respect to the nature of customer demand and technical feasibility); and fourth, the time frame required for ramp-up (the longer the time scale, the higher the risk). Against all these criteria, Iridium was a high-risk project. But there's no reason radical innovation has to be high-risk. As we will see, it is possible to de-risk bold new strategies through low-cost, low-risk experimentation. **Imagination and prudence are not mutually exclusive.**

I believe that many companies are *too* willing to make big, risky bets. Between 1996 and 2000, companies in the S&P 500 wrote off more than $226 billion in the form of extraordinary charges against earnings. During this time they recorded only $62 billion of extraordinary gains. A significant proportion of the write-offs came from acquisitions that failed to live up to their (typically overhyped) advance billing, from new business bets that never paid off and from venture investments gone bad. Let's be honest: In recent years investment bankers and VCs have talked big-company executives into doing the *stupidest* things. The challenge is not to avoid taking risks, but to get much, much smarter about how to de-risk grand aspirations.

I believe in revolutionary goals and evolutionary steps. When Julian Metcalfe and Sinclair Beecham, the founders of Pret A Manger, set out to create food that was fresh, preservative-free, healthy, tasty *and* affordable, they were embarking on a revolutionary journey. The first Pret store opened in 1986, the second in 1990. In the intervening four years, the founders lurched from challenge to crisis and back again as they struggled to perfect a business concept that would scale up. Like virtually every other successful industry revolutionary, Pret was not an overnight success. However bold the vision, a company has to get *there* from *here*, one step at a time. So the choice is not between being bold and foolhardy on one hand, and cautious and timorous on the other. Instead, like a seasoned climber attempting a new and unfamiliar peak, a company faces the challenge to prepare rigorously and move prudently.

Radical innovation comes in all sizes. A couple of years ago, an employee at Virgin Atlantic noticed a bit of empty curb space at Heathrow Airport. In a matter of days, and on his own initiative, he secured the rights to the space and laid out a plan for Virgin to build a curbside check-in kiosk. As a result, Virgin became the first airline at Heathrow to offer its business-class passengers the convenience of getting a boarding pass without having to stand in a check-in line. Soon, check-in times were measured in seconds instead of minutes. Over the past decade, dozens upon dozens of similarly "radical" ideas—from seatback videos to onboard manicures—have allowed Virgin Atlantic to differentiate its services from its larger rivals.

What makes an idea radical is not the size of required capital investment, nor the timetable for payback. Instead, a radical idea is one that upends some industry convention, significantly changes customer expectations in a net-positive way, dramatically alters the pricing or cost structure of the industry or changes the basis for competitive advantage within the industry (i.e., changes the assets or competencies required for success). Enough small ideas that meet some or all of these criteria can have a big impact on the distribution of market share and profits across an industry.

Look down the long sorry list of companies that have fallen on hard times, and you will quickly discover that it isn't prudent yet radical innovation that typically imperils a company's future; it is an overweaning affection for precedent, convention and incrementalism. Given this, you may want to do a quick inventory of the improvement initiatives, capital investments priorities and new product programs that are currently getting attention in your company: How many of these meet the test of being radical? If it's a scant fraction, mediocrity is the best result you can hope for. In the end, radical innovation is the only way for newcomers to succeed in the face of enormous resource disadvantages and the only way for incumbents to renew their lease on success.

With every wrinkle in the fabric of history, new wealth gets created and old wealth gets destroyed. It will be no different as the age of progress gives way to the age of revolution. The question is, **Who will create the new wealth and who will squander the old?** The revolutionaries have already laid their hands on enough wealth to ransom all the world's potentates several times over. In early 2002, in the midst of the worst downturn to ever hit the PC business, Michael Dell was leading a company whose market value was $10 billion more than that of Ford and General Motors combined. At the same time, Southwest Airlines, a quintessential industry revolutionary, had a market value nearly double the combined worth of AMR and UAL, the parent companies of American Airlines and United Airlines, respectively. Vodafone, a British company that came from nowhere to assemble a global network of mobile phone operators, boasted a market value of $162 billion in January 2002, more than twice that of telecom stalwart AT&T. And in less than ten years as a public company, Kohl's, the Wisconsin-based retailer that reinvented the department store around "no hassles" shopping, had accumulated a market value equal to that of both Sears and JCPenney—a particularly noteworthy accomplishment when one considers that Kohl's operated just 320 department stores to Sears' 863 and Penney's 1,111. The evidence is unequivocal: In a world of diminishing returns to incrementalism, smart revolutionaries will capture a disproportionate share of the new wealth.

Companies today are rightly obsessed with satisfying shareholders. Spin-offs, de-mergers, share buybacks, tracking stocks, value-based management programs—all these things release wealth, but they don't *create* wealth. Neither do mega-mergers. These strategies don't create new wealth because they don't create new business models, new markets, new sources of competitive advantage or new customers. So while they may deliver onetime gains to shareholders, they don't fundamentally change a company's long-term earning potential. Industry revolutionaries are in the business of creating new wealth. You won't find them playing shell games with shareholders. Any company that wants to thrive in the age of revolution is going to have to do more than wring a bit of wealth out of yesterday's strategies. Revolutionaries don't release wealth, they create it. They do more than conserve, they build. In truth, CFOs and CEOs have mistaken the scoreboard for the game. They have spent too much time trying to manipulate quarterly earnings and the share price, and too little time trying to build their company's capacity for radical innovation. Shareholder wealth may be the score-board, but the game is radical innovation.

TOWARD CAPABILITY

Any company that hopes to stay relevant and vital in turbulent times must be capable of creating strategies that are as revolutionary as the age we live in. This raises a question you may already be asking yourself: Where do new wealth-creating strategies come from? The strategy industry—all those unctuous consultants, self-proclaimed gurus and left-brain planners—doesn't have an answer. They all know a strategy when they see one—Look! Twenty-two "profit zones"!—but they don't know where new strategies come from. They don't have a theory of strategy creation, much less any insight into how to build a deeply embedded capacity for strategy innovation.

Perhaps strategies come from the annual planning process—that well-rehearsed ritual found in almost every organization. Consider the planning process in your own company. What adjectives would best describe it? Those in column A or column B? Unless your company is truly exceptional, you'll probably have to admit that the descriptors in column A are more apt than those in column B.

___A___	___B___
Procedural	Creative
Reductionist	Expansive
Extrapolative	Inventive
Elitist	Inclusive
Easy	Demanding

The notion that strategy is "easy" rests on the mistaken assumption that strategic planning has something to do with strategy making. Of course strategy appears easy when the planning process narrowly limits the scope of discovery, the breadth of involvement and the amount of intellectual effort expended, and when the goal is something far short of revolution. The assumption that strategy is easy says more about the inadequacies of our planning processes than the challenge of creating industry revolution.

Giving planners responsibility for creating strategy is like asking a bricklayer to create Michelangelo's *Pietà*. Any company that believes planning will yield revolutionary strategies will find itself caught in a prison of incrementalism as freethinking newcomers lead successful insurrections. If the goal is to create new strategies, you might as well dance naked round a campfire as go to one more semisacramental planning meeting.

No wonder that in many organizations, the whole notion of strategic planning has been devalued. How often has it produced any radical value–creating insights? No wonder corporate strategy has become little more than deal making. No wonder consulting companies are doing less and less "strategy" work and more and more "implementation" work.

Perhaps revolutionary strategies come from "visionaries" like Bill Gates (Microsoft), Anita Roddick (The Body Shop), Jeff Bezos (Amazon.com), Howard Schultz (Starbucks) and Michael Dell (Dell Computer). Many, if not most, industry revolutions have their genesis in the vision of a single individual who often ends up as CEO or chairman. Yet today's vision is often tomorrow's intellectual straitjacket. **All too often a company outruns the visionary's headlights, and then crashes and burns.** Just remember Apple Computer, where Steve Jobs, the poster boy for missed opportunities, resisted efforts to license the Macintosh operating system to other companies. Improbably, after having been booted from the company he helped to create, Jobs got a second chance when he took up the CEO reins again in 1997. Yet however miraculous Apple's more recent turnaround, the company will forever be a footnote in the history of the computer industry—in large part because of the myopia of the company's founders. Likewise, Dell Computer will be similarly doomed if its top management is unable to escape a PC–centric view of the computer industry. The mainframe was eclipsed by the minicomputer, which was in turn eclipsed by the personal computer. DEC became the second–largest computer company in the world when IBM was slow to respond to the threat of minicomputers, and Dell became the most dynamic company in the PC business when IBM, Compaq and others were slow to reinvent their business models. Yes, there will one day be a post–PC world, and if Dell is going to thrive in that world, it will need to reinvent itself just as thoroughly as it has reinvented the PC industry.

Visionaries don't stay visionaries forever. Few of them can put their hands on a second vision. Worse, their compatriots become dependent on the visionary's prescience, thus abdicating their own responsibility for envisioning new opportunities. More times than not, a fading visionary who is also CEO or chairman unwittingly strangles a company's capacity for radical innovation. That is why visionary companies seldom live beyond their first strategy.

Of course most companies are not led by visionaries; they're led by administrators. No offense, but your CEO is probably more ruling–class than revolutionary. So don't sit there staring at the corporate tower hoping to be blinded by a flash of entrepreneurial brilliance. Administrators possess an exaggerated confidence in great execution, believing this is all you need to succeed in a discontinuous world. They are accountants, not seers. Visionary CEO or sober–suited apparatchik, neither is likely to be an ever–flowing font of radical innovation.

Maybe some of you have sat through a business–school case study—a 90–minute striptease where some creaky professor undresses a management principle that has been enrobed in 20 pages of colorless prose. Suppose the case being discussed concerns a hugely successful company, and the professor is in the midst of an elaborate and elegant post hoc analysis ...

... So you see, they developed a killer application by exploiting a disruptive technology that allowed them to capture increasing returns from their unique core competencies, thereby creating a new ecosystem with a deep, untapped profit pool.

In the midst of such blather did you ever think to yourself, "Wait a minute, was this success the result of some terribly incisive strategic thinking, or was it pure dumb luck?" Luck or foresight? Where does strategy come from? That's a damn good question.

Consider the genesis of three revolutionary strategies:

When her husband left their home in Littlehampton, England, to pursue a lifelong dream of riding horseback from Buenos Aires to New York, Anita Roddick was left to fend for herself and her daughters. To support her family, Anita opened a small cosmetics shop in nearby Brighton, filling cheap plastic bottles with goo. From this seed grew The Body Shop, a worldwide retailer of funky, politically correct cosmetics.

Just before his 58th birthday, Mike Harper, the acquisitive CEO of ConAgra Inc., suffered a heart attack. After an extended stay in intensive care, Mike left the hospital with a commitment to changing his dietary habits. The newly health–conscious CEO challenged his company to create a line of good–for–you products that would be equally great tasting. The result was Healthy Choice, a line of nutritious frozen dinners that quickly became the leader in its category. The Healthy Choice brand now spans more than 300 products—from breakfast cereals to snack foods to deli meats to ice creams—that had more than $15 billion in sales in 1999.[4]

What do Pez dispensers—those little plastic heads that dole out candy—have to do with one of the world's hottest Internet start-ups? Plenty. Just ask Pierre Omidyar. His fiancée was a committed Pez collector. How, Pierre wondered, could he help his girlfriend feed her Pez passion? The answer: an online, person-to-person trading community where Pezheads could buy and sell their weird collectibles. Pierre's idea blossomed into eBay, the Web's premier auction site, where more than 2 million members place a million bids a day. As eBay's founder, Pierre is credited with transforming everything from classified ads in small-town newspapers to the pompous practices of the world's elite auction salons.[5]

Luck or foresight? Where do radical new business concepts come from? The answer is this: **New business concepts are always, always the product of lucky foresight.** That's right—the essential insight doesn't come out of any dirigiste planning process; it comes from some cocktail of happenstance, desire, curiosity, ambition and need. But at the end of the day, there has to be a degree of foresight—a sense of where new riches lie. So radical innovation is always one part fortuity and one part clearheaded vision.

If the capacity of an organization to thrive in the age of revolution depends on its ability to reimagine the very essence of its purpose and destiny and to continually create for itself new dreams and new destinations, we are left in a quandary. How do you increase the probability that radical new wealth-creating strategies emerge in your organization? Can we turn serendipity into capability?

The quality movement provides a useful analogy. Thirty years ago, if you had asked someone, "Where does quality come from?" they would have replied, "From the artisan" or perhaps, "From the inspector at the end of the production line." Quality came from the guy with magical hands at Rolls-Royce, who spent weeks hammering a fender around a wooden form, or from the white-coated inspectors at the end of the Mercedes-Benz production line. Then Dr. Deming came along and said, "We must institutionalize quality—it has to be everyone's job. That guy down there on the shop floor, with ten years of formal education and grease under his fingernails, that guy is responsible for quality." With 30 years of hindsight, it's easy to forget how radical this idea was. In Detroit, auto execs said, "You gotta be kidding! Those guys down there are saboteurs."

It took many companies a decade or more to grasp the notion of quality as a capability, and American car makers have still not closed the quality gap with Toyota and Honda. But the challenge is no longer quality. Neither is it time-to-market, supply chain management or e-commerce. Today the challenge is to build a deep capability for business concept innovation—a capability that continually spawns new business concepts and dramatically reinvents old ones.

Like Deming, Juran and the early leaders of the quality movement, we're going to have to invent new practice. If you had wanted to benchmark best-of-breed quality in 1955, where would you have gone? The answer's not obvious. There was no Deming prize; no ISO 9000. Yet the quality pioneers were undeterred. They invented new practice, built on a new philosophical foundation. Like them, we must aspire to more than "best practice," for most of what currently passes for best practice innovation is grounded in the age of progress; it's simply not good enough for the age of revolution.

Creating a companywide capacity for radical innovation will be no less challenging than creating an organization infused with the ethos of quality—and this time it can't take ten years. And it won't—not if you're willing to kick off the lead boots of denial; not if you're willing to dump all that useless management theory you picked up back there in the age of progress; not if you're ready to climb over the walls of your cubicle and take responsibility for something more than your "job."

THE POSTINDUSTRIAL ENTERPRISE

Reflect for a moment on just how little management wisdom has changed over the past hundred years. At the beginning of the twentieth century, Frederick Winslow Taylor was the world's best-known management guru. His principles were simple: Decompose your processes into their constituent parts, excise or redesign activities that don't add value, then put your processes back together again. For one hundred years Taylor's "scientific management" was masquerading as reengineering, business process improvement, and ERP and CRM and a dozen other acronyms for faster, better, cheaper.

Nearly everything we know about organizing, managing and competing comes from an age in which diligence, efficiency, exactitude, quality and control were the complete secrets to success. The management disciplines we inherited from the industrial age are the unquestioning servants of optimization. These disciplines are the product of a world where industry boundaries were inviolable, where customers were supplicants and where business models were assumed to be nearly eternal. That world may be long dead, yet optimization still regularly trumps innovation.

And despite all the pro-innovation rhetoric that one encounters in annual reports and CEO speeches, most still hold the view that innovation is a rather dangerous diversion from the real work of wringing the last ounce of efficiency out of core business processes. Innovation is fine so long as it doesn't disrupt a company's finely honed operational model. A hundred years on from Frederick Taylor, innovation is still regarded as a specialized function (the purview of R&D or product development), rather than as a corporation-wide capability. In most companies, the forces of perpetuation still beat the forces of innovation to a pulp in any contest. As change becomes ever less predictable, companies will pay an ever-escalating price for their lopsided love of incrementalism.

In the years ahead, we must build companies that are as full of radical innovation as they are of diligent optimization. There can be no either/or here, there must be an *and*. In the end, the goal is not innovation for its own sake. Given a choice, most of us would prefer quiet continuity to perpetual revolution. But the choice is not ours. Discontinuous change is the defining characteristic of the postmodern world. Even so, radical innovation is simply a means to an end—and that end is "resilience"—both corporate and personal: the capacity to thrive no matter what the future throws at us.

Resilience is what has allowed America to prosper for more than 225 years with only a single major internal disruption—the Civil War. Over that long span, America has changed all out of recognition—culturally, materially and technologically. It has metamorphosed from an agrarian society to an industrial powerhouse—and morphed again to become a supercharged information economy. It has cleansed itself of slavery, defeated the barbarisms of Nazism and Communism—and set back the ticking hands of the Doomsday Clock. More recently, it has led the international community in defending civil society from the scourge of terrorism.

In contrast, hundreds of governments and scores of constitutions have come and gone in the past two centuries—houses of straw against the gale force winds of change. America's resilience, like that of all long-lasting constitutional democracies, is based on a series of seemingly irreconcilable opposites, tensions held in perpetual creative balance: Coherence and diversity. Community and activism. Strength and compassion. Bravery and prudence. The spiritual and the material.

Resilience is based on the ability to embrace the extremes—while not becoming an extremist. As Charles Simeon, a prominent eighteenth-century English pastor, put it: "Truth is not in one extreme and not in the middle, it is in both extremes." The thesis and antithesis of the modern corporation are optimization and innovation. Both of these extremes must be embraced and transcended.

MOST COMPANIES DON'T DO PARADOX VERY WELL. They are filled with accountants and engineers who have an instinctive aversion to dichotomies and contradictions. But the postindustrial company can't be all one thing or all another. Instead, it must be all of many things—all focus *and* all experimentation, all discipline *and* all passion, all evolution *and* all revolution, all optimization *and* all innovation—*all*. Discipline, alignment and control will always be virtues, but they can no longer be the only or even the dominant virtues. Any company that hopes to survive the next ten years, let alone the next hundred, will have to be a paragon of penny-pinching efficiency on one side and unbridled creativity on the other. The accountants and the engineers are going to have to learn to love the poets and the dreamers.

It's easy to forget that the large-scale industrial company is the product of human imagination. Go back 150 years and you find chaotic and fragmented craft-based industries. In mastering the virtues of scale, control and discipline companies such as Du Pont, General Motors, Siemens and Shell invented the modern corporation. In so doing, they created incredible efficiencies and brought a cornucopia of goods and services within the reach of Jane and John Mainstreet. Now the times call for another burst of organizational invention, for we can be sure that the companies that learn to flourish in the age of revolution will be as different from the paragons of the industrial age as those companies were from their craft-based predecessors.

The good news is that no company has yet managed to build the epitome of a postindustrial enterprise, though a few companies like GE, Nokia, UPS, Cemex and Charles Schwab have challenged themselves to do so. So you're not starting from behind. The bad news is that creating an organization that is fit for the age of revolution is a lot harder than digitizing your business model. While there are a clutch of industrial-age virtues that will survive the shift to a postindustrial world, there are great swaths of management and organizational orthodoxy that will not. Expunging these superannuated beliefs won't be easy; making innovation a systemic capability will be even harder. Yet the payoff is nothing less than the chance to soar on the winds of change.

Whether what you now hold in your hands is simply shelfware or a powerful tool for radical innovation depends on you. You've been told often that change must start at the top—that's rubbish. How often does the revolution start with the monarchy? Nelson Mandela, Václav Havel, Thomas Paine, Mahatma Gandhi, Martin Luther King: Did they possess political power? No, yet each disrupted history; and it was passion, not power, that allowed them to do so.

Most of us pour more of our life into the vessel of work than into family, faith or community. Yet more often than not the return on emotional equity derived from work is meager. The nomadic Israelites were commanded by God to rest one day out of seven—but He didn't decree that the other six had to be empty of meaning. By what law must competitiveness come at the expense of hope? If you're going to pour out your life into something, why can't it be into a chalice rather than down a drain? For every one of us, it is our sense of purpose, our sense of accomplishment, our sense of making a difference that is at stake—and that is more than enough.

Never has it been a more propitious time to be an activist:

○ Intranets and corporation-wide e-mail are creating something close to an information democracy. The information boundaries that used to delineate corporate authority are more permeable than ever.

○ More than ever, senior executives know they cannot command commitment, for the generation now entering the workforce is more authority-averse than any in history.

○ It is universally apparent that we are living in a world so complex and so uncertain that authoritarian, control-oriented companies are bound to fail.

○ Increasingly, intellectual capital is more valuable than physical capital, and it is employees who are becoming the true "capitalists."

○ Millions of employees are now shareholders as well—they are suppliers and owners.

Activists are changing the shape of companies around the world. At Sony, a midlevel engineer challenges top management to overcome its prejudice against the video-game business. "We don't make toys!" they protest. He badgers, plots and schemes. Against all odds he persuades Sony to develop the PlayStation—a phenomenally successful video-game console that in 1998 accounted for more than 40 percent of Sony's profits. He keeps pushing. Finally Sony sets up a Computer Entertainment division and commits itself to making the computer more than a soulless business machine.

A Web-besotted computer scientist and a gadget-loving market planner join forces at IBM in the early 1990s. Their quixotic goal is to turn IBM into an Internet-savvy powerhouse. They establish a bootleg lab and begin building Webware. They organize an underground lobbying effort that turns a disparate and far-flung group of Webheads into a forceful community of Internet advocates. Their grassroots efforts become the foundation for IBM's emergence as the e-business company.

So don't tell me it can't be done. Only ask yourself if you have the guts to lead the revolution.

Dream, create, explore, invent, pioneer, imagine: do these words describe what you do? If not, you are already irrelevant, and your organization is probably becoming so. If you act like a ward of your organization, you'll be one, and both you and your company will lose. So if you're still acting like a courtier or a consort, bending to the prejudices of top management, buffing up their outsized egos, fretting about what they want to hear, getting calluses on your knees—stop! You're going to rob yourself and your company of a future that's worth having. No excuses. No fear. If you're going to make a difference in your company, these have to be more than T-shirt slogans.

In the new industrial order, the battle is not democracy versus totalitarianism or globalism versus tribalism, it is innovation versus precedent. Ralph Waldo Emerson put it perfectly when he said, "There are always two parties—the party of the past and the party of the future, the establishment and the movement." Which side are *you* on?

Just as nineteenth-century America opened its doors to all those who believed in the possibility of a better life, the twenty-first century opens its doors to all those who believe in the possibility of new beginnings. In the age of revolution it will matter not whether you're the CEO or a newly hired administrative assistant, whether you work in the hallowed halls of headquarters or in some distant backwater, whether you get a senior-citizen discount or whether you're still struggling to pay off school loans. Never before has opportunity been more democratic.

Do you care enough about your organization, your colleagues and yourself to take responsibility for making your company revolution-ready? If you do, you have the chance to reverse the process of institutional entropy that robs so many organizations of their future. You can turn back the rising tide of estrangement that robs so many individuals of their sense of meaning and accomplishment. You can become the author of your own destiny. You can look the future in the eye and say:

I am no longer a captive to history.
Whatever I can imagine, I can accomplish.

I am no longer a vassal in a faceless bureaucracy.
I am an activist, not a drone.

I am no longer a foot soldier
in the march of progress.

I am a Revolutionary.

2

FACING UP TO STRATEGY DECAY

BEYOND THE BOOM

In the last, long economic boom, companies were often able to deliver respectable shareholder returns despite a dearth of any real business innovation. Six things made this possible: first, a doubling of the P/E ratio for shares listed on the New York Stock Exchange (fueled by a massive inflow of funds from retirement–conscious baby boomers); second, an unprecedented attack on corporate inefficiency, which buoyed earnings in many companies; third, a superheated market for acquisitions, which drove up corporate valuations; fourth, an army of newbie investors eager to bet big on fast–growing, loss–making companies; fifth, dozens of creative CFOs who, in their quest to report rapidly escalating earnings, were willing to push generally accepted accounting principles to the breaking point; and sixth, a huge boom in capital spending as companies poured billions of dollars into computer and networking equipment. The confluence of these forces produced the longest bull market in history. Between 1995 and 2000, the NASDAQ Composite Index rocketed from 755 to 4,696 and the Dow Jones Industrial Average climbed from less than 4,000 to nearly 11,500. There were many who claimed that the long stock market rally was proof that the business cycle had been suspended and that a new age of unprecedented productivity growth had dawned. They were wrong.

Trees don't grow to the sky. P/E ratios can't rise indefinitely. Efficiency programs eventually reach the point of diminishing returns. The scope for industry consolidation is finite. Naïve investors inevitably discover that earnings matter. Sleight-of-hand accounting can't forever disguise a decaying business model. And sooner or later, CEOs discover that IT spending doesn't always, or even often, lead to fatter margins. During the boom, a rising tide lifted all boats—some of which weren't entirely seaworthy. It was all too easy for top management to take credit for financial results that were attributable to the incredible and unsustainable dynamics of the stock market rally. In the end, the belief that a 20- to 30-percent annual stock market return is somehow "normal" was revealed to be a temporary, though potent, collective delusion. Over the long term, it is impossible for share prices to rise faster than corporate earnings. And during the next decade, earnings growth is going to be harder than ever to come by—thanks to more powerful and fickle customers, diminishing returns to efficiency programs, the relentless onslaught of disruptive technologies, the consultant-aided spread of "best practices" and the consequent erosion of firm-specific advantages, the corrosive impact of e-business on prices, more aggressive enforcement of antitrust law and the entry of new competitors from at home and abroad. In the post-bubble economy, every company is suddenly alone with its bootstraps. Given that, any company that hopes to outperform the mediocre average is going to have to make innovation an all-the-time, everywhere competence.

STRATEGY DECAY

Even in the midst of a stock market boom, it is not easy for companies to deliver top-quartile shareholder returns for more than a few years at a time—a fact that becomes immediately apparent if one studies the recent performance of the companies that make up the S&P 500. Because the S&P 500 is a listing of America's most valuable companies, the population of this index is constantly changing—companies that have fumbled the future fall out while fast-rising newcomers earn their way in. At the end of 2001, there were 284 companies that had managed to hold a spot in the index for every year since 1991. Of these companies, 15 failed to deliver top-quartile shareholder returns in even one year out of ten; 74 companies achieved top-quartile results in one year out of ten, 69 companies made it into the top quartile in two years out of ten, and 61 were standout performers in three years out of ten. There were only two companies—Centex and Computer Associates—that delivered top-quartile shareholder returns in as many as seven years out of ten, and no company did better than that. General Electric, one of America's most-admired companies, was one of 40 companies that achieved top-quartile results in four years out of ten. In total, there were only 25 companies, or less than 10 percent of the entire population, that managed to deliver top-quartile returns for five years or more out of the ten-year period. These are the odds your company faces if it hopes to outperform its peers. The odds are long because all strategies decay—they lose their economic potency over time—and because few companies know how to reinvigorate old strategies and invent new ones.

Just how much life is left in your company's strategy? How confident are you that your company's strategy is up to the task of delivering superior returns over the next several years? No company will embrace the cause of radical innovation unless it believes that strategy decay is inevitable. Companies that fail to face up to the reality of strategy decay suffer an all-too-familiar fate: They get "resized" in accordance with their suddenly diminished fortunes. The commitment to making radical innovation a corporation-wide capability should come long *before* your company's strategy starts to sputter. So you and your colleagues may want to ask yourselves the following questions:

○ How much more cost savings can our company wring out of its current business model? Are we working harder and harder for smaller and smaller efficiency gains?

○ How much more revenue growth can our company squeeze out of its current business model? Is our company paying more and more for customer-acquisition and market-share gains?

○ How much longer can our company keep propping up its share price through share buybacks, spin-offs and other forms of financial engineering? Is top management reaching the limits of its ability to push up the share price without actually creating new wealth?

○ How many more scale economies can our company gain from mergers and acquisitions? Are the costs of integration beginning to overwhelm the savings obtained from slashing shared overhead costs?

○ How different from each other are the strategies of the four or five largest competitors in our industry and how different from our own strategy? Is it getting harder and harder to differentiate our products and services from those of competitors?

○ How much competitive differentiation is our company's IT budget actually buying? Does it feel like our company is locked in an IT spending arms race with our competitors?

If you answered "not much" and "yes" more than a couple of times, your company's business model is already showing signs of strategy decay. The only way to confirm these suspicions is to dig deeper into the evidence.

UNSUSTAINABLE COST CUTTING— GETTING BLOOD FROM A STONE

Over the past decade the pressure on executives to produce an escalator of steadily rising earnings has been intense. This pressure spawned a myriad of initiatives aimed at cutting overhead, reducing labor and material costs and improving capital utilization. Outsourcing, six sigma programs, reengineering, e-procurement, restructuring, ERP and downsizing are all examples of efficiency-oriented programs. In many companies, this single-minded assault on inefficiency produced several years of double-digit earnings growth. Indeed, in many cases, earnings growth far outstripped revenue growth.

In the short run, profits can grow much faster than revenues. We often see this phenomenon in the early years of a major corporate turnaround. Corpulent companies go on a crash diet. Head count is slashed, assets are sold and costs cut. While revenue growth remains sluggish, margins quickly improve. But there's ultimately a limit to how much profit even the best-managed, most efficient company can squeeze out of any fixed amount of revenue. And as the most egregious inefficiencies get excised, it becomes harder and harder to reap big cost savings.

We have to be suspicious of any company that has been growing earnings substantially faster than it's been growing revenues, especially if it has been doing so for more than a couple of years. Let's take a few examples. Between 1995 and 2000, the ratio of net income growth over revenue growth was 67 for Cigna, 48 for Computer Associates, 43 for Colgate-Palmolive, 27 for ConAgra Foods, 18 for AMR (the parent of American Airlines), and 13 for Northrop-Grumman. Ask yourself, How long can a company grow earnings 13 times, 38 times or 67 times revenue? The answer is, Not for long. My research indicates that if a company's earnings growth exceeds its revenue growth by more than 5 to 1 for more than three years in a row, there's an 80-percent chance that it will face a major earnings shortfall sometime in the next three years. Put simply: There's a limit to liposuction.

While cost cutting has a way to run in Japan and continental Europe, many American and British companies have already reached the point of diminishing returns in their efficiency programs. In 2000, the average operating margin for the nonfinancial services companies in the S&P 500 was 16.2 percent. In 1996, the average operating margin for these same companies had also been 16.2 percent. Whatever the contribution of downsizing, ERP and other efficiency programs to lower costs, these initiatives haven't done much to fatten margins—at best, they've simply helped companies ward off the effects of steadily declining real prices.

This doesn't mean that companies should abandon their zeal for cost cutting. But it does suggest that unless a company has a way of reducing costs substantially faster and deeper than the industry norm, it will gain little in the way of an earnings or share price advantage.

UNSUSTAINABLE REVENUE GROWTH—
SPINNING YOUR WHEELS

Downsizing is a harrowing experience. A lot of former efficiency addicts are now eager to grow. But focusing on growth, rather than on the challenge of radical innovation, is as likely to destroy wealth as to create it. After some point, trying to squeeze more revenue growth out of a moribund business model is no easier than trying to squeeze out more costs. In the absence of radical innovation, a blind allegiance to growth can suck a company into zero-sum market-share battles or seduce it into paying exorbitant sums for customer acquisition. Worse, it can lead to an ill-conceived acquisition. When Daimler-Benz acquired Chrysler, it became a bigger company, but the hoped-for economies at DaimlerChrysler have yet to materialize. Interestingly, Porsche and BMW, both of which make many fewer cars than DaimlerChrysler, have much better margins.

The result of a growth obsession is often bigger revenues but not much traction in terms of additional profits—this seems to have been the case for many Internet start-ups. Let's flip our earlier ratio and look at revenue growth over earnings growth. If the ratio of revenue growth to earnings growth is more than 5 to 1 and has been so for a year or two or more, it suggests that a strategy meltdown is in progress or, in the case of a start-up, a solid business model has yet to be found. After all, a "revolutionary" strategy that doesn't produce earnings growth isn't revolutionary at all—it's just dumb.

Between 1995 and 2000, the ratio of revenue growth over earnings growth was 28 for Cinergy. For Nextel the ratio was 21, 15 for WW Grainger and 7 for Nike. Despite growing its top line by 2,633 percent, Waste Management saw its bottom line contract by 431 percent. While Staples' revenues grew by 248 percent over the five-year period, its earnings contracted by 19 percent. **Clearly, growth by itself is no substitute for radical innovation.** This is particularly true when growth is the product of a pyramid of acquisitions.

Companies that can grow revenue only by "giving away value" at close to zero profit are spinning their wheels—the engine's racing, but there's not much forward progress. Of course, there will be times when profits are scarce as a company "builds out" its strategy and amortizes its start-up costs (think Hughes and DirecTV). But in an existing business, a declining ratio of earnings growth over revenue growth is a sure sign of strategy decay—the strategy may not stink yet, but it's sure dead.

On the other hand, many companies have had a reasonably balanced ratio of revenue growth to earnings growth. Charles Schwab, FedEx, General Electric and Washington Mutual are just a few of the companies that delivered balanced profit and revenue growth in the years 1995 to 2000. While a balanced ratio is no guarantee of a sound strategy, a seriously unbalanced ratio usually indicates a decrepit strategy.

UNSUSTAINABLE GROWTH IN SHAREHOLDER RETURNS—
THE LIMITS OF FINANCIAL ENGINEERING

It is fashionable today to talk of "unlocking" shareholder wealth. The metaphor is telling. The assumption is that the wealth is already there—it's already been created—and with a little financial engineering, it can be set free.

To unlock shareholder wealth you get out of bad businesses—as Jack Welch did when he took over GE. You spin off companies that may command a significantly higher P/E than the parent company—witness the recent appetite for spin-offs and de-mergers at 3M (Imation), Hewlett-Packard (Agilent Technologies), AT&T (Lucent Technologies and AT&T

Wireless), PepsiCo (Tricon) and a host of other companies. You try to dump inflexible and expensive capital assets onto someone else via outsourcing. Of course there's a limit to how many bad businesses a company can divest and how many of its assets it can transfer to someone else's balance sheet. It's not surprising that after a couple of rounds of corporate restructuring, CEOs turn to share buybacks as the easiest way of plumping up share prices.

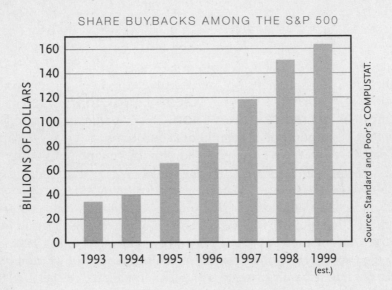

SHARE BUYBACKS AMONG THE S&P 500

Source: Standard and Poor's COMPUSTAT.

Share buybacks are one of the simplest and perhaps most simple-minded ways of unlocking shareholder wealth. Fresh out of ideas? No compelling investment opportunities? No problem! Take the cash being produced by today's businesses and return it to shareholders. We shouldn't be surprised that we've witnessed a record level of equity buybacks in recent years (see the graph "Share Buybacks Among the S&P 500"). After all, there's nothing on this earth with a shorter time horizon than a 60-year-old CEO sitting atop a mountain of stock options, racing his first coronary to the bank. And there's no way to get the share price up faster than buying back your own stock. Not surprising, then, that the number of share buybacks has grown apace with the number of share options held by senior executives in America's largest companies.

If downsizing is the quick fix for corporate obesity, buybacks are the instant cure for an anemic share price. In the five years through 1999, companies as diverse as Toys "R" Us, Cigna, PG&E, General Motors, US Airways, Times Mirror, Maytag and Bear Stearns bought back shares

US Airways	66	Dow Chemical	31
Times Mirror	60	R. R. Donnelley & Sons	31
W. R. Grace & Co.	57	General Motors	30
Tandy	53	Union Carbide	30
Reebok International	44	Autodesk	30
Knight-Ridder	43	DuPont	26
Ryder System	40	AMR	26
PG&E	39	Phelps Dodge	25
ITT Industries	39	Sunoco	25
Liz Claiborne	36	Nordstrom	24
Cooper Industries	34	Deluxe	23
Adobe Systems	34	Hershey Foods	22
Hercules	33	Delta Air Lines	22
Maytag	32	Textron	22
IBM	31	Allstate	21

Source: Standard and Poor's COMPUSTAT; Strategos calculations.

worth more than 30 percent of their market capitalization (see the table "Buyback Champs"). Buybacks are a way of rewarding shareholders despite a lack of apparent growth prospects. Indeed, between 1995 and 2000 the average compound annual revenue growth rate of the top 50 buyback champs was a measly 4 percent. That rate for the S&P 500 was 13 percent, and the 50 fastest-growing companies averaged 50-percent compound annual revenue growth. "Here," buyback CEOs seem to be saying. "We don't know what to do with the cash. You take the money and go see if you can find some better investment opportunities." Of course this is exactly what a CEO bereft of new strategy ideas should do! But it's no more sustainable than selling off assets.

There are dozens and dozens of companies that have, over the past few years, delivered healthy shareholder returns, but have at the same time generated little or no growth in their overall market value. (A few are listed in the table "Growth in Shareholder Returns Versus Growth in Market Capitalization.") These companies haven't created much new wealth.

When growth in shareholder returns significantly outpaces growth in a firm's market value (i.e., when share price is going up faster than the overall value of the firm), you can be sure there's a bit of financial legerdemain going on somewhere. A company that is relying exten-

GROWTH IN SHAREHOLDER RETURNS VERSUS
GROWTH IN MARKET CAPITALIZATION, 1994–1999

	Shareholder Returns 1994–1999 (annualized)	Growth in Market Cap 1994–1999 (annualized)	Difference
W. R. Grace & Co.	18.3	(31.2)	49.5
Dun & Bradstreet	12.9	(15.4)	28.3
Times Mirror	27.2	(2.3)	24.9
Fortune Brands	9.2	(7.4)	16.6
Philip Morris	8.5	(6.4)	14.9

Source: Standard and Poor's COMPUSTAT.

sively on sell–offs, spin–offs or buybacks to drive up its share price is admitting, however inadvertently, that its strategy is wheezing. Look down the list of the buyback champs and you won't see too many industry revolutionaries.

De–mergers, spin–offs, share buybacks and other techniques for unlocking shareholder wealth have built–in limits—at some point, there's no more wealth to "unlock." At some point you actually have to *create* new wealth. Stewards unlock wealth, radical innovators create wealth.

Of course, worse even than the share buybacks are the accounting gyrations that some companies go through in a vain attempt to prop up a feeble business model. Stuffing the channel at the end of the quarter, issuing pro forma earnings reports that ignore significant non-recurring charges, taking "extraordinary" write-offs in an attempt to boost future earnings growth by lowering the baseline, using off–balance sheet financing to deflect attention from a crushing debt load—a reliance on such devices is prima facie evidence of a significantly challenged business model. Having endured a painful lesson on the limits of aspirational accounting, post–Enron investors are demanding new accounting standards and even more transparency. In this climate, even the most imaginative CFO is going to find it hard to pretty up a butt–ugly business model by draping it in a gossamer veil of creative accounting.

The point is this: In too many companies, senior management has mistaken the scoreboard for the game. Quarterly earnings are the score; customer–pleasing, competitor–slamming innovation is the game. Wildly manipulating the numbers on the scoreboard is no substitute for learning how to play the game.

There is yet another option open to executives who are exhausting internal cost-cutting possibilities and have already pushed their accounting practices to the limit—the mega-merger. Hoping for a temporary respite from the law of diminishing returns, companies spent the last few years merging and acquiring at a record pace. The value of mergers and acquisitions announced globally in 2000 amounted to nearly $3.5 trillion (see the graph "Value of Announced Mergers and Acquisitions Worldwide"). In the United States alone, announced M&A activity totaled more than $1.7 trillion, roughly 14 percent of the value of all publicly listed companies in America. Nineteen out of the top 20 mergers in history, by size, were announced in the 18 months leading up to the end of the century. With virtually every company "in play," this superheated merger activity helped to buoy stock prices ever higher. But sadly, there is an in-built limit to industry consolidation. After all, if industry consolidation proceeded for another seven or eight years at 2000's breathless pace, there would be only one firm left in America. This seems an unlikely outcome! Indeed, in 2001, global M&A fell by half, amounting to just $1.7 trillion, and investment banks slashed more than 30,000 jobs.

Over the past few years it has been hard to pick up a financial magazine and not feel like someone who's just been transported to Jurassic Park. Everywhere you look there are dinosaurs mating: Exxon and Mobil, BP and Amoco, J.P. Morgan and Chase Manhattan, Norwest and

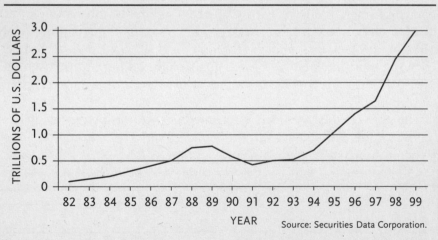

VALUE OF ANNOUNCED MERGERS AND
ACQUISITIONS WORLDWIDE

Source: Securities Data Corporation.

More than 50 percent of the senior executives of America's largest companies derive a significant portion of their compensation from stock options. Indeed, a $100 million stock option payout is not unusual. A few executives have reaped close to half a billion dollars in a single year by exercising their accumulated share options. And these are not hot, young CEOs building new fortunes, but tenured administrators running legacy companies. While the theory was that option-owning managers would work even harder to create new wealth, the reality has been somewhat different.

With most of their assets tied up in stock options, it's difficult for top management to diversify their own shareholdings. Hence they cannot easily offset the risk of holding a large hoard of one company's equity. Thus it's not surprising that option-rich executives are likely to be even more conservative and short-sighted than the average investor who has the freedom to diversify across many companies. With so much of their net worth riding on a single stock, and retirement just a few years away, senior executives can be expected to prefer low-risk strategies for pumping up the share price. Buying back one's own shares is a safer bet than betting on novel business concepts.

Most option plans are not tied to the relative performance of a company against the S&P 500 or any other index. According to the *Wall Street Journal*, of the 209 big stock option grants made by large companies in 1998, only 36 had any type of performance trigger.[a] Thus an executive could underperform the average and still cash in, as his company's stock price was on the rise. Worse, options are frequently repriced if a stock falls below the strike price——an option not open to outside investors who may find themselves underwater thanks to management's malfeasance. Even the *Wall Street Journal*, hardly known for begrudging wealthy CEOs their due, had to conclude that "these days CEOs are assured of getting rich, however the company does."[b]

A few compensation committees do set specific stock price hurdles that must be reached before the options can be exercised. Level 3 Communications grants its top executives options that can be exercised only if the company's stock outperforms the S&P 500 stock index. General Mills requires executives to hold on to most of the shares they buy when they exercise their options.[c]

The law of unintended consequences is ever at work. Rather than getting CEOs focused on growing the long-term value of their companies, stock options have seduced many into short-term, one-shot, price-pumping schemes such as share buybacks, spin-offs and mega-mergers. In too many cases executives are not managing in the best long-term interests of their shareholders; they are managing in the best short-term interests of themselves.

[a] Joann S. Lublin, "Lowering the Bar," *Wall Street Journal*, 8 April 1999.
[b] Ibid.
[c] Tamar Hausman, "Predicting Pay," Wall Street Journal, 8 April 1999.

Wells Fargo, American Airlines and TWA, Daimler–Benz and Chrysler, International Paper and Champion, Bell Atlantic and GTE, SBC and Ameritech, Pharmacia and Upjohn. Hundreds of other copulating couples dot the landscape. While some of these mergers are propelled by truly strategic considerations—global market access or industry convergence—many are simply the last gasp of cost–cutting CEOs who hope that by slamming together two lumbering incumbents, they will be able to lop off another $1 billion or so of shared overhead and show another 10,000 employees the door. Yet shareholders lose more often than they gain from such mergers. A 1999 study found that of the 700 largest deals completed between 1996 and 1998, more than half had actually diminished shareholder value.[1] These mergers follow a familiar course. The share price takes a bounce on expectations of future efficiencies, top management in the acquired company gets a Midas–like payout and in the months that follow the deal, the usual postmerger turmoil and ever-escalating integration costs wipe out nearly all of the expected benefits.

A recent study in the pharmaceutical industry suggests that the most notable impact of a merger is the loss of market share by the participating companies. Furthermore, the study finds little evidence that bigger companies are any more productive at discovering new drugs.[2] A significant minority of mega–deals, such as AT&T's purchase of NCR, Novell's acquisition of WordPerfect, Dow Jones & Co's purchase of Telerate and Quaker Oats's acquisition of Snapple Beverage (which was eventually sold to PepsiCo), turn out to be monumental stinkers, with the acquired company sold after an enormous write–off. Putting two drunks together doesn't make a stable person.

If there is a secondary logic to the wave of mergers sweeping the planet, it is the simple arithmetic of oligopoly. If you reduce the competitive intensity in an industry by reducing the number of independent competitors, profits are likely to go up. It's hard not to conclude that this logic has driven a number of telecom deals such as that between SBC and Ameritech. The industrial oligarchy loves an oligopoly: just enough competition to avoid direct government control; not enough to threaten a profitable sinecure.

Defending their merger plans, CEOs are often quoted as saying, "You have to be number one in your market to make any money". or "Only the biggest will survive." This rationale is largely specious. Size doesn't inoculate a company from rule–busting innovation. **Bulk is no bulwark against the onslaught of revolutionary new competitors.** And it's hard to mate and run at the same time. The merger–obsessed thinking in some executive suites seems to go something like this: "If we're a really, really big dinosaur, maybe we can survive the Ice Age."

In fact, for the top 1,000 publicly listed companies in America, the correlation between company size (revenues) and profitability (operating margins), whether measured over three, five or ten years, is no more than .004—a result that isn't statistically significant.[3] Put simply, there is no reason to expect that being bigger will make a company more profitable. Company size and imagination of the sort that produces new wealth-creating strategies are not correlated. Sure, size brings advantages, but in the age of revolution those advantages are often offset by disadvantages—inflexibility, internal politicking and sloth.

A final rationale for many mega-mergers is "synergy," or its twenty-first-century counterpart, "convergence." These words should send investors racing for the door. Here's what AT&T's CEO said in 1991 when his company acquired NCR: "I am absolutely confident that together AT&T and NCR will achieve a level of growth and success that we could not achieve separately. Ours will be a future of promises fulfilled." Here's what AT&T's CEO said in 1995 when NCR was spun off to shareholders: "The complexity of trying to manage these different businesses began to overwhelm the advantages of integration. The world has changed. Markets have changed." No shit, Sherlock. That's the age of revolution for you—all that damn change. Well, then, be careful about loading up the balance sheet with billions of dollars of fixed assets on the basis of something as ethereal as "synergy" or "convergence."

Yeah, there are going to be a lot more mega-deals in the years ahead, particularly in Europe and Asia, where there are still too many national-scale banks, airlines, car companies and insurance companies. And yes, a well-thought-out program of disposals and acquisitions can sometimes play a critical role in revitalizing a company's core strategy. A series of bold deals, culminating in the acquisition of Seagram's Universal unit, helped transform a 150-year-old French water treatment company, Générales des Eaux, into Vivendi Universal, one of the world's top three media and entertainment giants. But once the ownership cards have been reshuffled, top management still has to produce sustainable, profitable growth. And that takes genuine innovation. The 1990s produced a crop of ravenous deal makers—from Sandy Weill at Citigroup to John Chambers at Cisco to Bernie Ebbers at WorldCom and Chris Gent at Vodafone, from Bernie Arnault at LVMH to Dennis Koslowski at Tyco and Jean-Marie Messier at Vivendi Universal, among many others. In a few cases, the deal making was based on sound business logic. In other cases, the orgy of buying was nothing more than a giant pyramid scheme: Use a spate of acquisitions to fuel top-line growth; talk investors into giving your company a nose–bleed share price based on its growth record; use your vaunted share price to make yet more acquisitions, etc., etc. In the long term, such a strategy is completely unsustainable; but in the short term it can turn a vision-challenged CEO into a demibillionaire. In the end, deal making is no substitute for strategy innovation. Investment bankers can make a company bigger, but they can't make it more innovative.

STRATEGY CONVERGENCE— THE LIMITS TO BEST PRACTICE

In a recent survey, I asked more than 500 CEOs whether they believed the strategies of their major competitors had been getting more alike or more dissimilar. The number one answer: more alike. This is not good news. Do you remember Economics 101 and the idea of "perfect competition"—when everyone in an industry followed an identical strategy and had similar resources? You probably also remember the textbook result: Every company made just enough profit to survive and no more. It's the business equivalent of a subsistence economy. That's the inevitable result of convergent strategies.

In nearly every industry, strategies tend to cluster around some "central tendency" of industry orthodoxy. Strategies converge because successful recipes get slavishly imitated. All you computer industry executives who've been trying to imitate Dell's build–to–order business model, raise your hands! All you car company honchos who spent two decades trying to duplicate Toyota's lean manufacturing model, fess up! All you department store execs who've been using Wal–Mart as a case study in how to manage logistics, go ahead, admit it. Nothing wrong with imitation, of course, as long as you've achieved strategy differentiation in other areas of your business. *But all too often, a successful new business model becomes the business model for companies not creative enough to invent their own.*

Aiding and abetting strategy convergence is an ever–growing army of eager young consultants transferring "best practice" from leaders to laggards. When some big consulting company whispers in your ear, "We have a really deep understanding of your industry," what are they saying? Simply this: "We'll infect you with the same orthodoxies we've infected everyone else in your industry with." The challenge of maintaining any sort of competitive differentiation goes up proportionately with the number of consultants moving management wisdom around the world.

Outsourcing has been another powerful force for strategy convergence. As companies outsource more and more, the scope for competitive differentiation gets narrower and narrower. There's a reason Dell Computer hasn't outsourced its core IT processes and is no friend of cookie–cutter ERP solutions. Dell's business model is based on creating unique advantages out of IT—that's something that can't be easily done with off–the–shelf solutions.

Executives who spend much of their time attending the same trade shows, reading the same industry magazines and listening to the same e–biz pundits accelerate the pace of strategy convergence. In the end, strategies converge because everyone defines the industry in the same way, uses the same segmentation criteria, sells through the same channels, adopts the same service policies and so on. In fact, the typical definition of an "industry" is simply those companies that are all operating with the same business model.

In the airline industry the strategies of American, United and Delta are virtually indistinguishable—at least from the perspective of a customer. If tonight, while everyone was asleep, we randomly reassigned the top hundred executives from each of these airlines to their competitors, would you expect anything substantial to change in your flying experience? Despite a vibrant economy, the U.S. airline industry's return on sales was a meager 5 percent in 1999. With every downturn, the incumbents engage in a sort of intra–industry cannibalism, slashing prices in an attempt to steal each other's customers. Of course, cheapskate flyers will heartily applaud the spectacle of contestants chewing off each other's limbs, but investors may be less amused.

Or think about department stores. May Department Stores, Federated Department Stores, JCPenney, Sears and Dillard's have all underperformed the S&P 500 in the last decade. And no wonder—store layout, merchandise selection and service policies are boringly similar. Wal–Mart, Best Buy, Target and Kohl's are the standout performers. Each has a strategy that's distinctly different from traditional department stores.

In general, wealth–creating champions possess highly differentiated strategies. Sure they face competitors, but they have unique capabilities, unique assets, unique value propositions, and unique market positioning. You won't mistake a flight on Virgin Atlantic for one on United. You won't mistake a sandwich at Pret A Manger for a production–line burger. If a strategy ain't different, it's dead. At one time, Bernie Ebbers, the rebel who built WorldCom, claimed to be an enemy of strategy convergence. A stock analyst once asked Mr. Ebbers whether he was going to buy up cable television properties as AT&T's Michael Armstrong had done. Bernie's reply: "We're not going to do anything that he's doing."[4] How then, Bernie, do you explain your acquisition of MCI, a long-distance telephone company that competes head-to-head with AT&T? If ever there was an industry where strategies have converged, it's long-distance telephone service in the United States. Quick—name an important difference between the service offered by Sprint, AT&T and WorldCom MCI. You get my point. Bought for $30 billion in 1998, MCI was estimated to be worth around $3 billion in June 2001.[5] Not surprisingly, many observers now view MCI as an albatross round WorldCom's neck.

So how do you know if your strategy is converging with everyone else's? Well, if your company's revenue growth, return on investment, operating margins or P/E ratios are tightly clustered around the industry average, it's a good bet that strategies are converging. Have a look at the performance of the major U.S. airlines over a ten-year period (see the table "Key Financial Indicators for Selected U.S. Airlines, 1989-1999"). Who do you think has the most differentiated strategy here? Southwest's earnings grew nearly twice as fast as the industry average and its revenues even faster. It also has the healthiest operating margins by far. It should be no surprise that Southwest also has the most highly differentiated strategy. Southwest said, in effect, "If we're going to treat customers like cattle, we might as well develop a business model for cattle—no reserved seating, no meals, no fancy lounges and no in-flight entertainment." The airline industry is not unique. Strategy convergence tends to produce margin convergence—around a relatively low average.

Without radical innovation, a company will devote a mountain of resources to achieve a molehill of differentiation. The amount spent on advertising indistinguishable soft drinks, the millions of direct-mail so-

KEY FINANCIAL INDICATORS
FOR SELECTED U.S. AIRLINES, 1989-1999

	Average Operating Margin *1990-1999*	Compound Annual Growth in Net Income *1989-1999*	Compound Annual Growth in Revenue *1989-1999*
AMR (American Airlines)	6.1	3.7	5.4
Northwest	4.9	16.2	4.6
Delta Air Lines	4.2	9.1	6.2
UAL (United Airlines)	3.4	14.3	6.3
Southwest	**11.6**	**20.8**	**16.7**

Source: Standard and Poor's COMPUSTAT.

licitations trying to induce customers to switch from one credit card company to another, the millions of "free" miles given away by airlines to induce customers to remain "loyal" in the face of uniformly lackluster service, the marketing investment needed to get investors to pay attention to any one of the more than 3,500 mutual funds available in the United States, the resources expended in producing half a dozen look-alike television newsmagazines, the "incentives" car companies have to pay to move indistinguishable autos off dealer lots—these are just a few examples of the high-cost, low-impact futility of carbon copy strategies.

Is your company a victim of strategy convergence? If you have to answer yes to the following three questions, it probably is.

1. **Have we let others define customer expectations?** Sears, Roebuck let Wal-Mart and Target set customer expectations for value. Target went a step further and created a shopping environment substantially more inviting than Wal-Mart's warehouse format. Target's payoff: loyal shoppers from across the entire socioeconomic spectrum.

2. **Does competition within our industry feel like a zero-sum game where the only way to gain market share is through cutting prices and margins?** This has long been true within the American long-distance telephone business, where pricing gimmicks seem to be the only way to grab customers. In this case, tit-for-tat price battles serve only to ratchet down industry profitability.

3. **Are our performance metrics (revenue growth rate, operating margin, P/E ratio, asset turn, etc.) within a standard deviation of the industry average?** Performance metrics that conform to the industry average are usually evidence of a strategy that is no more than average.

Occasionally, strategy convergence verges on mass hysteria. This is, of course, what produced the dot-com bubble. While some observers, reflecting on the dot-com crash, have argued that the Internet spawned too much business innovation, the opposite was actually nearer the truth. Literally thousands of B2C and B2B companies were created between 1998 and 2000. Most of these companies had virtually identical business models—indeed, it was often possible to find 20 or 30 companies vying for the same narrow niche (e.g., creating an online market for buying and selling bulk chemicals). Moreover, each of these companies believed resolutely in first-mover advantages and therefore attempted to outspend competitors in building early market share. Services were given away for free, small fortunes were spent on advertising and computer capacity was built far ahead of demand. Of course, to get a first-mover advantage, you actually have to be a first mover, that is, you have to arrive at a truly unique point of view about a new opportunity *before* anyone else. This was the case for eBay, for Amazon, for ICQ (the instant messaging pioneer later bought by AOL) and for the handful of other Internet pioneers still standing. To reap a first-mover advantage, a company must be able to buy market share at a discount. This is possible only if potential competitors have not yet awoken to the new opportunity and are not, therefore, going to attempt to outspend you. When a clutch of companies all share the same broad view of a future opportunity, are building roughly similar business models, are equally well funded and intent on spending whatever it takes to build a preemptive market position, there is virtually no chance of buying market share at a discount. In such a case, there is no first-mover advantage—just a bloodbath. As the vast majority of dot-com entrepreneurs ultimately discovered, the fact that a business model is Net-based doesn't make it "revolutionary"; it is revolutionary only if it is different in some substantial, and profitable, way from other Net-based business models.

Gray-suited executives are just as susceptible to mass hysteria as T-shirt–wearing entrepreneurs—how else can one explain the $130 billion that European telecom companies dumped into third-generation wireless licenses in an orgy of competitive bidding? Outbidding similarly intentioned and deep-pocketed rivals for the right to spend further billions building out an infrastructure for a service facing uncertain demand is bold—but not necessarily smart. A folly of similar proportions occurred between 1997 and 2001 when, in a headlong rush, a few dozen United States–based start-ups buried $90 billion worth of fiber optic in the ground. A score or more of companies with identical visions and willing bankers managed to borrow nearly $400 billion and raise hundreds of billions more through equity offerings. At the end of this orgy of tunneling, less than 3 percent of the fiber was actually in use and dozens of bankruptcies had been announced, including PSINet, Winstar Communications, NorthPoint Communications and many more. A mania, defined as an excessively intense enthusiasm, is not the same thing as a competitively unique strategy. And when a mania is widely shared, there are going to be tears all around.

Right now, thousands of managers are spending boatloads of bucks to webify their business models—without any real understanding of whether those investments will create competitive differentiation. Efficiency–besotted execs can be forgiven for falling prey to the lurid come–on of IT consultants: Slash your inventories, cut your working capital, replace your call centers and get rid of all those paper–pushers. There is no doubt that e–business transformation yields unprecedented efficiency gains. Yet it's not easy to turn productivity into profits. And in the absence of competitive differentiation it's impossible.

If the Net's efficiency bonanza doesn't end up on the bottom line, where will it end up? In the pockets of customers. The thought that you can spend a couple of years and a mountain of cash turning your company into an e–business and end up with your margins just about where they started is none too comforting. But for many, probably most companies, this is exactly the fate that awaits them in the brave new world of e. Lest you think this is scare–mongering, consider, for a moment, the profit impact of the original e—electricity.

In their provocatively titled report, *Is the Internet Better than Electricity,*[6] Martin Brookes and Zaki Wahhaj, a pair of Goldman Sachs economists, studied the process of electrification at the beginning of the twentieth century. Their aim was to glean insights into the Internet's potential impact on productivity and profits. Electrification provides a useful analogy because, like the recent wave of IT spending, it produced dramatic efficiency gains and a redistribution of profits among various sectors of the economy. The fruits of electrification were divided among four groups: companies like General Electric and Westinghouse that made the equipment for electricity generation and transmission (think Accenture, Sun, IBM, Intel, et al.), companies that generated and distributed electricity (e–business consultants and application developers like Oracle and SAP), industrial companies which invested heavily to electrify their businesses (the bulk of the Fortune 500) and consumers.

During the more than 40 years covered in the Goldman Sachs study, the makers of electrical gear enjoyed the biggest profit boost, in part because of their lock on key patents (a particularly robust form of competitive advantage). Electricity generators did well for a while, then suffered dwindling margins and declining share values as competitors multiplied. But what was most remarkable was the impact of electrification on the profits of the industrial companies that rewired their factories and redesigned their processes to take advantage of the new technology. It is worth quoting Brookes and Wahhaj on this point:

> The industrials sector experienced profits growth below the growth of nominal GDP in each of the periods considered. Companies were becoming more efficient, using the technology of electricity to produce output more cheaply. But they were forced to pass these gains on to the consumer in lower prices instead of increasing profit margins. [p. 16]

Of course a few industrial companies grew their profits faster than GDP, but these were the exceptions. In the battle between producers and consumers over the spoils of increased productivity, the consumers won—at least in the case of electricity. Will the Internet be different? Certainly it will bring a productivity bonus to the U.S. economy. Robert Litan of the Brookings Institution and Alice Rivlin, a former Federal Reserve vice chairman, predict Internet-related savings ranging from $100 billion to $230 billion between 2001 and 2006. But that doesn't mean these savings will fatten corporate profits. Indeed, over the past decade, the share of U.S. capital spending going into IT zoomed from less than 20 percent to nearly 60 percent. Yet, as we saw earlier, average operating margins have barely budged over the last several years.

There are two reasons why the twenty-first-century version of e may be even harder on profits than its twentieth-century counterpart. First, to the extent that the Internet succeeds, over time, in reducing economic "friction," it will also zap profits. While Web-heads celebrate the dawn of "frictionless capitalism," they typically fail to note that companies often owe a majority of their profits to friction. Profit-producing friction comes in many guises:

○ For banks, insurance companies, auto dealers and many other industries, customer ignorance has long been a source of friction and a reliable profit center. Before the Internet, consumers found it difficult and time consuming to compare prices and features across multiple suppliers. Now we are moving toward a world of perfectly informed customers and zero search costs. Many companies are going to get a surprising lesson in the difference between customer inertia and real customer loyalty.
○ In the past, jewelers, bookstores, radio stations and all those category-killer retailers often enjoyed local monopolies. Minimum-scale economies limited the number of retailers that

could profitably serve any particular geographic area. But today, customers can shop the globe for the best deal. There are no more hostage customers.

○ Accountants, lawyers and financial advisors have long exploited knowledge asymmetries. They knew something you didn't know and charged you hefty fees to share their wisdom. But the cost of putting information on the Web is close to zero, so the margins from knowledge arbitrage are bound to fall.

○ Asymmetries in bargaining between buyers and suppliers are yet another source of friction. B2B exchanges threaten to even out these differences. A group of 40–plus retailers with nearly three-and-a-half times the buying power of Wal–Mart have come together to form the World Retail Exchange. On the flip side, Procter & Gamble, Coca–Cola, General Mills, Kellogg, Kraft Foods and other grocery suppliers have invested more than $250 million to build Transora, their own B2B mega–market. Whatever the out-come of these efforts, most suppliers will soon be facing a world in which there are no more weak customers. Every buyer will wield Wal–Mart's bargaining power.

○ Transaction costs, which represent information asymmetries between buyers and sellers, are another artifact of friction. In the years ahead, market makers of all sorts are going to find it harder and harder to make a living as the Net drives transaction costs ever downward.

Friction props up prices. As friction disappears, the challenge will be to invent new forms of competitive advantage faster than old ones disappear. For companies that have grown fat on friction, this will be no easy task. It doesn't take a heap of imagination to exploit the advantages of friction. But in our hyper-transparent world where the Net has left mediocrity no place to hide, competitive advantage will increasingly rest on an ability to create products, services and business models that are unique and utterly compelling. In the past, it mattered less that few companies were adept at radical innovation—they could coast on friction instead. So although e-business offers enormous scope for cost cutting, it may well be that the price–deflating impact of the Web, in the form of reduced friction, will overwhelm the efficiency–enhancing benefits of the Web for the vast majority of companies. This is not to argue that the Web will fail to offer companies the chance to invent new sources of friction—you can be sure Microsoft is working day and night to do just this. Microsoft's hope is that its Passport e–commerce registration system will be the turnstile through which every online shopper must pass, depositing his or her identity and a few coins along the way. Neither is the Internet going to erase all forms of off-line friction overnight. But in the medium term, the Net is going to exert a powerful deflationary impact on prices—of that there can be no doubt.

There is a second, subtler way in which the Internet may prove to be the enemy of profits: e-business transformation may contribute to strategy convergence. More and more, companies are using the same software platforms, be it SAP's R/3 ERP solution or Oracle's 9i database. More and more, companies are relying on the same handful of IT consultants—all of them organized along vertical industry lines—the better to share *your* best practice with your competitors. More and more, companies are outsourcing critical IT functions to a small club of specialists like EDS and IBM Global Services. And if the IT vendors have their way, erstwhile rivals will adopt common procurement policies and combine their purchasing power in B2B exchanges.

For too long, CIOs have seen their role as improving operating efficiency rather than creating competitive differentiation through radical innovation. As long as this is true, they will fall victim to e-biz vendors who bleat about the importance of IT as a source of competitive advantage, then urge their clients to outsource rather than operate, buy rather than build and embrace the best practices of competitors. If your company is going to spend better than half of its capital budget on IT, it better have a point of view about how it's going to use IT to create advantages unique to the industry!

Of course a Web-based strategy *can* create competitive advantage. AOL accomplished this with instant messaging. eBay did it with online auctions. In the pre-Web world, information technology powered innovative business models at Wal-Mart, Federal Express and a handful of other companies. But if you expect the Web to create wealth for *your* shareholders, your e-strategy better come wrapped inside a truly novel business model, one that offers customers unrivaled efficiencies or truly unique products and services. And these things aren't for sale by any e-consultant.

The collective delusion of the dot-com mob was that clicks, hits and visits could be readily translated into customers and revenues. The collective delusion of the Fortune 500 aristocracy is that productivity gains automatically translate into plumper profits. Any company that plans to make money from e will have to have a Web strategy that creates *unique* value for customers, confers *unique* advantages in delivering that value and is tough to copy. As different as Mustique is from the Jersey Shore—that's how different your company's Web strategy needs to be if it's going to create real competitive advantage. Of the many things the so-called new economy didn't change, here's one more: Sameness still sucks.

So no, Virginia, the Internet is not some profit bonanza—not even for big companies with seemingly well-entrenched positions. The Internet is simply one more force chipping away at profits and thereby increasing the importance of rule-busting, expectation-shattering innovation.

HONESTY FIRST

If you want to escape the cul-de-sac of diminishing returns, the first step is to admit that your current strategy, your dearly beloved business model, may be running out of steam. ***Strategy decay is not something that* might *happen; it's something that* is *happening.*** And it's probably happening faster than most folks in your company are willing to admit.

Working ever harder to improve the efficiency of a worn-out strategy is ultimately futile. Think of all those CEOs leading all those depressingly mediocre companies. How many of them are willing to stand in front of their shareholders or their employees and own up to the obvious—"Our business model is busted"?

Dakota tribal wisdom says that when you discover you're on a dead horse, the best strategy is to dismount. Of course, there are other strategies. You can change riders. You can get a committee to study the dead horse. You can benchmark how other companies ride dead horses. You can declare that it's cheaper to feed a dead horse. You can harness several dead horses together. But after you've tried all these things, you're still going to have to dismount.

The temptation to stay on a dead horse can be overwhelming. Take one example. In a recent six-month period, the percentage of teenagers who named Nike as a "cool" brand shrank from 52 percent to 40 percent.[7] By the time teenagers are sporting T-shirts that read, "Just Don't Do It," it's a bit late to start work on revitalizing your brand. The time to begin searching for new wealth-creating strategies is long before the horse stumbles. Today's stock market darlings would do well to reflect on the fate of Hewlett-Packard, Xerox, Compaq Computer, Novell and dozens of other highfliers that fell to earth when they couldn't escape the gravitational pull of moribund strategies.

Sun Microsystems' chief technology officer has estimated that 20 percent of his company's in-house technical knowledge becomes obsolete each year.[8] Sun sees itself as being on a never-ending hunt for new strategies. America's major television networks, dusty relics in an era of 500-channel satellite television, have been somewhat less than attentive to the risks of strategy decay. It's been nontraditional channels like MTV and Comedy Central that have pioneered edgy new shows (though it's hard to argue that *South Park* advances the art of television programming). Twenty years ago, television networks were a bit like *Time* magazine—broad and shallow, with something for everyone. Now television is like a 30-foot-long magazine rack filled with specialty rags: The Classic Movie Channel, The Golf Channel, Animal Planet, MTV and dozens more. Television has been parsed into hundreds of tiny markets. Just over the horizon looms full video Webcasting, which will turn television into a whatever-you-want, when-you-want-it medium. In the 1991–92 season, the four major networks had an audience share of 76 percent. By the 2000–2001 season that had tumbled to 51 percent.[9] Says Robert A. Iger, the former head of ABC and now president of Disney, "We used to think the possibility existed that the erosion was going to stop. We were silly. It's never going to stop. As you give customers greater and greater choices, they are going to make more choices."[10] **DENIAL IS TRAGIC. DELAY IS DEADLY.**

Why do so many companies once a decade have to suffer through a performance crisis and the management upheavals that typically ensue? The answer is that they can't bring themselves to abandon a seriously out-of-date business model. To create new wealth, a company must be willing to abandon its current strategy, at least in part, before it goes toes up.

In the age of revolution, the future is not an echo of the past. While every executive understands this intellectually, it is quite another thing to stand in front of the members of your organization and your investors and boldly confront the demon of decay. But investors and employees are smart enough to know that sooner or later every company has to do a strategy "uninstall."

Without an explicit recognition of the onset of decay, there is little incentive for a strategy reboot. It is imperative, therefore, that you and everyone else in your organization be alert to the signs that your company's business model is approaching its "sell by" date—unless, of course, you particularly relish the chance to manage a turnaround.

So start with the truth. Executives must be willing to be brutally honest about the rate at which their current strategy is decaying. Most senior executives grew up in a world where business models aged gracefully and where incumbency was often an overwhelming advantage. That world is gone. Get over it. Anyone who fails to recognize this fact puts his or her company's future success in grave jeopardy. Executives and employees in every company have a set of little lies they tell themselves to avoid having to deal with the reality of a faltering strategy. Like an alcoholic who claims to drink only socially, managers often claim a dead business model is only sleeping. Here are some of the most-used lies:

"It's only an execution issue."
"It's an alignment problem."
"We just have to get more focused."
"It's the regulators' fault."
"Our competitors are behaving irrationally."
"We're in a transition period."
"Everyone in our industry is losing money."
"Asia/Europe/Latin America went bad."
"We're investing for the long term."
"Investors don't understand our strategy."

Sometimes people in a company will walk around a dead strategy for years before admitting that it has expired and gone to strategy heaven.

So what are the little lies that get told in your company? Recently, I came across the corporate magazine for one of America's largest insurance companies. In this magazine the CEO was quoted as saying, "Insurance is very complex, I think people will always need agents." That's at least a medium-size lie. Quotesmith.com, along with a bunch of other new insurance infomediaries, can easily imagine a world without agents, as can anyone who has bought insurance this way. Oh yeah, we may still need claims agents for a while longer, but sales agents? Don't be too sure. Every business model is decaying as we speak.

If you want to lead the revolution you have to search for signs of diminishing returns in your efficiency programs, for evidence of unsustainable revenue growth or creeping convergence. Be honest: Has "corporate strategy" been more about financial restructuring and mega-deals than about business concept innovation? Are you counting on some e-business whitewash to cover the cracks of a crumbling business model? You have to have the courage to speak candidly about the fragility of success in a discontinuous world. Never forget that good companies gone bad are simply companies that for too long denied the reality of strategy decay.

The nub of the matter is this: What will it take to get your company to reinvent itself? Will it take a competitor's success—a benchmark so clear and unequivocal that you will be forced to move? That's what it took to prompt Merrill Lynch to embrace online trading. But if you wait until a competitor hands you a paint-by-numbers kit, you're going to end up producing something highly unoriginal. Will it take a direct and immediate crisis—a threat so close you can smell failure on its breath? If the threat is already breathing in your ear, you're unlikely to escape without a mauling. Or does it take only a sense of the enormous possibility that exists in the age of revolution to get you and your company totally jazzed about the opportunity for radical innovation? In 1986, Lorenzo Zambrano, the newly installed chairman of Cemex, a regional Mexican cement producer, saw the chance to turn the global cement industry on its ear. Over the next 15 years, Cemex became the fastest-growing *and* most profitable cement company in the world. It's no coincidence that Cemex was also widely regarded as one of the most innovative companies in the world.

In the age of revolution, every company must become an opportunity-seeking missile—where the guidance system homes in on what is possible, not on what has already been accomplished. A brutal honesty about strategy decay and a commitment to creating new wealth are the foundations for strategy innovation. But you can't be an industry revolutionary unless you've learned to see the unconventional. You won't have the courage to abandon, even partially, what is familiar unless you feel in your viscera the promise of the unconventional. And you can't create radical new business concepts, or reinvigorate old ones, unless you first understand what a business concept actually is. So that is where we will turn our attention next.

3
BUSINESS CONCEPT INNOVATION

CAN YOU THINK BEYOND NEW PRODUCTS?

Can you think beyond "more of the same"? Can you imagine products and services that have the power to profoundly change customers' expectations? Can you conceive of entirely new business models? What about unconventional strategies for breathing new life into old business models? Can you envision pulling apart an industry and putting it back together in a way that creates new value? In most organizations there are few individuals who can think holistically and radically about *business concept innovation.*

Say the word "innovation," and the average middle manager will conjure up an image of a product-line extension (Diet Coke with Lemon) or a big bucks R&D project (nanotechnology, fuel cells, pharmacogenomics and the like). The first type of innovation seldom produces a torrent of new wealth, nor is it likely to arrest the fading fortunes of a firm stuck with an out-of-date business model. The second type of innovation occasionally produces big returns (like the multibillion-dollar payoff on a blockbuster drug) but also requires an appetite for equally outsize risks. Product development and corporate R&D are well-recognized functions in most companies—yet radical, rule-busting innovation seldom comes from either of these traditional sources.

Product-focused innovation is often more incremental than radical—it seldom challenges the basic conception of the product or the service. Of course there are exceptions—real product breakthroughs occasionally change the future of an industry. The video tape recorder, the Apple Macintosh computer, the ATM card and AOL's instant messaging service are some standout examples. **INCREMENTAL INNOVATION IS BETTER THAN NO INNOVATION AT ALL, BUT IN AN INCREASINGLY NONLINEAR WORLD, ONLY NONLINEAR IDEAS ARE LIKELY TO CREATE NEW WEALTH.**

Radical innovation is innovation that has the power to change customer expectations, alter industry economics and redefine the basis for competitive advantage. The notion of competitive advantage is very important here. An idea may appear to be radical in the sense that it changes customer perceptions (for example, the ability to buy pet food online), but if the idea doesn't produce a defensible source of competitive advantage, it is radical only in the most superficial sense—a point many dot-com entrepreneurs failed to understand. By definition, a bona fide competitive advantage is both unique and difficult to duplicate. A central goal of radical innovation is the invention of new sources of competitive advantage. Few product-line extensions or product enhancements (for example, a TV with a built-in DVD player) meet the test of radical innovation. Correspondingly, they have limited power to generate new wealth.

Virtually every industry can be characterized by a set of improvement curves that define the pace of progress. One of the most famous is Moore's Law, which posits a doubling of the ratio of semiconductor performance to price every 18 months or so. An improvement curve measures progress in a key performance metric over time. Typical metrics include cost of customer acquisition, time to market, direct manufacturing cost per unit, number of defects per thousand products and reported customer satisfaction. When it is successful, radical innovation dramatically alters the shape of an important improvement curve. For example, when Kodak pioneered the single-use camera, it created a significant dislocation in the cost curve associated with the manufacture of 35mm cameras. Indeed, Kodak's cheap and cheerful cameras sell for less than the annual cost savings typically achieved by Canon or Nikon in the production of traditional 35mm cameras. The single-use camera also changed customers' perceptions and habits. How many parents would trust a ten-year-old with a Nikon camera? Yet few would think twice about giving a child a disposable camera to use at the beach or a friend's birthday party. This kind of innovation is far more profound and has far more impact than incremental product enhancements.

Another limitation of traditional product innovation is that it is often confined to the physical product or the actual service. Yet the product is only one of several components that comprise the overall business concept. Thinking in terms of business concepts rather than products significantly extends the potential scope for innovation. It may be possible, for example, to build a radically different business concept even when the product itself is a virtual commodity. This is what Dell Computer accomplished in the PC business. A personal computer made by Dell is virtually indistinguishable from one made by HP or Compaq. Dell is not a product innovator. Yet Dell has innovated extensively in the way it builds and distributes PCs. And the 2:1 margin advantage that Cemex enjoys over its traditional competitors in the cement business is not the result of product innovation. It derives instead from Cemex's ability to spawn and deploy a steady succession of process innovations.

A product-centered view of innovation leads to blind spots—neglected opportunities for new thinking that are likely to be exploited by less myopic competitors. Product innovation is to business-concept innovation as bicep curls are to strength training—important, but only a small part of a much bigger challenge. Our interest is in innovation that is not only *radical* but also *extensive* in that it views every component of the business concept as a potential candidate for rule-breaking innovation. A business concept that differs from industry conventions along several dimensions is typically the most difficult for convention-bound incumbents to emulate.

Every new idea can be judged in terms of these two criteria: To what degree does the idea depart from industry norms (how radical is it)? and to what extent does the idea stretch beyond the product to encompass other elements of the business concept (how extensive is it)? Using these criteria, it is easy to see why companies like IKEA, eBay, Southwest Airlines, MTV, ReplayTV, Dell Computer, NetJets, Starbucks, Kohl's, Pret A Manger and XM Radio, among many others, truly qualify as industry revolutionaries.

Ask yourself what percentage of your company's product development projects, improvement initiatives and capital investment programs are aimed at producing radical innovation? Any company that

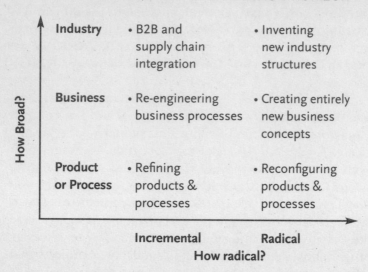

hopes to outperform its mediocre peers will need to have a significant percentage of its projects, programs and initiatives in the upper right-hand quadrant of the matrix above.

So what about science? What about the kind of innovation that wins Nobel prizes? Companies like Boeing, Merck and Intel depend on R&D to produce breakthrough products and to redefine the performance envelope of existing products. R&D can be outrageously expensive (in 2002 the cost to develop a new drug was around $800 million).

Struggling as it does to push back the frontiers of knowledge, R&D is beset by uncertainties. Multimillion–dollar R&D programs often grind to a halt when they encounter intractable scientific problems. And even in the best cases, payback periods can stretch out to a decade or more. As an example, it took JVC and Sony nearly two decades to master the science of video recording. Given this, it shouldn't be surprising that technological prowess is no guarantee of above–average returns. In a recent five–year period, each of 21 U.S. companies was awarded 1,000 patents or more. These companies are America's technology superstars. Yet as a group, their earnings per share grew only 70 percent as fast as the average for the entire S&P 500 over the same five–year time frame. No wonder many companies are reining in corporate R&D and tying research budgets ever more tightly to the near–term priorities of operating units.

Science seeks to discover what is not yet known. Business concept innovation has a more modest goal—to imagine what has not yet been done. While the financial rewards can be spectacular in both cases, business concept innovation is, on average, less risky than fundamental technology innovation (where risk is the probability of failure multiplied by the minimum required investment). New scientific knowledge typically comes at a steep price. By contrast, **the imagination required to invent new business concepts comes cheap.** And while business concept innovation is never risk-free, there are ways, as we will see, of reducing those risks through low-cost experimentation and short-loop market feedback cycles. Radical innovation does not need to entail radical risk taking, nor should it.

Many companies have a difficult time in assigning an exact dollar value to the returns they get from their R&D spending—yet year after year they devote 2, 5 or even 10 percent of revenues to it. I would argue that companies should be spending a like sum on experiments aimed at reinventing existing business concepts and inventing new ones. One company with which I am acquainted recently decided to set aside 10 percent of its billion-dollar-a-year capital budget for projects that met the test of being "radical." Over each of the next five years, an additional 10 percent of the capital budget will be devoted to projects that challenge conventional thinking. If divisional managers fail to come up with such projects, their capital budgets will be cut proportionately. In this case, the CFO is sending a clear message to operating executives: Above-average performance requires investment proposals that defy industry-average thinking and deliver better than industry-average rates of improvement.

In the end, it is imagination, not investment, that drives innovation. The goal of this chapter and the next is to help you improve your capacity for the kind of radical, extensive innovation that thrills customers and dismays competitors. In the chapters that follow, you will meet some of the individuals and companies that have become adept at business concept innovation. But first, let's get some practice in thinking radically about business concepts. Let's speculate about what could be. As a start, let's imagine a radically new business concept—a global cyber business school.

CYBER B-SCHOOL

Maybe you're midcareer and would like to go to business school but don't relish the prospect of uprooting your family and putting your career on hold for two years while you attend a top-flight B-school. Or maybe you simply can't afford the exorbitant fees charged by those ivy-clad institutions. Could the way you buy business education change as dramatically over the next ten years as the way you buy books (Amazon.com), trade shares (E*TRADE), or get your news (Yahoo!)? You bet. Let's try a little thought experiment, one that will illustrate the kind of wrenching innovation that will destroy old business models in the age of revolution.

Start with the salient characteristics of a typical top–ten B–school:

○ *Geographically defined:* Faculty and students live within 20 miles of campus.

○ *Tough to get in:* Admission requirements include an honor-student GPA and a ninetieth percentile score on the Graduate Management Admissions Test—for starters. On average, fewer than one out of five applicants gets accepted.

○ *Classroom-based:* The typical format is one professor, 80 students, and a badly photocopied case.

○ *Few "stars":* Twenty percent of the faculty have world–class reputations as "gurus," the rest don't. Stars earn as much as 90 percent of their income from outside teaching and consulting.

○ *Egalitarian pay structure:* The salary differential between the "stars" and newly hired assistant professors is typically no greater than three to one.

○ *Publish or perish:* To get promoted, young faculty must publish within a narrowly defined "discipline." Peers within that discipline review their research. Faculty are generally unwilling to participate in multidisciplinary research and teaching.

○ *Young customers:* For the core M.B.A. program, customers are college graduates, roughly 25 to 30 years of age, with three or four years of work experience.

○ *Student numbers:* Top business schools admit anywhere between a couple hundred and around 1,000 M.B.A. students per year.

○ *High tuition:* Fees can amount to as much as $20,000 per year and even more.

○ *Inflexible program of study:* The M.B.A. program comprises two years of intensive residential study with 20 classroom hours per week and classes offered at set times.

○ *Academic research:* For faculty, the unstated goal is to publish "the maximum number of pages in journals read by the minimum number of people." Most research never gets applied. Even the best faculty find it difficult to pry research money out of the dean.

The top ten business schools in America turn out fewer than 7,500 M.B.A. graduates a year. In a world of 6 billion people, what is the size of the unfilled demand for high-quality business education? The vast majority of would-be business students is relegated to a second-class education or none whatsoever. As market economies take root in Eastern Europe, Asia, Latin America, and the Indian subcontinent, the demand for management education will soar. Failure to meet this demand could slow the speed of economic development in some parts of the world. Is there room for a new business model in business education? Yeah, acres of room.

Imagine that Paul Allen, co-founder of Microsoft, or George Soros, the global financier, decides to establish a cyber management school—let's call it the Global Leadership Academy. The first step is to skim two or three star professors from each of the ten best business schools and ten or so of the most cerebral partners in the leading consulting companies—the ones who've written groundbreaking books. Faculty are attracted to GLA by the chance to make a global difference in the quality of management—something that's difficult to do when your distribution channel is limited to a few hundred 27-year-olds each year. Faculty members are given equity in the new venture and a guaranteed income of $1 million per year. The new venture can afford these salaries because it is built on a very different economic model from a physical B-school. Instead of putting one professor in front of 80 students, GLA puts one professor in front of 100,000 students—through live satellite broadcasts and Webcasts. GLA also builds a network of local tutors around the world, affiliated with second-tier universities. These tutors meet occasionally with students and can facilitate online discussions of cases and lectures. Students can share insights in custom-designed chat rooms.

GLA's admission requirements are unlike those of traditional B-schools. To enroll, an applicant must simply submit three letters of recommendation from individuals outside his or her family. The first letter must describe some sort of "against the odds" accomplishment—perhaps overcoming drug addiction or helping to raise younger siblings after the death of a parent. The second letter must describe the applicant in a leadership role, however humble, and the third must outline a contribution the applicant has made to the community.

GLA's costs are largely unrelated to the number of students it serves. Indeed, it wants as many "customers" as possible in order to better amortize its fixed investment in online courseware and faculty salaries.

Though the entrance requirements may appear to be "soft," there is a demanding exit exam. Those who pass it get a degree from GLA. Those who don't get a certificate outlining their specific educational accomplishments. GLA charges students a flat fee of $2,000 per year, irrespective of how quickly they progress through the program. Dedicated students can finish the program in three years.

In some traditional business schools, students are given a limited number of "points" with which they can bid for admission to the classes of the most popular teachers. There are no oversubscribed courses at GLA. Every student learns from the best. The elite faculty supervises the development of Internet-based curricula and delivers key lectures.

GLA abandons the traditional discipline-based M.B.A. program and opts for an issue-based curriculum instead. Courses include "Profiting from Strategic Alliances," "Unleashing Innovation," "Building Digital Strategies," "Accessing Global Capital Markets," "Inspiring a Gen-X Workforce" and other cross-discipline issues.

With a 50 percent gross margin, GLA is able to build a first-rate research team around each faculty member. Freed from the burden of repetitive teaching, and with a cadre of first-rate researchers, faculty members dramatically raise their research output.

While GLA doesn't have a hundred-year history as a noble university, the chance to study with the world's best business minds attracts a flood of students. The collective "brand" of the faculty soon outshines the brand of any offline university.

GLA's early success astonishes traditional business schools. Unlike first-generation distance learning programs pioneered by Duke University and other schools, GLA offers its students the very best faculty in the world, rather than those willing to live near some particular university. Business education begins to resemble investment banking and basketball, where the stars get paid star salaries. Traditional business schools that seek to emulate GLA find themselves caught in a thicket of intractable issues:

How do we sign up faculty from "competing" business schools?

How do we manage the tensions when one faculty member gets paid 10 or 20 times what another faculty member gets paid?

How do we pay star rates, given a brick-and-mortar overhead structure?

How do we blow up the functional chimneys that prevent us from building an issue-based curriculum?

> How do we justify high tuition fees when students can get the
> best faculty in the world for 90 percent less?

After three years of dithering and debate, Harvard, Wharton, Michigan, Northwestern and the London Business School join forces and launch their own virtual B-school. But internal squabbling and the challenge of managing a five-way alliance hamper their efforts. Oxford, Cambridge and other universities still struggling to build old-economy business schools simply give up.

An all-star B-school in cyberspace. Will this new business model materialize? Without a doubt. **New business models are more than disruptive** *technologies*, **they are completely novel business concepts.** They are more than *replacements* for what already is. Instead, they open up entirely new possibilities.

BUSINESS CONCEPT INNOVATION

New business models sometimes render old business models obsolete. For example, it's easy to imagine Internet-based phone calls, based on packet switching, largely supplanting phone calls made on dedicated voice circuits. More often, new business models don't destroy old models, they just siphon off customer demand, slowly deflating the profit potential of the old business model. Sears still has a hardware department, and Craftsman is a great brand, but The Home Depot has captured a huge portion of the burgeoning demand in the do-it-yourself market. Digital photography is not going to kill the film business in one fell swoop, but it may maim it by capturing a significant part of the "imaging" demand.

The goal of business concept innovation is to introduce more strategic variety into an industry or competitive domain. When this happens, and when customers value that variety, the distribution of wealth-creating potential often shifts dramatically in favor of the innovator. It's not value that "migrates" within and across industries, but the locus of innovation. Companies in one part of an industry will sometimes sit idly by while their strategies converge, while elsewhere some radical upstart creates a new business model and a gusher of new wealth. For example, Wal-Mart's bargaining power has allowed it to suck a lot of wealth out of its suppliers, but it would be only half right to say that value has "migrated" toward Wal-Mart. What actually happened was that Wal-Mart succeeded in doing something that few of its suppliers or competitors had done: inventing an entirely new and oh-so–attractive business concept—the super efficient hypermarket with "everyday low prices."

Business concept innovation is *meta*–innovation, in that it changes the very basis for competition within an industry or domain. The *American Heritage College Dictionary* defines "meta–" as "beyond" or "more comprehensive." Because it is nonlinear, business concept innovation goes *beyond* incremental innovation. Because it takes the entire business concept as the starting point, it is more comprehensive than innovation that focuses solely on products or technology.

Let's take cosmetics as an example. **When was the last time you caught your breath as you walked past the cosmetics counter in some big department store?** When was the last time you stopped, looked around and thought, "This is *so* cool"? Never? Well, that's no surprise. The way cosmetics are merchandised and sold has hardly changed over the past couple of decades. If you parachuted into the cosmetics section of a major department store, could you immediately tell whether you were in Macy's, Saks Fifth Avenue, Bloomingdale's or one of their competitors? If the product names were disguised, could you immediately distinguish the Estée Lauder counter from the Lancôme counter? Probably not. No wonder the cosmetics industry has been in a funk.

Think for a minute about the cosmetics business concept. High–end beauty products are sold almost exclusively in upscale department stores and account for as much as 20 percent of store profits. Manufacturers jealously control the display of their products, with counters and staff dedicated to each brand. Salesclerks, who are often paid by the manufacturers, are on commission and trained to be pushy—to *sell* you something rather than just let you *buy* something. If you want a lipstick of a particular shade, you'll have to wander from counter to counter, trying to remember if that Chanel lip gloss over there is an eensy-weensy bit less pink than the Lancôme lipstick you're holding in your hand. Many times you have to ask a clerk to see a particular product—most are displayed under glass–topped counters. Merchandising often relies on a "gift–with–purchase," a freebie that shoppers increasingly take for granted.

Sephora, a French–born cosmetics chain, recently acquired by the luxury giant LVMH, is on a global growth tear. Why? Because it's been ripping up the cosmetics rule book. Walk into a Sephora store, and you'll be blown away. In front of you is a wall of video screens. The staff are robed in black, each wearing one black glove, the better to show off delicate perfume bottles. They work for a flat salary. The store layout is black and white and oh–so–sleek. You'll find beauty-related books, magazines and videos; poetry inscribed on gleaming columns; and more than 600 different brands. But the biggest wow factor comes from the way Sephora displays the merchandise. Virtually every perfume in the world is arranged alphabetically along a wall. There's a lipstick counter with more than 365 hues, arranged by color. Face and body products are organized by category, rather than by manufacturer. You'll find everything from the hip (Urban Decay) to the *très chic* (Lancôme). Premium and mass–market brands often end up side by side. There's a fragrance organ—a multitiered rack of essences—where staff can tell you just what's in your favorite perfume and direct you to other similar fragrances. All the products are on open display. Pick them up, test them—even the lipsticks. There are no gifts. This is a temple of beauty, with the consumer as goddess.

Don't take my word for it, listen to Marianne Wilson of *Chain Store Age*:

> By the combined force of its ambience, design and merchandise
> mix, Sephora blows away all other competitors in its category.
> And it does so without the gift–with–purchase clutter, hard sell
> and often haughty sales people that define much of department
> store beauty retailing. In fact, what I most liked about Sephora
> was the egalitarian way it treats both shoppers and merchandise.[1]

By the spring of 1999, Sephora had captured 20 percent of the French retail cosmetics market. Within 18 months of opening its first U.S. out–let in Manhattan, Sephora had opened an additional 49 stores across the United States, and had plans to open as many as 200 more. Myron E. Ullman III, architect of Sephora's international expansion, has his own view on what Sephora is all about:

> Retailing is about change. I can't think of a single retail concept
> that hasn't changed that is now doing very well. That's why we
> have a group in Paris who sit around and do nothing else but
> think of different ways to do things. Chief among their tasks is to
> keep [our] flagships so stunning that people are compelled to
> walk in. When our customers stroll down Fifth Avenue, we want
> them to say to themselves, "Should I go to the Museum of
> Modern Art or should I go to Sephora?"

Sephora has trashed the typical cosmetics business model:

	Traditional Model	Sephora Model
Sales staff on commission	Yes	No
Gift with purchase	Yes	No
One brand per counter	Yes	No
Manufacturer controls display	Yes	No
Easy to sample	No	Yes
Shop unmolested	No	Yes
Easy to compare products	No	Yes
Customer in control	No	Yes

Without a doubt, this is business concept innovation.

With Sephora, the cosmetics makers lose their control of the sales force, product display and merchandising—the very things they relied on for competitive differentiation at point of sale. Major ouch! Some cosmetics manufacturers, afraid of angering department stores, have refused to let Sephora handle certain product lines. You won't find Es-tée Lauder's MAC, Bobbi Brown and Aveda lines at Sephora. Nor will you find Chanel's makeup lines—not, at least, for now.

Business concept innovation starts from a premise that the only way to escape the squeeze of hyper-competition, even temporarily, is to build a business model so unlike what has come before that traditional competitors are left scrambling. **When it's most effective, business concept innovation leaves competitors in a gut-wrenching quandary:** If they abandon their tried-and-tested business model, they risk sacrificing their core business for a second-place finish in a game they didn't invent, with rules they don't understand; yet if they don't embrace the new model, they forgo the future. Damned if they do and damned if they don't—that's business concept innovation at its best.

Business concept innovation is not a way of positioning *against* competitors, but of going *around* them. It's based on *avoidance*, not *attack*. Here's the key thought: *what is not different is not strategic.* To the extent that strategy is the quest for above-average profits, it is *entirely* about variety—not just in one or two areas, but in all components of the business model. Business concept innovation often falls short of this lofty goal, but that's the objective.

Consequently, a capacity to first identify, then deconstruct and re-construct business models lies at the heart of a high-performance innovation system. If your company is not experimenting with radically different business models, it's already living on borrowed time.

UNPACKING THE BUSINESS MODEL

To be an industry revolutionary, you must develop an instinctive capacity to think about business models in their entirety. There are many ways of describing the components of a business model. I have created a framework that is complete, yet simple.

A business concept comprises four major components:

- ○ Core Strategy
- ○ Strategic Resources
- ○ Customer Interface
- ○ Value Network

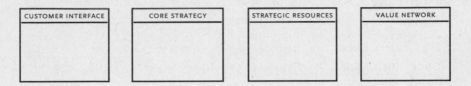

Each of these components has several subcomponents, which will be described later in this section. For each element I have also suggested a few questions that should help you think more deeply and deftly about opportunities for business concept innovation. The fact is that most companies have *business concept blind spots* that prevent them from seeing opportunities for innovation in many parts of the business concept. In this chapter we'll remove those blind spots.

The four core components are linked together by three "bridge" components:

- ○ Core Strategy → *Configuration* of Activities → Resource Base
- ○ Core Strategy → Customer *Benefits* → Customer Interface
- ○ Resource Base → Company *Boundaries* → Value Network

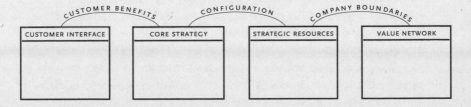

Underpinning the business model are four factors that determine its profit potential:

○ Efficiency
○ Uniqueness
○ Fit
○ Profit Boosters

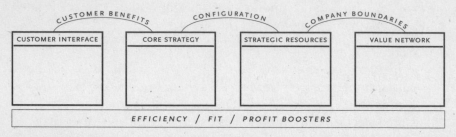

Core Strategy

The first component of the business concept is the *core strategy*. It is the essence of how the firm chooses to compete. Elements of the core strategy include the business mission, product/market scope and basis for differentiation.

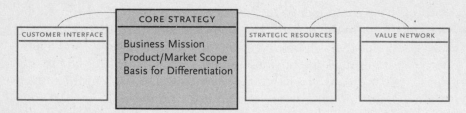

1. The Business Mission: This captures the overall *objective* of the strategy—what the business model is designed to accomplish or deliver. The business mission encompasses things such as the "value proposition," "strategic intent," "big, hairy, audacious goals," "purpose," and overall performance objectives. It implies a sense of direction and a set of criteria against which to measure progress. It is often unstated and often constrains a company's view of potential business concepts. A change in a company's business mission doesn't necessarily result in business concept innovation. But when a company brings a new or very different business mission into an industry dominated by companies with roughly similar business goals, the result may be business concept innovation. This was the case when Virgin exported its lifestyle-oriented, entertainment-focused business mission to the airline business. Traditional air carriers had business missions focused on maximizing the operational efficiency of their airlines. Virgin's business mission was focused on fun, value-for-money and customer feel-good factors. Anyone who has flown on Virgin will have noticed the difference this makes.

Example: Although it has long styled itself as "The Document Company," Xerox's implicit business mission has focused on copiers and copying. This definition created a *business concept blind spot* that allowed Hewlett-Packard to build a commanding lead in the printer business. With most of their documents stored electronically, individuals use their printers, rather than copiers, to reproduce documents. You can argue that HP is also a "document company," but its business mission focused on printing rather than copying. After falling far behind, Xerox amended its business concept to include printing. 'Tis a pity for Xerox that this business concept innovation didn't occur a decade earlier.

Ask yourself: What is our business mission? What are we becoming as a company—can we describe a "from" and a "to"? What is our dream? What kind of difference do we want to make in the world? Is our business mission sufficiently broad to allow for business concept innovation? Is our business mission as *relevant* to customers as it might have been in years past? Most important, do we have a business mission that is sufficiently distinguished from the missions of other companies in our industry?

Thought: A business school that sees its business mission as granting degrees to residential students, rather than addressing the world's "management deficit," will have little incentive for business concept innovation.

2. **Product/Market Scope:** This captures the essence of *where* the firm competes—which customers, which geographies, and what product segments—and where, by implication, it doesn't compete. A company's definition of product/market scope can be a source of business concept innovation when it is quite different from that of traditional competitors.

Example: Amazon may have started as an online bookseller, but its goal is to become the Wal–Mart of the Internet—offering products as diverse as videos, personal electronics, lawn and garden supplies, tools, toys and much more. Leveraging its easy–to–use customer interface, Amazon seems intent on increasing its share of online purchases to the detriment of single–segment Web retailers.

Ask yourself: Could we offer customers something closer to a "total solution" to their needs by expanding our definition of product scope? Could we increase our "share of wallet" as well as our share of market by expanding our scope? Would a different definition of scope allow us to capture more of the life cycle profits associated with our product or service? **Are there types of customers that have been generally ignored by companies in our industry?**

Thought: What if banks expanded the scope of their debit card offerings to include children? Wouldn't it be great if your daughter had her own debit card and her allowance was automatically transferred to her bank account each month? She could spend the available funds with her debit card. No more worrying about lost allowances, and no more arguments about whether you remembered to pay her or not. 'Tis a pity that Visa or MasterCard haven't thought of this.

3. Basis for Differentiation: This captures the essence of *how* the firm competes and, in particular, how it competes *differently* from its competitors.

Example: You don't know Jonathan Ives, but you know his work. At 30 years of age, the quirky Londoner was appointed head of Apple Computer's industrial design division. It is Ives, after all, who was responsible for the iMac, the curvy, translucent machine that has redefined what a computer should look like. For years, the PC was the ugliest thing in your house. It looked like a disemboweled robot with cords and cables spilling everywhere. And it came in only one color—deadly, boring beige. Why? Because most of the companies making PCs had an industrial products heritage—they were filled with engineers not artists. The iMac sold 400,000 units in the first month after its introduction, and introduced an entirely new dimension of differentiation—aesthetics—into the computer industry. And in early 2002, Apple did it again with the new iMac—a radically new computer design with a footprint smaller than a dinner plate and a new ergonomic "floating" flat panel display.

Ask yourself: How have competitors tried to differentiate themselves in our industry? Are there other dimensions of differentiation we could explore? In what aspects of the product or service has there been the *least* differentiation? How could we increase the differentiation in some of these dimensions? Have we searched diligently for differentiation opportunities in *every* dimension of the business model?

Thought: You can take $250 out of a cash machine with a piece of plastic. But if you want to check in to a $250–per–night hotel room, be prepared to give your life history at check–in. This is absurd. You take money out of the ATM, but you take nothing from the hotel but the soap. By the time you arrive, you've already guaranteed your room with a credit card, and they have your name on file, so why do you have to go through the whole check–in rigmarole? Why not use your credit card as a room key? Will it happen? Yep. Holiday Inn is planning a new hotel near the Atlanta airport where consumers will be able to use their credit cards as room keys.[2] Hey guys, ATMs have been around for years—what took you so long?

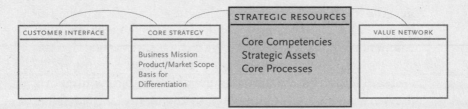

CUSTOMER INTERFACE

CORE STRATEGY

Business Mission
Product/Market Scope
Basis for
Differentiation

STRATEGIC RESOURCES

Core Competencies
Strategic Assets
Core Processes

VALUE NETWORK

Strategic Resources

Every competitive advantage worthy of the name rests on unique firm–specific resources. Dramatically changing the resource base for competition can be a source of business concept innovation. Strategic resources include core competencies, strategic assets and core processes.

1. **Core Competencies:** This is what the firm *knows*. It encompasses skills and unique capabilities.

Example: Disney, a company with roots in animated films and theme parks, has become a force to be reckoned with on Broadway. Theatrical productions are lavish entertainment, and who knows lavish better than Disney? By transporting its core competencies in stage design (what is a theme park, but a giant stage?) and storytelling to Broadway, Disney's blockbuster *Lion King* was the winner of six Tony Awards and one of the highest-grossing musicals of all time. *Lion King* quickly became more than a Broadway production and a movie, launching a blockbuster franchise that spawned TV spin-offs, books, toys and theme-park attractions. When, on occasion, Disney has diversified into areas where there is less of a core competence connection, as with its purchase of the ABC television network, success has been much harder to come by.

Ask yourself: What are our core competencies? What do we know that is (a) unique, (b) valuable to customers, and (c) transferable to new opportunities? What are the deep benefits that our core competencies allow us to deliver to customers? How could we deploy those benefits in new ways or in new settings? What difference could our core competencies make if we introduced them into industries where competitors possess very different skills? Are there skills we don't currently possess that could undermine the role our traditional competencies play in some overall customer solution? What new competencies should we be adding to our business concept?

Thought: The skills eBay applies to the problem of creating an online, consumer-to-consumer marketplace are very different from the competencies a newspaper relies on in running its classified ads section. A newspaper would face a daunting challenge if it wanted to run real-time, coast-to-coast auctions. When business concept innovation changes the competence base of an industry, it puts traditional players at a profound disadvantage, which is, of course, the goal of business concept innovation.

2. Strategic Assets: Strategic assets are what the firm owns. They are things, rather than know-how. Strategic assets can include brands, patents, infrastructure, proprietary standards, customer data and anything else that is both rare and valuable. Using one's strategic assets in a novel way can lead to business concept innovation.

Example: I think it's unlikely that Barnes & Noble will ever match Amazon.com's success as an online retailer. But Barnes & Noble has one strategic asset that Amazon.com can't match—its prime retail locations. Barnes & Noble has used this asset to deliver new forms of value to customers. First it sprinkled comfy sofas and overstuffed chairs amid the acres of books. Next it built coffee bars in its bookstores. Then it started scheduling poetry readings and music recitals. All this has transformed Barnes & Noble into a leisure destination—something more akin to a community center or the old town square than a bookstore.

Ask yourself: What are our strategic assets? Could we exploit them in new ways to bring new value to consumers? Could our strategic assets be valuable in other industry settings? Can we build new business models that exploit our existing strategic assets—that is, can we imagine alternate uses for our strategic assets?

Thought: How likely is it that a company making earth–moving equipment would become a fashion icon? Despite the long odds, this is exactly what Caterpillar, the macho manufacturer of heavy machinery, has managed to do. Caterpillar started selling "Cat" branded work boots in 1995 and sold 3 million pairs that first year; by 2000 they had sold 26 million pairs. Cat branded shoes, apparel, toys and accessories will be sold in over 600 stores by 2003. Caterpillar's worldwide sales of licensed merchandise totaled nearly $1 billion in 2000. Making it one of the most powerful licensed brands in the world—up there with Coca–Cola and Harley–Davidson. *The raw mechanical power of the Caterpillar brand, that yellow-and-black image of heavy machinery once known only to construction workers, is now attracting hip young urbanites.* What strategic assets has your company overlooked?

3. Core Processes: This is what people in the firm actually do. Core processes are methodologies and routines used in transforming inputs into outputs. Core processes are activities, rather than "assets" or "skills." They are used in translating competencies, assets, and other inputs into value for customers. A fundamental reinvention of a core process can be the basis for business concept innovation.

Examples: Dell's build–to–order system is one of its core processes and a powerful example of business concept innovation. Drug discovery is a core process for every pharmaceutical company. It is also a process that has been radically reinvented in recent years through bioinformatics, which makes it possible to rapidly screen thousands and thousands of compounds. Toyota's lean manufacturing was a process innovation that turned the car industry on its ear.

Ask yourself: What are our most critical processes—that is, what processes create the most value for customers and are most competitively unique? What is the rate at which we are improving these processes? Is that rate of improvement accelerating or decelerating? Can we imagine a radically different process that would deliver the same benefit? Are there opportunities for step function improvements in the efficiency or effectiveness of our processes? Could we borrow nonlinear process ideas from other industries? Conversely, could we use our process expertise to transform some other industry?

Thought: Have you ever had a house built? How long did it take? A year? Two years? A few years ago the San Diego–based Building Industry Association sponsored a seemingly ridiculous contest. Two teams were pitted against each other—each would try to build a house in less than four hours, using traditional materials. The teams planned every second of the building process with military precision. They struggled to invent new technologies, such as cement that would dry in a matter of minutes. They broke the work down into subtasks that could be carried out in parallel. While one group was laying the foundation, another would frame the walls, and another would build the roof. The frame would get bolted to the foundation in large sections, and the roof would be lifted onto the framing with the help of a crane. Each team brought hundreds of construction workers to the site, and every tradesman was given an intricately choreographed role to play. Improbably, one team managed to build its three–bedroom bungalow, complete with landscaping, in less than *three* hours. Of course the contest had a logic—**ONLY BY PUSHING THE PEDAL TO THE METAL, BY REACHING FOR THE SEEMINGLY IMPOSSIBLE, IS IT POSSIBLE TO ESCAPE THE LIMITS OF CURRENT PROCESSES AND DISCOVER NEW POSSIBILITIES.** But don't you dare call *this* process reengineering—it's far more radical. So what kind of process innovation would allow you to transform *your* industry?

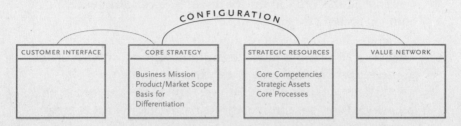

Configuration

Intermediating between a company's *core strategy* and its *strategic resources* is a bridge component I'll call *configuration*. Configuration refers to the unique way in which competencies, assets and processes are *combined* and *interrelated* in support of a particular strategy. It refers to the *linkages* between competencies, assets and processes and how those linkages are managed. The notion of configuration recognizes that great strategies (and great business models) rest on a unique blending of competencies, assets and processes.

> **Example:** Prior to its ill–fated acquisition by Daimler–Benz, Chrysler had gained a substantial amount of advantage from the way it uses "platform teams" to orchestrate the functional disciplines involved in producing and marketing a vehicle. Most car companies are organized by function–design, engineering, manufacturing, marketing and sales. Employees sit in functional "silos" and are often more loyal to their function than to any particular car program. The result is a lot of friction, suboptimal trade–offs and development delays. Chrysler used a new building to unite functional specialists around vehicle platforms, employing a team structure it first used in the development of the built–to–thrill Viper sports car. Each platform team has representatives from every function.

They sit together in a stadium-sized room, where each employee has a line of sight to every other employee. In the new configuration, it's clear that an employee's first loyalty is to the success of the program he or she is working on, not to some distant functional head. Chrysler's American competitors possess roughly similar technical knowledge, strategic assets, and processes, but Chrysler was the first American car company to configure all of these into boundary-breaking platform teams. This is one reason Chrysler came to be regarded in the 1990s as one of the most innovative car companies in the world.

Ask yourself: How do we manage the interfaces between different assets, knowledge and processes? Have we configured our assets, skills and processes in unique ways? Has anyone in our industry or domain configured their strategic resources in an unconventional way? Do they gain any advantage from this configuration? Can we imagine very different configurations from what we have at present?

Thought: If your bank is like most, it sends you one statement for your credit card, another for your mortgage, another for your checking account, another for your savings or investment account, and still another for your car loan or any other borrowing you may have. The blizzard of statements you receive each month reflects the internal configuration of most banks—each product area is a separate profit center. It also reflects banks' eagerness to borrow money from you at one rate (what they pay you on a certificate of deposit, for example) and lend it back to you at a higher rate (the interest you pay on your credit card debt, for example). Virgin Money, the innovative financial services arm of Sir Richard Branson's far-flung empire, offers customers a radically different approach based on a completely different configuration of banking resources. The Virgin One account works like this. Imagine you have a $200,000 balance on your mortgage, with an 8 percent interest rate. Imagine further that your monthly paycheck amounts to $8,000. When your paycheck is electronically deposited into your Virgin One account, your mortgage balance is immediately reduced by $8,000. Then, as you write checks during the month from the same account, your mortgage balance creeps back up. In this way, you're earning the equivalent of 8 percent on the money from your paycheck that sits in your One account. Compare that with what most banks give you on your checking account. Now let's say you splurge on a Tahitian holiday and end up with $10,000 of credit card debt. Instead of paying this down over a period of months and being subject to the typically exorbitant interest rates charged by credit card companies, you pay the credit card bill out of your One account. Your debt goes up by $10,000, but you're being charged interest at only 8 percent. And when, a few months later, you pay in that $20,000 inheritance from grandma, it reduces your debt by a similar amount, and therefore earns an effective 8 percent interest rate—far better than what you could get on a deposit account. The radical premise behind the Virgin One account is this: you are one person with a single overall level of indebtedness. Your bank shouldn't treat you like you're suffering from a case of multiple personalities, nor should it gain financially from the fact that it is configured in a way that makes it impossible to consolidate your borrowing and savings into a single account.

Customer Interface

The third component of the business concept, *customer interface*, has four elements: fulfillment and support, information and insight, relationship dynamics and pricing structure. The Internet has caused a radical shift in how producers reach consumers.

1. **Fulfillment and Support:** This refers to the way the firm "goes to market," how it actually "reaches" customers—which channels it uses, what kind of customer support it offers and what level of service it provides.

   Examples: Commercial radio, a $17 billion industry that has seen little technological change since FM 40 years ago, is ripe for revolution. If you commute to work by car in the United States, you have probably endured hours of bland, commercial-ridden radio. Most urban markets offer a scant handful of programming formats: Top 40, country music, classical music, hard rock, news radio and maybe a sports station or two. And if rush hour traffic wasn't frustrating enough, drive-time radio typically subjects the harried commuter to 20 minutes of advertising per hour. And if your journey spans a few hundred miles, you'll find that your favorite station soon fades to static. Thankfully, XM Radio and Sirius Satellite Radio are reinventing the way news and entertainment get delivered to your car. Both companies offer a "satellite radio" service that pumps out up to 100 channels of CD-quality radio to a small satellite receiver that can be mounted in a car or at home. The service, which covers the United States, costs listeners $10 per month. Within a few months of its launch, XM Radio had become the fastest-selling new audio product in 20 years. Satellite radio's new best friends are car companies, and factory-installed satellite radio will soon be available from GM, Honda, DaimlerChrysler, Ford and BMW. Sony and other consumer electronics firms are offering after-market radios that can be plugged into the car or carried indoors. A compact Walkman version is on the way. No longer will radio listeners be hostage to the bland and banal advertising-supported stations that typically populate the radio dial. Will folks pay $10 a month for something they used to get for free? **Well, water is free, and broadcast TV is free, and yet Perrier and DirecTV have managed to take billions of dollars out of consumers' pockets.** XM Radio might just be the next blockbuster based, as it is, on a radically different fulfillment model.

With iPhoto, Apple is transforming the way the humble snapshot gets stored, printed and shared. A key spoke within the iMac's digital hub, iPhoto helps shutterbugs import, organize, edit and store digital images with a graceful GUI that makes removing red-eye, cropping images and producing soundtrack supported slideshows intuitively simple—all without the need of third-party software. Among iPhoto's menus is a "share panel" that provides the option of one-click ordering of prints in various formats, from contact sheets to greeting cards. Images can be easily shared by posting them to an Apple-provided personal home page. If that weren't enough, iPhoto offers photographers the option of having their pictures professionally published, quickly and effortlessly, in a custom-made book of photographs and captions printed on acid-free glossy paper and bound in an elegant linen cover. As competitors focus on bulking up RAM and ROM, Apple has realized that digitally savvy customers also value memories of a more personal nature.

Ask yourself: How do we reach customers? What does a customer have to "go through" to buy our products and services? To what extent have we built our fulfillment and support system for our benefit rather than our customers' benefit? Could we make the process of fulfillment and support substantially easier or more enjoyable for customers? What would it look like if we designed our support and fulfillment processes from the customer backward? Could we dramatically reduce search costs? Could we provide customers with truly honest data for comparison shopping? Have we removed every element of customer aggravation in the support and fulfillment process?

Thought: Today Americans give to charity a smaller percentage of their income than ever before. We are so wrapped up in our lives, so constantly busy, that we have hardly a moment to think about doing good for anyone but ourselves. Could business concept innovation change this? Is there another way of linking donors to worthwhile causes—another "fulfillment" mechanism? Of course. One thing that blunts the impulse to give is the bureaucracy that intervenes between the giver and the beneficiary. You give to United Way or some religious organization that pools your money with other gifts and directs those funds to projects around the world. You have only a vague sense of where your money goes and no direct feedback on the difference it makes. Most of us wouldn't consider putting our financial investments in a "blind trust," but this is essentially what happens when we give to charity. What if you had the chance to pick the exact projects to which you'd like to contribute? What if you got a monthly report on the good that was being done? What if you were able to pick projects that were sized to the amount you could afford—projects where you could feel your contribution made a critical difference, whether it was $100, $1,000 or $100,000? What if you could easily build a portfolio of specific charity projects that reflected your own personal interests—be it abolishing hunger, ending child labor, reducing deforestation or saving souls? Instead of United Way, it would be Your Way.

So let's establish a website called givemore.org. A small team of people will vet charity projects submitted from around the world. They will be assisted by local review teams. One project might be to build an orphanage in Rwanda, another to help a struggling church in Byelorussia and another to help teens at risk. Each project will be posted to the Web. While today you can get a long list of charities on the Web, you can't easily make donations to specific projects. At givemore.org, project listings will include the amount of funding needed, the expected benefits and the supervising organization. The review team will rate each project on some cost/benefit criteria. You will know what portion of your contribution is going to be absorbed by overhead and administrative fees. Projects will be posted by government agencies, churches, long–standing charities and responsible individuals. Potential donors will go online and select a project from a menu of worthy causes organized by need and geography. They will get regular e-mail updates on the progress of their projects. Every year givemore.org will arrange a trip for large donors so they can review the impact of their giving on-site. With givers no longer divorced from the heartwarming gratitude of recipients, giving just might soar. Is this all a fantasy? Yeah, but it'll happen. **Do you have a fantasy about how your company can reinvent its connection to customers?**

2. **Information and Insight:** This refers to all the knowledge that is collected from and utilized on behalf of customers—the information content of the customer interface. It also refers to the ability of a company to extract insights from this information—insights that can help it do cool new things for customers. It also covers the information that is made available to customers pre- and postpurchase.

Example: Dell Computer uses information to link itself tightly to its customers and to build barriers to entry for less Web-savvy competitors. Dell's largest customers, big companies that buy millions of dollars of hardware every year, access Dell products via custom–tailored "Premier Pages." These Web pages are configured to reflect the IT and procurement policies of each corporate customer. An employee who wants to buy a computer from Dell will have access to a special page that generates dynamic price quotes based on prenegotiated volume discounts. The Premier Pages also let employees know what product configurations have been approved by their company's IT executives. Corporate procurement managers can view each outstanding order submitted by their company's employees, give their approval and submit the order to Dell. By tightly coupling its online selling process with the procurement policies of its big customers, Dell has given itself a powerful "easy to do business with" advantage. Dell exploits information in other ways, as well. Each time it builds a PC, it gives the machine a unique five-digit alphanumeric code. A customer can go to Dell's support site, enter that code and get the original configurations of that machine as it was shipped, the days left on its warranty, where it was shipped and all the driver files and utilities. No monopoly lock-in here. Rather, Dell uses the twine of information to bind itself ever more tightly to its customers.

Ask yourself: What do we actually know about customers? Are we using every opportunity to deepen our knowledge of our customers' needs and desires? Are we capturing all the data we could? How do we use this knowledge to serve them in new ways? Have we given our customers the information they need to make empowered and intelligent purchasing decisions? What additional information would customers like to have?

Thought: A senior executive of a large supermarket chain once told me of some research that suggested a top-quartile customer in an average store would spend 50 times more in a year than a bottom-quartile customer. The top-quartile customer lived locally, shopped a couple times a week, had a family and was reasonably well off. The bottom-quartile customer was just passing through or didn't have a family, and wasn't so well heeled. I started thinking about this data. What if it were true? Every supermarket has an express lane for customers with "10 items or less." But who uses that lane? Bottom-quartile customers. Top-quartile customers are waiting in line with an overstuffed cart—they've come to buy more than beer and cigarettes. Why, I began to wonder, wasn't there a line for customers who spend $5,000 or more in a year? Why didn't these shoppers have someone to help them load their groceries into their BMWs and Volvos? While many supermarkets give loyalty cards to their customers, few seem to have used the information gathered to provide truly differentiated service to their best customers.

3. Relationship Dynamics: This element of the business model refers to the nature of the *interaction* between the producer and the customer. Is the interaction face to face or indirect? Is it continuous or sporadic? How easy is it for the customer to interact with the producer? What feelings do these interactions invoke on the part of the customer? Is there any sense of "loyalty" created by the pattern of interactions? The notion of relationship dynamics acknowledges the fact that there are emotional, as well as transactional, elements in the interaction of producers and consumers, and that these can be the basis for a highly differentiated business concept.

Example: There's probably no company in the world that works harder to build genuine relationships with its customers than Harley–Davidson. The Harley Owners Group boasts 450,000 members. Every year Harley–Davidson sponsors a rally where the tattoo contest is one of the most keenly anticipated events. As the company says, **"It's one thing for people to buy your products. It's another for them to tattoo your name on their bodies."** BMW makes awesome motorcycles, but when was the last time you saw a bicep that read "Bayerische Motoren Werke"?

Ask yourself: How do we make our customers *feel*? What is the range of emotions that a customer experiences in his or her interactions with us? Have we invested in our customers? Could we reinvent the customer experience in ways that would strengthen the sense of affiliation the customer has with us? Where can we exceed customer expectations and raise the hurdle for competitors? What are the dozen greatest customer experiences in the world? Is there anything about those experiences we could replicate in our relationship with customers?

Thought: Perhaps nowhere is the alignment between customer expectations and the actual service experience more out of whack than in health care. A senior health-care executive recently described the current state of the U.S. health-care experience as follows: "Prison inmates and hospital patients have a lot in common. Both are subjected to excessive questioning, stripped of their usual clothing and possessions, placed in a subservient, dependent relationship and allowed visitors only during certain hours." Adventist Health System, one of the largest church-affiliated hospital groups in America, is seeking to change this sorry state of affairs. It has examined each stage of the patient experience and has identified opportunities to revolutionize service delivery. A couple of examples: Instead of answering the same questions over and over again, patients will be given a Web-based "portable health record" that travels with them from clinical experience to clinical experience. Another innovation is the elimination of visiting hours. Family members will have visiting privileges 24 hours a day, even in the emergency room. While creating some inconvenience for the staff, this idea has greatly reduced litigation expense in the hospitals where it has been instituted. When a health event goes wrong, the family is less likely to point fingers at anonymous health-care providers if they were there and know the doctors and staff did all they could do for the patient.

4. **Pricing Structure:** You have several choices in what you charge for. You can charge customers for a product or for service. You can charge customers directly or indirectly through a third party. You can bundle components or price them separately. You can charge a flat rate or charge for time or distance. You can have set prices or market-based prices. Each of these choices offers the chance for business concept innovation, depending on the traditions of your industry.

Examples: While traditional insurance companies are just that—traditional—devoting themselves to the age-old practice of selling fixed-rate auto insurance policies by the year, Britain's Norwich Union has overturned this industry orthodoxy by offering its customers insurance by the mile. Rather than pay to protect a car that is sitting in the garage while you work from home, carpool or travel by train or plane, you just pay for insurance when you're actually on the road. Using a global-positioning system, pay-as-you-drive customers are charged an insurance premium that is based on how often, when and where their cars are used. A novel pricing structure, to be sure.

In pre-Web times, when you purchased a CD, you were compelled to buy whatever tunes the producer chose to include. Consumers rebelled against this model in amazing numbers with the launch of Napster in 1998. Napster's users, as many as 20 million at its peak, weren't looking primarily for "free" music—they just wanted to make their own choices of which songs to include on their CDs. Since the days of Napster, a whole industry supporting user–selected downloadable music has emerged, including producers of portable MP3 players, CD–R drives and software for organizing and sharing playlists. Napster's legal successors, PressPlay and MusicNet, although backed by big record labels, have not yet achieved the Napster magic with their limited selection, crippled song versions and digital time bombs which disable your downloads should you stop subscribing to the service. Sooner or later, someone will invent a music download service that captures the hearts and wallets of Napster's former fans. At its heart will be a new pricing algorithm—one that allows customers to buy individual tracks and record them on any device of their choosing.

Increasingly, General Electric, Rolls–Royce and Pratt & Whitney—the world's leading makers of jet engines—don't sell a product. They sell "power by the hour." When airlines buy one of Boeing's ultra–long–range 777s, scheduled for launch in 2003, they'll get a pair of GE 90 engines that come with a fixed–price maintenance agreement pegged at so many dollars per flight hour. After all, airlines don't really want to own jet engines; they want guaranteed up time. Many Internet service providers used to charge by the hour for connect time. No more. Most now have a single monthly charge no matter how long you're online.

Ask yourself: What are you actually charging for? What is the dominant pricing paradigm in your industry? Can you break it? Do you really know what customers think they're paying for? Can you more closely align what you charge for with what customers actually value? Does the existing pricing structure implicitly penalize some customers and subsidize others? Can you change this?

Thought: What you charge for and what your customers think they're paying for are often quite distinct. Your pricing structure and a customer's value structure are not the same things. When I buy a magazine I pay for information or entertainment. When I buy a razor I pay for a cleanly shaven face. A company that understands a customer's value structure—the value that is placed on each of the benefits received—is in a great position to be a pricing innovator. If I visit the *New York Times* or the *San Jose Mercury News* online, I get the reporters or columnists that write for those particular papers. But why can't I go to a site that lists the top–100 columnists and news reporters, along with the titles of their latest stories or editorials? That way, I'd pay for and get to read the writers I most enjoy.

Customer Benefits

Intermediating between the *core strategy* and the *customer interface* is another bridge component—the particular bundle of *benefits* that is actually being offered to the customer. Benefits refer to a customer-derived definition of the basic needs and wants that are being satisfied. Benefits are what link the core strategy to the needs of the customer. An important component of any business concept is the decision as to which benefits are or aren't going to be included in the offering.

CUSTOMER INTERFACE	CORE STRATEGY	STRATEGIC RESOURCES	VALUE NETWORK
Fulfillment & Support Information & Insight Relationship Dynamics Pricing Structure	Business Mission Product/Market Scope Basis for Differentiation	Core Competencies Strategic Assets Core Processes	

Example: It used to be that when you bought a car, you bought sheet metal and rubber. Now, if you buy a luxury sedan, you get a car bursting with ancillary benefits: 24/7 roadside service, expense reimbursement when your trip is interrupted by car trouble, a loaner when your car is in for major service and a free car wash with every service. GM's OnStar system provides a 24–hour concierge who can secure a restaurant reservation or direct you to the nearest zoo. If your airbags deploy, OnStar automatically contacts emergency services and gives them your location. Having trouble locating your car in an airport parking lot? Call OnStar from your cell phone, and they'll flash your car's lights and sound its horn. They'll even unlock the doors remotely if you've been a particularly silly prat and locked your keys inside. OnStar may fall short of industry revolution, but it's certainly raising the ante for luxury car makers and it's just the beginning of what car makers hope will ultimately be a cornucopia of services that will generate a continuing stream of revenues long after the vehicle has been purchased.

Ask yourself: What benefits are we actually delivering to customers? Are there ancillary benefits that the customer might value? What's the core need we're trying to address? Have we defined that need broadly enough? Conversely, are we delivering benefits that customers don't really care about? Can we change the benefit bundle in ways that will surprise customers and frustrate competitors? What's the context in which the product or service is used? Does that context suggest the possibility of enlarging the benefit bundle?

Thought: Imagine you want to build a patio behind your house and you go online to check out a DIY superstore. You provide some information on the size of patio you want to build, the style of your house and your budget. A virtual architect then presents a couple of dozen plans from which you can choose. The program automatically resizes each plan to fit your available space. Once you've made your selection, a virtual contractor generates a list of all the tools and materials you're going to need and a construction blueprint. You can remove from the list any item that you already have. In a few hours a truck delivers everything you're going to need on one pallet. You print out a detailed construction guide from the website. When you make your purchase you get a telephone number to call for help if you should run into any problems. Now that's a

FINDING THE REVOLUTION

uniquely tailored bundle of benefits, and it could be the basis for some real business concept innovation for The Home Depot, Orchard Supply or some other big home-improvement retailer.

Value Network

The fourth component of a business model is the *value network* that surrounds the firm, and which complements and amplifies the firm's own resources. Today many of the resources that are critical to a firm's success lie outside its direct control. Elements of the value network include suppliers, partners and coalitions. The design and management of the value network can be important sources of business concept innovation.

1. Suppliers: Suppliers typically reside "up the value chain" from the producer. Privileged access to or a deep relationship with suppliers can be a central element of a novel business model.

Example: Pret A Manger, the UK-based fast-food chain specializing in freshly made gourmet sandwiches, uses a network of mostly small suppliers to provide it with a broad range of additive-free ingredients. Since ingredients are delivered fresh to each Pret store every day, there are no long supply lines of frozen French fries or sesame-coated buns. This allows Pret to change their menu frequently—adding a new menu item every two weeks or so. It also minimizes inventory costs. Pret's imaginative suppliers are always on the lookout for new and interesting ingredients. One supplier located a source of crayfish, flown in daily from China. In early 2002, the most popular sandwich on Pret's UK menu was a crayfish and rocket lettuce sandwich. Burger King may have a hyperefficient supply chain, but when was the last time a supplier brought forward an idea that turned into a BK menu favorite? Beating the hell out of suppliers over price may be fashionable, but this isn't likely to be a recipe for business concept innovation.

Ask yourself: How effectively are we using suppliers as a source of innovation? Do we regard them as integral to our business model? Do we gain competitive advantage from the way we manage the linkage with our suppliers (lightning speed, dramatically reduced inventory costs, etc.)? How closely are our business goals aligned with those of our suppliers?

Thought: Now more than ever, it is possible for companies to off-load noncore activities onto suppliers. Technology has steadily reduced the costs of communication and coordination. Industry standards, such as GSM in the cell phone business, have simplified the interface between different components of a system. Enormous economies of scale in the manufacture of high–volume "core products" such as semiconductors have made it necessary for downstream assemblers to rely on just a few suppliers. Add to this ever shorter product life cycles and a premium on flexibility, and it is easy to see why companies are becoming less vertical. Yet every company must guard against "outsourcing" things that might become critical sources of competitive differentiation. Once you've outsourced something to some big IT company, you can write it off as a source of competitive advantage.

2. Partners: Partners typically supply critical "complements" to a final product or "solution." Their relationship with producers is more horizontal and less vertical than that of suppliers. *An imaginative use of partners can be the key to industry revolution.*

Example: The success of Microsoft's Windows platform is in large part due to the support Microsoft has lavished on its software development partners. Making it easy for independent software vendors (ISVs) to write for Windows increases the number of applications running on Windows and further strengthens its market position. Microsoft's support includes offering development tools to ISVs that make it easier to write software for the Windows O/S, helping young companies get access to capital and offering them co–marketing opportunities, hosting dozens of developer events around the world and running a dedicated website that provides developers with extensive online support. In 1999, the Microsoft Developer Network included over 10,000 ISVs.

Ask yourself: Can we look at the world as a global reservoir of competencies? What opportunities might be available to us if we could "borrow" the assets and competencies of other companies and marry them with our own? How could we use partners to "punch more than our weight"? How can we use partners to achieve greater flexibility, focus more tightly on our own core competencies, build a first-mover advantage or offer a more complete "solution" to customers?

Thought: A lot of "suppliers" would like to become "partners"—that is, they want to be more than order takers competing on price. Here's what this implies. First, you have to take responsibility for something more than a minor component in the overall solution. You need to take responsibility for an entire system or product. Second, you may have to be willing to share some of the commercial risk. To win an exclusive contract from Boeing to supply jet engines for a super–long-range derivative of the 777, GE had to behave like a partner. It agreed to put up as much as half of the $1 billion needed to launch the 777 derivative, thus reducing Boeing's development risk. Third, you have to work hard to make sure that your contribution is truly differentiated in a way that makes a difference to end consumers. This means you can't rely on your immediate downstream customer for your understanding of end–consumer needs. You must build your own point of view about what those end customers really want. If you're Dell or HP, the Taiwanese company that makes your computer monitors is a supplier. Intel is a partner. Every supplier would like to become "Intel Inside." But this won't happen unless you stop thinking of yourself as a supplier.

3. Coalitions: Business concept innovation often requires a company to join together with other, like-minded competitors in a coalition. This is particularly likely to be the case where investment or technology hurdles are high or where there is a high risk of ending up on the losing side of a winner–take–all standards battle. Coalition members are more than partners, they share directly in the risk and rewards of industry structure innovation.

Example: Airbus Industrie, a consortium of France's Aerospatiale Matra, Germany's DaimlerChrysler Aerospace Airbus, British Aerospace, and Spain's CASA, is one of the world's most successful coalitions. In 2001 Airbus rang up 274 orders for new aircraft compared to Boeing's 272. This was the second time in three years that Airbus booked more orders than Boeing. With Lockheed gone, and McDonnell Douglas now part of Boeing, Airbus is all that stands between the world's airlines and a Boeing monopoly.

Ask yourself: Can we look beyond our own resources and markets and imagine new resource combinations that could create new markets and services? Can we co-opt other firms into a "common cause"? Can we use their resources to alter the competitive dynamics of an industry? Can we use a coalition to bring a highly risky project into the realm of feasibility? Can we use a coalition to attack the entrenched position of an industry incumbent?

Thought: Business-to-business "hubs" and "exchanges" have yet to live up to their promise, but they represent a potentially intriguing new type of coalition. In April 2000, 11 of the world's largest retailers, including Target, Safeway, Marks & Spencer and Tesco, announced the formation of the Worldwide Retail Exchange, a global buying consortium. Within two years of its founding, the WWRE had grown to 59 members. Sears, Carrefour, Metro AG, J Sainsbury plc and Kroger joined forces to form a competing B2B market, GlobalNetXchange. In both cases, member companies hope the exchange will help them counter the enormous buying power of Wal-Mart, which emerged at the end of 2001 as America's largest company, with $217 billion in revenues. Wal-Mart has its own proprietary exchange, Retail Link, and any supplier that wishes to do business with Wal-Mart must do so over this private exchange. Whatever the ultimate fate of these new coalitions, it is a good bet that they will ultimately change the distribution of bargaining power within the grocery industry. Through the 1990s, companies merged in hopes of capturing global procurement economies. Hubs and exchanges may eventually

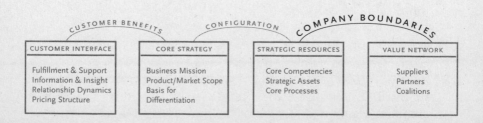

CUSTOMER BENEFITS	CONFIGURATION	COMPANY BOUNDARIES	
CUSTOMER INTERFACE	**CORE STRATEGY**	**STRATEGIC RESOURCES**	**VALUE NETWORK**
Fulfillment & Support Information & Insight Relationship Dynamics Pricing Structure	Business Mission Product/Market Scope Basis for Differentiation	Core Competencies Strategic Assets Core Processes	Suppliers Partners Coalitions

constitute a kind of "virtual" merger that allows companies to pool bargaining power while avoiding the panoply of complex integration issues that bedevil full-fledged mergers.

Company Boundaries

Intermediating between a company's *strategic resources* and its *value network* are the firm's *boundaries*. This bridge component refers to *the decisions that have been made about what the firm does and what it contracts out to the value network.* Again, an important aspect of any business model is the choice of what the firm will do for itself and what it will outsource to suppliers, partners, or coalition members. Changing these boundaries is often an important contributor to business concept innovation.

Example: The PC industry's spectacular growth was driven by innovative boundary decisions by IBM, Microsoft and Intel. Twenty years ago the computer industry was dominated by vertically integrated companies such as IBM, Data General and Digital Equipment Corp. These companies made their own silicon chips, created their own proprietary operating systems, manufactured their own computers and often wrote application software. The PC, with its open standards, changed all that. Microsoft did the operating system. Intel did the chips. Hundreds of suppliers from California to Taiwan to Ireland made specialized components such as SCSI cards, sound chips, monitors and disk drives. Thousands of independent software vendors wrote applications, and assemblers, such as Dell, shipped the finished products to customers and handled technical support. Horizontal specialization allowed component manufacturers to reap enormous economies of scale as they were no longer limited to selling through their own channels, under a single brand. It gave the assemblers complete freedom to incorporate the very latest technology and the most cost-competitive components in the finished product. Indeed, it is difficult to believe that a vertically integrated company could have sustained the pace of innovation witnessed over the past couple of decades in the PC business.

Ask yourself: Have you looked critically at where you draw the boundary between what you do and what you don't do as a company? Is there a chance to change industry rules by "deverticalizing" your industry, as Microsoft did in the computer business? How explicitly do you think about the opportunity to change the boundaries, vertically and horizontally, that distinguish the activities of various industry participants?

Thought: In the age of progress, companies were organized like hierarchies, where internal transactions were governed by some central authority and every business unit was 100 percent owned by the parent company. While this structure allowed, in theory, for a lot of internal coordination, as, for example, when General Motors sources engines for several model lines from a single factory, the sheer size of these hierarchies, and top management's distance from the market, often made them slow and unresponsive. In our increasingly turbulent times, resilience has become a critical virtue. The pursuit of flexibility and resilience has had a profound impact on corporate boundaries. In recent years, companies have been eager to shed fixed assets by outsourcing their manufacturing to companies such as Flextronics and Solectron, and turning their data centers over to EDS, IBM Global Services or other IT service providers. Companies have increased their workforce flexibility by hiring thousands of contract workers who can be let go when demand retracts.

Even pharmaceutical companies are beginning to question the benefits of vertical integration. Many of the big drug companies have been shedding functions amid the growth of new horizontally oriented pharmaceutical companies. Traditional drug companies are finding that clinical trials are becoming increasingly expensive, with clinical approval times nearly doubling in the last few years. In response, they are handing this function over to a growing number of CROs (contract research organizations). Covad, one of the largest of the CROs, uses its proprietary IT systems to manage patient data and rapidly screen the results of biochemical assays, all with the goal of quickly deciding which trials are worth pursuing and which should be abandoned. As drug companies struggle to cope with steadily escalating R&D costs owing to breakthroughs in genomics and proteomics, they have started to selectively outsource drug discovery to the new biotech companies and to companies that specialize in the various phases of the drug discovery process. Drug marketing is the latest of the major drug company functions to be outsourced.

A growing number of marketing service companies are focused on crafting new product launch strategies, drafting marketing plans and designing customer pull–through programs.

Undoubtedly, deverticalization and outsourcing decisions are occasionally no more than quick expedients for CEOs under the gun to shave expenses. In these cases, the quest for resilience may jeopardize important core competencies. Yet the fact remains that vertical integration, which was in the past a response to high transactions costs (which could be lowered by bringing key functions inside the corporate boundary), is becoming less critical in a world where real–time information allows for transparency and trust between business partners. Nevertheless, something that is outsourced usually ceases to provide a competitive advantage, unless a company has a unique and proprietary relationship with its partners. While being "virtual" may bring flexibility, the capacity to earn above–average profits still depends on having a defensible competitive advantage.

Wealth Potential

To be an industry revolutionary you need a point of view about how you're going to use each component of the business concept as a lever for rule–breaking innovation. You also need a compelling story about how this innovation will generate new wealth.

There are four factors to consider in determining the *wealth potential* of any business concept:

○ the extent to which the business concept is an *efficient* way of delivering customer benefits;
○ the extent to which the business concept is *unique*;
○ the degree of *fit* among the elements of the business concept; and
○ the extent to which the business concept exploits *profit boosters* that have the potential to generate above–average returns.

Let's take each of these in turn.

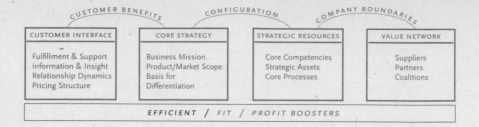

CUSTOMER INTERFACE	CORE STRATEGY	STRATEGIC RESOURCES	VALUE NETWORK
Fulfillment & Support Information & Insight Relationship Dynamics Pricing Structure	Business Mission Product/Market Scope Basis for Differentiation	Core Competencies Strategic Assets Core Processes	Suppliers Partners Coalitions

CUSTOMER BENEFITS   *CONFIGURATION*   *COMPANY BOUNDARIES*

EFFICIENT / FIT / PROFIT BOOSTERS

Efficient

To create wealth, a business model must be efficient in the sense that the value customers place on the benefits delivered exceeds the cost of producing those benefits. Many new business concepts founder on this very point—there's just no margin! Many Web–based retailers started with the idea that they could survive by selling goods below cost. The hope was that advertising revenues would compensate for negative retail margins. That dog didn't hunt. The largest of the large online retailers, ValueAmerica, went bankrupt in August 2000, and another, Buy.com, subsequently announced a new policy of "selective price increases."

> **Examples:** Southwest Airlines has a business model that delivers air travel to budget–minded fliers more efficiently than any of its major competitors. With its point–to–point route structure, all–737 fleet and flexible work practices, Southwest has the lowest seat–per–mile cost of any major airline. Despite Southwest's low fares, it has one of the healthiest margins in the airline business.
> **However, having an efficient business model does not mean having the lowest costs.** Midwest Express Airlines doesn't match Southwest's fares, and Southwest would never claim to deliver the "best care in the air," as Midwest does. Filet mignon with lobster, a roll with butter, spinach, mandarin salad and chocolate banana–split cake—when was the last time you ate like this in coach? That's a typical meal on Midwest Express. The company spends an average of $10 per passenger on meals, compared with Southwest's 20¢. (You can get peanuts really cheap when you buy in bulk.) Midwest offers its coach passengers two–by–two seating, with five more inches of knee room and four more inches of hip room than usual coach seats. Midwest earns healthy profits because it tightly controls costs in other areas—

it flies an older fleet of mostly DC–9s, and it operates out of a low–cost hub, Milwaukee. The same coach fare that would buy a distinctly mediocre service experience on American or United buys a near–first–class experience on Midwest. No wonder the airline has been rated by *Travel & Leisure* magazine as the best domestic airline, and no wonder its stock has outperformed the Dow Jones Industrial Average. While Southwest offers less service for a much lower price than traditional airlines, Midwest offers more service for about the same price. Both companies have highly efficient business models.

Ask yourself: Have we tested our assumptions about the value customers will actually derive from our products or services? Do we understand in detail the costs we will incur in providing that value?

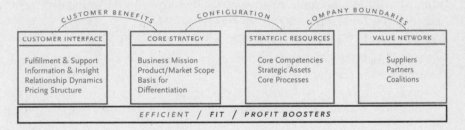

Fit

Consanguinity is a ten–dollar word that means "fit." A business concept generates profits when all its elements are mutually reinforcing. A business concept has to be internally consistent—all its parts must work together for the same end goal. Almost by definition, a company with mediocre performance is a company where elements of its business model work at cross–purposes.

Example: Four Seasons Hotels and Resorts, Inc., based in Toronto, runs the largest chain of luxury hotels in the world and defines "pampered" in nearly 20 countries. The company's success comes from the fact that every aspect of its business model— property location, staff selection and training, architecture, quality of decor, service levels and catering—is focused on making you feel like a head of state. Few companies achieve the kind of consistency so much in evidence at Four Seasons. For example, on a recent first–class flight from San Francisco to London, on an airline that shall remain nameless, there was an elegant caviar service at the beginning of the flight, and a breakfast at the other end that featured a plastic tub of Wheaties with a pull–off paper lid. Talk about a jarring inconsistency! This is how cereal is sold at McDonald's, and not quite what is expected for a $10,000 roundtrip airfare.

Ask yourself: Do all of the elements of the business model positively reinforce each other? Are there some elements of the business model that are at odds with other elements? What's the degree of internal consistency in our business model? Is there anything that looks anomalous to customers?

Profit Boosters

Of course what you actually want to know is not whether your business model is going to be profitable, but whether it's going to be *really* profitable. **THERE ARE A DOZEN PROFIT BOOSTERS THAT CAN PUSH PROFITS INTO ORBIT.** The trick is to figure out a way of bolting one or two of these profit boosters onto your business concept.

These profit boosters can be grouped under four categories:

- ○ Increasing Returns
- ○ Competitor Lock–Out
- ○ Strategic Economies
- ○ Strategic Flexibility

You need to get acquainted with each of these profit boosters. They are what distinguish so–so profits from returns that make investors swoon.

The first two, *increasing returns* and *competitor lock-out*, are synonyms for monopoly. Business concept innovation is, after all, the search for temporary monopolies. While revolutionary business concepts tend to undermine entrenched monopolies, a business concept with strong monopolistic tendencies can often withstand a prolonged assault from would–be rivals before crumbling. In general, the stronger the monopoly, the greater the innovation necessary to unseat the incumbent. In this sense, business concept innovation is the quest for strategies that are, insofar as possible, impervious to further bouts of business concept innovation. Got that? To be clear, I am not using the word "monopoly" in a legal sense—I am merely referring to strategies that tend to be self-reinforcing. You don't have to engage in predatory tactics or set out to be a robber baron to create a business concept that ends up yielding monopolylike profits.

Economists start with an assumption of perfect, atomistic competition. They look at any firm earning above-average profits as an anomaly. Industry revolutionaries start with an assumption that the entire goal of strategy is to create *im*perfect competition. To them, strategy is all about building quasi monopolies. To an economist, above-average profit represents "market failure." To a strategist, it represents a killer business concept. The problem for economists is that there are a lot of anomalies these days. Microsoft's Windows operating system, Delta's control of gates in Atlanta and Salt Lake City, Intel's PC architecture and the patents behind the DVD are all examples of quasi monopolies. Recently, economists such as W. Brian Arthur and Paul Romer have discovered what savvy innovators have known all along: some business models, by their very nature, have built-in monopolies.

Increasing Returns

Founded more than 800 years ago, Oxford and Cambridge universities are two of the oldest examples of "increasing returns." Their continued dominance in British higher education is attested to by the fact that they are often known simply as "Oxbridge," a class of two that eclipses all other British universities. Imagine you're a brilliant young physicist who one day hopes to win a Nobel Prize. Where do you want to go to do your post-doctoral research? That's simple—to a university that already has a clutch of Nobel Prize winners. You also want access to the best Ph.D. students, who are, of course, attracted to the best faculty. The best attract the best— this virtuous circle has allowed Oxford and Cambridge to dominate British academia for the better part of a millennium. It wasn't Microsoft and W. Brian Arthur that invented increasing returns.

The term *increasing returns* simply refers to a competitive situation where the rich tend to get richer, and the poor, poorer. It denotes a flywheel effect that tends to perpetuate early success. Those who are ahead will get farther ahead, and those who are behind will fall farther behind. Perpetual motion is almost as rare in business as it is in physics, and every business model ultimately encounters some sort of friction, but a business concept characterized by increasing returns can produce fat profits for an immodestly long time. The notion of increasing returns is subtly different from the notion of scale. In an industry such as chemicals, which is characterized by significant economies of scale, you have to be big to win. In industries with increasing returns, if you win early, you're likely to *get* big. Economies of scale are largely static; increasing returns are dynamic.

To benefit from increasing returns, a business model must harness one of three underlying forces: network effects, positive feedback effects, or learning effects.

1. Network Effects: Some business models benefit from a strange kind of value multiplier known as the "network effect." In some cases, the value of a network increases as the *square* of the growth of the number of "nodes," or members in the network. If you model the growth of a business concept that exploits the network effect, you get a diagram that looks like the power curve for nuclear fission or the infection curve for a virulent virus.

Examples: eBay is a classic example of network economies. You wouldn't go to an auction site that had only a dozen items for sale. But as the number of participants (nodes) increases, the chance you'll find what you want, or find a buyer for what you don't want, goes up geometrically. If you have something to buy or sell online, why *wouldn't* you go to eBay? With 42 million registered users and over 79 million items for sale in 8,000 categories, eBay has exploited the dynamics of the network effect to the hilt. Where the value of the network is a function of the *number of members in the network*, there will be increasing returns for those who start earliest, work hardest and build the biggest network. As their network gets bigger and bigger, it gets harder and harder for latecomers to build equivalent networks, and there is less and less incentive for customers to switch networks.

Network effects also account for the triumph of Visa, Master-Card and American Express as truly global credit cards. The more merchants who accept these cards, the more likely you are to carry them. The more likely you are to carry them, the more merchants are apt to accept them. Another virtuous circle.

Ask yourself: Do we have a business concept that taps into the network effect? Can we find opportunities to create network economies where none currently exist? If not, can we somehow hitch our business concept to the network multiplier?

2. Positive Feedback Effects: *Positive feedback effects* and *increasing returns* are sometimes used interchangeably to denote a situation where success breeds success. But I'd like to use *positive feedback effects* in a more limited way—to refer specifically to the way one uses market feedback to turn an initial lead into an unbridgeable chasm for competitors. A firm with a large base of users, and a way of rapidly extracting feedback from those users, may be able to improve its products and services faster than its competitors. As a result, its products become better yet, and it captures even more customers. Another virtuous circle ensues.

Example: AOL has systematically exploited insights derived from its customer base to provide the easiest online service, and has steadily pulled ahead of other branded Internet portals. The better the content and online experience, the more users AOL attracts. The more users AOL attracts, the more advertising revenue it gets. The more advertising dollars it gets, the more it can afford to invest in upgrading and expanding its services, thus attracting more users. This positive feedback effect also works with advertisers. The more users, the higher the ad rates AOL can charge. The higher the ad rates, the more AOL can spend on differentiating its site and offering. The more it spends on making its site and content even better, the more users it attracts. Positive feedback effects are the hub in the virtuous circle of customer learning and improvement.

Ask yourself: Where's the flywheel that will perpetuate our early success? Where are we creating a virtuous circle of increasing returns? Where could we create positive feedback effects within our business model? Can we set up a very short learning cycle that will allow us to improve our products and services faster than anyone else? Should we be heavily discounting our products or services, or giving them away for free as a means to generate positive feedback effects that would allow us to outpace competitors?

3. Learning Effects: More and more industries are knowledge-intensive. A company that gets an early start in accumulating knowledge, and then continues to learn faster than its rivals, can build an almost insurmountable lead. Knowledge accumulation is often highly correlated with experience. (Remember

Boston Consulting Group's experience curve?) **The notion is simple: the application of knowledge begets new knowledge.** This is particularly true in cases where the critical knowledge is both complex and tacit—complex in the sense that it represents the fusion of several different types of knowledge, and tacit in that it is not easily codified.

Example: In an industry—be it manufacturing semiconductors or strategy consulting—characterized by strong learning effects, it is difficult for latecomers to intercept the knowledge-building progress of the leaders unless they change the knowledge base of the industry. Learning effects gave Sharp and Toshiba dominant positions in the manufacture of flat screen displays. In the early years, flat screen manufacturing yields were disastrously low. But perseverance paid off. For a long while, Sharp and Toshiba enjoyed virtual monopolies in the single most valuable component of a laptop computer. Hundreds of millions went to the bottom line. Of course, over time all knowledge tends to get commoditized—it gets acquired from suppliers, equipment manufacturers, ex-employees or through reverse engineering. As this has happened, new competitors have entered the flat screen display business.

Ask yourself: What parts of our business model might be subject to learning curve effects? Where does accumulated volume count, and how much does it count as a percentage of total costs? Are we taking full advantage of every opportunity to learn? Are we building that learning into our products and services on a real-time basis?

COMPETITOR LOCK-OUT

When you find a window of opportunity, the goal is to crawl through it and lock it behind you. You want *all* the loot, and you don't want to have to fight for it. Ghastly business, fighting. Always a chance that some of *your* blood may get spilled. **That's why really slick business models lock competitors out through preemption, choke points and customer lock-in.**

1. Preemption: Where there is great potential for increasing returns, merely being first may be enough to put competitors out of contention. It's terrific when the first punch is a knockout blow. In industries that are R&D-intensive or that have high fixed costs, there's often no second place—you're either first or you're nowhere.

Examples: Imagine that Early Bird, Inc., has just sunk $200 million into developing a new software product. In its first year of operation it finds 5 million customers for its WormFinder software, which sells for $250 a pop. That's $1.25 billion in revenue. With a variable cost of $50 per copy (to cover manufacturing, distribution, advertising, and admin), Early Bird's direct costs amount to $250 million. That leaves $1 billion—a 500 percent return on its R&D investment. If it's smart, Early Bird will sink a couple of hundred million dollars back into R&D to bolster its lead. Slow As Snails, Inc., enters the market 10 months late with a competing product and manages to sell only 1 million copies. At $250 a pop, Snails' gross is $250 million. With variable costs of $50 per copy, Snails' gross profit is $200 million. That barely covers its own development costs. Going forward, there's no way it will be able to match Early Bird's escalating R&D investment. Now Early Bird has the chance to play vulture. It drops its price to $150 and the market expands to 11 million customers, of which Early Bird has 8.5 million. Its revenues inch ahead to $1.275 billion, but it is still making a very healthy gross profit of $850 million. Meanwhile, Slow As Snails matches Early Bird's price and rakes in only $225 million on 1.5 million customers. After deducting direct costs of $75 million, Slow As Snails can afford only $150 million for ongoing R&D. It may take another couple of rounds for the fight to be over, but Slow As Snails is going down. A business concept with this kind of fixed-cost leverage offers the fleet of foot the chance to create an almost unassailable position.

First-mover advantages are never absolute, but they are often pivotal in industries with a rapid pace of technological development and relatively short product life cycles. If you get in late, you're going to be fighting the U.S. Marines with slingshots and bottle rockets. Preemption requires a great product, a capacity to learn fast, and a willingness to double up your bets. Being first means nothing if you're trying to sell something nobody wants or if it takes you forever to respond to customer input. Apple may have been first with handheld computers, but the Newton was so woefully underdeveloped that it left the door wide open for the PalmPilot.

Johnson & Johnson pulled a Newton with its groundbreaking coronary "stent," a tiny metal frame that props open cholesterol–clogged arteries. Three years after the product's launch in 1994, it was closing in on $1 billion in revenues, and had a 90 percent market share and gross margins judged to be as high as 80 percent. But J&J left the stent window wide open. The company's overambitious pricing ($1,595), sluggish pace of product refinement, and offhand treatment of cardiologists opened the door for followers like Guidant Corp. and Boston Scientific Corp. Forty–five days after it launched its competing product, Guidant claimed a market share of 70 percent. J&J ultimately abandoned the market. Pre-emption without follow–through ain't worth squat.

Ask yourself: Do you risk becoming a perpetual follower? Are there any first–mover advantages implicit in your business concept? Where do you plan to preempt, and how do you plan to follow up on that? How are you going to turn being first once into being first again and again?

2. Choke Points: The famed military strategist Karl von Clausewitz called it the "command of heights." My colleague Peter Skarzynski calls it "choke point control," but the idea is the same. Whether it's 1452 and you're Sultan Mehmet II building a fortress to control the Bosphorus or it's the new millennium and you're trying to gain control of the cable television infrastructure that will allow broadband Webcasting, the logic is the same. Whoever owns the choke point collects the toll. If you're unwilling to pay up, you're locked out.

Examples: In 1984, AT&T gave up direct access to its customers by agreeing to spin off the Baby Bells as part of its divestiture agreement. With this decision, AT&T not only gave up the physical line into the home but also the right to bill those cus-tomers, as long–distance billing was included in the local bill and the Baby Bells became sole owners of the local customer data. Now, as the dust settles from the great telecom shakeout, it is glaringly apparent that what still really matters is the physical connection to the customer. As digital subscriber line (DSL) providers like Covad, NorthPoint, Teligent, Winstar and countless other newcomers file for bankruptcy, the Baby Bells have emerged from the shakeout as the winners in the local market. The Telecommunications Act of 1996 was supposed to open the local market. But the Baby Bells had no incentive to give up their chokepoint—control over all connections to the local network—and they didn't. While staying within the letter of the law, which required that new entrants be allowed to connect to the local phone switches, the Baby Bells found amazingly creative ways to slow this process down—to the point where many newcomers either gave up or went bankrupt. With the local line still the bottleneck and the last-mile rollout of DSL slowed to a snail's pace, most of the so-called Next Generation backbone carriers, companies such as Williams and Level 3 that had been busy laying high bandwidth fiber between major cities, also found themselves in deep pooky. (If you need a picture here, imagine a super highway with no exit ramps.) And it wasn't just the DSL entrepreneurs and the fiber optic barons who paid the price for the Baby Bells' stranglehold on local access. As the broadband rollout faltered, so too did the prospects of companies making telecom hardware, providing Web-hosting services or hoping to provide interactive television and a host of other bandwidth-hungry services. The telecom shakeout serves as a multibillion-dollar lesson in choke point control. But the fact is that the stronger a company's choke point, the greater the incentive for competitors to blast a path around it. The Baby Bells' stranglehold on local access, and their leisurely approach to rolling out their own DSL services, provided a big opening for cable television companies eager to sell high-bandwidth cable modems to residential customers. Many tele-com experts believe that the Baby Bells overplayed their hand and will ultimately lose a big chunk of the broadband future to the cable television companies, which also own a last-mile connection to the home.

Microsoft's Windows may be history's most effective choke point. It is virtually impossible to build a PC, write a software application or create a document without, in some way, sending a check to Microsoft. All of us who've passed through the Microsoft toll gate should be thankful for one thing: Internet Protocol (the standard that governs how packets of data are sent across the Internet) and HTML (the standard that governs how information is displayed on the Internet) are not only open, they're in the public domain. That must drive Bill Gates nuts, yet he should be grateful, for if anyone owned IP and HTML, Bill would probably be the second-richest person on the planet.

Choke points come in many shapes and sizes: a technical standard, control of some costly infrastructure, preferential access to a government buyer, a patent or a prime location. Other choke point examples include the "anchor" store in a mall, Gatorade's prime position on the sidelines of every NFL football game, De Beers' historic control over the distribution of diamonds and a critical patent. A truly strategic business concept lets you command the heights.

Ask yourself: Is there some standard, some protocol, an interface or a bit of infrastructure that you could uniquely own? Are you creating any assets that will be critical to the success of other companies—so critical that you can effectively charge a "toll"? Are there some scarce assets or skills that you'd like to deny your competitors? Can you lock up these assets or skills in some way?

3. **Customer Lock-in:** Competitor lock-*out* often means customer lock-*in*. But even when you can't lock out *all* your competitors, you can lock in *some* of your customers—through long-term supply contracts, proprietary product designs that keep them coming back for upgrades and add-ons or control over a local monopoly. There are many ways you can tie up your customers, but you have to be careful. A customer that *feels* locked in is a particularly angry beast. You gotta use velvet ropes.

Examples: U.S. airlines have earned graduate degrees in customer lock-in. First there's the matter of gates. Competition-phobic air carriers moved swiftly after deregulation to consolidate their control over so-called fortress hubs. During the 1980s, the Justice Department approved every airline merger that was presented to it. The result? A fellow traveler can tell where you live simply by looking at the frequent-flyer luggage tag that adorns your carry-on—yeah, that gold-colored emblem of your slavery. You got a US Airways tag? You probably live in Pittsburgh or Charlotte. Continental? Houston or Newark.

America West? Phoenix. TWA (poor sod)? St. Louis. Northwest? Detroit or Minneapolis, maybe Memphis.

Fortress hubs have been wildly successful, as lock-in strategies go, provoking some in the U.S. Congress to label airlines "unregulated monopolies." Few fliers are dumb enough to believe that the new spate of proposed semi-mergers and co-marketing agreements (American and US Airways, United and Delta, Northwest and Continental) is really about "seamless travel." They're about better lock-in.

Frequent-flyer cards are an even more intricate set of manacles. Fail to fly enough with your airworthy monopolist, and you'll get stuffed into steerage on *every* flight. You'll never tally up enough miles for that second honeymoon either. You're not Platinum? Not 1K? Then don't even bother to ask an airline employee for a favor unless you're fully prostrate or more than halfway through a myocardial infarction.

Customer lock-in is just a fancy way of saying "switching costs." Once you've bought Microsoft Word and learned to navigate its Byzantine "features," you'll be well and truly on the hook. To Microsoft you're more than a customer, you're an annuity. Unless someone comes along with a truly radical new software business concept, you're going to be buying upgrades from Microsoft for a looooong time. Indeed, in a recent year, around half of Microsoft's software revenues came from upgrades. Talk about customer lock-in! You could escape the clutches of Philip Morris and a two-pack-a-day nicotine habit easier than you could wriggle free of Redmond Bill.

Only Intel has anything close to Microsoft's lock on customers. A few years ago Intel's co-founder and chairman, Gordon Moore, was asked whether he had been worried that his company's x86 chip architecture would be supplanted by new technologies such as RISC (reduced instruction set computing). His answer was telling: "No ... we had this tremendous advantage: all of the software that people had bought that ran on our instruction set."[3] Intel may be paranoid about many things, but a new chip architecture that would knock it out of the PCs is probably not one of them. Customer lock-in? Handcuffs, straitjacket and leg irons. Indeed, after years of trying, AMD has only recently taken a significant chunk of the microprocessor market in low-end PCs. And customers are glad for the alternative.

GE's jet engine deal with Boeing is a rather more palatable form of customer lock–in. GE's financial support for Boeing's development of the long–range 777 came with a price—Boeing would agree to sell the new 777 with GE engines *exclusively*. Lock–in is okay when the customer asks to be tied up.

All in all, be careful of customer lock-in. Lock-in is great while it lasts, but the moment those cuffs are off, your customers may well go for your throat.

Ask yourself: Could this business concept reduce our customers' ability or desire to buy from other suppliers? Is there anything in this business concept that would induce customers to limit their freedom of choice? How could we bind our fate with the fate of our customers even more tightly?

Strategic Economies

Unlike operational efficiencies, strategic economies don't derive from operational excellence, but from the business concept itself. Strategic economies come in three varieties: scale, focus and scope.

1. Scale: Scale can drive efficiencies in many ways: better plant utilization, greater purchasing power, the muscle to enforce industrywide price discipline and more besides. Industry revolutionaries often consolidate fragmented industries. Any company that gets caught behind the consolidation curve and misses the chance to build scale advantages will be left at a notable disadvantage.

Examples: Wal–Mart consolidated Main Street retailing and reaped unimagined scale economies in logistics and purchasing. While scale economies tend to perpetuate the success of big incumbents, revolutionaries look for industries that are still fragmented or for scale advantages that haven't yet been tapped. Imagine starting a business one day and 16 months later having your 29 percent stake valued at $315 million. Another sickening Internet story? Not quite—it's a story about Brad Jacobs and heavy equipment rentals. Jacobs got his start in the garbage hauling business. Having watched that business consolidate, he thought there might be a chance to bring scale economies to the highly fragmented rental market for air compressors, cranes, forklifts, generators and the like. United Rentals has consolidated more than 200 companies. After merging with a big competitor, United Rentals surpassed Hertz to become the largest equipment renter in the country, with over 600 locations.[4]

Ask yourself: Does our business model offer us the chance to build scale advantages? Where does size pay off in this business concept? Will the scale advantages outweigh any loss in flexibility?

2. Focus: A company with a high degree of focus and specialization may reap economies compared with competitors with a more diffused business mission and a less coherent mix of services or products. Focus is not about efficiency in a cost sense; it's about efficiency in a don't-get-distracted, get-all-the-wood-behind-one-arrow sense.

Examples: Focus is how little Granite Construction, Inc., of Watsonville, California, competes successfully with industry giants such as Morrison Knudsen and Bechtel. Granite Construction doesn't build chemical plants, and it doesn't do urban rail projects. It will, however, pave just about anything, be it an airport runway, a driveway or a section of interstate highway. Sales amounted to $1.2 billion in 1998, double what they were five years before. The company has a portfolio of more than 30 gravel pits that supply paving materials. It also makes its own ready-mix concrete and asphalt.

Focus is what lets BMW take on the might of Ford and GM in the luxury car business and win. Large companies often impose competing and ambiguous demands on their various divisions. Certainly this seems to be the fate that befell Cadillac—how can one explain products like the Cimarron and the only slightly less insipid Catera? What BMW loses in scale, it makes up for in single-minded zeal. Is there anything else on this planet so tightly put together as a 325i? BMW is a pure, sweet note; Lincoln and Cadillac have often sounded like ill-disciplined orchestras still tuning up. If BMW is ultimately swept up in merger fever, its new owners would do well to leave the Bavarian car-meisters alone.

Ask yourself: Does our business concept have a laserlike focus? If not, do we run the risk of trying to "boil the ocean"? What advantages would we gain by being more narrowly focused? What economies of scope would we lose if we were more focused?

3. Scope: The idea here is almost the inverse of focus. A company that can leverage resources and management talents across a broad array of opportunities may have an efficiency advantage over firms that cannot. Scope economies come from sharing things across business units and countries: brands, facilities, best practice, scarce talent, IT infrastructure and so on.

Example: Maybe you drink Moet & Chandon champagne, or perhaps your tastes run to Dom Perignon and Krug. Perhaps you carry a Louis Vuitton handbag or briefcase or wear a Tag Heuer watch. Your fragrance may have come from Christian Dior or Givenchy. And maybe that soft cotton shirt you're wearing came from Thomas Pink of Jermyn Street. Buy any of these brands and you're enriching the substantial coffers of LVMH, the world's premier luxury brands company. The company's chairman, Bernard Arnault, a.k.a. The Pope of Fashion, built LVMH into an $11.6 billion high-fashion juggernaut to capitalize on the substantial economies of scope that exist in manufacturing and marketing luxury goods. Scope economies come in a variety of flavors: channel power and access to distribution channels, economies in buying ad space and running high-tech distribution centers and the chance to move experienced management teams into acquired businesses to help revitalize elite but stuffy brands. While Prada and Gucci have recently made significant acquisitions of their own, they lag far behind LVMH in the race to build a *de luxe* powerhouse. No one in the rarefied world of platinum-plated brands doubts that Bernard Arnault is an industry revolutionary.

Ask yourself: Where are the potential economies of scope within our business concept? Can we find any "dual use" assets— things we can exploit in more than one business? What skills could we leverage across businesses, countries, or activities?

Strategic Flexibility

In a fast-changing world, with unpredictable demand cycles, strategic flexibility can generate higher profits by helping a company stay perfectly tuned to the market and avoid getting trapped in dead-end business models. Strategic flexibility comes from portfolio breadth, operating agility and a low breakeven point.

1. **Portfolio Breadth:** Focus is great, but if the world moves against you, you may lack other options. Linking the fortunes of your company to the fortunes of a single market can be a high-risk gamble. A company with a broad offering may be more resilient in the face of rapidly shifting customer priorities than a more narrowly focused competitor. **A portfolio can consist of countries, products, businesses, competencies or customer types.** The essential point is that it helps to hedge a company's exposure to the vagaries of one particular market niche.

   Examples: Given the vagaries of drug development and approval, most pharmaceutical companies feel it necessary to support the development of a broad portfolio of drugs. A broad portfolio increases the chances that a company can sustain high levels of R&D year in and year out, rather than have its R&D budget whipsawed by the changing fortunes of one or two products. It also raises the odds of coming up with an out-and-out blockbuster.

   Ask yourself: What are the advantages of a wide portfolio of products or businesses? How can we hedge our bets in this business concept? Does this business concept force us to put all our eggs in a rather small basket? Is the reduction of earnings variability, for example, a positive strategic benefit?

2. **Operating Agility:** A company that is able to quickly refocus its efforts is better placed to respond to changes in demand and can thereby even out profit swings.

   Example: Given the fact that Dell Computer owns few fixed assets, it is able to quickly reconfigure its selling approach and product line to suit changing market conditions. As one senior Dell executive put it, "We don't have to change bricks and mortar to change our strategy." Contrast that with Sears's 800-odd stores or GM's aging plants. Some business models are inherently easier to reconfigure than others—these are the ones that will endure in the age of revolution. Web-based businesses may offer the ultimate in flexibility. You can change a product description overnight, test a dozen different ad ideas and have the data back in 24 hours, and experiment with different price points—it's as if Web business concepts were made out of Play-Doh instead of steel and cement.

Ask yourself: How quickly does the demand function in our business change? Is there an advantage to investing in flexibility (i.e., in processes and facilities that would allow us to respond rapidly to shifts in demand)? Could we earn consistently higher profits if we were able to respond more quickly to changes in demand, or to changes in input needs (e.g., were able to quickly incorporate the latest components in our designs)?

3. Lower Breakeven: A business concept that carries a high breakpoint is inherently less flexible than one with a lower breakeven point. Capital intensity, a big debt load, high fixed costs—these things tend to reduce the financial flexibility of a business model. In doing so, they also reduce strategic flexibility, in that they make it more difficult to pay off *one* thing so that you can go on and do *another* thing.

Example: For several decades Japanese car companies have been working to reduce the breakeven point of a car model. If you can break even on 50,000 units, instead of 250,000, you can trade that for a broader product range aimed at narrower consumer segments. More recently, the advantages of strategic flexibility have induced many companies to "de-capitalize" their business models.

Ask yourself: Does our business concept give us a lower breakeven point than traditional business models? How could we tweak the business model to lower our breakeven point even further? What would be the benefits of a lower breakeven point? Could we use a lower breakeven to buy ourselves more flexibility or deliver more variety to customers?

Of course, none of these profit boosters can turn an awful product into a smash hit. On the other hand, a great business concept can sometimes compensate for a mediocre product—indeed, for years this is just what drove Apple aficionados nuts about Microsoft's success. For more than a decade, Microsoft's operating system was much less user-friendly than the Mac's, but Microsoft's profit boosters yielded an unprecedented financial windfall.

BECOMING A BUSINESS CONCEPT INNOVATOR

There are two reasons you must develop an instinctive ability to picture innovation in terms of novel business concepts, and competition as rivalry between business models. (Remember, the building blocks of a business concept and a business model are the same—a business model is simply a business concept that has been put into practice.) The first is so you can construct a well-developed business case around *your* billion-dollar insight. **Half-baked ideas don't get funding.** The second is so you can escape the hold the existing business model has on your imagination and your loyalties.

A successful business model creates its own intellectual hegemony. Success turns *a* business model into *the* business model. In *Dealers of Lightning*,[5] a cautionary tale for any preternaturally prosperous company, Michael Hiltzik pins down the reason Xerox failed so miserably to capitalize on the innovations that poured out of its Palo Alto Research Center. In the copier business Xerox got paid by the page; each page got counted by a clicker. In the electronic office of the future, there was no clicker—there was no annuity. How would one get paid? The hegemony of the pennies-per-page business model was so absolute that it blinded Xerox to an Aladdin's cave of other possibilities.

Many of the choices that define your company's business model were made years ago. Those choices were shaped by the logic of another age. In the fading glow of success, they may seem like inevitabilities. But they're not. It is your job to turn those inevitabilities back into choices. You do this by subjecting each element of the existing business model to fresh scrutiny: What are the alternatives? Does this choice still have merit? How would a company free of our prejudices tackle this? In decomposing the existing business model you create degrees of freedom where tradition reigns.

There are 25-year-old engineers in Silicon Valley who dream in Technicolor business concepts. But if you've been stuck for a decade in some functional chimney or you inherited a strategy from the village elders or you were taught to venerate "industry best practice," then thinking in terms of business models won't be a natural act for you.

So begin to practice. Pick the worst service experience you've had in the last year, and think about the business model that failed to meet your expectations. How would you change it—element by element? Find an industry where everyone seems to be stuck in the same cul-de-sac, and invent an exit strategy for one of the companies. Pick a company you care about—one you think deserves to be more successful than it is—and try to imagine a breakout business concept, your own equivalent of the cyber B-school. The great advantage of a business concept is that it is infinitely malleable. It is, at the outset, only an intellectual construct. So pretend you're a kid again—with a very big Lego set, one that allows you to remake the very foundations of commerce. This isn't some meaningless exercise. This is mental training for industry revolutionaries.

4
BE YOUR OWN SEER

DO YOU HAVE THE PENETRATING AND UN-
clouded eyes of a revolutionary? Do you just know what's coming next? Is it real and inevitable and three-dimensional for you? Can you see, really see, a kick-ass opportunity for business-concept innovation? Is it so seductive that you can't even imagine turning your back on it?

Are you the voice of opportunity in your company? Are you the champion of the unconventional? Do you know how to break through the hard, parched soil of ignorance and dogma to find a gusher of an opportunity? Are you a source of strategic diversity? In the age of revolution you have to be able to imagine revolutionary alternatives to the status quo. If you can't, you'll be relegated to the swollen ranks of keyboard-pounding automatons.

There are too many individuals who cannot yet escape the dead hand of precedent. Too many who are not fully vested in the future. Too many who cannot distinguish between their heritage and their destiny. Is this you? Wanna do something about it?

Look around you. Look at the individuals and companies that have been champions of business-concept innovation. Do this, and you will see that rule-busting, wealth-creating innovation doesn't come out of corporate planning. It doesn't usually come from some corporate "incubator" division. It doesn't come out of product development. And it doesn't often come from blue-sky R&D. More and more, innovation comes, not from the triumph of big science (important as it is in removing physical constraints to innovation), but from the triumph of contrarianism (which leaps over the mental constraints). It is the idiot savant, who asks a fresh question and then answers it using parts that already exist, who is so often the author of the new. That's because industry revolution is conceptual innovation. It comes from the mind and soul of a malcontent, a dreamer, a smart-ass, and not from some bespectacled boffin or besuited planner.

FORGET THE FUTURE

From Nostradamus to Alvin Toffler, individuals and organizations have long been obsessed with trying to see the future. The goal is to somehow get advance warning of "what will be." Yet in my experience, industry revolutionaries spend little time gazing deeply into the future. While there are some aspects of the future that are highly probable—the cost of bandwidth will go down, our ability to manipulate genes will go up—most of what will constitute the future simply can't be known.

In 1984 the *Economist* magazine conducted a little study.[1] They asked 16 individuals to make predictions about 1994. Four Oxford economics students, four finance ministers, four corporate CEOs and four London dustmen ("garbage collectors" to Americans) were asked to predict the pound/dollar exchange rate ten years hence, the rate of inflation among OECD countries, the price of oil, and other macroeconomic unknowables. Not surprisingly, when 1994 rolled around, the forecasts turned out to be wrong. For example, the consensus forecast for OECD inflation was 8 percent. In actuality, it was barely 4 percent. Think about the difference that makes if you are trying to pick a discount rate to apply to a long-term capital investment. Interestingly, it was the finance ministers who made the least accurate forecasts. The best were made by the CEOs—who tied for first place with the dustmen. Yet even they produced forecasts so wrong as to be worthless.

Recently I heard the chairman of one of America's leading high-tech companies poke fun at a *Popular Science* article of some decades back that had predicted that the world's first computer, then just invented, would one day weigh one ton instead of 20. The corporate boss then made his own prediction: Within the next 20 years it would be possible to store the visual and aural data of an entire lifetime—the entire multimedia experience of a person's life—on a device no bigger than the proverbial credit card. I couldn't help but wonder whether someone writing 20 years from now would find this prediction equally amusing. When it comes to predicting the future, humility is a virtue.

Forecasting attempts to predict what will happen. This is largely futile. As Samuel Goldwyn once said, "Only a fool would make predictions—especially about the future." Recognizing this, companies have sought ways of coping with the future's inherent unpredictability. One response is to rehearse a range of futures via *scenarios*. Scenario planning speculates on what might happen. The goal is to develop a number of alternate scenarios as a way of sensitizing oneself to the possibility that the future may be quite unlike the present. By focusing in on a few big uncertainties—what might happen to the price of oil, how the Green movement might develop, what could happen to global security—scenario planning lets a company rehearse a range of possible futures.

Scenario planning has many strengths, but it is not, by nature, proactive. Its implicit focus is on how the future may undermine the existing business model. In that sense it tends to be defensive—what might that big bad future do to us?—rather than offensive—how can we write our will on the future? There is little in scenario planning that suggests a firm can proactively shape its environment, that it can take advantage of changing circumstances right now. At least in practice, it is more often threat-focused than opportunity-focused. It is more about stewardship than entrepreneurship. Companies must do more than rehearse potential futures. After all, **the goal is not to speculate on what might happen, but to imagine what you can make happen.**

Another response to the future's inherent unpredictability is to become more "agile." Strategic flexibility is certainly a virtue in uncertain times. The ability to quickly reconfigure products, channels and skills is essential to maintaining one's relevance in a world that is shaken, not stirred. But agility is no substitute for a vision of a radically different business model. Agility is great, but if a company is no more than agile, it will be a perpetual follower—and in the age of revolution even fast followers find few spoils. **Companies fail to create the future not because they fail to predict it but be-**

cause they fail to imagine it. It is curiosity and creativity they lack, not perspicuity. So it is vitally important that you understand the distinction between "the future" and "the unimagined," between knowing what's next and imagining what's possible.

To even talk about "the" future is a misnomer. There is no one future waiting to happen. While certain aspects of the future are highly probable (the earth will still be spinning tomorrow), there is little about the future that is inevitable. IKEA didn't have to be. eBay didn't have to be. Southwest Airlines didn't have to be. The future is the creation of millions of independent economic actors. Was Cubism inevitable in art? Was deconstruction inevitable in literature?

SEE DIFFERENT, BE DIFFERENT

You can't be a revolutionary without a revolutionary point of view. And you can't buy your point of view from some boring consulting company. Nor can you borrow it from some rent-a-guru. You have to become your own seer, your own guru and your own futurist.

Seeing over the horizon, finding the unconventional, imagining the unimagined—innovation comes from a new way of seeing and a new way of being. Learn to see different, learn to be different, and you will discover the different. Not only that: You will believe it—deeply. And maybe, just maybe, you will build it. How to see. How to be. Two more critical steps in your training as an industry revolutionary.

Listen to Amazon's Jeff Bezos, talking to *Wired* magazine:

People have been telling me that everything that could be invented has been invented. This is insane.
Look at Napster—this guy in his dorm room, one person with no funding, a little bit of software, and he launches this thing and nine months later the music industry is petrified. Think what this implies about the power of an idea to change the world.

Well, maybe the idea behind Napster, downloadable tunes, hasn't yet changed the world, but it's certainly forcing some big changes in the music industry. If truly novel ideas are rare, which they are, it isn't because they are inherently scarce, but because few people are capable of first recognizing and then challenging the dogma that surrounds them.

A company that has not cultivated a capacity to imagine radical new business concepts, or is unable to dramatically reconceive existing business concepts, will be unable to escape decaying strategies. You know that tired old saw, "You have to be willing to cannibalize your own business"? Well, how likely is it that a company will cannibalize an existing business unless it has some incredibly compelling alternatives in view? I don't think the problem is that companies are unwilling to cannibalize themselves. I think the problem is that they don't have enough good reasons to cannibalize themselves. When was the last time you hung on to a good option when you had a much better option in view? It's simple. You have to have some very attractive birds in the bush to loosen your grip on the bird in your fist. But it's not always easy to spot the birds in the bush. That's why you must learn to see different and be different.

Many times, what's required is not a vision of an entirely new business, but a fresh view on how to reinvent an existing business. Too many companies are too quick to give up on what they perceive as a mature or unattractive business. When Cemex, the Mexican cement producer, felt itself threatened by the specter of foreign competitors entering its home market, it sold off its noncement interests and proceeded to reinvent its core business so thoroughly and profoundly that the company ended up with gross margins nearly double the average of its global rivals. So yes, you need to be on the lookout for good reasons to cannibalize yesterday's success, but new thinking can also help you reinvent yesterday's success. After all, however attractive, a bird in the bush is still in the bush.

Alan Kay, who fathered the personal computer while at Xerox's Palo Alto Research Center, is a font of zippy aphorisms. One of my favorites: "Perspective is worth 80 IQ points." Alan knows that **A FRESH WAY OF SEEING IS OFTEN MORE VALUABLE THAN SHEER BRAIN-POWER.** Impressionism. Cubism. Surrealism. Postmodernism. Each revolution in art was based on a reconception of reality. It wasn't the canvas, the pigments or the brushes that changed, but how the artist perceived the world. In the same sense, it's not the tools that distinguish industry revolutionaries from humdrum incumbents—not the information technology they harness, not the processes they use, not their facilities. Instead, it is their ability to escape the stranglehold of the familiar.

The essence of strategy is variety. But there is no variety in strategy without variety in how individuals view the world. Do you see differently? Do you have a point of view that is, in at least some respects, at odds with industry norms? The point is simple: You're going to have to learn how to unlock your own imagination before you can unlock your company's imagination. You must become the merchant of new perspective within your organization.

So what are ways we can school ourselves in the art of seeing past the familiar to the truly novel? The rest of this chapter describes a variety of disciplines that will help you imagine what could be. They fall into two broad categories: Be a novelty addict, and be a heretic.

BE A NOVELTY ADDICT

A whole lot of what's changing simply can't be seen from where you're sitting. You have an obstructed view. You have to get off your butt and search for new experiences, go to new places, learn new things, reach out to new people. In the age of revolution, the most dangerous words are "need to know." How the hell do you know what you need to know? You must find a way of continually surprising yourself. Sure the future is unpredictable, but what you don't know but could is much more important than what you don't know and can't. You must become a novelty addict.

FIND THE DISCONTINUITIES

Would-be revolutionaries, intent on discovering uncontested competitive space, think about the future very differently from prognosticators and scenario planners. They know you can't see the future. Their goal is less to understand the future than to understand the revolutionary portent in what is *already changing*. More specifically, they are looking for things where the *rate of change* is changing—for inflection points that foreshadow significant discontinuities. Those who fail to notice these nascent discontinuities will be rudely awakened by those who were paying attention.

They are also looking for things that are changing at *different rates*. Sooner or later, the thing that is changing more quickly will impact the thing that is changing more slowly—in other words, rates of change between different phenomena ultimately converge. For years the cosmetics industry assumed that women were interested only in glamor, that their sense of self-worth was directly proportional to the sparkle in a man's eye. As Charlie Revson, the founder of Revlon, once put it, "We sell hope in a bottle." As women gained their economic independence, the image of women as "eye candy" lagged farther and farther behind the reality of their changing self-perception. This lag was exploited by The Body Shop, Lush, Aveda and other New Age cosmetic brands with their implicit message that glamor is fine, but sometimes you just want to pamper yourself a bit and take good care of your skin. *Change differentials* often point to revolutionary opportunities.

Here's a visual illustration. Imagine that you attach one end of a piece of elastic to a hardback book. You begin pulling the other end. Slowly the elastic stretches. The book doesn't move. But when you reach the limit of the elastic, the book starts moving with a jerk. The "slack" disappears when some revolutionary says, "Wait a minute. Why is this thing just sitting there when everything around it is moving?" The car selling paradigm in the United States is stuck in neutral. While "category killers" consolidate distribution in other industries, car retailing remains a patchwork of mostly local dealerships. While you can get 24/7 tech support for your home computer, you can get your car serviced only between 8 A.M. and 5 P.M., and only Monday through Friday. While you can comparison-shop a dozen different TV brands at Best Buy, no equivalent auto superstore carries the full range of leading brands. Yeah, there are a lot of legal restrictions that have delayed dealer consolidation, but sooner or later it's going to happen. Right now, auto retailing in the United States is a glaring anomaly.

Or think of how little auto styling has changed over the last decade. Can you tell an Altima from a Camry from an Accord at 100 meters? Parking lots are seas of conformity. Now visit a dance club in Tokyo filled with Dankai Jr. kids—the rebellious offspring of Japan's baby boomers. You'll find multihued hair, clothes that are aggressively ugly and fashion colors that are so loud they practically scream at you. In short, you won't find anything that reminds you of Japan's blue-suited, look-alike salarymen. So why hasn't this new style been reflected in auto design? That's exactly the question Yoshiki Honma, a boyish 33-year-old designer at Honda, asked himself. His answer? The Fuya-Jo, a slab-sided vehicle that is one part car and one part dance club. The car has seats that look like high-backed barstools, mammoth speakers in the doors, a gearshift that looks like a microphone, an instrument panel meant to resemble a deejay's mixing table and storage space designed for skateboards and snowboards.[2] For now the Fuya-Jo is just a concept car, but it reflects a recognition at Honda that youth culture has changed a lot faster than automotive design over the past decade. This change differential creates an opportunity for a company with the courage to abandon conformist styling norms.

It's not enough to know what's changing. You also have to be aware of things that are changing at different rates, for it is the juxtaposition of the two that points to opportunities for industry revolution. Discontinuities and change differentials—that is where you look for inspiration.

Try to find the pattern in these three revolutions in sports equipment:

○ A couple of decades back, Prince pioneered oversized tennis rackets, and it is still the number–one brand in the industry. The frying–pan–size rackets have a giant sweet spot that helps propel off-center shots across the net.
○ Calloway invented the Big Bertha line of golf clubs, and Eli Calloway has become the patron saint of hackers everywhere. With an enlarged hitting area and perimeter weighting, the clubs dramatically increased the odds that high–handicap golfers could get the ball airborne and flying straight.
○ Elan was the first ski manufacturer to introduce super–sidecut, or "parabolic," skis, an innovation that has given the ski equipment industry a much needed boost. With a broad tip and tail, and a narrow waist, the new skis help even the most nonathletic skiers lay down curvaceous tracks.

What discontinuities were these three innovations exploiting? Beyond materials technology, they were exploiting the fact that baby boomers are the first generation in history that refuse to grow old. They may not have the hand–eye coordination they used to have, but they still love the sound of a tennis ball hitting the sweet spot. They don't have quite the rotation they used to, but they still want to hit the living daylights out of a golf ball. Their knees are a bit dodgy, but they still want to make turns like Hermann Maier. Come to think of it, Viagra's been exploiting the same discontinuity: Seniors who refuse to grow old gracefully and want great sex right up to the end.

Here are some essential questions for every wannabe revolutionary:

○ Where and in what ways is change creating the potential for new rules and new space?
○ What is the potential for revolution inherent in the things that are changing right now or have already changed?
○ What are the discontinuities we could exploit?
○ What aspect of what's changing can we come to understand better than anyone else in our industry?
○ What's the deep dynamic that will make our new business concept oh–so–relevant right now?

If you don't have an answer to these questions, there is virtually no chance you or your company is going to be an industry revolutionary.

Nearly two decades ago, in his book *Megatrends*, John Naisbitt posited that information would become a critical source of competitive advantage and that the "information float" would disappear as a way to make money. He argued that customers would demand a combination of "high tech" and "high touch." Instead of forcing technology on consumers, companies would learn how to use technology to improve service. He described a world in which hierarchies would give way to networks, and companies would become more virtual. He also hypothesized a shift from reliance on institutional help to more self-reliance in everything from health care to pensions. He foresaw a world in which consumers would use their wallets to enforce their values. Data mining, call centers, 24/7 customer support, outsourcing, supply chain integration, "green" energy, companies against animal testing—all these things are logical outgrowths of the forces Naisbitt described in 1984. How effective was your company in harnessing these discontinuities to create new business models and new sources of competitive advantage? If your company got caught behind the curve, it wasn't because these trends were invisible; it's because they were ignored. If you're paying attention to discontinuities, there's little that will surprise you. It's pretty simple. **Individuals who get startled by the future weren't paying attention.** One person's inevitability is another person's rude awakening. The question is, are you paying attention?

If you're an American, I'd like to give you a little test. How often did you watch ABC's *Monday Night Football* last autumn? If you're a middle-aged man, chances are you saw several games. Now ask yourself, how often did you watch an entire episode of TNN's *Raw*, a production of the World Wrestling Federation, which is also broadcast on Monday nights? Chances are, you didn't see even a single show. And you probably didn't read *If Only They Knew*, the best-seller co-authored by Chyna, one of the WWF's so-called divas. And yet, in a recent television season, *Raw* outdrew *Monday Night Football* by 47 percent among males aged 12–24. Now I'm not suggesting you watch the sweating hulks and surgically enhanced women who populate the WWF. On the other hand, if you work for a company that wants to sell something to young American males, you may need to get a bit closer to this particular fringe.

Or let's say you're in the music business, or the fashion industry, or merely want to know where the tastes of Gen Y urbanites are heading. Better get yourself down to one of Rio's funk balls in order to experience the world's most exotic and electrifying urban dance scene. The music, with its highly explicit lyrics and pounding rhythms, is the cultural signature of young Brazil. Having grown out of Brazil's *favelas*, the hillside shantytowns that are home to millions of Brazil's poor, funk is now going mainstream, just as rap did in the United States. Reaching far beyond Brazil, "favela chic" is inspiring fashion designers and music producers around the world. So have you done anything in the last year that has given you the chance to immerse yourself in something new, something strange, something that is on the verge of *happening*?

A novelty addict is always on the hunt for what's new, what's different, what's unexpected and what's changing. Every discontinuity prompts a "where does this lead" question. Let's practice. We'll start with a particularly noisome discontinuity. A recent study suggested that the average middle manager gets 190 messages a day: 52 phone messages, 30 e-mail messages, 22 voice mails, 18 letters, 15 faxes and so on. I don't have to tell you, this is a discontinuity. In the old days, when someone sent you a letter, they didn't expect to receive a response for at least a week. When they sent a fax, they expected a next-day response. Now, when they send an e-mail, they expect a reply within an hour or so. But it gets worse. With instant messaging, people know when you're online, and when they send you a message, they expect you to interrupt what you're doing and answer them immediately. It used to be that secretaries kept the world at bay—until downsizing turned middle managers into receptionists and filing clerks. It may be that we've taken accessibility to the point where meaningful work will simply grind to a halt. How ironic that in a world populated by "knowledge workers," there is virtually no time left to think. You may be able to manage the present in tiny splinters of time, but you certainly can't innovate if your attention has been smashed into minute-sized shards. This is a discontinuity. Can you see an opportunity in this? Let's take it a step further.

In a recent cartoon, a dad and his young daughter are walking along a beach. The dad is dressed in suit and tie and has a briefcase in one hand. His daughter is wearing her bathing suit. As she vainly tugs at her father's sleeve, he says, "Not now, dear, Daddy's working." Where don't you work these days? We are tethered to our jobs to an extent that is almost feudal. But there are opportunities lurking inside the insidious discontinuity of 24/7 accessibility. What about an electronic gatekeeper that could scan phone calls, e-mails, voice mails and even faxes? Caller ID? Hah! I want automatic message screening. Every couple of hours a little menu would pop up on my computer screen telling me who was queuing for my attention. I could tell my digital gatekeeper who I was willing to communicate with in a given day or week and how important it was that I make contact with any given individual. I could also tell it when I was willing to be interrupted and when I was not. (Imagine never, ever having a telemarketer interrupt dinner again!) I could assign a different level of "interruptability" to different times of the day or week. People and issues that exceeded some urgency threshold would get to break through into my consciousness. People below the threshold wouldn't get through. I could also give a few people (family) an "attention override" privilege that would let them intrude anytime. Trust me, some revolutionary is going to help us regain control of our fragmented lives. There's a billion-dollar opportunity inside this discontinuity. You get the point? Keep asking yourself, What's changing? What's the opportunity this presents? Do this at least a dozen times a week. Get addicted to change.

Imagine the possibilities when an entire organization is alert to discontinuities. Recently, General Motors launched a number of initiatives aimed at getting everyone plugged into the future. In one, a diverse cross-section of individuals identified 19 broad change categories (e.g., global urban culture, entertainment in everything) that encompassed more than 100 discontinuities. Every discontinuity was illustrated by a visual image in order to help individuals connect with what's changing. The goal was to use this inventory as the backdrop for every serious strategy discussion. After years of playing catch-up, GM is learning that you have to pay close attention to the discontinuities if you're going to get anywhere close to the bleeding edge of change.

SEARCH OUT UNDERAPPRECIATED TRENDS

There is no proprietary data about the future. Whatever you can know about what's changing in the world, so can everyone else. So you've got to look where others are not looking. The good news is that *most people in an industry are blind in the same way— they're all paying attention to the same things, and* not *paying attention to the same things.* For example, if you work at Shell or Schlumberger, you know a lot about the three-dimensional representation of complex information. Complicated computer models portray seismographic data in a rich graphical format. This is how petroleum engineers "see" underground. Likewise, the folks at Pixar, the computer animation company, are experts at visualization. Now talk to a senior partner in a big accounting company. How much does this person know about complex graphical modeling? Not enough. If you want to understand the financial performance of a large global company, you have to comb through columns of black and white data, searching for variances and calculating financial ratios. Ugh! Why isn't this information presented in three dimensions, dynamically? Why can't you "fly" over the globe, and "drop into" your German subsidiary? See that red mountain over there? That's inventory, and it's growing. See that lake over there? That's one of those famous "profit pools," and it's shrinking by the hour. See all those people massed at the border? Those are your employees leaving for better opportunities. You get the idea. But you can't get the picture—yet, at least not from any of the traditional financial software vendors. Odds are it won't be an accounting company or a well-known software company that reinvents the display of accounting data. But there's little doubt that Excel will one day look as antiquated as green ledger paper.

Next time you go to an industry conference or pick up a trade magazine, ask yourself, What is *no one* talking about? Search for what's not there. There's a reason that outsiders typically reinvent industries. The outsiders come from a different context—one that allows them to see new possibilities. William Gibson puts it beautifully: "The future has already happened, it's just unequally distributed." The future may not have happened yet in your industry, or your company, or your country, but it has happened somewhere. Revolutionaries are experts at *knowledge arbitrage*—moving insights between the hip and the un-hip, the knowing and the unknowing, the leading edge and the trailing edge. So get a bigger keyhole!

FIND THE BIG STORY

Next, search for transcendent themes. One of the reasons many people fail to fully appreciate what's changing is because they're down at ground level, lost in a thicket of confusing, conflicting data. You have to make time to step back and ask yourself, **What's the big story that cuts across all these little facts?** For example, consider five seemingly unrelated trends:

○ In most developed countries, people are getting married later in life. No longer do people expect to find a mate while still at school.
○ More people are telecommuting or working from home. Home-based businesses are one of the fastest-growing parts of the economy.

○ The number of single-parent families has been steadily increasing. Single parents are run ragged trying to balance work and family—personal time is a rare luxury.
○ New social standards governing the behavior of people at work make it ever more difficult to form romantic relationships with co-workers.
○ E-mail and the Internet absorb more and more of people's time. All the hours in front of the PC are hours of aloneness—unless virtual communities fill all your social needs.

Can you see an overarching theme here? It's individual isolation. We're living in a world where it is more and more difficult for people to find time to connect. So you should have been able to anticipate the success of online dating sites like Matchmaker.com and AmericanSingles.com. Right? Recognizing patterns in complex data is a bit of an art. Some of it is just raw, conceptual ability. But if you've ever won a game of Scrabble or solved a challenging puzzle, you'll do fine. Keep a list of things that strike you as new or different. Every once in a while, scan that list and search for broad themes. If you can get above the trees, you'll have a view that few others can match.

FOLLOW THE CHAIN OF CONSEQUENCES

The world is a system. Something changes here, and it will affect something over there. Yet most people stop with first-order effects—they don't have the discipline to think through the knock-on effects. Jim Taylor, coauthor of *The 500-Year Delta* and dedicated trend-watcher, predicted a 10,000 Dow Jones Industrial Average in 1992. Here's how he did it:

> I saw a number that estimated how much people were going to save as they got older. About 15 million people a year would become 50 years old, and they would throw a lot of liquidity into the market. So I made a prediction that the Dow would pass through 10,000. When you see a trend, it's a matter of asking, "What would this mean?"

Paul Saffo, director and Roy Amara Fellow at the Institute for the Future, makes the point this way:

> I think about it as "orders of impact." First order, second order, etc. When an earthquake happens you have a whole series of waves

that follow. The first order of the auto was the horseless carriage. The second order was the traffic jam. The third-order impact was the move toward the suburbs. This led in turn to the creation of huge metropolitan areas.

No executive or manager should be surprised by the recent spate of books on corporate values and "loyalty." This concern around how to build organizational cohesion is the second-order effect of a first-order change: the steadily declining ratio of supervisors to operators or managers to staff in corporations. To cope, companies need a solid value system because more and more they must rely on people's judgment. Whenever you see something changing, begin to work through the chain of consequences. Get in the practice of asking a series of "and then what" questions. As you learn to do this, the future will become less and less of a surprise to you.

DIG DEEPER

Sometimes creating proprietary foresight is just a matter of slogging through more data. You can't create economic value out of a superficial understanding of what's changing. For example, a short news item noting that some teenagers are spending more time online than in front of the TV is of almost no value. The real question is, Which kids are going online? Where are they going online? What, exactly, is it about the on-line experience that is more compelling to them than television? How much time do they spend online in a given day or week? What do they find cool or geeky online? And so on.

Faith Popcorn's BrainReserve interviews 4,500 consumers across 16 product categories every year. They also have a TalentBank of 6,000 experts globally who are subject area experts. No wonder Popcorn sometimes sees the tectonic plates moving before others do—she's digging deeper. You probably can't spread your interests this broadly, but you can pick a few things to understand far more deeply than you do. Genetics, Generation Y, deregulation, ubiquitous computing, the market for online software services, the global revolution in how pensions are funded—every year pick a couple of the big things that are changing and resolve to dig deep.

KNOW WHAT'S NOT CHANGING

The deep needs of human beings change almost not at all. Go back to Aristotle and the wants of man—little has changed. What changes is how we address our wants. Change gives us better tools. Opportunities come when we can imagine how to use our new tools to address our deepest desires. As Jim Taylor puts it, "The nature of human beings is the eye in the middle of the hurricane." We want to be loved, we want to be known, we want to communicate, we want to celebrate, we want to explore, we want to laugh, we want to know, we want to see new vistas, we want to leave some footprints in the sands of history. Any discontinuity that allows you to slake one of these thirsts more fully is an opportunity in the making.

If you think about human beings for a minute, you shouldn't be surprised that the Web was a chat room before it was a department store, or that Internet porn generates as much revenue as online book sales, and ahead of online airline tickets.[3] To be an industry revolutionary, **you must be as perfectly attuned to the timeless as to the ever-changing.** You must also let yourself be informed by the recurring themes of history. History has much to teach you about how discontinuities will play themselves out. For example, advances in genetics are slowly turning humans into creators. History suggests that the battle between the spiritual and the scientific over the proper use of genetic knowledge may be as heated as Galileo's clash with the Catholic Church over humankind's place in the cosmos and Darwin's run-in with creationists.

The speed of the Internet's takeoff surprised most people, but that it happened should have been no surprise—because the interstate highway system provided an almost perfect historical analogy. The automobile had existed for around 50 years before the interstate highway system began to connect communities across America. Within a decade of the interstate's introduction suburbs were springing up, city centers were withering, corporations were building office towers in what had been cornfields and commuters were commuting. It wasn't the car per se, but the ability to connect communities that changed the distribution of work and commerce. Likewise, computers had existed for about 50 years before the Internet took off. Before the Net, computers had been islands of computational power. Once connected, they began to transform society in ways even more dramatic than the interstate highway but also in ways that are entirely consistent with timeless aspects of human nature.

SEE IT, FEEL IT

You don't fall in love with a photograph or a resume, you fall in love with the experience of being with someone. In a similar way, you can't understand a discontinuity merely by reading about it, you can understand it only by living it. To be fully grounded in what is changing, you must move from the analytical to the experiential. Let me share a couple of examples. A few years back I was working with a large Nordic firm, perched on the edge of the Arctic Circle. This company was filled with brilliant engineers who designed technologically brilliant products that were boring to look at and sometimes difficult to use. I broke the bad news—if they wanted their products to be highly desirable and highly relevant, they were going to have to learn something about global lifestyles. Off the engineers trooped—to Venice Beach in California, to Greenwich Village in New York and down The Kings Road in London. They saw trendy style-setters wearing the latest fashion accessories. They came across people who had pierced every possible protuberance. They saw how designers in other fields were using colors and shapes in new ways. And they didn't see any of their competitors. How do you explain lifestyles with an overhead projector? Face-to-face with the edge, the engineers "got it." They went back and designed products in crazy hues with edgy designs and easy-to-use customer features.

People don't embrace an opportunity because they see it, they embrace it because they feel it. And to feel it, they have to experience it. If you want to teach someone in your organization about a discontinuity or give them a glimpse of a bold, new opportunity, you're going to have to design an experience. To create a demo, or a prototype, or even tell a compelling story, you have to do some mental prototyping. You need more than a fragment of an idea. You have to build a story around it: why this is important, what difference it will make, who will care, how people will use this, what it will look like, taste like and more. Radical alternatives are hard for people to imagine. You have to build a bridge between the world you're living in and the world everyone else is living in.

It's not always easy to make something new and ethereal, real and tangible. But think of this: Ask just about any kid to draw a picture of heaven, and you'll get back an imaginative illustration. If an eight-year-old can draw a picture of paradise, you have no excuse.

GET A ROUTINE

Swim in the new. Sounds easy, but the ocean is a big place. How do you avoid drowning in data? You need some kind of routine. I can't tell you what your routine should be, but I can say what works for some folks.

John Naisbitt's routine for finding the edge is simple: He reads newspapers from around the world for several hours each day, hunting for patterns in things that get reported but don't yet generate a lot of ink. Marc Andreessen, the inventor of the Internet browser, has a different routine:

> Pay attention to things that are taking off, even if they're only taking off at a small scale. One of the things that surprised me about the Internet is the number of things that I was aware of when they were small-scale things, not commercial, that are now picking up users and attention. Even if I was skeptical at the time, in most cases these are now billion-dollar companies. So you want to pay attention to small-scale successes because they're probably going to become large-scale successes.

What are your routines? How often do you pick up a magazine you've never read before? How often do you go to an industry convention for an industry you know little about? How often do you hang out with people who are very different from you? Are you on the fringe or in the hinterlands? Can you name a half dozen nascent trends? Find the small things, play an imaginary game of "scale up," and then ask, If this thing became really big, what kind of a difference would it make? Who would be affected?

Each of us tends to discount what is new and small. As a discipline, **start exaggerating what is new and small.** You're not investing in these things, for goodness sake, you're simply opening your mind to new possibilities.

Faith Popcorn's BrainReserve is a lightning rod for cultural discontinuities. Says Popcorn:

> We do something called "Brailleing the Culture"–monitoring the top 10 of everything. Anytime we see something that is weird, we key in on it. We look for things that are not part of the puzzle. How come *Touched by an Angel* was big on TV? How come the Dalai Lama is on posters? Don't dismiss the weird.
>
> We ask people, "What's sitting on your night table?" We're looking for culture hogs. They have to see everything, go everywhere. They're always on to the next thing.
>
> We look for cultural lingo. We review the soundtracks of sitcoms. We review the top 10 CDs, and what the artists are saying.
>
> I love to watch what new 12-step programs are emerging—recent ones are for people addicted to chat rooms or online pornography.

Popcorn isn't looking for fads, for cultural ephemera, but for the tip of deep icebergs, for leaves carried along by powerful currents that would otherwise be almost imperceptible. The weird are the harbingers. If you dismiss the stuff that strikes you as weird, you have virtually no chance of finding the new. What's the hippest club in your city? Have you ever been there? What's the trippiest video game out there? Have you played it? Go ahead, do a little cool hunting.

Jim Taylor of Iomega takes yet another tack:

> I watch the evolution of art, especially folk art. It's a wonderful precursor of what's changing in society. Look at the cubists in the 1930s. First it was art, then the structure of building and finally the structure of most organizations. Right now we're seeing the "outsider" movement in art—it's creating a sense that everyone is an artist.
>
> I also pay attention to a set of deep underlying questions: What's the big idea in society and how will it play itself out? What's the latest technology that's about to be generalizable [about to go mass market]? What's the latest organ they can grow in a test tube?

Artists have few constraints. Like magnifying glasses, they collect and concentrate the diffused light of cultural change. Taylor knows this. He also knows that if you develop a set of questions to ask yourself as you encounter the unfamiliar, you will increase the odds of actually taking away some meaningful insights.

John Seely Brown, for years the head of Xerox's famed Palo Alto Research Center, favors travel as a routine for discovering the new. A while back, he took a 7,500-mile motorcycle trip across America, entirely on back roads. Hundreds of conversations with people across America put Seely Brown in touch with what's changing away from the coasts. Says Seely Brown, "Everywhere one goes there's a chance to learn something. You keep asking, 'What's causing this?' . . . for example, a teenager doing something weird on the street. It's really active listening."

Insights come out of new conversations. All too often, strategy conversations in large companies have the same ten people talking to the same ten people for the fifth year in a row. They can finish each other's sentences. You're not going to learn anything new in this setting. Travel is still the fastest way to start a bunch of new conversations. It has the added benefit of turning the background into the foreground. When you travel to an exotic destination you're suddenly reminded of how much you take for granted and how there are alternatives to the familiar habits of your life. It was his experience with the casual warmth of Italian coffee bars that gave Howard Schultz the idea for Starbucks.

Familiarity is the enemy. It slowly turns everything into wallpaper. Travel makes you a stranger. It puts you at odds. It robs you of your prejudices. If you can't travel, find a good bookstore and pick up the *Globe & Mail* (Toronto), *The Daily Telegraph* (London), *The South China Morning Post* (Hong Kong), *The New Straits Times* (Singapore) or some other foreign newspaper, or find them online. If your understanding of what's changing in the world comes from network television news, the *Wall Street Journal*, and *Time* magazine, you're going to miss the future.

BE A HERETIC

It is not enough to be a novelty addict. You must be a heretic as well. Heretics, not prophets, create revolutions. You can immerse yourself in what's changing, but you'll only see the opportunities to leverage change in novel ways if you can escape the shackles of tradition. There is much that individuals cannot imagine simply because they are prisoners of their own dogma. In this sense, the challenge is not long-term thinking but unconventional thinking. **The real issue is not the present versus the future but the orthodox versus the heterodox.**

There is an enormous danger in viewing what's changing through the lens of what already is. People saw plastic, when it was first invented, as a substitute for existing materials—steel, wood and leather. (Remember Corfam shoes?) Eventually, plastic got the chance to be plastic. Can you imagine a hula hoop, compact disc or videotape made out of anything else? In the age of revolution the future is not just more of the past—it is profoundly different from the past. Whether or not you succeed in escaping the past is, in a way, quite irrelevant. The future's going to get invented, with you or without you. But if you want to build the new, you must first dismantle your existing belief system and burn for scrap anything that is not endlessly and universally true.

Ask yourself this question: What are the industry dogmas my company has knowingly chosen to violate? Can't think of any? Then don't expect to outperform industry averages. Industry revolutionaries create strategies that are subversive, not submissive. To do this, you must deconstruct the belief system that prevents individuals in your organization from imagining unorthodox strategies.

In most companies it is virtually impossible to redesign business models without first challenging the dominant mental models. Mental models spring out of and reinforce the current business model. A business model is a "thing." The mental model is a set of beliefs about the "thing." The mental model reflects the "central tendency" of beliefs around the key business concept design variables:

○ What is our business mission?

○ What is our product/market scope?

○ What is the basis for differentiation?

○ What core competencies are important?

○ What strategic assets do we need to own?

○ What core processes are critical?

○ How can we best configure our resources?

○ How do we go to market?

○ What kind of information do we need to serve customers?

○ What is the kind of relationship we want with customers?

○ How do we price our products and services?

○ What is the particular benefit bundle we deliver?

○ How do we integrate with suppliers and partners?

○ What profit boosters can we exploit?

The more successful a company has been, the more deeply etched are its mental models. In even moderately successful companies, most people take 90 percent of the existing mental model as a given. Design choices made years earlier are seldom revisited. It's difficult to imagine revolutionary strategies when you start with nine-tenths of your brain tied behind your back. Design choices of long ago are seldom challenged in the absence of a crisis. Even then, it often takes a new management team to pull out the old beliefs by their roots. You and your colleagues must learn how to systematically deconstruct the existing set of beliefs around "what business we're in," "how we make money," "who our customers are" and so on.

The first step in your training as a heretic is to admit that you are living inside a mental model—a construct that may not even be of your own making. Alan Kay tells a wonderful little story about how he came to recognize this deep truth:

On the third day of a conference at a Buddhist center, I asked people why they put their palms together several times a day. The Buddhists believe that the world is an illusion, but we have to go along with the illusion for efficiency reasons. When they put their hands together it is a semicolon, an acknowledgement that whatever they may think is going on right now is largely a fabrication of their own mind.

For much of life we simply go along with the illusion—yeah, this is the only way to sell a car, get a date or sell perfume. But every once in a while you need to put your palms together, pause, step outside yourself and examine what you believe and why. And in the age of revolution you have to do this more consistently and consciously than ever before.

You have to know that things are not as they seem—and you must know this at such a deep level that you can challenge the very foundations of what others regard as axiomatic. We are all caught inside theories, inside constructs. Most of us spend our lives elaborating someone else's theory—about how to run an airline or publish a magazine or sell insurance. New facts are either absorbed into the construct or rejected. Seldom do the constructs themselves get altered. The challenge is to break the construct—or at least bend it a bit. To do so, you must first acknowledge that you are inside the construct. Jim Taylor puts it like this: "The more you pay attention to information that supports your worldview, the less you learn. There tends to be a convergence in what any group of people believe is important, despite what might really be important out there."

The problem with the future is not that it is unknowable. The problem with the future is that it is different. If you are unable to think differently, the future will always arrive as a surprise. You know that old bumper sticker, "Question Authority"? Well the authority you most need to question is the authority of your own long-held beliefs. This isn't about pricking someone else's conventions. We are all reassured when the world conforms to our prejudices. But confirmation of what you already believe is a complete waste of time. **YOU MUST LOOK FOR DISCONFIRMING EVIDENCE, FOR THINGS THAT DON'T FIT, FOR THINGS THAT ARE AJAR.** This is hard, because it forces you to write off your depreciating intellectual capital—you must admit not only that you do "not know" many things but that you "wrongly know" many things.

SURFACE THE DOGMAS

So how do you cultivate contrarian tendencies and surface the dogmas in your company? One simple device is to ask yourself and your colleagues, What are ten things you would never hear a customer say about our company or our industry? For example, no customer is ever going to say, "The airline treats its customers with dignity and respect." Few customers would ever say, "It's easy to shop for a better rate on electricity." Fewer still would say, "Banking is fun," or "Hotels always have great food." Once you've identified what customers wouldn't say, ask yourself why they wouldn't say those things. What orthodoxies do they reveal? What opportunities do these orthodoxies create for some unorthodox newcomer? And finally, what would happen if we turned this orthodoxy on its head?

Another way in is to ask, What are the ten things that all the major competitors in this industry believe in common? Then ask, What would happen if each of these assumptions were inverted? What new opportunities would present themselves? How would customers benefit? Clearly, not all industry beliefs are stupid. There's a difference between dogma (the earth is flat) and physics (things fall downward rather than upward). It is seldom a good idea to defy physics. Nevertheless, much of what people in an industry will tell you is God-given is merely human-made. It is your job to turn certainties back into choices.

Time again for a little practice. Think for a moment about the orthodoxies in the American health-care industry. The sick are considered patients, not consumers. Health-care providers dispatch cases, they don't build relationships. The goal is to cure illnesses rather than promote wellness (you don't get reimbursed for wellness). Insurers are in the business of dodging risks rather than improving the health of a population. The entire industry has been organized from the payor backward rather than from the consumer forward. This has led to the greatest orthodoxy of all: Americans spend too much on health care. Says who? As compared to what? Do doctors perform unnecessary procedures? Yes. Do hospitals perform needless tests? Sure. Is there room for huge economies? Yup. So cut the waste. But before going any farther down the health-care rationing road, someone needs to challenge the assumption that American citizens believe they are devoting too much of their resources to health care.

How can anyone say what percentage of their income aging baby boomers might be willing to pay for health care? The question's never been put to them. Today it is employers who decide how much is too much when it comes to health care. It is employers—who are purchasing agents, not consumers—that contract with health-care providers and insurance companies. Imagine if we let purchasing agents choose our toilet paper, or our cars or the kind of food we eat. We'd all be using single-ply toilet tissue, driving puke-green Chevy Luminas and eating the kind of food you buy in bulk at warehouse clubs. We wouldn't put up with that. Why do we put up with employers telling us how much health care we can have? Managed care, which is more accurately described as managed reimbursement, isn't a revolution—it's just the health-care version of vigorous cost-cutting. There's nothing nonlinear about it. Whether we ever get a real revolution in health care will depend on whether anyone ever succeeds in taking a wrecking ball to the edifice of industry orthodoxy.

NEVER STOP ASKING WHY

Like children, heretics play an endless game of "why" and "what if." If you've been paying attention to what's changing, you can play a very intelligent game of "what if." For example, What if everything in the world were able to communicate with everything else? What would a vending machine want to talk about? "Hey, it's hot, and at this rate I'm going to be out of orange sodas in a couple of hours." What would a fuel pump say? "Oh, hi there, Jaguar XK8. I know you need premium fuel. That's what I'll pump." What would a refrigerator say? "My sensors tell me there's something rotten down in the crisper drawer."

Wayne Huizenga asked "why." Before AutoNation, no major car dealer had ever gone public. Says Huizenga:

> Every one of the dealers told me that Ford and General Motors
> and all the manufacturers would never let a publicly held
> company own a new-car dealership. And I'd always ask, "Why?" I
> never got a good answer. So we put some gentle pressure on the
> manufacturers and made it happen.

Revolutionaries simply ask "why" more often than the rest of us.

CELEBRATE THE STUPID

We've all been taught that good answers are more important than good questions. What was true in first grade is infinitely more true when you're in front of the board or your boss. But new questions are at the heart of business concept innovation—and if you're going to ask "why," you've got to be prepared to look foolish once in a while. Listen once more to Marc Andreessen:

> If your goal is to create something new and big, you're going to
> have to do something that everybody else will laugh at—so that
> becomes the test. If they're not laughing at it, and you don't get

turned down a few times, it's probably not a great idea. In other words, if it's something that makes everybody nod their heads and say, "Yeah, that makes sense," there are probably already a dozen people doing it.

Only stupid questions create new wealth. Of course, there are stupid stupid questions, and there are smart stupid questions. I remember asking a senior executive in one of America's leading hotel chains, "Why is it that someone who checks in at two in the morning has to check out at the same time as the guy who checks in at two in the afternoon?" When I got a blank stare I barged ahead. "Why can't you just have everyone check out 20 hours after they checked in? If I arrive at three in the afternoon, I'll have to check out at eleven the next morning. But if I arrive at ten in the evening, I can keep the room until six P.M. on the day of departure." The hotelier looked at me with a face full of condescension. "Gary," he said, "you don't understand the hotel industry." "That," I replied, "is my comparative advantage." I suggested he go study Hertz. When you rent a car at Hertz, they don't ask you to bring it back at noon. You have it for 24 hours. And the hotel operator has an advantage Hertz doesn't have—the rooms never move. No one promises to leave the room in Chicago and ends up leaving it in Milwaukee instead!

Or take another hotel example. Have you ever noticed that hotel hangers are often designed to make them impossible to use at home? The implicit message to guests is this: We think you're a thief so we've designed our hangers to be unusable anywhere else. Hmmm, not a very welcoming thought, is it? Now, what if you take something from the minibar and forget to report it when checking out? You'll still get charged for it—that's why the hotel takes your credit card data. Can you already see the unconventional solution to the problem of disappearing hangers? Put a sign behind the closet door, "Hangers $5, help yourself." Presto, you've turned the closet into a profit center. How hard was that? And the person who checks the minibar—well, he or she can check the closet as well. The point is, guests sometimes need an extra hanger. Here's a way to meet their needs and make a buck or two at the same time. So why is it that no one in the hotel industry has thought of this? Maybe it's because you don't ask stupid questions—like, how could we make the closet profitable—when you're an industry expert. What makes this particular bit of conventional thinking even more absurd, is that one of those useless hangers may well be holding up a bathrobe with a little card tucked into the pocket that reads, "If you choose to take this robe home with you, a $75 charge will be added to your account." But trust me, every industry is filled with dozens of similarly silly absurdities—but you won't spot them unless you're willing to ask a few silly questions.

In many companies the premium placed on being "right" is so high that there is virtually no room for speculation and imagination. If you insist on being incontrovertibly right, you will never be new. It's that simple. The fear of being wrong is so strong in many organizations that any idea not backed by a Dumpster of data is automatically suspect. The training given M.B.A. students and managers reinforces this tendency. In course after course the message is driven home: The quality of your analysis counts for more than the quality of your imagination. John Naisbitt explains:

> Academics are afraid to go beyond their data. Alfred North Whitehead said that a proposition doesn't have to be right, it just has to be interesting. Academics don't understand how liberating it is not to have to be right. When you have to be right you become a prisoner.

So students get steroids for the left side of their brain, while the right side gets put on a starvation diet. How absurd. Analysis can help you avoid truly bad strategies, but it will never help you find truly great strategies.

GO TO EXTREMES

Pick a performance parameter that's important in your business—time, cost, efficiency, quality, speed, whatever. Push this to extremes and ask, Why not? Pushing boundary conditions to the limit is one of John Seely Brown's favorite tricks for blowing up orthodoxies.

> My heuristic is, "Take it to the limit and see what happens." Xerox wants to make copiers that make less noise. I told our people that this wasn't an interesting problem. If you ask us to make a machine that makes no noise, that gets interesting. They said, "That's impossible." I said, "Not if the copier has no moving parts." The question led to a radical shift in architectures in terms of how to think about copiers, printers and mechanical systems. You'll see some radical products from Xerox that came from exploring impossible questions.

Think of every strategy conversation as your own personal version of the X Games. Get radical.

Revolutionaries find a way to transcend trade-offs. They just hate it when someone says you can have A or you can have B, but you can't have both. Toyota's "and" was a car that was economical to buy *and* of high quality. Where Mercedes-Benz and Chevrolet gave consumers an either/or, Toyota offered an "and." Look around. Where have people accepted "ors" when they would have rather had "ands"? Take one example. There are many who believe we have an educational crisis in America. Our kids live in a culture literally saturated with entertainment. The number of alternatives to homework grows each year: *South Park* or algebra—that's a tough one. Unless teachers can find a way to make learning educational and fun, media moguls will be the real teachers in America. "Edutainment" was the original idea behind *Sesame Street.* No wonder it became one of the most popular kids' shows in history—it offered an "and" instead of an "or."

This is how John Naisbitt puts it:

> You just have to hang out with the paradoxes, hang out with the contradictions until you understand them. When there is a perceived contradiction, I like to look for something that helps to resolve the contradiction. A lot of people have an either/or mentality. We get the Internet and everyone says, "Well newspapers are going to go away." It's not either/or. There will be a change in the mix, that's all.

Bridle whenever you hear an "or." Search for novel solutions that make trade-offs unnecessary.

DISTINGUISH FORM FROM FUNCTION

Why did people think the Internet would kill newspapers? Because they saw newspapers as a form (ink smeared on dead trees) rather than as a function (sifting through all that happens in a day and selecting out what's really important). While the form of a newspaper may disappear, its function certainly won't. If a newspaper company sees itself in the business of running giant printing presses and distributing newsprint, it may one day be rendered irrelevant. If it sees itself as a current events editor, it will learn to live as happily online as off.

One way of distinguishing function from form is to substitute a verb for a noun. Richard Kovacevich, chief executive of Wells Fargo bank, provides an example: "Banking is essential, banks are not." Banks are things—bricks and mortar. Banking is a function. If I can divorce the function from the thing, I can think about how to deliver the function in radically different ways.

There are some IT executives and technologists who argue that computing is about to enter the "post–PC era." High-capacity networks, linked by powerful hub computers, will feed data to millions of information appliances. International Data Corporation has estimated that by 2005 more information appliances—including set-top boxes, screen phones and handheld computers—will be sold than PCs. Couple this with online application service providers that remove the need for you to load up any software other than a browser, and you have a major threat to the existing PC business model—a threat that Microsoft is taking very seriously. The company's .Net initiative is aimed at using its XP operating system as the base for a wide range of new Web services. The company is also experimenting with set-top boxes for interactive television, has launched a video game device, is working with Intel on a new software/hardware platform for mobile phones and more besides. Yes, the PC will probably survive for another decade or two, but there's little doubt that the form of computing will change dramatically over the next few years. Any company that can't distinguish between form and function will get caught inside an obsolete form factor.

START A NEW CONVERSATION

In most companies there is no distinction between a conversation about radical new possibilities and a conversation about how to eke out another percentage point of gross margin. The same standards of analytical rigor are applied to both—whether the subject is the return on a new piece of production machinery or the chance to create an entirely new market. Strategy conversations at GE Capital are labeled "dreaming sessions." Questions about internal rate of return and EVA are disallowed. No one mistakes them for budget meetings. A conversation about an opportunity for radical innovation is supposed to be fun, open-ended, and inquisitive. It ends with a set of hypotheses to be field-tested. An operational conversation is supposed to be business-like, bounded, and filled with certainties. It ends with an implementation plan. In fact, there are a number of ways in which an operational conversation can be distinguished from a strategic conversation.[4]

Operational	*Strategic*
FOCUS	
Present focus	Future focus
Certainties	Possibilities
"Real"	"Play"
NATURE OF KNOWLEDGE	
Knowledge confirmation	Knowledge development
Static language	Dynamic language
Analytical	Experiential
Authoritative	Hypothetical
CONVERSATIONAL RULES	
Advocacy	Dialogue
Reach for closure	Open new conversations
Need for expertise	Need for generalists
Get a decision	Test a hypothesis

The next time you toss out an idea for turning your industry inside out, and someone asks you for an NPV, take a minute to educate them on the difference between a strategy conversation and an operational conversation. Then tell 'em to cut you some slack! The disciplines I've described here are reliable ways to help you discover opportunities for business concept innovation. Yet there's no surefire, mechanical process for creating a bold new "aha." Instead, you must marry a thorough understanding of your company's existing business concept with the wide-eyed curiosity of a precocious five-year-old. Phrases such as "disciplined imagination," "routine creativity" and "informed intuition" capture the challenge. You already understand the part about being disciplined, well informed and following a routine, but what about imagination, creativity and intuition? These qualities have been bred out of you—first by school, then by work. **Yet you can, and must, regain your lost curiosity. You must learn to see again with eyes undimmed by precedent.** What is familiar and drab must become wondrous and new. The goal of this chapter has been to help you regain your innocence.

Profound insights come out of a cocktail of unexpected problems, novel experiences, random conversations and newly discovered facts. The goal is to mix this cocktail again and again. Indeed the goal is to be the mixer—to encompass within yourself and your team all the elements that combine to produce bursts of deeply creative insight. Not only is this an individual imperative, it is an organizational imperative. No single individual can encompass all that is changing in the world. Your cocktail shaker is just so big.

5
CORPORATE REBELS

YOU UNDERSTAND THE REVOLUTIONARY

imperative. You feel it in your bones. You're vibrating with excitement at the thought of doing something new, building something radical, and you can't shut up about it. But your industrial-era boss, with a black belt in corporate gamesmanship, is immune to your ramblings. Every time you start to pitch your idea you get "the look"—you know the one I mean—the look that says, "Who hired this idiot, anyway?"

So whaddya do? Beat your head against the walls of your cubicle? Throw yourself in front of the chairman's limo? Bide your time until the morons recognize your genius and promote you? Take early mental retirement? Enroll in a seminary? Steady on. There's another option—a path, too-seldom trod, that is rocky and steep but leads to opportunity. It is a path unfamiliar to corporate types, but well known to thousands of otherwise powerless individuals who've succeeded in knocking history out of its grooves.

A middle-aged woman who takes on the Marcos oligarchy in the Philippines. An African-American woman who refuses to sit in the back of the bus. A group of mothers who press lawmakers to stiffen drunk-driving penalties. A 12-year-old kid who founds an environmentalist group that ultimately attracts 25,000 members. A Czech poet who stands up to totalitarianism. These are the people who change the world. And you can't change your own company? Give me a break.

Of course no one is going to give you permission. You're not going to get a "mandate" from on high. But you've got to decide. Are you a courtier, kissing corporate butt? Or a rebel challenging your company to reinvent itself? Are you there to buff up top management's outsized ego, or are you there to help your company stay relevant in a revolutionary world? If it's the latter, you're going to have to learn to punch more than your weight and to cast a much bigger shadow across your organization than you do right now.

FROM SUBJECT TO CITIZEN

Let's start with the facts. Big, complicated social systems (such as the company where you work) don't get changed from the top—not unless they're already on the verge of collapse. To understand why, take a minute and imagine the traditional corporate pyramid, with senior management at the top and the minions—sorry, I mean the valued "associates"—at the bottom. Where in the pyramid are you going to find the least genetic diversity? Where are you going to find people who have most of their emotional equity invested in the past? Where will you find the folks who are most tempted to venerate history? The answer to all three questions is "at the top." Now ask yourself, Who holds the monopoly on setting strategy and mapping out corporate direction? The same small group. Is this stupid or what? No wonder there is so little business concept innovation in most companies. No wonder it's newcomers who create most of the new wealth.

The organizational pyramid is a hierarchy of experience. Senior executives got promoted for doing one thing very well. But sooner or later, the organization must learn how to do another thing. Today the competitive terrain is changing so fast as to make experience irrelevant or dangerous—you can't use an old map to find a new land. If you're a senior executive, ask yourself, After two or three decades of industry experience, am I more radical or more conservative? Am I more willing to challenge conventions or less willing? Am I more curious than I've ever been in my adult life, or less so? Am I a radical or a reactionary?

Am I learning as fast as the world is changing? Senior executives have the same chance to be radicals as everyone else—but it is hard, because they have more to unlearn. Look at a company that is underperforming, and invariably you will find a management team that is the unwitting prisoner of its own out–of–date beliefs. When it comes to business concept innovation, the bottleneck is at the top of the bottle.

Rousseau once said, "Law is a very good thing for men with property and a very bad thing for men without property." The worshipful observance of precedent is a very good thing for those who sit at the top of organizations, because precedent protects their prerogatives. It rewards the skills they've perfected and the knowledge they've acquired in running the old thing. But precedent and a narrow distribution of strategy-making power is a very bad thing for anyone who wants to create a new future.

For business concept innovation to flourish, the responsibility for strategy making must be broadly distributed. Top management must give up its monopoly on strategy creation. In this sense, you can't have innovation in business models without innovation in political models.

Every company is comprised of four distinct models (see the figure "Creating Space for Business Concept Innovation"). On the bottom is the "operating model." This encompasses what people actually do on a day–to–day basis—how they're organized, what activities they perform, how they interact with customers and what processes they run. Sitting atop the operating model is the "business model." This represents all the choices, conscious and unconscious, the company has made about the various components of its business concept. On top of the business model is the "mental model," which encompasses all the beliefs that in-

CREATING SPACE FOR BUSINESS CONCEPT INNOVATION

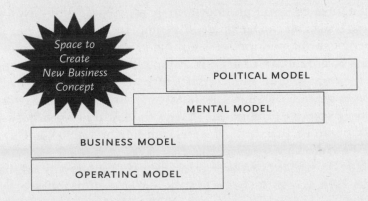

dividuals hold about what drives success in their industry. It is the prevailing set of dogmas or orthodoxies about what customers to serve, what those customers want, how to price, how to organize, which distribution channels to use and so on. Finally, on top of everything else is the "political model."

The political model refers to the way power is distributed throughout an organization and, in particular, the distribution of power to enforce mental models. So ask yourself, Who in your organization has the power to kill an idea and keep it dead? Who can make you feel like an imbecile just by saying, "We tried that five years ago and it didn't work"? Who can rule unconventional options "out of bounds"? Who has the last word on whether to try a new experiment? In most companies, political power is highly concentrated at the top of the organization, and precedent is a despot.

In a highly successful company the operating model, business model, mental model and political model are all perfectly aligned—each one sits squarely atop the one below. Human resource professionals call this "alignment." And **alignment is fine——if the world isn't changing. But perfect alignment destroys any chance of innovation, because it brooks no dissent and allows no alternatives.** Alignment is the enemy of business concept innovation.

In a discontinuous world, business models don't last forever. And when they begin to decay, the temptation is to pour human energy and capital into improving the efficiency of the operating model. But better execution won't fix a broken business concept. Ultimately, you need to invent new business concepts or dramatically reinvent those you already have. Yet there is no way of innovating around the business concept unless you can first move your company's mental model off dead center. You have to upend deeply cherished beliefs. You have to create some misalignment between the mental model and the business model. This is why you must learn to be a heretic. But there's a hitch. You won't succeed in changing your company's mental model unless you first push the political model off-kilter and temporarily redistribute the power to make strategy. Put simply, if the power to create strategy and enforce mental models is narrowly distributed, you may find it difficult to get heard. When's the last time your CEO invited *you* to address the Executive Committee? When's the last time your boss's boss told the board that the company was counting on *you* to come up with the next great business concept?

So how do you overthrow top management's monopoly on strategy making? Well, you're not going to stage a palace coup. You're not going to shoot a senior vice president. Instead, you must become an activist. You must build a powerful grassroots constituency for business concept innovation. You must help to build a hierarchy of imagination, where an individual's share of voice in strategy making and innovation is a function of imagination and passion, rather than position and political power.

The good news is this: rule–busting change can start anywhere. Ever hear someone say, "Change must start at the top"? What utter rubbish. How often does the revolution start with the monarchy? Have you ever seen Queen Elizabeth II out in front of Buckingham Palace, waving a placard that reads, "We want a republic"? Nelson Mandela, Václav Havel, Mohandas Gandhi, Susan B. Anthony, Martin Luther King—how often has profound change started at the top? Indeed, the fact that America has suffered but one civil war owes much to the principles of constitutional democracy enshrined in the Constitution. These principles create ample opportunity for change to emerge from below. It is not Congress that sets the social change agenda in America, it is activists.

Do the names Peter Benenson, Florence Kelly, Samuel Hopkins Adams, Irving Stowe, Sarah Brady and Linda Carol Brown mean anything to you? Perhaps not, but you may well have enjoyed the fruits of their activism. Benenson was the founder of Amnesty International. Kelly was a consumer and labor activist who established the National Consumer's League and fought for the passage of minimum wage, child labor and working hour laws. Adams was a muckraking journalist who was instrumental in getting the Pure Food and Drug Act passed in 1906. Stowe helped organize Greenpeace. Brady, whose husband James Brady was shot during the attempted assassination of Ronald Reagan, is one of the most effective gun–control activists in America. Her lobbying helped bring about the Brady Bill, which requires a five-day waiting period on all gun purchases. Brown was the gutsy, young African–American student who tried to enroll in an all–white school in Topeka, Kansas, in 1950, prompting the landmark Supreme Court case *Brown vs. Board of Education of Topeka*, which declared the racial segregation of schools to be unconstitutional. These individuals and thousands of less celebrated activists badgered, harangued, organized, plotted, schemed and ultimately prevailed. What they lacked in power they made up for in passion. They were citizen–activists.

The resilience of a democratic government rests not on one person, one vote, but on its capacity to give voice to the activists, provide a platform for the aggrieved, and harness the energies of those dissatisfied with the status quo. A democracy is a free market for causes—be it feminism, environmentalism, right–to–life, racial equality, or a hundred other movements. Those who lead these causes and shape society's agenda are truly citizens. The rest of us are subjects. It is unfortunate that the idea of democracy has become so enervated and the individual's sense of responsibility to the community so diminutive that they both can be summarized in the slogan, "One person, one vote." One person, one vote represents not the full ideal of democracy, but its most minimal precondition. If you exercise the rights of citizenship only once every four years, at the polling station, can you really claim to be a citizen? Likewise, if you willingly relinquish your responsibility to influence the destiny of the organization to which you devote the majority of your waking hours, can you really claim to be anything more than an employee?

Take a moment and reflect on the tragic price humankind so often pays when a society is unable to reshape itself through peaceful activism, when there is no escape valve for the disaffected and the disgruntled. Genocide, coups and bloody uprisings become the only way to alter policy. Is it any different inside companies? Many companies suffer for years under mediocre leadership before the generals, sorry, the shareholders demand a change of the guard. Instead of being tied to a stake and shot, discredited CEOs take early retirement for "personal" reasons.

American constitutional democracy has survived two and a quarter centuries of unprecedented social and technological change. Democracy in America and elsewhere in the world provides more than an escape valve for the disgruntled; it provides the means for altering the very foundations of the political institutions themselves—in the case of the United States, through the legislative process and, ultimately, Constitutional amendments. In the same way, if companies are going to thrive in the age of revolution, they are going to have to become less like autocracies and more like democracies. And if you want to be a corporate citizen, rather than a subject, you're going to have to learn to be an activist.

Activists are not anarchists. They are, instead, the "loyal opposition." Their loyalty is not to any particular person or office, but to the continued success of their organization and to all those who labor on its behalf. They are patriots intent on protecting the enterprise from mediocrity, narrow self–interest and veneration of the past. They seek to reform rather than to destroy. Their goal is to create a movement within their company and a revolution outside it. Here's how Webster's defines a movement: "a series of organized activities by people working concertedly toward some goal." By contrast, a revolution is the "overthrow of a government, form of government, or social system." A movement is what you create to raise consciousness and mobilize resources inside your company. A revolution is what you want to foist on your competitors.

Activists are "tempered radicals."¹ They are committed to their company, but they're also committed to a cause that is at odds with the pervading values or practices in their organization. They behave as responsible members of their organization, but they are also a source of alternative ideas and transformation. They challenge the status quo in two ways: first, by their refusal to "fit in" and, second, through their intentional acts to unbalance the status quo. They are idealists and non-conformists. But they're also street-smart pragmatists who know how to bend the political system to their own ends. They are cold-blooded hotheads.

You're probably asking yourself two questions: first, Why should I care? Why should I take a risk for a company that considers me expendable? Second, Is it really possible to change the direction of something as big and unwieldy as a company, particularly when one doesn't hold the levers of power?

For a decade now, senior management has been telling employees that they have no entitlements. There's no job for life, no sinecure, no guarantee. Take responsibility for your career. Stay current. Justify your job. But the flip side of no entitlements is no dependency. For years companies mistook dependency for loyalty. But you're no longer dependent, you have choices. Nevertheless, there are three good reasons to put your head above the parapet.

Reason #1: You deserve something more than a paycheck and stock options. Do you remember that famous line often attributed to John Lennon: "Life is what happens while you're busy making other plans"? Yeah, maybe there's a hereafter, but that's no excuse to treat life as a dress rehearsal. Ask yourself, Have you done anything in the last three years that you will talk about for the rest of your life? Just what are you working for? Material well-being, granted, but is that it? Individuals become activists because they know that their self-worth is determined by the causes they serve. You need a noble cause.

Reason #2: The organization isn't "them," it's "you." Stop whining about "them." That's just an excuse you use to justify inaction. Start thinking of your company as the vehicle for your dreams, as you writ large. That's not an ego trip, that's the truth. Every organization is no more or less than the collective will of its members. And you can shape that will.

Reason #3: You owe it to your friends and colleagues. Your company has a face—you see it every time you peer into the next cubicle or share a table in the cafeteria. Like you, these people deserve the chance to make a very cool difference in the world. They may lack your courage, but they yearn to create, and they're ready to dream. You're not doing this to pump up the value of the CEO's stock options; you're doing it to give ordinary people the chance to accomplish extraordinary things.

That's why you bother. But can it be done? Yes. You're about to meet several corporate activists who succeeded in changing the direction of some of the world's largest companies.

JOHN PATRICK AND DAVID GROSSMAN: IBM'S WAKE-UP CALL

Do you remember when IBM was a case study in complacency? Insulated from the real world by layer upon layer of dutiful managers and obsequious staff, IBM's executives were too busy fighting their endless turf battles to notice that the company's once unassailable leadership was crumbling around them. The company that took the top spot on *Fortune's* list of Most Admired Corporations for four years running in the mid-1980s was in dire need of saving by the early 1990s. Fujitsu, Digital Equipment Corp. and Compaq were hammering down hardware margins. EDS and Andersen Consulting were stealing the hearts of CIOs who had long been loyal to IBM. Intel and Microsoft were running away with PC profits. Customers were bemoaning the company's arrogance. By the end of 1994, Lou Gerstner's first full year as CEO, the company had racked up $15 billion in cumulative losses over the previous three years and its market cap had plummeted from a high of $105 billion to $32 billion. Armchair consultants were near unanimous in their views: IBM should be broken up.

Despite Gerstner's early assertion that IBM didn't need a strategy (the last thing he wanted was to start another corporationwide talkfest), IBM was rudderless in gale force winds. Yet over the next seven years, IBM transformed itself from a company that primarily sold boxes into a company that sold services and delivered end-to-end IT solutions. IBM Global Services grew into a $30 billion business with more than 135,000 employees. Fine, you may say, but IBM was still playing catch-up to Andersen, CSC, EDS, and a host of other IT service companies. Perhaps, but IBM's more recent transformation into the world's premier supplier of "e-business" solutions cannot be so easily gainsaid. By the end of 1998, IBM had completed 18,000 e-business consulting engagements, and about a quarter of its $82 billion in revenues was Net-related. In a few short years IBM had gone from being a metaphor for corporate sloth to being the first stop for any large company eager to become Net-enabled. Now how weird is that? **How did a company that had lagged behind every computer trend since the mainframe catch the Internet wave——a wave that even Bill Gates and Microsoft originally missed? Much of the credit goes to a small band of activists who built a bonfire under IBM's rather broad behind.** This is their story.

The first match was struck in the backwoods of IBM's empire, on a hilltop in Ithaca, New York, by a typically self-absorbed programmer. David Grossman was a midlevel IBMer stationed at Cornell University's Theory Center, a nondescript building hidden away in the southeast corner of the engineering quad. With access to a supercomputer connected to an early version of the Internet, Grossman was one of the first people in the world to download the Mosaic browser and experience the graphical world of the Web. Grossman's fecund imagination quickly conjured a wealth of interesting applications for the nascent technology. But it was an event in February 1994, as snow dusted the ground around the Theory Center, that hardened his determination to help get IBM out in front of what he knew would be at least "the next big thing," and might be "the ultimate big thing."

The Winter Olympics had just started in Lillehammer, Norway, and IBM was its official technology sponsor, responsible for providing all of the results data. Watching the games at home, Grossman saw the IBM logo on the bottom of his TV screen and sat through the feel-good ads touting IBM's contribution to the event. But when he sat in front of his

UNIX workstation and surfed the Web, he got a totally different picture. A rogue Olympics website, run by Sun Microsystems, was taking IBM's raw data feed and presenting it under the Sun banner. "If I didn't know any better," says Grossman, "I would have thought that the data was being provided by Sun. And IBM didn't have a clue as to what was happening on the open Internet. It bothered me."

The fact that IBM's muckety-mucks were clueless about the Web wasn't exactly news to Grossman. He remembers when he had landed at IBM a few years earlier, and everyone was still using mainframe terminals: *"I was shocked. I came from a progressive computing environment and was telling people at IBM that there was this thing called UNIX, there was an Internet. No one knew what I was talking about."*

This time, though, he felt embarrassed for IBM, and he was irked. After logging on to the corporate directory and looking up the name of the senior executive in charge of all IBM marketing, Abby Kohnstamm, Grossman sent her a message informing her that IBM's Olympic feed was being ripped off. A few days later, one of her minions working in Lillehammer called Grossman back. At the end of a frustrating conversation, Dave had the feeling that one of them was living on another planet. Ever persistent, Grossman tried to send the Olympic marketer some screen shots from Sun's website, but IBM's internal e-mail system couldn't cope with the Web software. That didn't stop IBM's diligent legal department from sending Sun a cease-and-desist letter, which succeeded in shutting down the site. Most frontline employees would have left it at that. But there was a bigger point that Grossman felt the rest of IBM was missing: Sun was about to eat their lunch. After everyone had come back from the Olympics, he drove down to IBM headquarters, four hours away, in Armonk, New York, to show Kohnstamm the Internet himself.

When he arrived, Grossman walked in unattended, a UNIX workstation in his arms. Wearing a programmer's uniform of khakis and an open-necked shirt, he wound his way up to the third floor—the sanctum sanctorum of the largest computer company in the world. Borrowing a T1 line from someone who had been working on a video project, Grossman strung the line down the hall to a storage closet where he plugged it into the back of his workstation. He was now ready for his demo—a tour of some early websites, including one for the Rolling Stones. As sober-suited IBM executives scurried through their rounds, Mick Jagger could be heard wafting out of the closet.

Two people in addition to Kohnstamm were present at that first demo. One was Irving Wladawsky-Berger, head of the supercomputer division where Grossman worked. The other was John Patrick, who sat on a strategy task force with Wladawsky-Berger. Patrick, a career IBMer and lifelong gadget freak, had been head of marketing for the hugely successful ThinkPad laptop computer and was working in corporate strategy, scouting for his next big project. Within minutes, Grossman had his full attention. "When I saw the Web for the first time," says Patrick, "all the bells and whistles went off. Its ability to include colorful, interesting graphics, and to link to audio and video content blew my mind."

Not everyone saw what Patrick saw in that primitive first browser. Says Patrick:

> Two people can see the same thing, but have a very different understanding of the implications. When Java first came along and you saw a little clown dancing on the Web page, some people said, "So what?" and others said, "Wow, this is going to change everything." Part of it is, I'm always intrigued by anything new. A lot of people did say, "What's the big deal about the Web?" but I could see that people would do their banking here and get access to all kinds of information. I had been using online systems like CompuServe for a long time. So for people who weren't already using online systems, it was harder for them to see.

Their passions fueled by the Web's limitless possibilities, Patrick and Grossman would become IBM's Internet tag team, with Patrick doing the business translation for Grossman and Grossman doing the technology translation for Patrick. Patrick would act as a sponsor and broker for resources. Grossman would develop intimate links with Netheads in IBM's far-flung development community. "The hardest part for people on the street like me," says Grossman, "was how to get senior-level attention within IBM." Patrick became his mentor and his go-between.

After seeing Grossman's demo, Patrick hired him, and they soon hooked up with another Internet activist within IBM, David Singer. Singer was a researcher in Alameda, California, who had written one of the first Gopher programs that fetched information off the Net. Grossman and Singer started building a primitive corporate intranet, and Patrick published a nine-page manifesto extolling the Web. Entitled

"Get Connected," the manifesto outlined six ways IBM could leverage the Web.

1. Replace paper communications with e-mail.
2. Give every employee an e-mail address.
3. Make top executives available to customers and investors online.
4. Build a home page to better communicate with customers.
5. Print a Web address on everything, and put all marketing online.
6. Use the home page for e-commerce.

The "Get Connected" paper, distributed informally by e-mail, found a ready audience among IBM's unheralded Internet aficionados. The next step was to set up an online news group of the sort that allowed IBM's underground hackers to trade technical tidbits. "Very few people higher up even knew this stuff existed," says Grossman. Within months, more than 300 enthusiasts had joined the virtual Get Connected team. Like dissidents using a purloined duplicator in the old Soviet Union, Patrick and Grossman used the Web to build a community of Web fans that would ultimately transform IBM.

As Patrick's group began to blossom, some argued that he should "go corporate" and turn the nascent Web initiative into an officially sanctioned project. Patrick's boss, Jim Canavino, disagreed. "You know," Canavino remarked to Patrick, "we could set up some sort of department and give you a title, but I think that would be a bad idea. Try to keep this grassroots thing going as long as possible." Patrick needed to infiltrate IBM rather than manage some splendidly isolated project team. It would be easy for others at IBM to ignore a dinky department, but they couldn't stand in the way of a groundswell. Still, Canavino wasn't above using his role as head of strategy to give the fledgling initiative a push. To avoid the danger of IBM quickly going from having no Web site to dozens of uncoordinated ones, Canavino decreed that nobody could build a website without Patrick's approval. Though few in IBM had any inkling of what the Internet would become, Patrick had become IBM's semiofficial Internet czar. Pretty good for a staff guy.

Patrick's volunteer army was a widely dispersed group of Net addicts, many of whom had been unaware that there were others who shared their passions. "What John ended up providing," says Grossman, "was the ability to articulate and summarize what everyone was doing and to open a lot of doors." In turn, "the kids in black" introduced Patrick to the culture of the Internet, with its egalitarian ideals and trial-by-fire approach to developing new technologies. When the Get

Connected conspirators gathered for their first physical meeting, remembers Grossman, **"the question on everybody's lips was how do we wake this company up?"**

Patrick gathered a small group of his Get Connected renegades, including Grossman, at his vacation house, set deep in the woods of western Pennsylvania. There they cobbled together a mock-up of an IBM home page. The next step was to get through to Gerstner's personal technology advisor, who agreed to make Lou available for a demo of the prospective IBM corporate Web site. When Gerstner saw the mock-up, his first question was, "Where's the buy button?" Gerstner wasn't a quick study, he was an instant study. But Dave and Patrick knew that an intrigued CEO wasn't enough. There were thousands of others who still needed to get the Internet religion.

Their first chance for a mass conversion came at a senior management meeting of IBM's top 300 officers on May 11, 1994. Having schemed to get himself on the agenda, Patrick drove his point home hard. He started by showing IBM's top brass some other Web sites that were already up and running, including ones for Hewlett-Packard, Sun Microsystems, the Red Sage restaurant in Washington, D.C., and a page for Grossman's six-year-old son Andrew. The point was clear: on the Web, everyone could have a virtual presence. Patrick ended the demo by saying, "Oh, by the way, IBM is going to have a home page too, and this is what it will look like." He showed the startled executives a mock-up of www.ibm.com, complete with a 36.2-second video clip of Gerstner saying, "My name is Lou Gerstner. Welcome to IBM."

Still, many IBM old-timers remained skeptical. Recalls Patrick: "A lot of people were saying, 'How do you make money at this?' I said, 'I have no idea. All I know is that this is the most powerful, important form of communications both inside and outside the company that has ever existed.'"

Shortly after the May meeting, Patrick and a few colleagues showed up at one of the first Internet World trade conventions. The star of the show, with the biggest booth, was rival Digital Equipment. Like Grossman before him, Patrick's competitive fires were stoked. The next day, when the convention's organizers auctioned off space for the next show, Patrick signed IBM up for the biggest display at a cost of tens of thousands of dollars. "It was money I did not have," admits Patrick, "but I knew I could find it somehow. If you don't occasionally exceed your formal authority, you are not pushing the envelope." Now that IBM's name was on the line, Patrick had a rallying point around which he could gather all of the company's various Internet-related projects.

Patrick was as concerned about the internal audience he wanted to reach as he was about the outside world. Here was his chance to seed his message across the entire company. He sent letters to the general managers of all the business units asking for anything they had that smelled like the Internet. They would only have to put in a little money, and he would coordinate everything. It turned out that IBM had a lot more Web technology brewing than even he had expected. But none of it was really ready to go to market. Still, by that December, Patrick was able to showcase IBM's Global Network as the world's largest Internet service provider and a Web browser that preceded both Netscape's Navigator and Microsoft's Explorer. IBM stole the show and became a fixture at every Internet World thereafter.

Constantly fighting IBM's penchant for parochialism, Patrick took every opportunity to drive home the point that the Web was a company-wide issue and not the preserve of a single division. At the next Internet World, in June 1995, he challenged his compatriots to leave their local biases at the door: "The night before the show, I got everybody together in an auditorium and said, 'We are here because we are the IBM Internet team for the next three days. You are not IBM Austin or IBM Germany.' That is part of the culture of the Internet: boundary-less, flat." The huge IBM booth generated a lot of curiosity among the show's other participants. When people asked Patrick to whom he reported, he said, "The Internet." When they asked him about his organization, he replied, "You're looking at it, and there are hundreds more."

Patrick was a relentless campaigner, spreading the good word about the Internet in countless speeches both inside and outside IBM. "Somebody would invite me to talk about the ThinkPad," he recalls, "and I would come talk about the Internet instead. I'd use the ThinkPad to bring up Web page presentations rather than PowerPoint slides." He also made himself very accessible to the media. People inside IBM would learn about what Patrick was doing by reading the newspaper. But even when talking to the media, Patrick's prime constituency was still the vast swath of unconverted IBMers. He just couldn't shut up about the Internet. Says Patrick: "If you believe it, you've got to be out there constantly talking about it, not sometimes, but all the time. If you know you're right, you just keep going."

While Patrick and his crew were throwing Internet hand grenades into every meeting they could wheedle their way into, Gerstner was fanning the flames from above. Gerstner's early belief in the importance of network computing dovetailed nicely with the logic of the Internet. Having bought into Patrick's pitch, Gerstner was ever ready to give IBM's Webheads a boost. He insisted that IBM put its annual and quarterly reports up on the Web well before most other companies were doing so. Gerstner also signed up to give a keynote address at Internet World, saying that the Internet was really for business. This was while Bill Gates and others were still dissing the Web as an insecure medium for consumer e-commerce.

Within IBM, Patrick became a trusted emissary between the company's buttoned-down corporate types and the T-shirted buccaneers who were plugged into Net culture and living on Internet time. Patrick had the ear of IBM's aristocracy, and his message was simple and unequivocal: "Miss this and you miss the future of computing." At the same time, Patrick convinced Grossman and his ilk that not everyone at head office was a Neanderthal. Says Grossman:

> I used to think that IBM at senior levels was clueless, that these guys had no idea how to run a company. But one of the many things that has impressed me is that the people who are running this company are really brilliant business people. Somehow we connected them to the street. Knowing how to shorten paths to those decision makers was key.

When IBM finally set up a small Internet group, with Patrick as chief technical officer, he insisted that the team stay separate from IBM's traditional software development organization. Patrick's logic: "I do believe there's a benefit in being separate, otherwise we'd have to start going to meetings. Pretty soon we'd be part of someone else's organization, and a budget cut would come along and we'd be gone."

Many of the folks in Patrick's fledgling organization weren't old enough to rent a car, and many were younger than his daughter.

Although IBM now had a formal Internet organization, Patrick and Grossman didn't disband their grassroots coalition. As the 1996 Summer Olympics approached, this group went through several watershed events. Patrick loaned Grossman out for 18 months to corporate marketing, which was in charge of the Olympics project. For the first time, the Olympics would have an official website, and IBM would build it. Grossman launched himself into building the Olympics website and was soon begging Patrick for extra bodies. "Patrick did the magic to get them hired," says Grossman, "and I morphed from doing the grunt technical work to being Tom Sawyer and getting other people to help whitewash the fence." Ultimately, more than 100 IBMers got involved.

To prepare for the Olympics, Grossman and his team had started developing websites for other sporting events such as the 1995 U.S. Open and Wimbledon. For the U.S. Open site, he gave a couple of college interns from MIT the task of writing a program to connect a scoring database to the website. "By the end of the summer," remembers Grossman, "we were sitting in a trailer, barely keeping together a website with a million people a day pounding away at it for scores. It was held together by Scotch tape, but we were learning about scalability." It was amazing, thought Grossman, that all of these people would come to a site merely for sports scores. IBM's second surprise came when it was caught off guard by the flood of global interest generated by a chess match between world chess champion Garry Kasparov and an IBM supercomputer named Deep Blue in early 1996. Corporate marketing had asked Grossman earlier to build the website for the match, but he was booked with too many other assignments, so the site was outsourced to an advertising agency that did little more than put up a cheesy chessboard. The day of the first match, the site was overloaded with traffic and crashed.

"Nobody had any idea this was going to be such a big deal," says Patrick. IBM went into panic mode. Grossman and a handful of IBM's best Web engineers jumped in to take over the site. They had about 36 hours to completely revamp the site before the next match. They got Wladawsky-Berger to pull a $500,000 supercomputer off the assembly line. The site didn't crash again, but the incident raised the anxiety level about the upcoming Olympics. If IBM was having difficulty running a website for a chess match, then what were the Olympics going to be like? The incident also succeeded in convincing a few more skeptics that the Internet was going to be beyond big.

IBM had to build an Olympics website that could withstand anything. Patrick went tin-cupping again, asking all the general managers to loan him their best people and their best equipment. He got not one supercomputer, but three. Grossman's team eventually grew to about 100 people. IBM was learning in the crucible of the world's most visible sporting event. By the time it was over, IBM had built the world's largest website (at the time), which withstood up to 17 million hits a day with few shutdowns. The content on the site was replicated in servers across four continents. IBM even learned how to do a little e-commerce when a demo site for online ticket sales attracted a flood of credit-card numbers and $5 million in orders.

For Patrick and Grossman, the Olympics was just one more high-profile way to show IBM the possibilities of the Internet. It was also an easy way to get funding for development. Admits Grossman:

I used the Olympics as a front basically. What I was doing, without telling anyone, was getting computing resources. I also thought the fastest way to get IBM to change was to work from the outside in. If IBM saw itself written about in the papers, then it would change faster than if we got mired in an internal process.

Grossman's on-the-fly development, in public no less, was the complete antithesis of IBM's traditional way of doing things, which was to push developers to perfect products before letting them out the door. It was the difference between improv comedy and a carefully rehearsed Broadway play. The old model didn't make much sense on the Web, where if something breaks, you can fix it universally without sending out millions of CD-ROMs with new software. You just fix the software on the server, and everyone who logs on automatically gets the new version. In the superheated development climate of the Web, there is a big premium on getting stuff out fast, learning quick, and improving the breed as you go along. Grossman and Patrick quickly concluded that creating Web-enabled software called for a new set of software development principles, which they summarized and shared with the burgeoning Web community within IBM:

Start simple, grow fast
Trial by fire
Just don't inhale (the stale air of orthodoxy)
Just enough is good enough
Skip the krill (go to the top of the food chain when trying to sell your idea)
Wherever you go, there you are (the Net has no bounds)
No blinders
Take risks, make mistakes quickly, fix them fast
Don't get pinned down (to any one way of thinking)

Much of the technology that Grossman and his crew first prototyped would later make its way into industrial-strength products. For instance, the Web server software developed for the Olympics evolved into a product called Websphere, and much of what his group learned formed the basis for a Web-hosting business that today supports tens of thousands of websites.

Following the Olympics, the Internet group turned its attention to proselytizing within IBM. Grossman, who had become the senior technical staff member on Patrick's team, set up an Internet lab to bring in executives from all over the company so they could experience the Web's possibilities. The group started a project called "Web Ahead" that worked to revolutionize internal IBM IT systems that had always had a low priority. For instance, the team took the old terminal–based corporate directory and wrote a Java application that gave it a great graphical interface and cool features. With a few clicks, employees could look up a colleague, see what computer skills he or she had, and then ask the directory to list every other employee at IBM with those same skills. These "Blue Pages" were an instant hit across IBM.

Patrick and Grossman never rested in their campaign to infiltrate the rest of IBM with their Internet thinking. The Internet group had only a few dozen people officially working for it, so Patrick was constantly pleading to borrow people (who were usually already part of his virtual team) from other departments. His most important ally was the team's ever–lengthening list of success stories. People could argue with position papers, but they couldn't argue with results. Repeatedly, Patrick put his whole organization on the line, and taking that risk and delivering results gave him credibility no fancy title or mega–budget could match. Patrick recounts how he co–opted line executives into sharing their resources:

> I have never been turned down on anything I have asked for,
> and I have asked for a lot. There was a lot of evangelizing and
> selling. I would go to a general manager and say, "I need you to
> pull some disk drives from the assembly line and I need your top
> engineer. What you will get out of it is unique. Your guy is going
> to come back to your group, and you are going to have a hell of a
> reference story to talk about. It will be great PR. We will make
> your stuff work on the Internet." I never did any name–dropping,
> but I didn't have to. Also, I was making a real commitment. I had
> 20 people working on these things.

Patrick was hard to refuse, partly because it was clear that he was fighting for the interests of all of IBM, rather than for the interests of his own little group. As he explains:

> I didn't have any allegiance to any one product group. Although
> I had a budget that came out of the software group, I didn't think
> of us as part of the software group. When somebody calls us and
> asks for help, we don't ask them for a budget code. We say, "Sure."

We have never been a threat to any other part of the company. From the beginning our goal was to help IBM become the Internet Business Machines company.

Patrick was quick to assure would-be donors that the relationships he was forging worked both ways. He would borrow people from various business units, but at any given time about a quarter of his own people would be out on loan to other units. Further, Web Ahead alumni were regularly posted to permanent positions across IBM. When that happened, he would tell his remaining staff, "We did not lose Bill, we colonized the network hardware division. Now there is one of us living there." Patrick also helped start an internship program called "Extreme Blue" that paired some of the brightest engineering students with top IBM researchers. When IBM later hires these students, few come to work in Patrick's group, but all will be part of his virtual network.

Again and again, throughout their Internet campaign, **Patrick and Grossman broke long-standing IBM rules and overstepped the boundaries of their own authority.** But because their cause was so thoroughly righteous and their commitment to IBM's success so visibly selfless, they got away with things that had often sunk careers at IBM. Then and now, Patrick is unapologetic:

> If you think of yourself as being in a box, with boundaries, you're not going to have any breakthroughs. I expect this of my people on my team, if they come to me and say, we failed because we didn't have the authority to do something, I'll say that's crazy.

Inside IBM and out, Patrick and Grossman are today recognized for their pivotal contribution to IBM's e-business metamorphosis. John and Dave's excellent activist adventure is full of lessons:

○ They were relentless in getting their message across.
○ They ignored hierarchy and directly lobbied Gerstner and his deputies for support.
○ They borrowed resources from wherever they could find them.
○ They enrolled true believers from the distant reaches of the IBM empire in a virtual network.
○ From the Kasparov–Deep Blue chess match to the Summer Olympics to the Blue Pages, they put their butts and their reputations on the line to prove new technologies and build demos that would make the Internet's possibilities real to the uninitiated.

○ Web Ahead developers produced the seeds of dozens of commercially viable products and services, which legitimized not only their own Web projects but everyone else's as well.

These two unlikely heroes—a software nerd and a corporate staffer—along with a pro-change CEO, helped give IBM the chance to do something it hadn't done for a couple of decades: lead from the front.

KEN KUTARAGI: SONY'S DIGITAL BANDIT

Throughout its history, Sony has had a knack for coming up with gee-whiz products, from one of the world's first transistor radios to tiny TVs to the Walkman, CD player (with Philips), and 8mm camcorder. Its archrival, Matsushita, may be bigger, but Sony's relentless innovation has made it synonymous with what's new and cool. Yet by the mid-1990s, Sony was in a deep funk. Its profits had sunk from a high of $1.3 billion in 1992 to a loss of $3.3 billion in 1995. Its foray into Hollywood had proved expensive and embarrassing, generating a $3 billion write-off in 1995. More worrying, Sony had mostly missed three of the biggest opportunities in consumer electronics: personal computers, cell phones, and video games. Compaq, Dell, HP, Toshiba and a dozen other companies had trounced Sony in PCs. Motorola, Nokia and Ericsson had run away with most of the cell phone business, and Nintendo and Sega had staked out the video game market.

All these new markets were either based on or quickly moving to digital technology. Yet Sony's historical strengths lay with analog technologies—of the sort found in televisions, VCRs, and tape players. With the exception of a handful of engineers scattered throughout the company, few at Sony were in tune with the digital revolution that was rendering analog technology obsolete and fueling entirely new businesses. One of the few cognoscenti, buried deep in a corporate R&D lab, was Ken Kutaragi. Lacking any formal mandate, Kutaragi launched a bandit project that eventually led to the establishment of the Sony Computer Entertainment division in 1993 and the introduction of the PlayStation video game console the following year. Less than five years later, the PlayStation business had grown to comprise 12 percent of Sony's $57 billion in total revenues, and an incredible 40 percent of its $3 billion in operating profits.[2] But more than simply being an astounding financial success, the PlayStation provided the springboard for Sony's leap into the digital age.

From his earliest days, Kutaragi had been infused with an engineer's curiosity. At the age of 10 he built a guitar amp for a friend. By the time he was a teenager he was putting together go-carts from old scooters. Unlike most of his peers, he grew up in an entrepreneurial household, working after school in the printing company his father had started following his return from World War II. After graduating from engineering school in 1975, Kutaragi applied for a job at Sony. The oil crisis had put a damper on hiring, and Kutaragi was one of only 46 male university graduates Sony took on that year.

Kutaragi's first job was to work on a liquid crystal display for calculators. The potential of LCDs captured his imagination. He explains:

> I thought it would be nice not just for calculators, but also for future televisions. I created a very small LCD TV set. Unfortunately at that time Sony was making CRT [cathode ray tube] TV sets, so this was not a mainstream area. I was the only one pushing for flat screen displays, and I was just an insignificant engineer.

His mini-TVs, which prefigured the Sony Watchman by about a decade, got stuck in the lab. Still a tinkerer, he was fascinated by the brand-new microprocessors that companies such as Hitachi, Intel, and NEC were just beginning to produce. He bought samples of the first 4-bit and 8-bit chips and reverse-engineered their simple instruction sets. He also explored the intricacies of CP/M, an early personal computer operating system. With this knowledge, Kutaragi created a computer system in the tiny laboratory he occupied. "It was a nice toy for me," he recalls.

Kutaragi's digital hobby came in handy in the early 1980s when Sony began replacing some of the electromechanical components in its tape decks and video recorders with digital microcontrollers. His frustrations in designing a chip to measure sound levels convinced Kutaragi that the development tools provided by the chip companies were inadequate. In response, he created his own hardware and software tools for developing chips aimed at audio and video applications. Ultimately, these tools became standard issue for all Sony engineers. By the mid-1980s, Kutaragi had become fully convinced that the digital revolution was inevitable. With dozens of companies being formed around the world to exploit the new technologies, Kutaragi started to get an entrepreneurial itch. "I was in corporate R&D, but I wanted to enter the business area," he says. In R&D he was heading up part of a project to develop the first-ever digital camera for the consumer market, the "Mavica." Instead of using film, it stored its images on a two-inch disk.

It was during this time that Kutaragi purchased one of Nintendo's first-generation, 8-bit video games for his eight-year-old daughter. "She begged me to play every day," says Kutaragi, though he readily admits he needed little encouragement. But two things about the Nintendo system disturbed him: its sound was awful, and the games were stored on magnetic cartridges. Ever the technical perfectionist, these shortcomings irritated Kutaragi. "Why," he asked himself, "did the game use such an unsophisticated magnetic storage system with such a sophisticated 8-bit processor?"

Convinced that he could make Nintendo's product better with the floppy storage system he had developed for the Mavica, Kutaragi tracked down the one salesman in Sony who had a relationship with Nintendo, and the two of them met with the game maker's head of technology. Kutaragi would have preferred to help Sony get into the video game business, but he couldn't find anyone internally who shared his enthusiasm for digital entertainment. Indeed, recalls Kutaragi, "When Nintendo introduced its first 8-bit system, no one in Sony mentioned it. They hated the product. It was a kind of snobbery. For people within Sony, the Nintendo product would have been very embarrassing to make because it was only a toy."

So began Kutaragi's collaboration with Nintendo and his bandit project. Ultimately, Nintendo decided not to use Kutaragi's floppy disk technology. Yet several of Nintendo's senior managers were intrigued by Kutaragi's unorthodox views and invited him to an offsite meeting in 1986 to further discuss the company's upcoming 16-bit system. Kutaragi suggested that Nintendo should let Sony make a special, digital, audio chip for its next game system. The new chip would greatly improve the machine's sound. Nintendo accepted.

Kutaragi's bold proposal left him with a problem. He was a researcher, not a businessman—he had no authority to strike a deal with Nintendo. To complicate matters, Sony had just embarked on an ill-fated foray into 8-bit computing with its line of MSX personal computers. Hoping to create an alternative to Microsoft's DOS operating system, a number of Japanese companies had converged around the MSX standard. The MSX project was something of a sacred cow within Sony as it was led by the son of Akio Morita, Sony's much-revered founder. Still, Kutaragi was unimpressed: "I hated the idea. We wanted to sell the MSX. But we saw the MSX as a subset of the PC. The MSX was no good at real-time graphics. Nintendo realized the importance of real-time entertainment. The architecture was totally different."

So Kutaragi kept his deal with Nintendo a secret. Only his boss, Masahiko Morizono, the head of R&D, was made aware of the budding relationship with Nintendo. Says Kutaragi, **"I realized that if it was visible, it would be killed."**

As the launch date for the new machine approached, Nintendo sprung a surprise on Kutaragi. The game maker wanted to release a joint statement touting Sony's new sound chip. Kutaragi's boss could no longer protect him. The project was out in the open. Kutaragi would have to come clean. Thus, he found himself in the unenviable position of standing in front of a group of furious senior executives trying to explain why Sony was helping a rival. Remembers Kutaragi: "They were upset. The executives hated to know that we were allied with Nintendo and were competing with an internal product [the MSX machine]. Many of them wanted to kill our project. But Ogha–san protected us."

Ogha–san was then president Norio Ogha, who later became Sony's CEO and chairman. Ogha was intrigued by the new market. In the end Nintendo was given permission to use Sony's chip, and the product's success brought Kutaragi some credibility—at least outside of Sony. When Nintendo started to think about developing a 32–bit system in 1989, the company wanted Kutaragi to contribute to its design. In addition to a better sound chip, Kutaragi still wanted to replace the magnetic–based storage device—this time with a CD–ROM drive.

Within Sony, Kutaragi was viewed with suspicion. If he was going to continue his collaboration with Nintendo, he would need to find someone who could help him make his case to top management. Trolling for sponsors, Kutaragi approached Shigeo Maruyama, one of Ogha's disciples within Sony Music Japan. Maruyama expressed interest in the project because a CD–based system would be able to play not only games but music as well. Using Maruyama as a conduit, Kutaragi asked Ogha to create a dedicated group around the Nintendo project that would sit outside Sony's major businesses. Kutaragi feared that without this separation, his project, and his dream, wouldn't survive. Ogha, who had years earlier resorted to the same tactic in creating the music division, agreed to put Kutaragi's fledgling business in a separate unit.

This was a very lonely time for Kutaragi. He felt isolated from the rest of the company. "I was the outsider," he says. "No one would use my team's technology for internal projects." Here he was, developing key components for Nintendo's next game machine, which was likely to generate hundreds of millions of dollars, and his colleagues were ignoring him. Kutaragi recalls: "We were in a separate facility. No one accepted our project. This was a very difficult time for me. I moved my project out of the headquarters building, and located in a different area of Tokyo."

Then in 1991, just when he thought things couldn't get worse, Nintendo backed out of the deal. This change of heart came after Kutaragi had already devoted two long years of his life to the project. Nintendo was frightened that a CD–ROM drive might weaken Nintendo's hold over the production of game software. Magnetic cartridges required longer lead times to produce and were much more expensive than CD-ROMs, but it was a technology that Nintendo controlled. Nintendo was concerned that a CD–based machine might weaken the company's position in the game software business, which was where the real profits lay.

With his project in tatters, Kutaragi was more lonely than ever: "People inside Sony hated us. I was aligned with Nintendo, so when they cancelled the project I was homeless. I was arguing that computer entertainment would be a very important area for the future of Sony, but no one agreed."

Undeterred, he once again approached Ogha through Maruyama. Kutaragi recalls: "I wanted to convince Mr. Ogha that we needed to make Sony a digital company, and the video game was the only project I could think of that would let us take a first step in this direction."

The MSX project, Japan's attempt to create its own PC operating system, had sputtered and died. Kutaragi saw game machines as Sony's best chance at becoming a digital company. But more than that, he wanted the company to make a commitment to computer entertainment. Sony sold millions of CD players, and by then there were digital components in most of its consumer electronics, but it still did not see itself as a digital company. The CD was seen as a replacement for vinyl records, rather than just one example of what would become an explosion of digital media. Kutaragi lobbied tirelessly to change this view. He explains:

> I convinced them that computer entertainment would be very important for the future of Sony. Sony's technology was analog-based. Analog would be finished by the end of the century in terms of being able to make a profit. The first age of Sony was analog, but it had to convert to a digital, information–based company in the future. No one realized that.

To underscore his commitment to the project, Kutaragi threatened to leave Sony if he wasn't allowed to proceed with his video game project. Not only that, he made an outrageous promise: If the company would fund his R&D efforts, he would create a platform for Sony's future growth. Ogha's go-ahead, when it came, reflected not only his reluctance to lose a creative engineer, but his annoyance that Nintendo had breached a contract with his own signature on it. Thus Nintendo's fears pushed the start button on Sony's PlayStation.

Kutaragi wanted to give the project a grand name, Sony Computer Entertainment, to match his grand vision for how chip technology would one day carry Sony far beyond games. At first, Ogha wasn't convinced. Recalls Kutaragi:

> I proposed the name to Mr. Ogha. I didn't want the project to be seen as games, I wanted a more sophisticated image. Mr. Ogha, said, "It's a very big name." Sony Music Entertainment, that's big business, but what is Sony Computer Entertainment? That is not a big business like Sony Music or Sony Pictures.

Despite the reservations, Kutaragi's project got the outsized name.

Already Kutaragi could envision an opportunity to vest bland business computers with fun, personality and emotion. Two years of development came and went before Kutaragi and a handful of engineers completed the PlayStation. The 1–million–transistor chip underneath its plastic shell was one of the first to combine a 32–bit processor, a graphics chip, and a decompression engine on the same piece of silicon, otherwise known as a *system-on-a-chip*. Launched in Japan at Christmas 1994, the PlayStation was the first 32–bit game machine on the market. It would be a full year and a half before Nintendo released its next-generation system, the Nintendo 64. In a market where being first with the fastest is everything, Sony had pulled off a coup.

Sony's sterling brand name and the machine's engineering superiority gave the PlayStation a rapid liftoff. As sales shot skyward, Sony Computer Entertainment was awarded divisional status within the company, but Kutaragi was not immediately appointed as its president. Instead, he was asked to head up the division's engineering efforts.

Where Nintendo had been notorious for taking a tough line with game designers, Sony coddled independent game developers and made it easy for them to design games for the PlayStation. The PlayStation quickly became the world's top–selling game machine. Kutaragi, the onetime outcast, became CEO of the division in March 1999, when his boss moved on to become Sony's deputy CFO. By the end of its 1999 fiscal year, Sony had sold 55 million PlayStations worldwide and 430 million copies of video game software. Over 3,000 different game titles were available. All told, Sony Computer Entertainment racked up $6.5 billion in revenues, with a mouth–watering 17 percent operating margin, compared with 5 percent for the company as a whole (see the table "Sony

Computer Entertainment Growth in Revenues and Operating Profits as Percentage of Corporate Profits").

SONY COMPUTER ENTERTAINMENT GROWTH IN REVENUES AND OPERATING PROFITS AS PERCENTAGE OF CORPORATE PROFITS, 1995–1999 (IN BILLIONS OF YEN)

	FY95	FY96	FY97	FY98	FY99
Sony Computer Entertainment Revenue	35	201	408	700	760
Sony Computer Entertainment Operating Income	n/a	(9)	57	117	137
Sony Corporate Operating Income	(167)	235	370	520	339

Kutaragi had proved himself. Former critics were now praising his courage and perseverance. He had made good on his promise. The returns on his bandit project had kept Sony afloat through the Asian financial crisis in 1997 and 1998, contributing nearly half of the company's profits. And Sony Computer Entertainment had become the company's second-largest business, surpassing Sony Music and Sony Pictures and second only to Sony Electronics. For a company that had staked billions on hardware-software synergy, Sony Computer Entertainment was proof that integration could pay off. Sony's software partners would sometimes spend as much as $40 million developing and marketing a single new game—that's the kind of budget more typically associated with Hollywood blockbusters. Video game software had come to generate more revenue than movie ticket sales. Nor was the PC safe from the onslaught. In 1998, software produced for dedicated game machines captured more than two-thirds of all the revenue derived from entertainment software. PC-based titles took the other third.

But Kutaragi's ambitions for Sony were far from sated. With sales of the PlayStation still climbing, Kutaragi began working on his next development masterpiece, informally known as the PlayStation II. Even though he was now CEO of Sony Computer Entertainment, he led the engineering team that set out to design the new machine. More than just a game machine, the PlayStation II would be built around a 128-bit processor called the "Emotion Engine," a chip Sony claimed to be three times faster than a Pentium chip of the same vintage. The new chip would be able to render images and movement more realistically than a Silicon Graphics workstation. Costing a cool $1 billion to develop, the chip would be powerful enough to recognize speech and render characters that could be controlled down to their facial expressions. The PlayStation II would play DVD movies, as well as all 3,000 CD-ROM games developed for the original PlayStation. Its graphics would be comparable to an animated movie, its sound quality superior to that of a music CD and its computing power more than that of a high-end PC. Plus, it would connect to the Internet because, as Kutaragi says, "Communications is the biggest entertainment of all for humans. Even the telephone is a form of entertainment." Kutaragi's hope was that the PlayStation II would become a "home server" that would link households to all kinds of broadband services. A senior executive at Sony described the PlayStation II as an entirely new *dohyou*, using the Japanese word for sumo ring.

But even this groundbreaking product was just one step toward an even bolder goal. Explains Kutaragi:

> My intent is to create a new type of entertainment. Music has a 1,000-year history, movies have a 100-year history, but the computer is new. The microprocessor is a 30-year-old product, and IBM and Intel want to use it as an enhanced calculator. They are focused on productivity in the office, not entertainment. Spielberg saw our demonstration and he said, "Wow." Lucas thinks the PlayStation II can deliver his dream to the home. They did not expect that this type of technology would be available in this decade.

What Kutaragi is describing is nothing less than some future melding of TV, film, computers, music, and the Internet. Whether Sony will actually make this happen remains to be seen. But there is no doubt that the PlayStation II is more than just a game machine, and a few of the world's digerati wondered whether Sony might have Intel or Microsoft in its sights.

Yeah, Kutaragi could have left Sony and started his own video game company, but then he wouldn't have been able to leverage Sony's considerable marketing muscle, manufacturing capability and money. Kutaragi muses:

> If I had started this business as a venture outside a big company, it would have worked, but the moving speed would not have been fast enough. Sony had great human resources, capital and

manufacturing capability, but it did not have a vision at that time. But my team had the vision. We wanted to use Sony's infra-structure to enhance the time to market. If we were a Silicon Valley company, we would have created another Silicon Graphics. But our ambition is bigger than to be another Silicon Graphics.

In spring 1999, Sony announced a restructuring that placed Sony Computer Entertainment at the core of the company, and Kutaragi joined Sony's corporate management team. Kutaragi's odyssey from ignored engineer to corporate mogul provides a real-life seminar in what it takes to make a great company greater still:

○ Start with a vision that is so bold and seductive that it is capable of sustaining you when others try to shut you down.
○ Don't start with grand projects; start with something you can achieve right now, with your own resources (such as that first sound chip for Nintendo).
○ Go underground if you have to, even if the price is isolation.
○ Don't ask permission until you have achieved an early success and are ready to scale up.
○ Be willing to put your job on the line for what you believe.
○ In a world where most people can't see beyond the next quarter, perseverance pays.

In his new role, Kutaragi is no less intent on changing the world than he was as a lonely engineer. From exile to divisional CEO, an activist indeed!

SHELL'S RENEWABLE RADICAL

When he joined Royal Dutch/Shell's planning group in 1993, peering into the future was Georges Dupont-Roc's job. But Dupont-Roc was more than a soulless planner playing scenario mind games. He was a dreamer and a doer. He could see a world of opportunities for Shell that lay beyond fossil fuels, a world so compelling and real that he was willing to abandon the safety of his anonymous staff job to become a highly visible champion of renewable energy. Before he was done, Dupont-Roc had convinced his century-old company to make renewable energy Shell's fifth core division, alongside exploration and production, chemicals, oil products and natural gas.

As head of planning for the energy group, Dupont-Roc's job was to "look at the world energy scene and understand long-term issues that might have an impact on various sources of supply." In doing so, he became intrigued with the challenge of meeting the energy needs of a world with a rapidly increasing population in a way that would be environmentally sound and capable of sustaining economic development. Eager to deepen his thinking, Dupont-Roc sought out the world's energy experts at both universities and other corporations. He visited experts at MIT, Berkeley, Boeing and Mercedes-Benz in his quest to develop a view on how the world energy system would evolve and what role renewable energy sources—such as sun, wind and wood— would play. In 1994, he put his findings into a seven-page report, immodestly titled "The Evolution of the World's Energy Systems."

The report looked out not 5 or 10 years, but more than 50! **Even for an oil company accustomed to making investments in exploration that don't pay off for 10 or 20 years, the scope of Dupont-Roc's report was audacious.** But it was also grounded in a wealth of hard data about the progress of energy over the previous 100 years and what this might mean for the future. During the past century, world GDP had grown an average of 3 percent a year, supported by a supply of available energy that had grown at a 2 percent annual rate. During that time, the annual worldwide consumption of energy had increased from the equivalent of 4 barrels of oil per person to 13. Given these historical trends, Dupont-Roc came up with two potential story lines for the next century. The first one, which he labeled "sustained growth," assumed that energy consumption would continue to grow at its historical rate, in which case people would be burning the equivalent of 25 barrels of oil per capita by 2060. The second alternative, dubbed "dematerialization," assumed that energy growth would become somewhat disconnected from GDP growth as information technology, biotechnology and lighter materials improved energy efficiency. In this case, people would be consuming the equivalent of only 15 barrels of oil a year by 2060.

In Dupont-Roc's view, the sustained growth scenario was the most probable. It assumed that energy efficiency would continue to increase at 1 percent a year, the same as it had for the past century. For the dematerialization scenario to occur, energy efficiency would have to increase at twice the historical rate, a phenomenon that had never occurred for more than a few years at a time. Even if dematerialization did take hold, it would begin in the fully developed nations and take several decades to spread to underdeveloped regions. However Dupont–Roc cut the data, he couldn't see any way to avoid an energy supply squeeze as the world's population grew and as the environmental perils of fossil fuels became ever more inescapable. Says Dupont–Roc: "I saw the potential for renewable energy sources to reduce their cost and take market share from traditional energy sources, going from a small niche to a serious competitor in the way that oil did at the beginning of the twentieth century."

To convince his skeptical colleagues, Dupont–Roc drew a powerful analogy. He pointed out that in the beginning, oil had been a niche product, used almost exclusively in lamps and stoves. In 1890, even after 20 years of 8 percent annual price declines because of improved refining and production techniques, the market share for oil was still only 2 percent compared with coal and wood. It wasn't until Winston Churchill switched the British Navy from coal to oil, in order to give ships more power and make their emissions less visible, that oil started to become the world's dominant source of energy. Dupont–Roc was simply reminding his colleagues of what they already knew: energy markets take a long time to develop. Every time energy consumption increased, the market diversified to meet those growing needs—from coal to oil and from oil to gas and nuclear. Wasn't it possible that renewable energy would come next—both from existing renewable sources like solar and wind and from other renewable sources yet to be exploited? Wasn't renewable energy one of history's freight trains? You could either jump on board before it gathered speed or get run over. Under the sustained growth scenario, Dupont–Roc figured that renewable energy would be fully competitive with oil, gas, and other traditional types of energy by 2020 (see graph "Energy Market Share, 1860–2060").

Dupont–Roc reminded his colleagues that, in the early stages, it was impossible to predict exactly which technologies would eventually triumph. In the early part of the century, for instance, the zeppelin looked like a surer bet than the airplane, and even electric cars looked more promising than those powered by combustion engines. An aluminum car powered by an electric battery broke the land speed record in 1899, clocking in at 105 kilometers per hour. On the last page of Dupont–Roc's report were excerpts from an article titled "What May Happen in the Next Hundred Years" from the *Ladies' Home Journal,* December 1900. One of the entries predicted, "There will be Air–Ships, but they will not successfully compete with surface land and water vessels for passenger traffic. They will be maintained as deadly war vessels by all military nations."

Obviously, there is no such thing today as British Blimpways. Dupont-Roc was saying that the future's big trends, such as how much energy 10 billion people will need, can be fairly guessed at, but the details, exactly which technologies will provide that energy, are more difficult to discern. For this reason, he advocated a technology–agnostic approach to renewable energy: experiment with everything from solar to wind to biomass (burning wood and other renewable resources) to geothermal. The goal would be to take options on a wide range of renewable energy sources.

Dupont-Roc wanted more than a nod to renewables from Shell's top brass. He was after more than a PR campaign to assuage the environmentalists. He wanted an ironclad corporate commitment. But first he would have to buttress the case for renewables. Dupont-Roc argued

ENERGY MARKET SHARE, 1860–2060

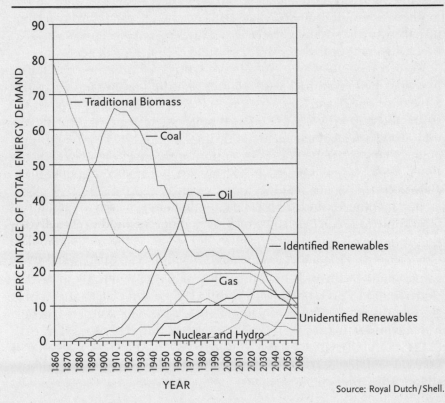

Source: Royal Dutch/Shell.

that the cost of making solar panels, growing trees and converting wind into electricity would drop at a rate similar to the decline in the cost of producing oil during the late 1800s. His report showed that during the 1970s and 1980s the cost of making solar panels declined 15 percent a year and that during the 1980s and early 1990s the cost of electricity from wind turbines had drifted downward at the rate of 10 percent per year. Wind energy was already competitive in some markets. Solar panel costs would continue to decline through advances in silicon manufacturing, thin-film technology and the scaling up of manufacturing. Through better cloning techniques and genetic manipulation, trees could be made to grow faster and burn hotter. In the meantime, production of hydrocarbon fuels would continue to rely on mature technology, and oil companies would be forced to go deeper offshore or look for smaller pockets of oil in older fields.

"I wasn't saying that oil was a dead business," recalls Dupont-Roc, "but that new energy segments would be able to improve their productivity faster and become competitive in the marketplace." Under his sustained growth model, the use of fossil fuels would continue to rise moderately until about 2020 or 2030, when renewables would come into their own and allow the total energy supply to keep growing at a time when energy from fossil fuels would be hitting a plateau.

Not everyone was immediately convinced by Dupont-Roc's thesis. In part, their skepticism was based on the disappointing results achieved in Shell's earlier experiments with renewable energy. In the 1970s, the company started a small solar energy project. But by the mid-1980s, after having spent about $100 million, it shut the business down. Photovoltaic energy was simply not cost-effective yet. In the 1980s, Shell also experimented with nuclear energy in a joint venture with Gulf, a dalliance that produced a $500 million write-off. By 1994, all that had survived of Shell's earlier experiments were a small photovoltaic research unit in Holland and a small forestry business with operations in Uruguay and Chile.

Undeterred, Dupont-Roc published his short strategy paper and began spreading the word about the new promise of renewables. He traveled from one Shell operating company to another, giving 80 speeches in 20 countries over the span of 18 months. Says Dupont-Roc, "Shell people were surprised that we were saying this sort of thing. **IT WASN'T POLITICALLY CORRECT TO TALK ABOUT A WORLD IN WHICH FOSSIL FUELS DIDN'T DOMINATE**." Others suspected that it was all just a PR exercise. Yet every time he told his story, it got stronger:

People would contribute to my stories by giving more examples and providing clarification, which I would feed back into my model. It was a bit of a democratic debate. The biggest thing I learned was not to be arrogant. Shell people have a reputation for being arrogant, of trying to push a story instead of sharing it and trying to hear what other people have to say.

Finally, Dupont–Roc got his chance to give his presentation to Shell's executive management committee. He received a cautious endorsement. His case was helped by the steady trickle of positive feedback Shell's top management had been getting from country managers who were pleased to see Shell leading a dialogue about new energy sources. The fact that Greenpeace had succeeded in mobilizing public opinion in opposition to Shell's plans to sink an old oil platform in the North Sea also added urgency to the renewables cause. With Shell getting pummeled in European newspapers, top management was especially receptive to any ideas that would make their company more environmentally friendly.

The executive committee asked Dupont–Roc to prepare a business plan outlining how Shell might poke its toe into the water of renewable energy. They were perhaps looking for nothing more than a token, but this was just the opening that Dupont–Roc needed to make his concept of a renewable energy business a reality.

Tree huggers notwithstanding, Dupont–Roc knew that he had to make his proposal financially credible if it was ever to see the light of day. He was certain that renewables would become economical over the next couple decades, but couldn't say exactly when or how. During the mid-1980s Dupont–Roc had been leading a drilling project in the North Sea when the collapse in oil prices forced everyone to find innovative ways to reduce the project's costs (through three–dimensional seismic technologies, subsea satellites and unmanned platforms). He was sure a similar wave of innovation would one day push renewables into the energy mainstream. But if Shell waited for that inflection point, it would be too late. Shell would lack the experience to catch up to those who had started earlier.

In the fall of 1995, Dupont–Roc sidestepped all of Shell's numerous barons during a one-hour meeting with the chairman in which he asked for $25 million to test the commercial potential of some renewable energy business concepts over a three–year period. Dupont–Roc wanted to concentrate on the two areas where Shell already had some competence: solar energy and biomass (specifically, the growing of trees for power generation). In photovoltaics, he wanted to automate the way solar cells were made and increase energy plant production from the equivalent of 2 megawatts of power a year per plant to 20 megawatts a year. His goal for biomass was to demonstrate that Shell could grow trees sustainably, harvest them and produce wood fuel for no more than the cost of natural gas. "We had to convince the chairman that Shell could do something real and credible," says Dupont-Roc. By the end of the meeting, the chairman gave him his $25 million.

Dupont-Roc had the cash, but he still had to enlist the support of the local line executives who control people and facilities across Shell's global empire. Applauding his speeches was one thing, but actually dedicating resources to a nascent business project was another. With his little band of warriors, which included three other people at Shell Central in London, he embarked on a new campaign. "It was very exhausting. We had to convince the chief executives of the operating companies to help us," he says. Dupont-Roc chose his targets carefully. If the operating companies were too big, the project would get lost. If they were too small, it might prove too distracting. So he focused on about two dozen of Shell's medium-sized operating companies. Typical reactions would be, "We are sorry, we're trying to rationalize our oil operations," or "The local strategy cannot support renewables—although we support you." Finally, his team narrowed the candidates down to about a dozen medium-sized subsidiaries. These test beds had the advantage of representing different types of economies and climates. Some of the experiments failed, and some were unqualified successes. In Germany, for instance, Dupont-Roc had to temper the local enthusiasm. He reflects:

> You have to keep a balance between retaining some type of
> central steering and letting the local initiative develop. In
> Germany, they went a little overboard. They started looking at
> solar heating, wave power, and wind power, which was good, but
> it was trying to do too much. We said, "We don't want to go that
> far right now." You have to remain focused or you will fail.

By the time the executive committee reviewed Dupont-Roc's progress in December 1996, he was well ahead of plan. His group had planted 300 hectares (741 acres) of trees in Uruguay and had set up a 3-megawatt, photovoltaic demonstration plant in Holland. The committee was thrilled. Even though the three-year trial period was not yet up, it asked him to come back with a plan to substantially expand his renewable activities. This time he developed a broad 15-year business plan for an entirely new division, which would not only expand the scope of Shell's biomass and solar power activities but also create a platform for entering two new areas: wind and geothermal. In preparing the plan, Dupont-Roc consulted about 20 senior executives throughout Shell who helped him fine-tune the commercial aspects of the plan. They would grill him: "What are you selling me? How will you produce it? In what countries? Who will find the customers?" When he finally presented the plan to the executive committee in June 1997, it was concrete. Its target was to create a portfolio of businesses by 2010 with assets in at least 20 different countries, $100 million in profits, and a 15 percent annual earnings growth rate. The businesses would be run locally, but a central team in London would assist in replicating successful ventures across the corporation.

Shell now faced a choice: it could either house the subsidiary within an existing division or create an entirely new one. It decided to pursue the latter option so that the business would be more visible and have a chance to grow. In the fall of 1997, the company established Shell International Renewables with a commitment to invest $500 million in the venture over the following five years. While Dupont-Roc was gratified that all his speeches and lobbying had finally paid off, he was profoundly disappointed that he wasn't asked to head up the new unit. Unfortunately, Shell was still an aristocracy, and he wasn't a blue blood. The job went instead to a more senior executive who had recently been reorganized out of his job in the chemicals division. Nevertheless, Dupont-Roc was heartened by the fact that his vision, aligned as it was with the tides of history, had helped to create the first major new division in Shell in decades. After staying to help the ex-chemicals executive set up the new renewables business and jump-start a geothermal energy project, Dupont-Roc quietly resigned to work for the French energy company TOTALFINA.

Despite his departure, Dupont-Roc left an indelible mark on Shell. By 1999 the first batch of trees, which had been planted in Uruguay under his watch in 1996, was ready to be harvested, and a new 20-megawatt solar panel factory was up and running in Germany. In South Africa, Shell International Renewables was marketing home solar systems to 50,000 people who lived too far away to get electricity from the power grid—the largest commercial rural electrification project ever to be based on solar power. It was also installing 10,000 solar home systems in Bolivia. In Germany and Holland, it opened a handful of solar–powered service stations where people driving electric cars could charge up in an environment–friendly way. And it was combining solar home systems with biomass–fueled power plants in a "Sun Station" project that provided electricity for 80 homes, a mosque, a government building and 11 street lamps in a village in Indonesia.

Back when the renewables business was still a $25 million project trying to prove itself, Dupont–Roc received a postcard from a politician in the French Alps, where he had grown up. The postcard showed two children playing in front of an extraordinary mountain scene, with a quote from the French novelist Antoine de Saint-Exupéry: "We do not inherit the land from our forefathers, we borrow it from our children." Shell's chairman Mark Moody–Stuart would later repeat these words in a 1998 letter to shareholders.

Dupont–Roc's success is instructive:

○ Invest relentlessly in your own learning. The endless meetings with experts and academics gave Dupont–Roc the weapons and armor he would need to win his arguments inside Shell.
○ There's no substitute for impeccable data. While data alone is seldom enough to convince a company to do bold, new things, shoddy analysis will sink an activist's career before it even begins.
○ A great cause (e.g., a cleaner planet and sustainable development) is as important as a great business case.
○ If you're not willing to be an apostle, don't expect anyone else to be.
○ Use analogies and experiences from your company's own history to buttress your credibility. Dupont–Roc's analysis of how oil, natural gas, and nuclear power had come to complement earlier energy sources was a powerful argument for renewables.
○ Start small. Small successes are the platforms for big successes.

David Grossman, John Patrick, Ken Kutaragi and Georges Dupont–Roc. They worked within the system, fomenting discontent, mobilizing kindred spirits, leading outlaw projects and, ultimately, changing the destiny of some of the world's largest, most complicated companies. They were citizen–activists.

So where do you start? How are you going to organize a movement? Do you have what it takes? What can you actually learn from Ken and Dave and John and Georges? Read on.

6

GO AHEAD! REVOLT!

EVERY DAY COMPANIES GET BLINDSIDED

by the future. Every day dozens of organizations find themselves suddenly on the defensive, struggling to adapt a decrepit business model to someone else's business concept innovation. Yet the future never arrives as a surprise to *everyone* in an organization. Someone, somewhere, was paying attention. For these heretics and novelty addicts, tomorrow's opportunities are every bit as real and inevitable as today's sunrise. But too often the seers feel isolated and impotent. They don't know where to begin in building a grassroots movement, even though the principles of activism aren't classified and there's no secret handshake. Over the decades, social campaigners of all types have constructed a highly practical theory of activism. How sad that the principles of activism are virtually unknown to citizens of the corporate realm.

Every senior executive claims to "embrace change," and every CEO solemnly warns that "change is the only constant." Isn't it rather odd, then, that the principles of activism haven't been drilled into the head of every employee? After all, most social systems get changed by activists not by the elite. Yet I've never come across a company-sponsored training program that teaches the rank and file how to be activists. Let's end this strange omission, shall we? There's plenty we can learn from Dave Grossman, John Patrick, Ken Kutaragi, and Georges Dupont-Roc, profiled in the previous chapter, about how to organize a movement.

HOW TO START AN INSURRECTION

STEP 1: BUILD A POINT OF VIEW

As an activist, you need a point of view (POV), which includes the following:

○ What is changing in the world?
○ What opportunities do these changes make possible?
○ What are the business concepts that would profitably exploit these changes?

If you understand the principles of business concept innovation, if you've learned how to be your own seer, then you're well on your way to developing your own POV.

It is rare to come across an individual who has a well-developed point of view about an opportunity for industry revolution. **Most folks stand for nothing more than more of the same.** This is much to your advantage. A sharply articulated POV is a sword that lets you slay the dragons of precedent. It's a rudder that lets you steer a steady course in a world filled with people blown about by fad and whim. And it's a beacon that attracts those who are looking for something worthy of their allegiance.

A POV must meet four tests: it must be credible, coherent, compelling and commercial. To be credible it must be based on unimpeachable data. A POV can be as bold and far-reaching as your aspirations, but it must have a foundation in fact. Georges Dupont-Roc demonstrated clearly and unequivocally that several renewable energy sources would become cost-efficient by the year 2020, if not before. He showed Shell's executive team that the cost per kilowatt-hour of renewable energy had been falling around 10 percent to 15 percent per year for several years. Project that forward, add in the cost of meeting stringent environmental standards for fossil fuels, and you can make a well-informed judgment about the point at which renewable energy sources will become a viable alternative to carbon fuels. It's also clear, given the technical hurdles involved, that any company that hopes to reap profits from renewable energy sources needs to start investing now.

John Patrick and David Grossman also had the tide of history on their side. Although the Internet was still a nascent phenomenon when they began agitating within IBM, there was plenty of hard data describing its rapid growth. There were also many analogies from history that suggested the inevitable triumph of any technology that would allow people to better connect and communicate. They may have been in front of the curve, but there was a curve. Rhetoric isn't enough. You need to wade hip-deep in data to make sure you really understand what's going on. You have to be ready to back up your bold assertions. And you must clearly separate what can be known from what is unknowable—don't claim to know things you can't.

A POV must be coherent. The pieces of your POV must fit together and be mutually reinforcing. Corporate executives and their well-trained attack dogs will sniff out the slightest bit of inconsistency in your story line. Logic lapses are not allowed. This doesn't mean you have to have perfect perspicuity, but there's no excuse for muddled thinking. I often see would-be activists demolished when, in their enthusiasm, they defy logic. I witnessed one young activist in a large software company pitching a new product to his CEO. "This will be on everybody's computer. Everyone will use it every day," he gushed. The CEO's eyebrows moved closer together. "Other than the browser, e-mail, and word processing, what applications get used by everyone, every day?" he inquired. The activist's balloon starting hissing air. "Well, none," he had to admit. "And what is it about your application," the CEO pressed further, "that will create some new standard of ubiquity?" The balloon was now a flaccid bit of rubber. The would-be activist never got a second chance. Passion is no substitute for a coherent point of view.

Facts and logic are not enough, though. If you're going to enroll others in your dream, you must speak to their hearts as well as their intellects. You must be ready to tell people why your particular cause will make a difference in the world. If you can present your POV as a story (what happens to the world if we *don't* harness renewable energy sources) or as a picture (like the Web page featuring Grossman's six-year-old son), it will be that much more emotionally compelling. Many assume that only numbers talk. That's stupid. Only economists think we're perfectly rational. Beauty, joy, hope, justice, freedom, community—these are the enduring ideals that attract human beings to a cause. What is the ideal that makes your POV truly worthwhile?

If you want your company to *do* something, your POV must be commercial as well as emotionally compelling. If you can't describe how your business concept will generate wealth, you won't get far as a corporate activist. This doesn't mean you have to have a pro forma P&L accurate to two decimal places. It does mean your POV must point to a bona fide commercial opportunity. Anticipate the basic commercial questions: What's the value proposition for a customer? How will this create competitive advantage? What are the cost dynamics? Where is the flywheel of increasing returns? Your business concept may not yet be fully fledged, but you must demonstrate you are attending to these questions. Somewhere in all the enthusiasm and purpose must be the beginnings of a story about wealth creation.

A POV that is credible, coherent, compelling and commercial may rise to the standard of an *ideology*, which the *Random House Webster's College Dictionary* defines as "a body of doctrine or thought forming a political or social program." Civil rights is an ideology. Democracy is an ideology. Christianity is an ideology. A vision of computers vested with the power and intelligence to display human emotion is an ideology. A belief in the power of renewable energy to sustain economic development without imperiling the planet is an ideology. **AS AN ACTIVIST, YOU MUST BUILD YOUR OWN IDEOLOGY.** Start your journey with a sense of destiny. Don't be afraid to dream big, like Kutaragi–san and Dupont–Roc. As one of my activist friends once put it, "If you're going to fish, use a big hook." Setbacks are inevitable. You will lose many battles in the process of winning the war. It is your ideology that will sustain you and from which you will draw courage. Know that you have a *righteous* cause—one that is in tune with what's changing, one that is inherently worthwhile, one that will help your company stay relevant in the age of revolution.

STEP 2: WRITE A MANIFESTO

These are the times that try men's souls. The summer soldier and
the sunshine patriot will, in this crisis, shrink from the service
of their country; but he that stands by it now, deserves the love
and thanks of man and woman.

George Washington ordered these words read to his soldiers at Valley Forge, on Christmas Eve, shortly before crossing the Delaware. They are the first lines of a polemic written by Thomas Paine, the American revolutionary and pamphleteer. Paine's most famous work, *Common Sense*, was the manifesto for the American Revolution. Over the course of two centuries his powerful words and timeless principles have been used again and again to resist the authoritarian designs of despots and dictators.

You, too, must become a pamphleteer. It's not enough to have an ideology; you have to be able to pass it on, to infect others with your ideas. Like Thomas Paine, you have to write a manifesto. It doesn't have to be long. A contagious manifesto will do the following:

○ Convincingly demonstrate the inevitability of the cause—here's why it is right, right now.
○ Speak to timeless human needs and aspirations—here's why you should care.
○ Draw clear implications for action—here's where to start.
○ Elicit support—here's how you can contribute.

There are hordes of people in every organization who bitch and moan about what their company *should* be doing. But how many ever take the trouble to write a passionate and well-reasoned call to arms? Ideas that are flaky appear even more so when committed to paper. Conversely, ideas that are inherently strong get even stronger through the discipline of writing.

Think of your manifesto as a virus. What can you do to make it even more infectious?

○ Search for "data bombs" that will explode upon reading— incontrovertible facts that challenge prejudices and create urgency.
○ Find simple phrases and powerful analogies that people can use as "handles" to pick up your ideas and pass them around. (Don't you love the description of the PlayStation II as an "emotion engine"? Those two words say loads about Sony's view of the future of computing. They make a very complicated idea instantly portable.)
○ Stay constructive. Don't criticize. Don't rehearse past failures. Don't look for culprits.
○ Provide broad recommendations, but don't argue for a single, do-or-die course of action. Remember, you're launching a campaign

that will need to go forward on several fronts. At this point you have to stay flexible on tactics.

○ Keep your manifesto short. You're not getting paid by the word. Patrick's "Get Connected" was a simple 6-point treatise on how the Web would transform business and large-scale computing. Dupont-Roc's manifesto, "The Evolution of the World's Energy Systems," was only 7 pages. A 40-page white paper isn't a manifesto—it's a consultant's report, and it will never get read.

○ Make it opportunity-focused. A manifesto is more likely to get passed around if it focuses on the upside rather than the downside. Where's the big win?

○ Sometimes you need a stick. There are some whose love affair with the status quo borders on obsession. Like a reluctant Pharaoh, unwilling to free the Israelites from bondage, the only way they're going to change their minds is if you convince them that things are bad and getting worse. Every company sits on a burning platform. If you don't know where yours is burning, go find out. Maybe it's an online competitor that's about to rip your margins to shreds. Maybe it's just the hard fact that your company is underperforming and you've run out of ideas for propping up the share price. Maybe it's that you're living on Internet helium and you have no idea how to produce sustainable profits. Do a fast-forward—make it abundantly clear when and how the existing strategy is going to run out of steam.

Expect to hear dozens of reasons for *not* doing something. When timid, backward-looking souls go scrambling for an escape hatch, bolt it shut.

> *Escape hatch*: "It's not happening as fast as you say."
>   *Bolt*: "Oh yes it is, and here's the data to prove it."

> *Escape hatch*: "You can't make any money with that kind of a business model."
>   *Bolt*: "Someone already is, and here's how they're doing it."

> *Escape hatch*: "We don't have the skills to do this."
>   *Bolt*: "But we could get them, and here's how."

> *Escape hatch*: "We don't have the bandwidth to deal with this right now."
>   *Bolt*: "We have no choice. Here's what we should stop doing."

Escape hatch: "Someone already tried this, and it didn't work."
   Bolt: "They didn't try it *this* way."

Your manifesto must build a case for your *intellectual* authority. The depth of your analysis, the quality of your thinking and the clarity of your reasoning must shine forth from every page. It must also wrap you in a cloak of *moral* authority. Moral authority comes from a cause that is both economically sound and undeniably in the best interests of the organization and its members. Your manifesto must contain nothing that would suggest your primary motivation is selfish. You're not some product champion trying to get your little widget built, or some corporate hack trying to defend a budget. You can't afford to be sectarian or parochial if you want to change the world. Martin Luther King spoke for African–Americans, but he called on all Americans to embrace justice and equality. Unlike Malcolm X, he was inclusive rather than exclusive. He understood that America could never live up to its promise if it relegated some to a permanent state of despair. It is no crime to be self-interested, but if you are *only* self-interested, your manifesto will be quickly and rightfully dismissed.

Your manifesto *must* capture people's imagination. It must paint a vivid picture of *what could be*. It must inspire hope. Your manifesto must challenge people to look the future in the eye, however disconcerting it may appear. It must deal forthrightly with the little lies that people tell themselves to avoid the discomfort of change. It must make inaction tantamount to corporate treason. But most of it all, it must ignite a sense of possibility.

STEP 3: CREATE A COALITION

You can't change the direction of your company all by yourself. This is a lesson that even corporate chairmen eventually learn. As founder and chairman of Silicon Graphics, Inc., Jim Clark fought a long–running and often bitter battle with SGI's CEO, Ed McCracken. Clark was eager that SGI go "down market" and produce workstations at the upper end of the PC price range. McCracken was loath to sacrifice fat margins to serve "out-of-scope" customers. Unable to change McCracken's mind, Clark eventually quit.

Even chairmen have to seduce, cajole, and convince to get things done. Granted, it's easier when you control capital budgeting and compensation, but it still ain't a walk on the beach. Most CEOs are good at exhortation and arm twisting, but this is seldom enough to re–vector a large company. To do that, you have to build a broad coalition. **In**

building a coalition, you transform individual authority into collective authority. It is easy to dismiss corporate rebels when they are fragmented and isolated, and don't speak with a single voice. But when they present themselves as part of a recognizable coalition, speaking in a single voice, they cannot be ignored. This is the simple principle behind all collective action, be it a labor union organizing a strike or a trade association lobbying politicians. I have yet to see a company in which a few hundred or even a few dozen like-minded employees can't substantially impact corporate direction. The very fact that they *are* organized and *are* speaking from conviction is a powerful message to corporate leaders.

There is another reason to build a coalition. Most new opportunities don't fit neatly into any of the existing organizational "boxes." While there were scores of Netheads spread out across IBM, the Internet opportunity couldn't be shoehorned into any one division. Likewise, computer entertainment at Sony and renewable energy at Shell lacked natural organizational homes, at least to begin with. In creating a cross-company coalition, one is recognizing that the resources, brains and passion needed to bring a new opportunity to fruition are broadly distributed. You are creating a magnet for people who harbor the same revolutionary tendencies you do, wherever their current organizational home is. A movement is not a box on the organizational chart; it's an ink blot that has bled all over the formal org chart. It's a splat, not a department.

The first step in building a coalition is to recognize that you are not the only prescient, frustrated, yet ultimately loyal individual in your company. You're not the only one who "gets it." The second step is to begin to identify potential recruits. Start by asking these questions:

○ Who is already in your orbit? Surely you've already been talking to some folks about your revolutionary ideas.
○ Are there staff groups or task forces in the company that might be naturally inclined toward your point of view?
○ Are there any cross-company initiatives you could tap into?
○ Who across the organization might have a stake in the success of your campaign?
○ What are the news groups or e-mail distribution lists you might hijack?

Maybe you can't write like Thomas Paine, but then he didn't have the Web. Put your manifesto up on an internal website. Build an e-mail list of those you think might share your views. Create an online forum where people can share their perspectives and help elaborate your manifesto. Locate outside experts who can lend your cause credibility. Invite network members to brown–bag lunches and after–hours soirees where you can scheme and plot and remind each other that you're not all crazy. Create opportunities to work together on some ad hoc project. Coalitions get stronger when they focus on a common task. Be inventive. Look for involvement vehicles like the Internet trade shows John Patrick used to mobilize IBM's early Internet converts.

Stay underground, at least initially. Use the network to help strengthen your business case and identify opportunities for early action. As your recruits start talking to colleagues in their own spheres of influence, the virus will spread. Don't be impatient. If you map the infection curve of a virus, it is initially flat. But at some point the exponential arithmetic of the network effect takes over, and the infection rate soars. Don't be overquick to present top management with a go/no–go decision. It's easy to shoot one pheasant out of the sky; it's a bit harder to bring down an entire flock. Keep building your flock.

And remember, you have an advantage that top management often doesn't. Most of the folks who report to them are conscripts, but you're building an all–volunteer army. Conscripts fight to stay alive, volunteers fight to win. Your goal is to enroll and embolden the latent activists. If you build strength from below, top management will ultimately come to you. Georges Dupont–Roc got his chance because a chorus of support for renewable energy was echoing off the walls of Shell's worldwide organization.

STEP 4: PICK YOUR TARGETS AND PICK YOUR MOMENTS

Sooner or later, the movement has to become a mandate. The "Get Connected" coalition became "IBM, the e–business company." Dupont–Roc's informal network of renewables fans turned into a $500 million commitment. In most companies, these commitments aren't made by the Birkenstock–wearing, Volvo–driving, ponytail brigade. Activists create movements, they don't create mandates. That's why **activists always have a target——a someone or group of someones who can yank the real levers of power.** You need to know who in your organization can say "yes" and make it stick. It may be a divisional vice president, it may be the CEO, or maybe it's the entire executive committee.

At Sony, Kutaragi knew his project was doomed unless he got the CEO onboard early. Sony's aristocracy was actively hostile to the idea of video games. After trying several approaches, Kutaragi established a relationship with Maruyama, who helped him lobby the CEO. At IBM

Grossman managed to engineer an Internet demo for Lou Gerstner. Later, when Gerstner's likeness spoke from a Web page to a throng of IBM senior managers, the Internet die was cast. For Dupont-Roc, the pivotal moment came when he was asked to present to Shell's senior executive group.

All too often, corporate rebels are inclined to look at senior management as out-of-touch reactionaries, rather than potential allies. This is self-defeating. Their support is the object of the whole exercise. Few of them are stupid, and most are no more venal than you or I. Arrogant? Sometimes. Ignorant? Often. But that doesn't make them irredeemable. You must find a way to help them see what you see, to learn what you have learned and to feel the sense of urgency and inevitability you feel.

So you've identified your targets. The next step is to understand them. What are the pressures they face—from Wall Street, from customers and competitors? What issues top their agenda? What objectives have they set themselves and the company? Which of them is searching for help and ideas? Be ready to bend your objectives to fit their goals. Sony had been struggling to demonstrate that hardware/software synergy was more than a concept. After Sony's initial debacle in Hollywood, Ogha was eager for another chance to justify Sony's foray into software and media. Kutaragi was ready to scratch Ogha's itch. Do you *really* know where the top guys itch? You gotta find out.

Often the top guy is easier to convince than the divisional barons one level down. Shareholder expectations hang over the head of the average CEO like Damocles' sword. With a corporate vantage point, the CEO is often less likely to be defensive and parochial than a divisional VP. In many companies, you find the "Gorbachev syndrome": there's a cautiously unorthodox leader at the top and a sea of discontent down below. Like Gorbachev, the CEO wants the organization to adapt and change. Likewise, ordinary citizens want a better life. It's all too obvious to them that the system doesn't work. The ones that are most difficult to convince are those in the middle—the city bosses, the *nomenklatura*, the vice presidents who feel most threatened by a new order of things. The recalcitrant middle can long resist the exhortations of an isolated and embattled CEO. But it's much more difficult for them to hold out when they are caught in the vise of a reform-minded CEO and a committed and revolutionary rabble. Savvy corporate leaders, such as Ogha and Gerstner, know this. They're more than willing to use the heat of the activists' passions to thaw the frozen middle in their own organizations.

Getting access to the top isn't always easy. "Invitations" often have to be engineered. Court the executive assistants, the adjutants and the bag carriers. Find out who the top guy respects and relies on. Find out who writes the speeches. Know what customers the senior execs care most about—they may provide a back channel of influence. In other words, plot all the various avenues of influence that lead to your desired targets. Invite these people to your offsites, hook 'em up to your e-mail list, do a demo for them. Use your network to work all the approach routes simultaneously.

Make a list of all the events and occasions when you might get a chance to directly influence your targets. What are the meetings, workshops or conferences that your targets regularly attend? See if you or one of your network members can get on the agenda. Keep your pitch short. Entice and intrigue, don't harangue. Think of the gatekeepers and high-profile events as "strategic infection points"—opportunities to educate, entertain and enroll. To activists, the whole world's a stage. Every event is an opportunity to advance their POV. Patrick and Dupont-Roc gave dozens of speeches. As with skilled politicians, it didn't matter what question they were asked; they gave the answer they wanted to give. They were endlessly opportunistic. Every impromptu meeting, every hallway conversation was a chance to win another convert.

Sooner or later, you'll want to go one on one with your targets. Pick your moment carefully. You're waiting for the stars to align—you want the groundswell to have reached a critical mass; you want to catch your targets at a point when they're rooting around for a new idea; and, in an ideal world, you'll time your big pitch to some external event that adds credibility and urgency to your case (such as the frenzy of environmental outrage produced by Shell's decision to sink an offshore platform). Get all this right, and top management won't think you're a rebel; they'll think you're a godsend.

Your big moment may not be planned. It may happen unexpectedly—in a company cafeteria, at a trade show. Always have your elevator speech ready. Know what you want to ask for—keep it small and simple. Make it easy to say yes.

STEP 5: CO-OPT AND NEUTRALIZE

Saul Alinsky was one of America's most accomplished twentieth-century radicals. His book on how to organize a movement, *Rules for Radicals,* is a classic.[1] In the mid–1960s he went to Rochester, New York, to lead a campaign on behalf of the city's black community. Mary Beth Rogers describes his approach:

Alinsky, in something of a self-parody of his own tactics, threatened to buy 100 tickets to one of Rochester's symphony concerts and feed the predominantly black members of the local organization a dinner of baked beans a few hours before they went to the concert. The resulting "stink-in" would be a surefire attention getter. . . . There was no law against it. It might be fun. And it would probably get action quickly because the social elite wouldn't want "those people" to invade their activities again.[2]

Such tactics may work in the public sphere, but confrontation and embarrassment are seldom effective in a corporate setting. You are trying to disarm and co-opt, rather than demean and confront. Temper your indignation with respect.

John Patrick was extremely successful in drafting IBM's big guns into his cause. Given the scope of his ambition—to make the IBM Corporation Internet-ready—he realized that Gerstner's support would be necessary but hardly sufficient. With virtually no resources of his own, Patrick had little choice but to co-opt IBM's feudal lords. This took more than concerted lobbying. Patrick constructed a set of win-win propositions for key divisional leaders: Lend me some talent, and I'll build a showcase for your products. Let me borrow a few key people, and I'll send them back with prototypes for cool, new Internet-ready products. Patrick knew that reciprocity wins more converts than rhetoric.

Patrick didn't belittle, and he didn't berate. He worked hard to avoid an "us versus them" mentality. He wasn't trying to suck people and resources out of other divisions. He wasn't trying to build his own corporate fiefdom. He wasn't out there competing with the rest of IBM for customers. Divisional presidents saw him as a catalyst for change rather than as a competitor for resources and promotion. He wasn't cannibalizing their business; he was helping those businesses get ready for the future. In everything he did, it was clear that Patrick had the interests of the entire IBM Corporation at heart. In the beginning, he even lacked a formal organization. For all these reasons, he presented a very small target to his opponents.

Win-win propositions. Reciprocity. A catalyst not a competitor. Big impact, small target. These are vital principles for *your* campaign. Of course, it doesn't always work like this. The top brass at Sony saw Kutaragi's project as an impertinent challenge to their own MSX initiative. Companies have a finite number of resources, so expect a tug-of-war from time to time. But whenever you can, avoid expending political capital in highly charged head–to–head battles. At Shell, Dupont-Roc drew little fire because he never argued that renewables would replace fossil fuels. Indeed, he didn't think they would become fully competitive until 2020, long after the retirement of the existing divisional leaders. So yeah, you can stand on your soapbox and rant at the VPs. But to change your company, you're going to have to learn to co-opt at least some of the aristocracy into your revolutionary cause.

STEP 6: FIND A TRANSLATOR

You've been at it a while, and despite your best efforts you're having trouble getting heard. You talk, but you're not sure they comprehend. Don't be surprised. The very things that make you a revolutionary make it difficult to build a base of common understanding with the disciples of orthodoxy. Imagine how a conservative dad might look upon a kid who comes home with green hair and an eyebrow ring. Well, that's the way top management is likely to view corporate rebels. **Different experiences. Different languages. Different values. Different planets. This is why corporate revolutionaries need translators.**

John Patrick was a translator for Dave Grossman—someone who could build bridges between the Internet cultists and IBM's corporate cardinals. Patrick was a translator between geekdom and officialdom. But he did more than explain the intricacies of HTML to guys still in love with Big Iron. He helped to translate between the apparent chaos of the Web and the discipline of large-scale corporate computing; between the culture of "just enough is good enough" and the ethos of "zero defects"; between a half-baked technology and a zillion-dollar opportunity; between the agenda of the true believers (we just want to do "cool stuff") and the priorities of top management (those demanding shareholders, again). Patrick was also a credibility bridge. When top management asked, "Who *is* this guy, Grossman, and these kids in black?" he had an answer. "These guys care about IBM, they're not bomb throwers."

Patrick was also a translator between present and future. He found tangible ways of folding the future back into the present, starting with the Web sites built for sporting events. Each successive project gave long-term IBMers a better sense of what the new business model might look like in practice.

So if you're stymied, go find a translator—someone who is plugged into the future, who is naturally curious and who may be shopping around for an interesting point of view to sponsor. Senior staff and newly appointed executives are often good prospects. Both are typically in search of an agenda to call their own.

STEP 7: WIN SMALL, WIN EARLY, WIN OFTEN

People can argue with position papers, but they can't argue with success. All your organizing efforts are worth nothing if you can't demonstrate that your ideas actually *work*. Start small. Unless you harbor kamikaze instincts, search for demonstration projects that won't sink you or your cause if they should fail—and some of them will. You may have to put together a string of demonstration projects before top management starts throwing money your way. You don't run pell-mell down an unfamiliar path on a moonless night. Nor do companies blindly throw resources at untested business concepts. Commitment to a new business concept should never be presented as all or nothing—unless you're already way behind the change curve and some other company has taken all the risks. You have to help your company feel its way toward revolutionary opportunities, step by step.

Successful activists engineer a set of escalating experiments designed to test the new business concept and justify additional increments of investment. Without the original sound card he designed for Nintendo, Kutaragi would never have won the chance to do the PlayStation. Without Lillehammer, Deep Blue and a dozen other small wins, Patrick and Grossman would have never pushed IBM out in front of the Internet curve. Without a success in his first $25 million demonstration project, Dupont-Roc would have never shaken half a billion dollars out of top management's pockets. Activists are not daredevils. Revolutionary goals, but evolutionary steps—that's the way to think.

Be careful not to overpromise. Patrick's team called its alpha projects "experimental applications" to clearly distinguish them from IBM's thoroughly tested market-ready applications. There will be some who will wish you to fail. If your early experiments are too grand or you claim too much for them, and you then falter, you will provide enormous satisfaction to the skeptics. Search for small projects that offer the greatest potential impact for the smallest number of permissions, projects that will engender maximum visibility with minimum investment risk. You may have a grand strategy in the back of your mind, but you need to start with some little "stratlets." Keep asking yourself, What would constitute an early win? What could we do, right now, with the limited resources available within our network to build our credibility?

What could we do that would surprise the skeptics? What kind of success would others find compelling?

STEP 8: ISOLATE, INFILTRATE, INTEGRATE

Experiments that stay experiments are failures. The objective is to turn early experiments into radical, new wealth–creating business models with the power to change the direction of your company. For this to happen, you must eventually push your brood of baby projects out of the nest. In the early stages of your activist campaign, you may want to *isolate* your projects from the rest of the organization. Kutaragi moved himself and his team to a distant precinct in Tokyo, out of the line of fire of hostile executives. With a similar logic, IBM's PC business was originally housed in Boca Raton, Florida, far from meddlesome corporate staff and antagonistic vice presidents. To grow, new opportunities need to escape bureaucratic controls and orthodox thinking. They need their own place—a place where new ideas, new values and new teams can grow unmolested. This is the logic behind corporate "incubators," "internal venture divisions," and "skunk works." Sadly, most projects never escape the incubator, which is often little more than an orphanage for unloved ideas. Malnourished and secluded, few projects ever find foster parents.

Companies are often advised to "protect" new initiatives from the overweening control of the old guard, particularly when the new projects are built around a competing technology. But extended isolation will kill any project that requires a significant input of talent or capital or that is in any way complementary to existing businesses. For example, while IBM succeeded in "protecting" the PC business, that protection carried a stiff price. Physically cut off from the rest of IBM and from its broad base of capabilities, the PC development team had no choice but to turn to Microsoft and Intel for key software and hardware. The rest, as they say, is history. A similar fate befell many of the innovations spawned by Xerox's Palo Alto Research Center. Being 3,000 miles from headquarters guaranteed PARC a large measure of freedom, but it also made it difficult for Xerox to profit from PARC's endless stream of world–changing ideas. It's hard to drink through a straw that's 3,000 miles long.

Let's assume you are campaigning on behalf of something *big*. Sooner or later, a large–scale opportunity will require a large–scale resource commitment. This commitment is unlikely to be forthcoming if your project has been locked up too long in some business incubator.

You will need to convince a broad cross-section of key executives that your new business concept is essential to your company's future. Only then do you have a chance at winning the battle over resources. **To attract resources, you're going to have to make the leap from isolation to infiltration.** A powerfully argued position paper, regular speech making and high-profile demonstration projects helped Dupont-Roc to infect Shell with the renewable energy virus. He knew that if he couldn't get the rest of the organization to share his intellectual agenda, the renewables opportunity would never win the battle for resources within Shell. The resources that will make your dream a big commercial success have to come out of somebody's hide. Whoever's wearing that hide needs to be an ally. That will happen only if you've run a successful infiltration operation.

Sometimes you need more than resources. Sometimes the opportunity is not a *new* business, but a dramatic reconfiguration of the *existing* business. If you're a drug company, you can't put genomics in solitary confinement. If you're a retailer, you can't relegate e-commerce to some offline business incubator. Here you need more than infiltration, you need integration. Patrick wanted to change the very essence of IBM—rather than simply launch a new business. To this end he courted executives from IBM's operating divisions, searched for projects they would find relevant, trained and returned their people, and put his alpha-stage projects up for early adoption. It wasn't enough for Patrick to infiltrate IBM with his POV about the Internet; he needed to *integrate* the early experiments of the Get Connected cohort into IBM's major business groups. He didn't want the Internet to be a pimple on IBM's backside; he wanted it to be a virus in its bloodstream.

Sometimes an innovation makes it out of the incubator, but never gets integrated. GM's Saturn division is more than just an experiment. Saturn's sponsors were successful in infiltrating GM with their POV about the need for a "fresh-start" small car brand. Yet it is unclear just how many of the lessons learned in Saturn have been woven into the fabric of Chevrolet, Oldsmobile, Pontiac and GM's other brands. Indeed, in recent years it has appeared as if Saturn has become more like the rest of GM than the reverse. Integration requires more than a shared intellectual agenda. You are asking for more than capital and talent; you are asking the company to reinvent the core of who it is and how it competes. Your experiments must do more than attract resources away from incrementalist projects; they must take root throughout the organization and send out runners that will transform the landscape. It was John Patrick's hope that the Internet projects he transferred into IBM's operating divisions would ultimately seed a forest of local Web initiatives, and they have. This is the ultimate measure of success for a corporate activist.

Isolate. Infiltrate. Integrate. If you really want to change your company, you have to do it all.

ACTIVIST VALUES

Activists are the coolest people on the planet. They change big, complicated things with their bare hearts. They punch more than their weight. And when they fail, they fail nobly. To be an activist you need more than an agenda and a clever campaign. You need a set of values that will set you apart from the courtiers and the wannabes.

Honesty: Activists are truth tellers. They are authentic. They don't sacrifice their integrity for personal political gain. Their views cannot be bought and sold in the marketplace for perks and prestige. They speak the "unspeakables."

Compassion: Activists love the entire community. They are not interested in securing narrow sectarian advantage. Their goal is to create as big a legacy as possible for as many as possible.

Humility: Activists are terribly ambitious for their cause, but personally humble. They are arrogant enough to believe they actually can change the world, but they're not glory hogs. Their egos never get in the way of making something happen.

Pragmatism: Activists are more interested in action than in rhetoric. They're not searching for Utopia; they're trying to make stuff happen right here, right now. They prefer real progress to grand gestures.

Fearlessness: Activists are courageous. Their passion for the cause regularly overrides their sense of self-protection. They don't jump on land mines for the hell of it, but neither are they afraid to do battle with the defenders of the status quo.

Courage is, perhaps, the most important attribute of all. I have sat through hundreds of meetings where low-level employees soft-pedaled their convictions in an effort to protect the delicate sensitivities of top management. What came across as bold and uncompromising in a dry run presentation to their peers ended up as mushy and unconvincing when presented to top management. Afraid of bruising an ego or challenging a dogma, many would-be activists pull every punch and saw the sharp end off of every challenging point. In the end, every argument is so thoroughly padded with contingencies and qualifications that they might as well be firing cotton-ball bullets.

After Stalin's death, Khrushchev addressed the Supreme Soviet and denounced his predecessor's horrific crimes against the Soviet people. Many in the audience were stunned—the scale of Stalin's evil was mind-boggling. Finally, from the back of the hall, a voice rang out: "Comrade Khrushchev, you were there. You were with Stalin. Why didn't you stop him?" Momentarily flustered, Khrushchev's eyes raked the assembly. "Who said that?" he demanded. "Who said that?" he roared again. Those around the impertinent questioner sank lower in their seats. No voice was raised. No hand went up. After a terrible silence, Khrushchev said, "Now you know why." The questioner that day was no more willing to stand up to Khrushchev than Khrushchev had been willing to stand up to Stalin. The point was made. Luckily, there's no gulag in most companies. But activism still takes courage.

Listen, again, to Thomas Paine:

> Let them call me rebel and welcome, I feel no concern from it;
> but I should suffer the misery of devils, were I to make a whore
> of my soul.

If you find yourself saying a quiet "amen," then you're an activist.

The burden of radical innovation is not yours alone. To survive in the age of revolution, companies must become places where rule-busting innovation flourishes. In the next chapter we'll dig deep into several companies that have reinvented themselves and their industries again and again. From their experiences we can identify the key design criteria for building companies that are activist-friendly and revolution-ready.

7

GRAY-HAIRED REVOLUTIONARIES

ACTIVISTS SHOULDN'T NEED THE COURAGE OF
Richard the Lion-Hearted, the patience of Job or
the political instincts of Machiavelli to make a difference in their organizations. Sincere but bum-
bling activists often find themselves outgunned
and outmaneuvered by those who've sworn allegiance to the status quo. In the age of revolution
we need organizations that celebrate activism. Is
this possible? Can the fires of revolutionary fervor
be made to burn brightly throughout an organization, rather than only in small pockets of insur-
gency? As you'll see, the answer is a resounding
"yes." Indeed, unless a company can institutionalize activism, it's unlikely to be able to meet the
twin challenges of the age of revolution: reinventing itself and reinventing its industry.

REVOLUTION AND RENEWAL

Every organization, large or small, public or private, must be capable of innovating in two quite different ways. First, it must be capable of innovating with respect to its more orthodox peers. Consider, for a moment, the success of the University of Phoenix. With nearly 110,000 degree–seeking students taking classes on 110 campuses spread across 36 states, Puerto Rico and Canada, the University is the largest for–profit educational institution in America. While most universities see their "customers" as 18–year–olds, the University of Phoenix serves working adults of all ages who are eager to complete their university education. Founded in 1976, the University of Phoenix is truly an industry revolutionary. While the school doesn't have an Ivy League pedigree or endowment, its parent company, Apollo Group, has managed to build a business with a market value of more than $5 billion.

But it's not enough to innovate with respect to convention–bound competitors. A company must also be able to innovate with respect to its own past—this is often the more difficult challenge. The University of Phoenix has made a great start at reinventing its core business. The school currently has nearly 34,000 students enrolled in its pioneering online programs. Indeed, on its own, the University of Phoenix Online is bigger than all but a handful of traditional universities. With its own share listing, UoP Online was worth $350 million in early 2002. It's not a coincidence the overarching corporate values of the Apollo Group are innovation and inspiration.

Companies that are incapable of changing either themselves or their industry have no alternatives to retrenchment. They are the dead and

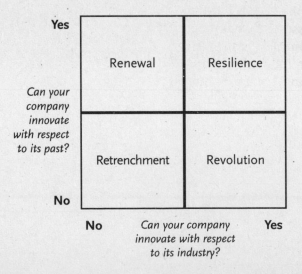

the dying, the no–hopers. They're acquisition fodder for more imaginative companies that will redeploy their skills and assets.

Companies that are incapable of leading an industry revolution are often slow–moving incumbents caught in perpetual catch–up mode. Think of Merrill Lynch and online trading, or Motorola and digital mobile phones, or Xerox and printers. All too often, incumbents reinvent their strategies only under duress—only when it becomes patently and painfully obvious that they've missed a critical opportunity. When they finally get around to the challenge of renewal, they do little more than ape the strategies of less orthodox competitors. However successful the ensuing makeover, top management deserves little credit, and even less recompense, for tagging along at the end of someone else's revolutionary parade.

On the other hand, the world is filled with one–strategy wonders—industry revolutionaries that were capable of changing an industry, but have yet to demonstrate that they are capable of changing themselves. Even the most brilliant strategy loses its economic effectiveness over time—this is the process of strategy decay. Any company that can't uncouple its long–term sense of identity from its initial strategy will end up as an industry footnote. Apple Computer, Body Shop, Kmart, Novell—these are just a few of the one–time industry revolutionaries who've never led a second revolution. Companies that have come to rely on a strong, entrepreneurial CEO find it particularly difficult to reinvent themselves. The simple fact is that most visionaries don't stay visionary forever. Renewal can't depend on a single individual having a second epiphany; rather the capacity for renewal must be baked deeply into the organization—into its attitudes, values, processes and systems.

Companies that are capable of both revolution and renewal are truly resilient—these are the companies that have the best chance of prospering in the tumultuous times that lie ahead. As we will see, there are revolutionaries like Charles Schwab (the pioneer of discount stock trading) that manage to reinvent themselves. And there are near hundred–year–old incumbents, like UPS and Cemex, that are able to reinvent both themselves and their industries. These are the "gray–haired revolutionaries," and they are the rarest breed of all. **Their gray hair comes not from years, but from the experience of having lived through several strategy "lifetimes."** They have done more than extend a legacy or enlarge a franchise. They have repeatedly turned themselves inside out and their industries upside down.

For every gray–haired revolutionary, there are dozens of incumbents still living off momentum and hundreds of start-ups that can't see beyond their IPOs. Even among the thin but vaunted ranks of gray-haired revolutionaries, there are no unqualified exemplars. There are no "excellent" companies. No company has totally cracked the code of the new innovation agenda. No company has yet fully internalized the new innovation regime with its focus on big, rule-busting ideas and radical entrepreneurship. But we can learn a lot from those that have made a start. In the pages that follow we'll learn from UPS, a company that has leveraged its unique competencies and assets to create a new multibillion-dollar business. We'll review the history of Charles Schwab, a serial innovator that has transformed itself into a quintessential e-business. Finally, we'll take an inside look at the unlikely success of Cemex, a company that has not only created new businesses and reinvented its core business, but has also committed itself to making innovation an everywhere, all-the-time capability.

UPS: GETTING OUTSIDE THE TRUCK

If you've ever had a cell phone break while under warranty, you know that all you had to do was call your wireless carrier and by the next day a new phone was on its way to you along with a prepaid postage label and a box to return the faulty phone. But did you know that if your carrier is Sprint PCS, the phone you sent back was never touched by a Sprint employee? Neither was the phone that was sent back to you. That new phone came straight from one of 500 warehouse and stocking locations throughout the country maintained by UPS, and the broken phone went to a cavernous UPS facility in Louisville, Kentucky, where its Service Parts Logistics business operates a repair operation. That's right, UPS brought you your new phone, and repaired your old one. And you thought all "Brown" did was deliver packages.

What is even more surprising is that this relatively new, and certainly creative, business is able to flourish in a highly disciplined, 95-year-old company like UPS with $30 billion in revenues and 370,000 employees. This is a company where, only a decade earlier, the decision to let employees decide how often to wash the company's ubiquitous brown trucks was hailed as a major break with the past. (Previously, a corporate policy had decreed that each truck was to be washed every day, whether dirty or not.) It's hard to imagine how such a buttoned-down place could give rise to a business that repairs returned cell phones, computers and medical equipment, and handles all the logistics to boot. Yet just two years after it had been formed, the

Service Parts Logistics was already ringing up hundreds of millions in sales. Moreover, this business is part of a larger UPS Logistics subsidiary that stores and delivers all Nike.com's shoes and helps Ford move its cars from factory to showroom. It took a mere five years for UPS Logistics to go from launch to an annual revenue run of $1 billion. "Within ten years," predicts former UPS Logistics CEO Dan DiMaggio (now president of UPS Supply Chain Solutions), "people will see us as a supply chain management company."

For most of its history, whether it was delivering parcels for department stores in the 1920s or for e-tailers in the 1990s, UPS maintained a maniacal focus on moving small packages efficiently from one place to another. In an engineering culture that prided itself on timeliness and accuracy, its drivers were measured to the second and trained in everything from how to hold their keys to what foot to put in their trucks first. In 1991, its highly focused corporate strategy statement was to "achieve worldwide leadership in package distribution." By 1999, that had changed to the much more expansive aspiration to "enable global commerce." UPS is aiming to do more than simply help its customers move their packages; it also wants to help facilitate the movement of the information and funds related to those goods. "We are always thinking about how to expand the definition of our markets," says recently retired senior vice president of corporate strategy Jack Duffy, of the company's new attitude. "We have all been trained to be constructively dissatisfied." It is that constructive dissatisfaction which helps UPS avoid being trapped by the constraints of its 95-year-old core business.

CEO Mike Eskew agrees with DiMaggio and Duffy's assessments of how the company is changing. "We've always been real good at analyzing the movement of goods as they go through our system," says Eskew, "and at trying to determine where to build buildings, and what kind of planes to buy, and where to position them. What we are doing more of now is helping our customers understand their information better, helping them streamline their processes, minimize their inventories and help them save some money. Really, what we are doing is to help streamline their supply chains."

This new outlook has been ten years in the making. UPS is a company that pays attention to small details and deviations. Duffy, a 30-year veteran, remembers working in New York City as a regional operations manager in the early 1990s: "Every day I would have to give a report to my executives about vehicles that broke down, the 100 packages that didn't get delivered, about the conveyor belt that broke down." It was this low fault-tolerance that alerted its executives to the early, subtle signs of strategy decay. UPS was still growing in the early 1990s, but the rate of growth, both in revenues and in the number of packages carried, was slowing. Margins were flattening. And the customer and employee satisfaction indexes that UPS measures religiously had peaked and were also flattening or declining slightly.

Rather than wait for a full-blown crisis, UPS decided to tackle the problems head-on, while the company was still healthy. It pursued a massive reengineering effort in which drivers were given more flexibility to determine their routes and generate sales leads. Suddenly it was okay to do things differently, as long as it did not affect the integrity of UPS's delivery network. The management ranks were trimmed 16 percent. Perhaps more important, the company's performance hiccup caused some to begin to question UPS's existing business definition.

This shake-up was all the more remarkable given that the company was still private at the time (its $5.5 billion IPO in 1999 would be one of the largest ever). For most of the century, the company was run as a partnership, which instilled a deep sense of responsibility in the senior executives. "We had a sense that we were given something, and we had to make it better," says Duffy. The senior management at the time decided to encourage some new conversations focused on a future that might extend beyond package delivery. They also came to the difficult conclusion that UPS would have to be willing to experiment with projects whose risk of failure was substantially greater than zero—not an easy decision for a conservative company, dominated by efficiency-minded engineers ever mindful of guaranteeing on-time deliveries.

Within this context, a group of about a dozen next-generation leaders in the company were chartered in 1995 to meet twice a month to explore possible new directions for the company. Named the Information Technology Strategy Committee (ITSC), the group included Duffy, soon-to-be CIO Ken Lacey and Eskew (who was then an industrial engineering VP). There were also representatives from international, UPS's package delivery airline, sales and engineering. "People got involved," recalls Duffy, "because here was a chance to reinvent the company—to create the future." The group's title reflected a belief that information technology would increasingly define the company's future. At the time, senior executives were also concerned that UPS was relying too much on outside vendors and consultants to keep abreast of changing technologies. The problem was, if UPS was hearing about some cutting-edge barcode technology from Gartner or a consultant, so were its competitors. The committee was a way for UPS to develop its own over-the-horizon radar.

UPS had already made a serious commitment to technology. It had introduced its electronic clipboard, the DIAD (delivery information acquisition device), in 1990 to replace the mounds of paperwork drivers previously had to fill out about each pick-up and drop-off. Information from each DIAD's barcode scanner poured into one of the largest private databases in the world and when the DIAD went wireless in 1993, UPS started leasing the largest private cellular network in the world. The company had a huge data center in New Jersey, and was building a redundant one in Atlanta, complete with server banks, mainframes and two sets each of power lines, fiber feeds, water mains, back-up generators, emergency battery rooms and hurricane-proof concrete walls. But the company had to figure out a way to make this information available to its customers while at the same time creating more efficiencies within its operations. But even as UPS's leaders were turbo-charging the core business with technology, they were also beginning to mull over the question of whether UPS had a future that extended beyond package delivery.

The goal of the ITSC was to create some time and space for reflection and exploration in what was otherwise a tightly controlled and tightly focused organization. The committee afforded its members the chance to learn about new trends, new technologies and new customer needs. Beyond that, it was a safe, nonhierarchical forum in which the implications of those needs, trends and technologies could be debated. The discussions ranged across a diverse set of subjects—from the implications of the then a-borning Internet, to bleeding-edge developments in robotics and mechanical engineering to ideas for how customers could benefit from the masses of information that coursed into UPS's vast data warehouses. Ultimately, the committee would bring in people from all over UPS (it touched at least a thousand other managers) in an attempt to mine the well of pent-up imagination that existed in the company. It also sought the views of outside experts and entrepreneurs. The members frequently went on field trips, and were taught early on how to use the Internet so that each of them could better understand its potential impact.

The ITSC was part seminar and part laboratory, part skunk works and part incubator—a place to think deeply and experiment quickly. Its members had the authority to decide whether or not to try experiments in each of their particular functions. "The group launched hundreds of projects and experiments directly, and probably inspired a lot more," says Duffy. The first thing it did was intercept e-commerce. Already in 1995, rogue Internet users within the company were putting up presentations, marketing materials, sales reports and other information on internal websites. Committee members interviewed these early users and came up with a set of best practices and guidelines for the company's internal use of the Web. They also recommended making package tracking information available to customers on the company's public website, which UPS did in 1995. The group authorized the development of software for large shippers that would link back into UPS databases, and the creation of software modules with standard interfaces that would plug into the enterprise software that its customers had already purchased from vendors such as SAP, PeopleSoft, Oracle or i2 Technologies. Customers such as eBay or Amazon.com would also use these interfaces as they sought to integrate UPS package tracking and returns management software into their own websites. UPS even created a corps of special e-commerce account managers whose job was to infiltrate customers' websites with these tools.

The committee also focused on improvements in material handling, which led to a five-year project to dramatically raise the level of automation at the company's main distribution hub in Louisville, Kentucky. The giant four-million-square-foot facility is filled with conveyor belts zig-zagging about, shoots, slides, digital cameras and barcode readers. Every night, UPS planes disgorge a mind-boggling multitude of packages into this labyrinth that then sorts them at a rate of 300,000 pieces an hour. What used to require legions of human package sorters is now done effortlessly by computer-driven machines. "A fundamental insight came out of the ITSC," says Duffy. "An understanding that we are a technology company with trucks versus a trucking company with technology." This significant insight was to prove the launching pad for a dramatic push into new market territory.

To get an early peek at emerging technologies, the committee created a corporate venture fund. The Strategic Enterprise Fund was started in 1997 and pretty much paid for itself through an early investment in an Atlanta-based B2B software start-up called Tradex which was sold to Ariba, netting UPS $200 million when it sold its Ariba shares near their peak in 2000. But unlike other corporate venture funds that were little more than an attempt to ride the dot-com boom, the UPS fund was set up from the get-go as a way to garner strategic insights. For instance, UPS was able to both profit and learn from Tradex, which helped UPS fine-tune its own software modules by being the first external company to adopt them.

"If you are going to have a venture fund, it should contribute back to the core entity," says John Wilson, who now runs the fund. "Before we make an investment," he explains, "both the fund and an operating unit within UPS have to agree there is a learning opportunity. It prevents an operating unit from making a bad investment and me from falling in love with a company." UPS always asked for board observation rights in the companies in which it invested, and that observer would always be pulled from the sponsoring operating unit. This helped to ensure that learning opportunities were fully exploited and that the Strategic Enterprise Fund didn't spend its money on completely tangential opportunities.

The venture fund served as a listening post, keeping UPS executives attuned to the ever-changing winds of technology and to innovations occurring outside the boundaries of their own experience base. It also helped them test their own conceptions of what business opportunities UPS might pursue in the future. The fund's purpose was threefold: to learn about new technologies that might be useful to UPS or its customers (and learn about them early); to be aware of rapidly emerging markets for which UPS might want to create new products or services; and to study novel business models to understand whether they posed any threat or could be adopted within UPS. So, for instance, the fund invested in a start-up called Savi Technologies to gain insight into the progress of radio frequency ID tags. While the cheapest tags (which currently cost about fifty cents each) are still too expensive to affix to every package, they could become a viable alternative to barcodes as their price drops. Similarly, the Strategic Enterprise Fund invested in Air2Web, a company that specializes in putting software applications on wireless devices. UPS also adopted Air2Web's technology and began to offer it as an additional way for customers to track packages, locate drop-off centers and figure out shipping costs.

The fund also helped UPS de-risk new opportunities in unproven markets and business models. One investment in particular prevented UPS from potentially wasting hundreds of millions or even billions of dollars. The start-up, Highpoint Systems, was developing specialized order entry software for grocery chains that needed to respond to the spate of home-delivery competitors such as WebVan and Peapod. In the fall of 2000, Highpoint's president helped UPS design a pilot delivery project with eight nonbranded trucks in a Northeastern city. The project tested the viability of delivering both groceries and dry cleaning. "We determined that the business economics would not be sustainable," says Wilson. Try as it might, UPS could not get the density of deliveries per hour up to a high enough level (six to eight was the goal) to make the business profitable. Everyone wanted deliveries at night, so the trucks and drivers stood unused during most of the day. Through its relationship with Highpoint, UPS confirmed that other such e-commerce grocery delivery businesses were running into the same problems. After a relatively inexpensive experiment costing a few million dollars (including the $1 million invested in Highpoint), UPS pulled the plug, an option that a company like WebVan did not have. In the end, it was a way for UPS to take an appropriately tentative stance on an opportunity riddled with uncertainty.

Though the strategy group was tasked to look beyond UPS's existing businesses, it didn't regard its mission as developing a diversification strategy. Rather, it was to find ways of leveraging the company's strategic assets and core capabilities to *create* new billion-dollar businesses under the broad umbrella of "enabling commerce." For instance, the committee pondered the fact that its drivers captured millions of signature every day on their DIADs, and wondered whether those signatures could constitute a proof of delivery, which would trigger an automatic payment between the recipient and sender. It was ideas like this that led to the launch of UPS Capital, which was established in 1998 as a separate subsidiary to create financial products related to the movement of goods. These included expedited C.O.D. payments, trade credit, credit insurance and electronic invoices. The strategy group also contributed to the formation of the service parts business in the same year.

Over the past five years, UPS's sense of what it is has changed dramatically. Who the company regards as its competitors has also changed. As the supply-chain outsourcing market develops, it will open up UPS to competition from more than just FedEx, Deutsche Post's DHL and the world's mail carriers. "We will end up competing with Accenture and IBM," says Duffy.

Going into logistics represents a major broadening of UPS's scope of operations. The small package delivery market is about a $100 billion industry, and UPS owns 30 percent of that. However, the global logistics and transportation industry is worth approximately $3 trillion—this includes about $1.5 trillion for physical transportation and another $1.5 trillion in other logistics-related services such as warehousing. That's a big opportunity—even for a $30 billion company. DiMaggio, who oversees the combined sales, product development and supply-chain consulting efforts for the logistics, freight forwarding and customs brokerage businesses, thinks the near-term addressable market within that much bigger opportunity is at least $150 billion—that's $150 billion worth of services that lie outside of UPS's traditional package transportation business. That's enough opportunity to keep UPS busy for quite some time—and to drive a whole lot of new growth. Indeed, while UPS's top-line growth was just 3 percent in 2001, the company's nonpackage segment, of which UPS Logistics is the biggest chunk, grew by an impressive 42 percent.

UPS will do anything it can to get a piece of that $150 billion market. Its UPS Logistics subsidiary manages warehouses, trucking fleets, ships, air cargo and all the information transfers required to get customers' inventories from factory to market. Sometimes it uses UPS trucks and planes, sometimes it contracts out to third parties—whatever makes the most sense for the customer. Of course, more than half the time it ends up using the UPS delivery network, driving even more volume through the UPS system and thus keeping it fully utilized.

As UPS broadened its vision to include the world of logistics, it was quick to realize that it didn't possess all the competencies that would be needed to succeed in the logistics space. Working diligently to acquire the new skills, the company has purchased a handful of smaller logistics players. Acquisitions were important in accessing new skills, but so were new hires. About three quarters of the employees who work at UPS Logistics come from outside the parent company and are conversant in the unique logistical challenges of industries such as health care, electronics and apparel.

By 2002, UPS had invested $800 million in its logistics business. But the $800 million didn't get spent all at once. Over and over again, DiMaggio has had to earn the right to up the stakes by meeting strict revenue growth and operating margin targets. UPS isn't going to take a flyer on some far-fetched dream. The logistics business has had to earn its right to explore new opportunity space, dollar-by-dollar.

"I'd be very disappointed if our growth rate in the logistics business was less than 25 percent," says DiMaggio, who sees his role as helping to decommoditize UPS's revenue streams. For instance, in a deal closed in early 2002, UPS won the right to revamp and manage the entire global supply chain of semiconductor equipment manufacturer Applied Materials. After months of carefully studying Applied's various logistics networks, DiMaggio's team suggested ways to rearrange the relationships between Applied and its customers and suppliers. "We're almost like consultants solving their business problems," says DiMaggio. He wants his customers to think of him as a trusted adviser, just like they would Accenture or IBM. Only UPS brings 88,000 trucks and 600 airplanes, as well as systems and software.

The story of how UPS created its service parts logistics business is indicative of how the company works its way into new opportunity areas. In 1998, the ITSC was looking at UPS's IT infrastructure and wondering if perhaps it could outsource some excess capacity in its warehouses, call centers or data centers. It explored these notions for six months, asking customers for their input. The data center management business proved untenable. There were also some challenging barriers to developing a third-party call center business. Michael Dell told a visiting UPS delegation that he would never outsource his call centers because that is one of the key ways his company learns about consumer desires and frustrations. But as the team kept mulling over ways in which it might use its assets to build businesses that would be nonthreatening to its current customers, it struck upon a quite different opportunity.

When UPS went to talk to computer makers like Dell and Hewlett-Packard, it noticed a common, albeit unvoiced, need. Hardware manufacturers all seemed to be having problems with managing their spare parts inventory. Duffy explains: "We came across an inefficiency that [original equipment manufacturers] had in terms of parts replacement—each OEM had their own system, even though most of the parts were standard. We realized that if we could consolidate all this, and then go to the IBMs, Compaqs and Dells, we could help them manage their parts inventory much more efficiently." Not knowing what repair challenge they might face next, computer technicians tend to keep a broad range of spare parts in the trunks of their cars. In an industry where the value of parts goes down every week, and many become obsolete within a matter of months, this "trunk inventory" was a huge waste.

For a company that makes a science out of getting things in and out of vehicles as quickly as possible, the very notion of "trunk inventory" was abhorrent to UPS. There had to be a better way. UPS could place the parts in a nationwide network of stock houses and manage them so that it could get a part to a technician within four hours of a call. UPS could also supplement these stock houses with same-day air delivery service via Sonic Air, a company UPS had acquired a few years earlier. After the service parts business was launched Sonic Air's revenue growth went from the low-single digits a year to 100 percent a year.

One key to renewal is the capacity to reinterpret your own history. In a way, the service parts logistics business was a reprise of an earlier UPS strategy. In the 1920s, department stores like Macy's, Saks and Gimbles each maintained their own fleet of trucks, just like IBM, Dell and HP maintained their own inventory of service parts in the 1990s. At the time, UPS founder Jim Casey convinced the otherwise fiercely competitive department stores to let UPS consolidate their deliveries. More than 70 years later, UPS would be consolidating and managing the global flow of spare parts for a group of otherwise bitter rivals in the computer industry.

Renewal is also about balancing what you are with what you could be. UPS has been able to do that by managing the tension between the need to experiment and grow while maintaining tight operational discipline within the core business. "We have [new] subsidiaries," explains Eskew. "They are nimble, entrepreneurial, innovative, quick. We tell them to try new things and fail small and fast. That is what our subsidiaries do. On the other hand our core company requires precision. You have to be deliberate and consistent across 200 countries because customers expect the same experience all across the world." The new and the old are tightly intertwined at UPS. New businesses such as UPS Logistics and UPS Capital are demand multipliers for the core business. Additionally, they leverage the enormous breadth of competencies UPS has assembled over the years. The new and the old play equally critical parts in the mosaic of enabling global commerce. A decade ago, few would have guessed that a company so disciplined in its quest to optimize what already is, could successfully create a capacity to explore what could be. Yet this is exactly what this gray-haired revolutionary has done.

LESSONS FROM A GRAY-HAIRED REVOLUTIONARY:

The essential foundation of UPS's capacity to leverage its assets and competencies are these:

○ An *out-sized aspiration* to grab a big chunk of the $1.5 trillion global logistics business—a sense of an enormous opportunity, there for the taking.
○ A *broad definition of business boundaries* (not package delivery but enabling global commerce), based on a deep understanding of the company's core competencies in transportation logistics, package tracking and handling and information systems.
○ A *learn-as-you-go* approach to new business development, which puts a premium on experimentation and rapid learning.
○ A willingness to bring in *new voices* to fuel the innovation effort. The ITSC tapped the imagination of hundreds of UPS employees as it explored the new growth options.

There are precious few companies that ever manage to create new multibillion-dollar businesses from within. Even more rare is an ability to reconfigure the profit engine in a company's core business. This is akin to changing jet engines in mid-flight. Yet this is exactly what Charles Schwab has accomplished—more than once.

CHARLES SCHWAB: BRICKS AND CLICKS

David Pottruck, president and co-CEO at Charles Schwab, puts it this way: "We're change junkies. We're addicted to change." Born a rule-breaker, Charles Schwab & Co. led its first revolution when it helped to create the discount brokerage industry by undercutting the steep fees of traditional brokers such as Merrill Lynch and PaineWebber. Its second revolution came with OneSource, a mutual fund supermarket that eventually let investors choose from more than a thousand different funds. Before OneSource it was difficult for investors to move assets between funds, and anyone with more than a few investments received a bewildering array of statements every month. By the late 1990s, Schwab's convenient one-stop shop for mutual funds had accumulated 10 percent of America's mutual fund assets in no-load funds and the company no longer relied so heavily on trading revenues. Between 1993 and 1998, the percentage of Schwab's revenues coming from commissions on stock trading had declined from 75 percent to 58 percent, attesting to the revolution in Schwab's business concept. Schwab's metamorphosis from discount broker to mutual fund powerhouse is only one of several strategy transformations Schwab has accomplished. Each metamorphosis has threatened to undermine historic sources of profitability, yet each has ultimately paid off by bringing customers fundamentally new benefits. Before OneSource, Schwab charged its clients a fee for the convenience of buying mutual funds in one place. Customers could avoid the fee by buying their no-load funds directly from the issuing investment companies. Irked that customers should have to pay more at Schwab than elsewhere, David Pottruck, then an executive vice president, was one of those who argued for doing away with the fee. Others at Schwab protested that this would cut the profitability of the company's mutual fund business in half. Ultimately the interests of the customer prevailed, and Schwab was able to recoup the lost fees by charging a small processing fee to the companies whose mutual funds Schwab was selling.

Schwab fought the cannibalization demon a second time when the company morphed itself into the nation's leading online broker. Deciding to make cheap Web trading available to all its customers was a gut-wrenching decision that slashed the company's commission for those trades by more than half. But by late 1999, Schwab boasted three million Internet customers with more than $260 billion in online assets (rival E*TRADE's assets were only one-tenth that size). With its Web offerings, Schwab recast itself as a new kind of full-service broker and entered the Age of Advice, coming full circle from its early days when it thought "advice" was a dirty word. "We are reinventing the full-service investing business and ourselves at the same time," says Pottruck. Schwab's conception of who it serves has also been a moving target. During its first decade, for instance, Schwab thought of itself as a no-frills broker that catered to sophisticated traders. Yet even within the discount brokerage industry, Schwab bucked conventional wisdom. Instead of sticking to a low-overhead, phone-based business, it started to build a network of branches. Chuck Schwab figured that people wanted to feel physically close to their money. This insight paid off handsomely when the company began to broaden its target audience. As investing became democratized—first through mutual funds, then via the Web—Schwab found that its branches were terrific for capturing neophyte investors because they gave Schwab bricks-and-mortar credibility. In 1999 customers opened more than one million new accounts at Schwab. Many of these investors had never had a broker before. In the process Schwab became one of the first "clicks-and-mortar" companies, with a business concept that optimized both its online and its offline presence.

Schwab's knack for reinvention and finding new business models has allowed it to thrive where others have foundered. It long ago zoomed past Quick & Reilly, its toughest competitor in the 1970s. From 1993 to 1998, Schwab's revenues grew at an average annual rate of 23 percent to $2.7 billion, and its earnings grew at an average annual rate of 24 percent to $350 million. During the same period, its stock price zoomed up 1,072 percent, as compared with 218 percent for Merrill Lynch and 164 percent for the S&P 500. In December 1998, Schwab's market capitalization surpassed that of Merrill Lynch for the first time ever. No one in the brokerage industry doubts that Schwab has been a revolutionary more than once.

IN LOVE WITH CUSTOMERS

SCHWAB HAS NEVER LET ITSELF BECOME TRAPPED IN ANY ONE PARTICULAR BUSINESS MODEL. Jeff Lyons, head of mutual fund marketing, says, "We have a hard time defining ourselves. We're uncomfortable with any of the labels." Rather, Schwab has always defined itself in terms of its cause, which is to serve investors by doing whatever it takes to help them secure and improve their financial lives. "When Chuck Schwab started the company," says John McGonigle, who runs the mutual funds group, "his goal was to make it a place where he would feel comfortable doing business as an investor. Chuck is the voice of the customer." One of the company's widely communicated and deeply held values is customer empathy, and Chuck Schwab is its foremost apostle. Says Bob Duste, CEO of Schwab Europe:

> I have never heard Chuck raving on about returns, profits or the share price. He is always talking about customers. He believes we need to do more to teach people how to invest—not for us, but for them. If we do right by the customer, he knows profitability will take care of itself. Chuck goes once a month to serve soup to old people at a Salvation Army kitchen. He says, "If they would have started early and planned, they could have avoided this, and it just breaks my heart. We have to have better products and reach more people."

Schwab's rank and file see their jobs not just as processing transactions, but as protecting some of the most precious things in a customer's life: the ability to send a kid to college, to support an elderly parent or to retire stress-free. "We think we're curing cancer," says chief strategist Dan Leemon.

Schwab has repeatedly found the courage to challenge industry dogmas by working from the customer backward. While other parts of the financial services industry seem to look on customer ignorance as a profit center, Schwab always assumes it is serving a very discerning customer—even when it is not. Comments McGonigle: "What distinguishes Schwab from most of the other financial services companies is that we presume that our customers are really smart and we're not going to pull anything over on them. We don't think we can fool them on fees or execution."

Schwab's unconventional strategies have often left competitors scrambling. It took Fidelity six years to fully embrace the idea of a mutual fund supermarket like OneSource because it was loath to carry competing products and surrender some of its management fees to other companies.

Schwab complements its customer worship with bold growth targets. Says Art Shaw, a senior VP:

Every year we feel we have to grow 20 percent. Every year we
have to say that last year is over, and we're starting from zero.
This creates an incredible desire to innovate. Only about 10
percent of large companies have grown both their revenues and
earnings 20 percent per year for five years in a row.

Schwab sees itself as addressing a nearly limitless market. Of America's
$15 trillion in savings, only 4 percent sits in discount brokerage
accounts, and Schwab itself holds only about $600 billion. Its goal is to
grab $1 trillion worth of assets before 2005 and nearly double its num-
ber of active customers to 10 million.

Besides its ardor for customers and ambitious growth goals, there
are two other forces powering innovation at Schwab. The first is the
opportunity that every employee has for wealth creation. Every
employee at Schwab is a shareholder. Says CFO Steve Scheid, "One of
the best financial disciplines is having your largest shareholder walking the halls thinking about serving customers." McGonigle, who previously worked at a giant bank, says, "At Schwab, the customer and the
shareholder are preeminent. At my bank they were theoretical constructs."

The other spur for innovation is a meritocracy that welcomes new
ideas. At Schwab the champions of innovation have been consistently
promoted out of rank and out of order. Jeff Lyons, John McGonigle and
Bob Duste were all activists who got early passes to an executive suite.
"Everyone in top management had a big idea when they were more
junior," says Susanne Lyons, Jeff's wife and another innovation activist
at Schwab. She adds, "Each of us did something with our idea and got
rewarded for it." Around Schwab, Susanne Lyons is known as the
"Queen of Segmentation." When she first arrived at Schwab in 1992
from Fidelity, Schwab's approach to customers was pretty much one
size fits all. Every customer had to call the same 1–800 numbers and
got the same plain–vanilla service, whether they had $3,000 in their
account or $300,000. But Lyons noticed that an elite group of customers
known as the "Schwab 500," which included some of Chuck Schwab's
friends and acquaintances, was getting special, personalized service
from a small team of eight account representatives. She thought, "Why
not replicate this on a much bigger scale? We could have these small
teams serving affluent investors." Her enthusiasm ran headlong into a
wall of resistance because most folks at Schwab thought the notion of
a premium service conflicted with the company's core value of treating the small investor well and every investor alike. So she started col-
lecting data on Schwab's more affluent customers and its most active

traders. She discovered that although they represented only 20 percent of Schwab's customer base, they accounted for an astounding 80 percent of its trading revenues. Now she had the ammunition to argue for the expansion of the Schwab 500 and to help her colleagues rethink their definition of "fairness." Why shouldn't investors who brought more value to Schwab get more value in return? Wasn't that simply fair? This logic won most people over.

Starting with the customers already in the Schwab 500, Lyons launched the service in 1994. It was targeted at investors who traded more than 48 times a year (later reduced to 24 and then to 12) or people with more than $100,000 in assets. Schwab started using Caller ID technology to automatically route calls from high-asset individuals to the special teams. A live person was available 24 hours a day, thus providing a level of round-the-clock personal service unmatched by traditional brokerages. Each eight-person team was given responsibility for a specific set of accounts, so that a customer could be assured of always talking to someone who really did understand his or her particular situation. Each team comprised individuals representing a broad spectrum of investment expertise. By 1999, around 750,000 customers were enrolled in Schwab 500, which had been renamed "Signature Services."

LEAPING ONTO THE WEB

Susanne Lyons's story is not unique. **Most of Schwab's mega-innovations have been built on a series of mini-innovations, driven by individuals who've learned to live inside their customers' skins.** Dramatic business concept breakthroughs such as Signature Services and schwab.com are more often the product of a string of rule-bending experiments than some grand strategic leap—more like a tireless climber bounding up a spiral staircase than Superman leaping over tall buildings in a single bound. In the same way that Schwab 500 prepared the way for Signature Services, a long string of technology-oriented experiments helped Schwab beat many of its traditional competitors to the Web.

A few of Schwab's early experiments with technology, such as its StreetSmart dial-up trading software, were modest successes, but most were dismal failures. In 1982, for instance, Schwab came out with the PocketTerm, a bulky, portable contraption that could receive stock quotes over the airwaves. In 1985, it unveiled SchwabLine, a device that, when connected to a phone line, would spit out quotes on an extra-wide roll of adding machine tape. Schwab also developed a slew of stock-trading software programs that bombed. Nevertheless, the young innovation addicts at Schwab were encouraged to build these early flying machines.

Every so often, Schwab's penchant for experimentation would turn up a winner. TeleBroker was an idea that came from outside Schwab. In 1989, a small start-up came to Schwab and demoed a technology that would allow investors to check quotes and trade stocks using the keypad on a Touch-Tone telephone. Schwab's call centers were constantly busy, and here was an inexpensive way to increase the number of calls it could handle without hiring more people. Duste, who was head of software engineering at the time, took the idea to a senior VP in the retail service group. He ran straight into trouble. Recalls Duste: "The business people thought this was a terrible idea. They thought customers would reject it because customers want to speak with a real person, or wouldn't be able to use the keypad. They couldn't understand it, because they couldn't imagine how it would be used."

Instead of arguing with them, Duste had two of his developers build a demo and roll it out in a pilot test. Customers found its deep, automated voice soothing and telephone trading highly convenient. Within six months, TeleBroker was available to all of Schwab's customers. As one Schwab manager puts it, "Around here the pilot is the first week of the rollout."

By 1995, about a fifth of Schwab's trading volume was going through TeleBroker and StreetSmart. And with the promise of the Internet glistening on the horizon, Duste worked with a few passionate technologists to build another demo to show Pottruck and Chuck Schwab that they could do TeleBroker on the Web. When Schwab saw the demo, he was dumbfounded. "I fell off my chair," he later told *Fortune*. Duste and his colleagues didn't write an elaborate strategy paper on how the Web would transform investing. Instead they gave Schwab and Pottruck a first-person, hands-on experience of Web trading. Pottruck immediately set up a Web-trading unit called e.Schwab. It was up and running on the Web by mid-1996 and attracted 25,000 customers in its first two weeks.

But as the Web blossomed, cracks in the e.Schwab business model started to appear. Customers who used e.Schwab were given a 40 percent discount off the company's usual charges, but Schwab was still twice as expensive as E*TRADE. And there was another catch: Schwab's online clients were not allowed to call Schwab's phone representatives or visit its branches—they had to agree to do all their business over the Web. A traditional Schwab customer who wanted to trade online had to set up a new account. Pottruck wanted to do away with this dual structure, but there was a lot of concern among the senior officers that doing so would hammer profits. They thought that encouraging traditional customers to trade online would cannibalize transaction fees. Conversely, it was feared that the fees generated by new online customers wouldn't be sufficient to cover the cost of in-person service at Schwab branches or phone help from Schwab's call centers.

But once again, the desire to do right by the customer overcame the initial concern over cannibalization. As one senior executive put it:

> We asked ourselves whether Internet trading was the right thing
> to do for the customer—and the answer was "yes." It would mean
> better information, more timely information, quicker access to
> their account, and so on. Once this was clear, we knew we had to
> make the move sooner rather than later. We couldn't wait
> until we had an ironclad business case. It's our responsibility, not
> the customer's, to figure out how to make money in the new
> Internet business model.

In January 1998, Web trading was opened up to all Schwab customers and e.Schwab was rechristened schwab.com. By the end of the year, 61 percent of all Schwab's trades were being completed over the Web. Between the first quarter of 1998 and the first quarter of 1999, Schwab gained nearly one million new customers (almost all of them online), commissions increased 60 percent, online assets doubled and total assets were up 33 percent.

Could Schwab have beaten Merrill Lynch and other traditional brokers to the Web without a succession of earlier mini-innovations? Most at Schwab doubt it. Customer behavior and business concepts seldom get changed in one fell swoop. **Schwab's relentless pursuit of a better customer experience had once again paved the way for a radical rebirth of the company's strategy.**

OVERCOMING ORTHODOXY

Success typically turns beliefs into unquestioned orthodoxy. Yet unlike most companies, Schwab has again and again challenged its deep-seated beliefs. For example, since the company's founding, Schwab has had an aversion to giving advice and hawking proprietary products. As a result, the company has avoided the kind of conflict-of–interest dilemmas that have bedeviled other investment firms. Schwab's image of studied neutrality has long been highly valued by customers. But a wave of newbie customers, who are far less sophisticated than Schwab's original high–volume traders, has forced the company to revisit this particular bit of dogma.

Explains Pottruck:

> For a long time we thought advice was a self–serving path. That was the reality we saw in the rest of the investing industry. Advice always had a self–serving motive, whether it was to push proprietary products or to get paid for the trade. So we said, "We don't give advice." We no longer have that luxury. Today, in excess of 50 percent of our new customers have no investing experience. They don't want us to just give them a brochure.

Schwab was able to move beyond the advice/neutrality impasse only once it realized that this was a false dichotomy—that values and habits could be separated. Says Art Shaw:

> Giving advice has nothing to do with our values, but avoiding conflict of interest does. Advice had a lot of connotations from the world we left behind—we had an allergic reaction to advice. So we had to ask a new question: "How do you give advice without a conflict of interest?"

So in 1994, Schwab launched AdvisorSource, a network of some of its independent money managers to which it began to refer customers who felt they needed counsel. The company has also launched several index–linked funds under the Schwab brand name, a move that lets Schwab keep more mutual fund profit in–house, but keeps the firm out of the stock–picking game. And of course it provides investment research tools on the Web as a form of self–directed advice.

The double whammy of September 11 and the economic recession pummeled the earnings of every financial services company—and Schwab was no exception. Like many other brokerages, Schwab announced a loss for the fourth quarter of 2001—its first loss since the stock market crash of 1987. But with client accounts totaling more than $840 billion, Schwab is still the undisputed king of the discount brokers. And those who know Schwab's people and their penchant for unconventional thinking and customer–centric innovation have little doubt that the company will emerge from difficult times stronger than ever. After all, innovation can't protect a company from a macroeconomic meltdown, but it can soften the blow and raise the odds of a rapid rebound.

LESSONS FROM A GRAY-HAIRED REVOLUTIONARY:

Schwab's capacity for relentless innovation is a product of:

○ *Outrageously ambitious growth* objectives that are simply unattainable without business concept innovation.
○ A *heart-felt customer empathy* that ensures that employees are always working from the customer in, rather than from their existing processes and offerings out.
○ An *innovation meritocracy* where great ideas win out, no matter where they come from.
○ *Rapid experimentation and prototyping* that let innovators test and define new ideas at a speed that leaves traditional competitors breathless.
○ A *loose and evolving definition of the service offering*, which ensures that Schwab doesn't get boxed in by its own orthodoxies.

So maybe your company isn't in a business that is quite as exhilarating as stock trading. Given all the changes in financial services over the past decade (deregulation, the explosive growth of the mutual fund industry and the market rally of the late 1990s), there have been a lot of opportunities for nimble incumbents and ambitious upstarts to change the rules. Perhaps you're asking, how do you innovate in an industry that seems completely and utterly boring? Good question. Where would you begin if your core business was cement?

CEMEX: NOTHING IS SET IN CEMENT

If there was ever any question that adversity breeds creativity, one need only take a drive through the hardscrabble city of Monterrey, Mexico's industrial capital and the headquarters of Cemex, the country's most innovative multinational cement producer. The cement industry isn't the most obvious place to search for examples of revolution and renewal, but then again, neither is Mexico. But Cemex is no ordinary clinker. As the third-largest cement company in the world, Cemex enjoys operating margins that are nearly twice as high as those of its two global rivals—France's Lafarge and Switzerland's Holcim. In 2001, a tough year in general for the world economy, Cemex's sales managed to expand a healthy 23 percent to $6.9 billion, and its profits grew at about the same clip, to $1.3 billion. Success on this scale would have seemed wildly improbable a scant decade earlier, when Cemex's very independence was threatened by the decision to open the Mexican market to foreign competition. With a peso–denominated balance sheet, Cemex faced a significant cost of capital disadvantage vis-à-vis its international competitors. (The 1994 peso freefall did not help matters, either.) But hardship isn't exactly a novelty in Northern Mexico, and Cemex's disadvantages forced the ambitious company to innovate in ways few of its competitors could have anticipated or matched. Along the way, Cemex proved there's no such thing as a mature industry, only mature thinking.

Cemex is proof positive **that new attitudes and new values can change an old industry**—in the case of Cemex, attitudes like curiosity and experimentation, and values like ambition and persistence. To put it simply, the more conventional the industry, the greater the power of unconventional thinking. "We understand our real business is helping our customers complete their construction projects," CEO Lorenzo Zambrano told a Stanford University audience in January 2002. "At the end of the day, no one *wants* to buy cement; they *want* to build a house or a bridge or a road." In contrast, the conventional attitude in this industry is: We make the cement, the customer worries about what to do with it. At the root of the company's restless innovation is an inbred dissatisfaction with the status quo and an unquenchable thirst for growth. "There is this ever–present search for something that is better than what we are doing," says executive VP of Planning and Finance Hector Medina. "We have a passion for growth," adds Juan Romero, president of Cemex Mexico.

This passion has spawned dozens of growth initiatives across the company—from GPS–guided delivery trucks to cheaper fuels to new methods for building houses in the developing world. Cemex has demonstrated a capability to reinvent its core business while explor-ing white spaces where new businesses may emerge. It stokes the fires of innovation by combining and recombining networks of curious people with diverse backgrounds who together find unorthodox solu-tions to customer problems.

Founded by Lorenzo Zambrano's grandfather in 1906, Cemex remained a venerable, family–owned enterprise until 1976 when it first offered shares on the Mexican stock exchange (its ADRs began trading on the New York Stock Exchange much later, in 1999). Zambrano, an engineer and Stanford–trained MBA, took over as CEO in 1985. Eager to push the company beyond its tradition–bound roots as a regional cement producer, Zambrano started by broadening the company's management team, hiring executives from a range of other industries. One of Zambrano's key hires was Gelacio Iñiguez as chief information officer. Starting from scratch, Iñiguez committed himself to building a common IT infrastructure throughout the company so that executives and plant managers could learn from each other and build a foundation of common business knowledge. "I knew we had to remove any barriers that would inhibit human interaction," recalls Iñiguez. "We needed to share practices from north to south and east to west."

Understandably, plant managers were less eager to remove the barriers that had long protected their local prerogatives. In the late 1980s, even basic phone service was often patchy. It was common practice among plant managers to tell their secretaries to take messages for incoming corporate phone calls, knowing it would take three or four hours for the caller to get another connection. In the meantime, the plant manager would be able to develop a well-reasoned answer to the corporate inquiry. This practice highlighted the appalling lack of communication within the company. Not surprisingly, one of Iñiguez' first steps was to install satellite phones at every plant.

Iñiguez was up against more than antiquated technology. Some of the more tradition-minded executives at Cemex thought that spending money on IT was a frivolous waste of money. They were initially dismissive of Iñiguez' efforts: "We don't need this approach—cement sells itself." At the time, this was a common perception both inside Cemex and across the industry. Demand for cement went up and down with GNP growth—that was simply a fact of life, or so the thinking went.

Undeterred, and with Zambrano's backing, Iñiguez pushed on. The satellite system served as the backbone for Cemex's budding internal computer network. It allowed Iñiguez to begin to install a computer platform that linked all the company's plants, warehouses and office locations. The goal was not standardization for its own sake, but rather a common platform that would enable common performance measures and the development of a common base of business knowledge. Once every plant was online, and reporting daily and monthly performance statistics, it would be easy to pinpoint opportunities to transfer local innovation across the company. While this was not exactly a new idea, it was a new idea for the cement industry. Around the world, cement was a classic local-for-local business. Transportation diseconomies limited the catchment area of any individual plant. Even large cement companies treated their plants as autonomous and largely disconnected outposts. From the beginning, Cemex management believed that ideas could be transported

around the world, even if cement could not. They were eager to build a platform that would expedite the spread of new ideas across Cemex.

The IT system was an essential tool for spreading information and learning among Cemex's plants. Before, if a plant manager wanted to improve a production process, he would have to send a written request to the central office for approval. All the reporting and approval lines ran vertically, up to headquarters in Monterrey. There was little sharing of information horizontally across production facilities and commercial organizations. Capital budgeting and planning were centralized but not terribly well coordinated. Plant managers regarded head office bureaucrats as poorly informed and prone to interfere, and were to be avoided at all costs (hence the drawn-out games of phone tag). Local managers reaped few benefits from being part of a company with operations across the Mexican isthmus.

The new IT system started gathering core production and sales data from every plant, making it available to executives on their desktops. The data was presented in a way that even a technophobe could understand—a map of Mexico served as the graphical user interface. The map was dotted with a dozen icons representing each plant. Any executive could click on a dot to obtain a chart of relevant operating data from that business unit such as sales, average energy consumption, number of work stoppages or raw material inventories. Zambrano became one of the most avid users of this system. "Every day at noon, Mr. Z. religiously would log into the executive information system and check what had happened in the last 24 hours," reports Iñiguez. The dots were color-coded green, yellow and red, with a red dot indicating that a plant or sales center was behind its budget forecast. If Mr. Z saw a red pulsating dot, he would personally call the manager of that plant and ask some rather pointed questions.

Suddenly tethered to headquarters by a reliable satellite phone system and computer network, local managers quickly learned that they had better have good answers when Señor Zambrano called. In self-defense, they started using the system themselves. If they saw a sister facility was achieving better results in, say, energy utilization per ton of cement produced, they'd call that manager to find out what he was doing differently. In this way, standard measures and transparent performance metrics fostered greater sharing and cross-collaboration between managers who had only recently ruled over cement-producing islands.

While Zambrano was shaking up the culture internally, he was also expanding externally. He watched warily as the cement industry began to consolidate in the developed economies. He realized that sooner or later Mexico would be compelled to open its long-protected domestic markets. With this in mind, Zambrano moved to sell off Cemex's mining and petrochemical interests—businesses he believed would be a distraction in the coming battle to defend Cemex's core business from foreign invaders. "We saw that our global competitors were all focussed on cement and that they were making investments all over the world," recalls Medina. It was clear to Mr. Z and his top lieutenants that Cemex would have to become a global consolidator itself, or else risk becoming consolidated. "We had to do this to survive," says Medina. So with the proceeds from the divestments, Cemex began doing some acquiring of its own, plunking down $1 billion for competitors in Mexico that might otherwise be attractive acquisition targets for Lafarge, Holcim or some other multinational.

Ever mindful of the company's high cost of capital (which hovered in the high teens, versus the middle single digits for its European and American counterparts), Zambrano challenged the organization to innovate in ways that would more than compensate for this cost deficit. The result: hundreds of opportunities for improvements in the manufacture and distribution of cement—improvements that rapidly migrated from plant to plant. One barometer of the way in which these mini-innovations produced macro results: Between 1989 and 1995, the company cut its workforce in half to 7,500, yet increased its cement-producing capacity by more than 20 percent. Another barometer: For the entire period between 1990 and 2001, sales increased at a 16 percent annual rate, while headcount only increased 4 percent.

Bulking up at home also prepared Cemex for its own preemptive leap overseas. Having used the specter of foreign competition to turbocharge innovation at home, Cemex was ready to export its learning via foreign acquisitions. In 1992, Cemex made its first foray overseas with its purchase of two cement companies in Spain. Those were followed by a buying spree that took the company from Venezuela, to Colombia, Egypt, the Philippines and the United States. Having once acquired a foreign cement company, Cemex was able to raise its operating margins as much as 20 percent. And with each acquisition, the timetable for achieving these results got shorter. It took 18 months for Cemex to bring its Spanish acquisitions up to the company's demanding benchmarks, while Southdown, a Houston-based cement company acquired in 2000, came up to standard in only four months.

Everyone at Cemex realized that the faster the company integrated a new acquisition, the faster it would earn back its investment, which would help to lower its effective cost of capital. Cemex found other creative strategies for addressing its cost of capital challenge, including placing its international assets on the books of its Spanish subsidiary (whose accounts were denominated in dollars) and pursuing a sophisticated interest-rate hedging strategy. By the end of 2001, Cemex had worked its cost of capital down to a competitive 8 percent.

In many companies, there is an unspoken belief that new ideas start at the top, with corporate R&D or new product development—and proceed from the center out. But the goal at Cemex is not centralization but learning. Zambrano, Medina, Francisco Garza (head of North America) and other senior executives realize that a lot of innovation is local. Correspondingly, operating units need the freedom and encouragement to try new things. In their quest to ensure that innovations don't stay local, Cemex executives have created a wide variety of cross-pollinating mechanisms such as cross-cultural teams that oversee merger integration, in-person monthly meetings of country managers, and computer-based performance metrics. For its part, Cemex never set out to build a computer network, *per se;* rather, it set out to build a learning and innovation network. And even the parent can learn. When Cemex acquired its Spanish operations, it noticed that the plants there were using coal as fuel. Cemex had spent years trying to figure out how to use cheaper coal for fuel, but had repeatedly failed to achieve the necessary fuel efficiency. Within months of the Spanish acquisition, the coal fuel technology had been transferred back to Cemex's Mexican operations.

Cemex is able to integrate its acquisitions rapidly because it possesses common processes and a common scorecard by which to measure performance. This allows Cemex to quickly determine where a newly acquired company needs to improve, and, just as important, where it may be able to contribute new learning to the rest of Cemex. The Cemex Way, as it is known, is implanted in newly acquired companies via a postmerger integration (PMI) team, whose members are among the most talented managers and functional experts in the company. Having landed on-site, the PMI team actively looks for frustrated innovators and savvy operators who have been ignored or undervalued by the previous management team. Unleashing this pent-up energy and imagination is a key part of the integration process. Sure, GE Capital and other serial acquirers rely on similar integration teams, but like its earlier IT innovation, this was a first for the cement industry. **And being first in your industry is all that is required for innovation to pay off.**

Cemex's $3 billion acquisition of Southdown in 2000 provides a case in point. Southdown was the second-largest cement company in the

United States when acquired by Cemex, yet its operations were highly decentralized. The central dispatch system used in Florida, for example, was not used in California. Each plant had its own IT and accounting department. There was no common performance scorecard, and thus no common "language" for sharing ideas. Francisco Garza, president of North American operations and trading, explains how Cemex reined in this accounting mish-mash: "Some plants would include their environmental costs [in their monthly reports], and others wouldn't. In the past, each plant would buy its own fuel oils. No more. These are non-negotiable. On the other hand, we allow them to try new fuels—in some places we can use waste oils or tires. They don't have to ask permission [to try something new] if it brings in more profit." So, crucially, the scorecard is not a straitjacket. It's not conformance that Cemex is after, but the freedom to pursue opportunities for radical improvement and visibility for new ideas that deserve to be widely emulated.

It is this tension between ensuring respect for best practice and, at the same time, encouraging innovation, that is the essence of the Cemex Way. The trick is to get rid of gratuitous variety without killing off experimentation. "We tackle this," says Medina, "by declaring very firmly that the way we do things is not established. If you have a better way to do things, people will be interested in spreading that practice around."

At Cemex, innovation is a collective act, not just the product of a single, brilliant thinker. It occurs at the juncture between different attitudes, outlooks and life experiences. Thus it requires people with a combination of skills working together to solve problems, who feel jointly responsible for success. If collaboration and trust are absent, innovation becomes difficult. That is why the PMI team does not arrive like a conquering army, giving orders and demanding compliance. Instead, they talk to the existing managers and employees, delve deeply into existing practices, and together come up with a better approach. "There is a lot of innovation that we do locally, but we are obsessive about transferring that from one country to another," says Juan Pablo San Agustin, head of Cemex's new business incubator, CxNetworks. Sharing best practices is fine, but it won't keep you ahead very long unless new best practices are being created and shared all the time. For instance, the Mexican plants adopted the coal-burning methods of the Spanish subsidiary in the early 1990s. More recently, another Spanish plant figured out how to use an even cheaper fuel in its kilns: petroleum coke. Normally, when petroleum coke is burned it produces gases with high sulfur content that build up in the kiln and cause blockages in its pre-heating tower. But a kiln manager in Spain found a way around this problem by changing the chemical composition of the raw materials so that they bind with the sulfur upon heating. Now this method, which has the added benefit of being more environmentally friendly, is being spread to Cemex's subsidiaries across the globe.

Sometimes outsiders can see opportunities that time and familiarity have rendered invisible to insiders. It was this thought that prompted Garza, then head of the Venezuelan operations, to suggest that the company convene a PMI-like team from managers of acquired companies and challenge them to come up with ideas for radical improvements to the operations back in Mexico. Garza led a group of 45 managers from Spain, Colombia, Venezuela and elsewhere who came to crawl through the mother ship. "The chairman was skeptical at first," says San Agustin, then a young Spanish executive who worked for Garza on this team, "but in six months we found close to $100 million in annual operations savings." Among other contributions, the multinational team found a way to streamline logistics, allowing Cemex to close two cement plants. As a result of this exercise, talent from the various countries began to cycle more regularly through executive positions within Mexico. "We decided that if we were going to be a truly multinational company, we would need to be multinational even at home," says San Agustin. These intersecting career paths are yet another highway for innovation at Cemex.

This collaborative approach to solving business problems is ingrained in the Cemex culture. For example, in the early 1990s, a group of Cemex managers, including Iñiguez, were trying to figure out how the company could take orders for ready-mix cement and deliver them on the same day. Because contractors often change their orders at the last minute, Cemex veterans believed that the idea would only work if Cemex was prepared to punish customers who changed their orders by charging a change fee. Moreover, giving customers the right to order with less than 24 hours' notice would dramatically complicate production scheduling. Iñiguez remembers telling the skeptics, "This is crazy, you can't punish customers." If simple logic wasn't enough to win the day, maybe a real world example would sway the skeptics. So Iñiguez and his fellow zealots pulled together a microcosm of Cemex— plant managers, salesmen, credit managers—and packed them to Houston to visit the city's 911 call center. After visiting the 911 dispatch center, the visitors retreated to a hotel to discuss what they had witnessed. Using the power of analogy to expand their horizons, Iñiguez asked, "A month ago you said it was impossible to put cement in a truck without more than 24 hours' notice—so how is Houston able to assemble a team of paramedics inside a truck within ten minutes in order to save a life?" Iñiguez made his point.

As a result of this thinking, Cemex set up a GPS dispatch system which was christened the Dynamic Synchronization of Operations or DSO. Today, Cemex's fleet of 1,500 cement-mixing trucks in Mexico are equipped with GPS locators and data terminals which allow them to be routed to construction sites based on ever-changing demand. The dispatchers are now able to guarantee delivery of cement within a 20-minute window, instead of the three hours that was previously the norm. Not only do customers get a substantially more responsive service, Cemex's delivery costs for ready-mix cement have also dropped by 35 percent. (Ready-mix cement accounts for about a quarter of Cemex's revenues, with the rest coming from bagged cement powder sold to contractors and consumers who mix it themselves.) Initiatives like the DSO are the reason Cemex is now a global benchmark for the innovative use of information technology.

Thus, the Cemex Way is not only a method for integrating acquisitions, it is also a recipe for collaboration that is replicated again and again across the company. "We bring together a network of people involved with any issue, and let them talk about the problems that come from a lack of collaboration or coordination," says Iñiguez, explaining Cemex's approach to problem solving in general. Cemex has been able to create a culture of experimentation where probing minds are welcome. "We are very good at hiring people who have this attitude of curiosity," says Medina. "They have a researcher's attitude."

WHAT MAKES CEMEX ONE OF THE MOST HIGHLY REGARDED EMPLOYERS IN MEXICO IS NOT THE, AHEM, GLAMOR OF THE CEMENT INDUSTRY, BUT THE OPPORTUNITY THE COMPANY AFFORDS TO AMBITIOUS AND CONTRARIAN INDIVIDUALS. They may be making cement, but no one at Cemex believes they have to live by the limits that constrain their competitors. As Mr. Z put it in that Stanford speech: "The Cemex Way ... [is] aiming at nothing less than to reinvent our company and our industry." Ask yourself, how often have you come across a company where dramatic reinvention is the cornerstone of the firm's espoused values? The key to keeping the spirit of reinvention alive, says Medina, is "to make sure that people don't think they've arrived, that they don't believe that success can be taken for granted."

Within Cemex, one of the most critical mechanisms for sharing ideas and challenging conventional thinking is the monthly country managers' meeting. Each month, Señor Zambrano meets with all of his country managers, sometimes in Monterrey, but often in cities outside Mexico. Few multinationals bring their country managers together on such a frequent basis, but Cemex believes frequent face-to-face communication is critical to the cause of innovation. At the meetings, executives compare detailed performance data and share breakthrough ideas. New approaches quickly rise to the surface in this setting, and the close personal relationships among key executives grease the skids for the staff transfers that are often required to move ideas across oceans. The top 50 officers, who make up what is known as the Key Value Creators group, also communicate regularly among themselves. And they, in turn, each mentor five to seven younger managers who are considered to be rising stars.

At lower levels, new ideas are developed and distributed via expert groups, or e-groups, that form around various processes and functions. For example, there is an e-group focused on plant operations that includes the best kiln operators, plant managers and cement grinders, who get together to swap ideas about how to cut energy costs, move to alternative fuels or find better sources for raw materials. There are also e-groups for logistics, finance, sales and so on. They communicate via discussion boards on the corporate intranet, by telephone and by occasional face-to-face meetings. Again, out of this diversity of viewpoints and interplay of ideas springs innovation.

Cemex sometimes goes to extreme lengths to foster a customer-centric view of its markets among its managers. For instance, consider its attempt to better understand the housing and construction needs of the urban poor in the developing world. Housing is one of the most basic human needs, yet many of world's poor find it difficult to afford even rudimentary shelter. Despite their meager means and lack of credit, some do manage to scrape together enough to build modest dwellings for their families. Cemex wanted to understand how its poorest customers managed to do this, and what, if anything, the company could do to help the poor house themselves. To this end, a team of Cemex managers put itself in the shoes of the poorest of the poor—literally. The company sent a group of about a dozen junior executives from logistics, sales, operations, planning, and marketing to live and work in a poor neighborhood of Guadalajara for a year. "In this year, we learned many things we didn't know because we are very far from these people in our thinking and way of life," reports Romero, who visited the colony himself, as did several vice presidents who reported to him.

Out of this cultural immersion came two new financing projects aimed specifically at the poor. In studying how the residents of one poor Guadalajara neighborhood saved money, the Cemex team discovered that many families participated in a sort of lottery, organized by a trusted community member. Each week, several dozen families would contribute a preset amount to the lottery. And each week, one family would claim the entire pot—enough to build a modest addition to a house. The lottery would continue, week after week, until everyone's number was eventually called. Those who won early would continue to contribute until the last family had received its pay-out. In effect, the lottery was a community-run savings plan. Drawing on their hard-won insights, Cemex marketers approached some of the organizers of these lotteries, typically women, and suggested that Cemex might help them set up similar financing pools with the exclusive goal of funding home-building projects. They called the program Patrimonio Hoy, which means "have your savings today." The idea was warmly received and soon Cemex had a team of women, the Avon ladies of cement, going door-to-door, signing up families for the new scheme. As an incentive, Cemex volunteered to provide construction advice, blueprints and a small amount of financing projects for the members of the pools. After the third year of the project, 13,000 families were participating. And the default rate on the incremental loans provided by Cemex was practically zero.

Cemex extracted a second insight from this field study. Much of the money used by local families to purchase building materials came from relatives working in the U.S. Further research revealed that of the estimated $8.5 billion that Mexican workers send back to their families every year, about 20 percent is used for construction. But much of this money is wasted because migrant workers are often compelled to pay substantial commissions, sometimes as much as 12 percent, to transfer their money. Moreover, once the funds arrive in Mexico, family members often spend the money on a party or on some other less-than-vital need. Another complicating factor was the fact that the wife or mother receiving the money in Mexico might not know how to get the best deal on construction materials. To address these issues, Cemex started a pilot project in Los Angeles in 2001 called Construmex. Under the scheme, Mexican workers can go to a Cemex office in L.A. and get help picking out the plans and material for a particular project. After being paid, Cemex communicates with a local distributor in Mexico, who assembles the materials and delivers them to the expatriate's relatives. The reinvention of the community lottery and the development of the expatriate funds-transfer service are both typically Cemex—

unconventional yet eminently practical ideas that were eagerly sponsored and quickly prototyped. And in both cases, the outcome was more customers buying more cement.

In the past few years, Cemex has begun taking steps to expand the scope of its business from merely making and selling cement to providing distribution and logistics services across the whole spectrum of the construction industry. "We have been working to become a complete supplier of construction materials, not only cement and concrete," says Romero. One way Cemex has done this is through Construrama, a franchising program for distributors and construction supply stores. In Mexico, more than 75 percent of Cemex's sales come from bagged cement powder. These bags are typically sold through small construction supply stores where cement makes up about half of their business. Cemex selected 1,000 distributors, out of 4,000 in the country, and started wrapping valuable services around its cement. "Our goal was to create competitive differentiation for something that is a commodity," says one executive. It may sound strange to treat cement as anything other than a commodity, but then, **does anybody fault Perrier for treating water as something more than H_2O?**

Cemex invested $10,000 in each store—enough to pay for a new Construrama storefront, Cemex signs, a computer and inventory-tracking software. Cemex also trained the distributors in marketing, financial planning, tax accounting and inventory control. "You are using your distributor as your hands," says Romero. Instead of just delivering cement to these distributors, Cemex now helps them design their stores, provides them with a barebones IT infrastructure, and helps them pool their purchasing power. In return it gets brand loyalty.

After being perfected in Mexico, Construrama is now being rolled out in other countries as well, but it's just one piece of a much larger puzzle. Cemex's goal is to become a mega-supplier of all construction materials to these distributors. Cemex doesn't intend on manufacturing a full range of building supplies, but it wants to put its vaunted logistics capability to work in managing the supply chain between the manufacturing companies and the distributor network.

In addition to more closely integrating its distributors into its operations, Cemex is also hoping to stake out a pivotal position in the construction materials supply chain and in late-2000 created a new business incubator, CxNetworks, to help it do so. Unlike other incubators born during the Internet boom, CxNetworks' purpose is not to spin out unloved ideas into IPOs, but rather to build new skills and relationships that can multiply the value of existing Cemex competencies and assets. The impetus for the formation of CxNetworks was a realization that the consolidation strategy that was fueling the company's growth would ultimately reach its natural limits—there are only so many cement companies to buy and improve. The goal of CxNetworks is to build new platforms for organic growth. In this sense, CxNetworks is not a sideshow, it is the main show. As Medina described it, "Cx-Networks is the transformation engine for Cemex."

"CxNetworks is a way of helping us develop other business relationships that can create value for Cemex," explains San Agustin, the incubator's leader. "It's not a stand alone attempt to create new businesses." CxNetworks has already spawned several nascent businesses including Arkio (a one-stop shop for professional home builders), Latinexus (a B2B exchange for the kind of maintenance, repair and operating materials bought by facility managers) and Neoris (an IT consultancy which grew out of Cemex's internal IT function). Just as Construrama links Cemex more tightly to its downstream distributors, the B2B exchanges are bringing efficiencies to the construction materials supplier network, while Arkio is bringing supply chain efficiencies to the house-building industry. Tellingly, these businesses are staffed with veteran executives, not 20-something Web-heads. For instance, Iñiguez transferred from his CIO position at Cemex to become the CIO of CxNetworks and Arkio's boss was formerly the CEO of Grainger's Mexican operations. "The new skills, developed in the new business models," says San Agustin, "will help to improve the blood of the company." Clearly, all of these people and ideas are expected, in some form or other, to eventually be pumped back into Cemex. CxNetworks is well funded, with up to 10 percent of free cash flow—about $100 million a year—available to it if necessary (although, in its first two years it tapped into less than half that amount). CxNetworks is, essentially, a business R&D unit seeking to leverage Cemex's distribution, logistics and IT competencies in new ways. But CxNetworks does not have a monopoly on new ideas. Every operating company is free to experiment on its own.

Indeed, Francisco Garza has charged his colleagues with the task of making innovation a deeply embedded and widely distributed capability. Although Garza was pleased with the outcome of the "reverse-PMI" project, which produced a multiyear plan for improving the Mexican operations, he felt that innovation needed to be more than a periodic project; nor could it be confined to a single unit, like CxNetworks. There is an expression in Mexico, "wearing the T-shirt." It is a metaphor for the kind of devotion shown by a football fan who wears a T-shirt emblazoned with the emblem of a favorite team. Garza wanted to make it possible for many people to wear the T-shirt of innovation and transformation—to get involved in the work of revolution and renewal.

In 2000, as an initial step toward this goal, Garza, along with Juan Romero, approved the formation of an innovation staff group within the Mexican operating company. By 2002, this group had grown to include nine full-time employees with responsibility for a $3.5 million annual budget. Carlos Gonzalez, innovation director at Cemex Mexico, and leader of the innovation team, comments on his first priority after taking up his responsibilities as innovation czar:

> We had been very innovative, but most of it had come from the top. We wanted to tap into more minds. So we started with a cultural study to identify the barriers. We were too hierarchical, did not have enough cross-cultural teamwork and we had no real established processes.

Overseeing the work of the innovation group is an "innovation board" comprised of five insiders (three Cemex Mexico VPs and two younger managers) and two outsiders (a supplier and a consultant). Working closely with the innovation board, and other senior executives, the innovation staff periodically commissions multifunctional teams from across the company to generate new ideas around major "platforms" or themes. By mid-year 2002, five platform teams were at work, searching for innovative answers to questions as diverse as how to achieve manufacturing breakthroughs, how to make it easier for customers to do business with Cemex, how to develop alternative uses of concrete, how to serve extremely poor customers and how to bring integrated solutions to builders and contractors.

Each platform team consists of 10 to 12 members who devote at least one day a week, over three or four months, to the challenge of generating new ideas and breakout proposals. Although team assignments "expire" after several months, the platforms may live on. (Platform themes are reviewed each year by the innovation board and may be carried forward for another year or retired.) Thus, over the course of a year or two, a platform theme may be addressed by a succession of teams. When a new platform is launched, or a new team formed, job postings are used to solicit talent from across the company. Most weeks, the team members assemble in Monterrey for a day to share ideas and work up detailed proposals. The innovation staff supports the work of the platform teams in many ways—by providing creativity training, leading brainstorming sessions, arranging field trips, bringing in outside experts and assisting with the design of exploratory projects.

After a period of research, learning and brainstorming, each team is expected to identify several "macro-opportunities" that will help to focus its creative energies. For example, the first "integrated solutions" platform team identified two macro-opportunities: helping contractors accelerate construction times and refocusing Cemex Capital on providing funding to builders in addition to its traditional role of extending trade credit to suppliers. **Like many of Cemex's micro-opportunities, these two grew out of a concerted effort to uncover the unarticulated needs of customers.** Platform team members would undoubtedly agree with the realization expressed by one Cemex officer: "We know we can reduce costs, but in the end, this is not a point of differentiation with customers."

One of the first innovation projects to be launched grew out of a conversation with a contractor who specializes in building low-income housing. Since the low income housing is financed by the Mexican government, the builder had no problem selling the houses. "But," as he told the platform team, "the problem is the time it takes to build the houses." In Mexico, house construction is even more labor intensive than it is in more developed countries. With construction workers flitting from job to job, the builder would lose up to 20 percent of his crew every week. As a result, the builder often missed his production targets.

Listening to such a complaint, most cement companies would say, "Sorry, your labor turnover is not our problem." But not Cemex. Not only did the builder's frustrations help to crystallize the team's thinking around a new micro-problem (speed of construction), but it also engendered a proposal for a practical solution. One way of reducing the labor intensity of construction, the team proposed, would be to use metal molds into which wet cement could be poured to quickly form walls and floors. These molds were already available in the States and Europe, but there were two obstacles to using them in Mexico. The first was that if you poured normal ready-mix sludge into them, air bubbles would form in the walls and make them structurally unsound. The second issue was that the molds were too expensive for most builders in Mexico to purchase. One of the members of the platform team, from the ready-mix business in Mexico, realized that just recently his area had developed a more fluid form of ready-mix that would be perfect for this application since it would fill up the molds more evenly. The second issue was addressed by creating a plan through which Cemex Capital would help builders finance the purchase of the required molds.

The innovation board approved the project and it was soon a successful new Cemex offering. Now, the contractor no longer has to build houses with a large crew and concrete blocks. He can put together a house with a handful of workers in three weeks. "Instead of just providing the ready-mix," says Gonzalez, "we are providing a new way to construct houses." And the best thing for Cemex is that the method requires about 50 percent more cement than before, which helps keep its plants running at full capacity. In the project's first year, Cemex expected 30,000 houses in Mexico to be built this way. Inspired by this success, another group was launched to help speed construction for smaller builders by developing Lego-like concrete blocks that would not require mortar.

Each platform team is expected to develop three specific investment proposals that can be taken to the innovation board for funding. Multiply this by the five platform themes, and the two or three teams that will be on each platform over the course of a year, and you get some sense of the range of experimentation that is being engendered by the new innovation group. The initial funding for the projects can range from a few hundred thousand dollars (when there are substantial uncertainties associated with the proposal) to several million dollars (when the business case seems rock solid). As an example, the metal molds initiative received $5 million in funding, while the Lego-block experiment was awarded a much more modest $250,000. As their experience with the innovation process has grown, the innovation board has become more and more willing to fund proposals that start out as something less than a sure bet. Explains Gonzalez:

[In the beginning], there was a tendency to straitjacket the project by going into too much detail. We realized that if the idea is powerful and well thought out, it will grow by itself. If you try to specify exactly the number of clients you're going to reach, or the number of units you're going to sell, people start trying to meet the exact numbers of the plan, instead of being open to wider opportunities. Cemex has a tradition of being very aggressive. So our people don't always expect to see an iron-clad business case. If the project is exciting, our folks will fund it. But when they do fund a project, they follow through very carefully—month-by-month.

Since most of the ideas that come out of the platform teams fit snugly within Cemex's core business, experimental projects are quickly transferred back into operating units. Gonzalez's innovation staff continues to monitor the projects once they reach the implementation stage, and regular reports go back to the innovation board. This visibility helps to ensure that nascent projects aren't ignored or abandoned by operating executives.

The innovation process within Cemex Mexico is also helping to build a cadre of freethinking, innovation-savvy managers. "It is leaving a genetic imprint on these people," says Gonzalez. When team members go back to their jobs or talk to customers, they take with them a probing mindset that questions conventional wisdom and searches restlessly for new avenues of growth.

Another component of the innovation process is an electronic Idea Bank designed to make it easy for employees to share their ideas, big or small. In rolling out the Idea Bank, members of the innovation staff visited plants, teaching employees about the system and encouraging them to contribute their ideas. In its nine months of operation, 504 ideas were submitted from across Cemex Mexico, and 40 were implemented. Employees who may not be comfortable using a computer can submit their idea on paper to a secretary who will enter the suggestion in the Idea Bank. Although many of the initial ideas were modest in scope (for example, a plan for recycling water), some were of sufficient magnitude to be forwarded to one of the platform teams.

At Cemex, the IT platform, the shared performance scorecard, the PMI process, the cross-company e-groups, the monthly meetings of country managers, the resources devoted to CxNetworks, the innovation board and innovation staff group, the platform teams and the Idea Bank are all components of a well-functioning "renewal engine." The fuel for this engine is a belief that is shared by virtually all of Cemex: Industry is not destiny. Here is a company that has never let itself be defined by the views that others have of its product or its prospects. It is a beacon to companies across the developing world that want to compete and win on the world stage. **Cemex's ability to continually reinvent both its industry and itself is a testament to the fact that at Cemex, nothing is ever set in cement.**

LESSONS FROM A GRAY-HAIRED REVOLUTIONARY:

Not only has Cemex succeeded at both revolution and renewal, it has also made a commitment to make innovation a ubiquitous capability. There are many things that underpin the company's capacity for revolution and renewal:

○ A *burning desire* to prove to the world that a Mexican company can out-compete all comers.
○ A *passion for finding and solving customer problems.*
○ A *dense network of lateral communication* and a *common performance scorecard* that facilitates the rapid transfer of new ideas.
○ Ever-changing *patterns of cross-corporate collaboration* that constantly combine and recombine ideas from a wide cross-section of employees.
○ A *deeply felt humility* that admits to the possibility that there's a better way of doing things.
○ A willingness to *push the boundaries* that constrain the definition of "served market."
○ A continuing investment in *creating the time and the space* for innovative thinking and real-world experimentation

ROUTES TO RENEWAL

By now it should be apparent that there are many routes to renewal and revolution. Sometimes renewal requires major portfolio changes. Generale des Eaux had a 130-year history as a French water services company before it started diversifying into pay-TV and telecommunications. After a buying spree that included Seagram's Universal Studios, mp3.com and the U.S. publisher Houghton Mifflin, the company rechristened itself as Vivendi. Today it is one of the world's leading media companies. Cable & Wireless, Disney and Bombardier are some of the other companies that have attempted a deal-driven metamorphosis. By definition, a major portfolio shift doesn't leverage many of a company's existing competencies or assets, yet it also doesn't require an extended period of organizational therapy—as the goal is not so much to transform the core business, as to escape what are perceived to be its inherent limits. There is, of course, a difference between megadeals of the sort that created Vivendi and highly targeted acquisitions designed to close specific competence gaps—such as the ones UPS has been making to buttress its logistics business. In general, pinpoint acquisitions have a higher success rate than do big deals aimed at a radical corporate makeover. The smaller deals involve less financial risk and are aimed at leveraging competencies and assets that already exist.

The inverse of the mega-acquisition is the mega-divestment. Hewlett-

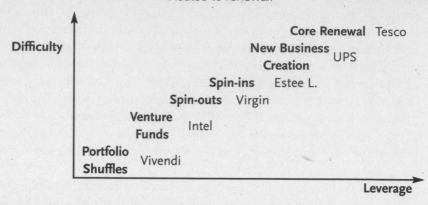

Routes to renewal:

Packard (Agilent), 3M (Imation) and AT&T (Lucent) are some of the companies that have disgorged major businesses in recent years. A company divests a business either because the unit is a perennial underperformer, dragging down the stock performance of the parent, or because it has great growth prospects that are not fully reflected in the valuation of the parent. For its part, Cemex sold off its noncement interests in order to focus its full attention on the task of reinventing its core business. Having reshuffled its portfolio, a company is still left with the challenge of innovating in ways that will lift its remaining or newly acquired businesses above the average.

Corporate venture funds constitute another route to renewal. As we saw with UPS, a venture fund can be a relatively low-cost way of learning about emerging opportunities; a way of taking options on the future. In May 1999, for example, two years before the launch of its Itanium 64-bit processor, Intel created the Intel 64 fund with $250 million earmarked for investing in hardware and software companies developing products that would exploit the new Itanium architecture. Intel, along with Johnson & Johnson and Microsoft, views venture investments as catalysts for renewal. Over the past few years, literally hundreds of companies established venture funds. Unfortunately, few saw these investments as vehicles for bringing new thinking and new technology into the core business. While UPS's Strategic Enterprise Fund won't invest in a business unless an operating executive sees an opportunity to learn something important from the new company, and must also be willing to supply an observer to sit on the young company's board, this tight coupling between venture fund investments and existing businesses is the exception, not the rule. For most companies, the logic of venture investing has been primarily financial—companies hoped to catch a ride on the IPO gravy train. When that train ground to a halt, many of the corporate VC wannabes simply closed up shop. And even for the strategic investors, venture funds can only do so much in revitalizing a core business. While Intel's venture fund has been financially successful (its $3.7 billion gain in 2000 amounted to one-third of Intel's profits in that year), it hasn't prevented the company from losing a significant amount of market share to competitors like Applied Micro Devices (microprocessors for PCs) and Sun (UNIX-based servers).

Closely related to venture funds are spin-outs. Here the goal is not to invest in outside start-ups, but to find and fund underexploited ideas that may be languishing within the hidden corners of a company. Spin-outs make sense when a business idea is clearly outside the company's scope. If venture funds were popular in recent years, corporate incubators were even more so, with more than 600 formed between 1995 and 2000. Yet these incubators haven't made much of a difference as far as shareholders are concerned. Since the ideas that get funded are, by definition, tangential, there is little that the new business can borrow from the core—beyond, perhaps, some cash, a few technical experts and a patent or two. This means the new ventures don't get much of a boost from their parent. As any VC will tell you, building a new business is hard work; there are dozens of failures for every unqualified success. Most companies have neither the patience nor the "mentor capital" necessary to shepherd nascent businesses into fully fledged companies. All too often, incubators were staffed with newbie managers who possessed little or no experience in actually scaling a business.

But again, there are exceptions. Sir Richard Branson's Virgin group is, essentially, a giant incubator which has "spun off" a clutch of successful companies—from Virgin Atlantic Airways to Virgin Money, Virgin Mobile (mobile phones), Virgin Trains and Virgin Cars. While these companies aren't publicly listed, nearly all of them involve outside investors and strategic partners. Virgin sees itself as a branded venture capitalist company. Each new company that Virgin forms has its own management team and its own capital structure. Virgin provides seed financing to the new ventures as well as its eponymous brand. Virgin doesn't have a "core" business. Its corporate function is dedicated to finding new opportunities, lining up an experienced management team, providing guidance and support and ensuring that the brand is well cared for. In short, Virgin is an exception. On average, spin-outs are a very poor substitute for genuine renewal.

I believe venture funds and spin-outs can play no more than a supporting role in the hard work of renewal. **For many companies, starting a venture fund or setting up an incubator is a little bit like putting a belly button ring on granny. It's an attention-grabbing ornament, but what granny needs is a liver transplant, not a navel ring.** In the end, the work of renewal comes down to two fundamental challenges: inventing new businesses that directly leverage the company's core competencies and strategic assets (I once termed these "white space" businesses because they exist in the white spaces between existing divisions or product offerings); and/or transforming the core business in some profound way. Logistics was a white space opportunity for UPS, as were Neoris and Arkio for Cemex. OneSource and Schwab.com represented radical transformations of Schwab's core business. Creating big new businesses and transforming old ones are organizationally difficult. In the first case, you have to move talent and cash into the new business—that means taking resources away from existing business unit leaders. You don't create a $1-billion-a-year business like UPS Logistics by putting a couple of 20-somethings and a million dollars in an incubator. Consequently, there's no way to build a substantial new business unless everyone in the company understands the new opportunity and is willing to sacrifice some talent and some cash to help make the new business a success. This requires a *shared point of view* about the new opportunity. On the other hand, to transform the core business, one must challenge long-held dogmas and practices. This requires that individuals be willing to write off at least some of the intellectual capital they have built up over the years. That's not an easy thing to do. Though they are organizationally challenging, core business renewal and white space business creation offer the greatest potential rewards, in that they leverage a company's accumulated skills, customer relationships, brands and capabilities.

The continued success of companies like UPS, Charles Schwab, Cemex, Microsoft and other gray-haired revolutionaries suggests it's possible to build substantial new businesses *and* fundamentally transform the core. When one digs deep, one finds that gray-haired revolutionaries share many qualities in common. These qualities suggest that there is a set of "design rules" for building companies capable of leading the revolution again and again. It is to these design rules that we now turn our attention.

8

DESIGN RULES FOR INNOVATION

WATCH A FLOCK OF GEESE TURNING AND swooping in flight, undeterred by wind, obstacles and distance. There is no grand vizier goose, no chairman of the gaggle. They can't call ahead for a weather report. They can't predict what obstacles they will meet. They don't know which of their number will expire in flight. Yet their course is true. And they are a flock. Complexity theorists describe this, and the many other examples of spontaneous harmony in the world around us, as order without careful crafting or order for free. The intricate play of the many markets that make up the global economy, the vibrant diversity of the Internet, the behavior of a colony of ants, that winged arrow of geese—these are just a few instances in which order seems to have emerged in the absence of any central authority. All of them have something to teach us about how revolutionary strategies should emerge in a chaotic and ever-changing world. Complexity theorists have demonstrated that by creating the right set of preconditions, one can provoke the emergence of highly ordered things—maybe even things like rule-breaking, wealth-creating strategies.

Order emerges out of deep but simple rules. Craig Reynolds has shown that with three simple rules, one can simulate the behavior of a flock of birds in flight.[1] Too many executives have been trying to design flight plans for their far-flung flock rather than working to create the conditions that would help their brood get off the ground and on their way to new and distant shores. They have spent too much time working on "the strategy" and not enough time working to create the preconditions out of which new wealth-creating strategies are likely to emerge.

Assembling grand strategies in the corporate tower is a futile undertaking in the age of revolution. This doesn't mean that top management is irrelevant. Far from it. But top management's job isn't to build strategies. Its job is to build an organization that is capable of continuously spawning cool, new business concepts and reinvigorating old ones. Its contribution is to design the context rather than invent the content. Its role is to operationalize the design rules for creating a deeply innovative organization—the design rules we see at work in our gray-haired revolutionaries.

So what are the rules for building habitually and perpetually innovative organizations?

DESIGN RULE #1: UNREASONABLE EXPECTATIONS

Listen to senior executives from a couple of gray-haired revolutionaries:

GE Capital: It is expected that we will grow our earnings 20 percent per year or more. When you have objectives that are that outlandish, it forces you to think very differently about your opportunities. If one guy has a 10 percent target and the other has a 20 percent target, the second guy is going to do different things.

Charles Schwab: We are a growth company. This is our charter. Every year you have to say that last year is over, and we're starting from zero. This creates an incredible desire to innovate.

Here's an experiment. Do a quick poll of 25 people in the middle of your organization. Ask them this question: "What do you believe would be a reasonable expectation for top-line growth this year?" Compute the average answer—is it 20 percent, 30 percent, or something substantially less ambitious? It is tautological but true: *No com-*

pany outperforms its aspirations. If most of your colleagues believe you are in a 5 or 10 percent growth business, you are. Their *beliefs set the upper limit on what's possible.*

I meet few individuals who truly believe their organization should be able to grow two or three times as fast as the industry average. Research across 20 industries over the past ten years shows that only one company out of ten managed to grow at double its industry average. I'm willing to bet that no more than one company out of ten has set itself the goal of growing at twice the industry average. And although a bold aspiration won't by itself produce a multitude of nonconformist strategies, its absence always yields bland, me–too strategies.

Whether the objective is growth in revenue, earnings or efficiency, nonlinear innovation begins with unreasonable goals. Modest aspirations beget incrementalism. Señor Zambrano and his colleagues at Cemex were not content to be a mediocre, mid–size Mexican company. Listen to Juan Pablo San Agustin, president of CxNetworks:

> I am very, very proud that we come from a developing country. If you have everything come easy to you, then you become lazy. But if you have to fight for everything, that becomes part of your competitive advantage.

The point is, Cemex's aspirations were completely unreasonable, given the company's starting point. Indeed, they were completely unreasonable even when judged by the performance standards of Cemex's supposedly world–class global competitors.

Strategy convergence, that pernicious margin killer, is the product of expectations convergence across an industry. I'll bet there aren't many people at American Airlines who believe their company can grow two times faster than United Airlines. In most companies, the majority of individuals believe there is some preordained, and typically uninspiring, "industry" growth rate—typically defined by the underlying growth rate of aggregate demand for what is seen as a more or less standardized product—that sets a cap on the growth rate of their own company. Yet unless one's expectations diverge from industry norms, there is little chance that one's ideas will diverge from industry norms. Only when people subscribe to unreasonable goals will they start searching for breakthrough ideas.

Convincing people in an organization that it is actually reasonable to strive for unreasonable goals is tricky. Mere exhortation is not enough. You have to demonstrate that it's actually possible to dramatically outperform the average—and you have to do this with real examples. Otherwise, the aspiration has no credibility. For example, ask your colleagues what they would do if they were in the lettuce business. You can't put a Pentium chip in a head of lettuce. It's not easy to digitize green leaves and send them zipping over the Internet. Yet thanks to Fresh Express and its imitators, the market for prewashed, precut, prepackaged lettuce (a salad in a bag) grew from nothing in the late 1980s to $1.6 billion by 1999. With a 38 percent market share, Fresh Express produces about 40 million pounds of salad per month. Eighty-one percent of Americans have purchased a prepackaged salad at least once. So send an e-mail to everyone you know in your company: **"Table-ready lettuce. $1.6 billion. If someone can do this with a vegetable, what the hell is our excuse?"** Never, ever believe you are in a mature industry. There are no mature industries, only mature managers who unthinkingly accept someone else's definition of what's possible. Be unreasonable!

One caveat: If you push for unreasonable growth goals, some folks in your organization will search for shortcuts—a mega-acquisition, deep price cuts, rebates. Don't let them get away with it. Only nonlinear innovation will drive long-term wealth creation.

DESIGN RULE #2: ELASTIC BUSINESS DEFINITION

Gray-haired revolutionaries aren't bound by a narrow self-concept. Their opportunity horizon is expansive and forever changing:

UPS: We are a technology company with trucks versus a trucking company with technology.

Charles Schwab: There are very few people here who feel they have a narrow business charter and have to defend their business against new models that will undermine those businesses.

GE Capital: We don't talk about market share because when people talk about market share it means they are defining their business too narrowly.

Who are we? This is, perhaps, the most fundamental question a company's employees and executives can ask themselves. How they answer it determines whether or not the company searches for unconventional opportunities. Too many companies define themselves by what they do, rather than by what they know (their core competencies) and what they own (their strategic assets). Thus they become prisoners of their existing business concept. For years, Xerox has defined itself as "The Document Company." So why, then, does Hewlett-Packard dominate the printer business? Printers handle documents—and are technically very similar to copiers. While "The Document Company" was a catch marketing slogan, it's not how Xerox employees saw their core business.

Here's how Michael Schrage, of MIT's famed Media Lab, views the challenges facing traditional universities as they seek to compete with newcomers like the University of Phoenix.

> Yes, MIT, Harvard and Berkeley are famous brands. But there's every reason to believe that market-oriented entities like [the University of] Phoenix have every incentive to be even more innovative than an MIT in crafting compelling online curricula and content. A decade hence, whose courseware sensibilities will be educating more people faster, better and cheaper around the globe?[2]

MIT certainly deserves credit for pushing the boundaries of its own business model. The school's OpenCourseWare initiative, announced in April 2001, aims to make the materials for all of the school's more than 2,000 courses available online. Yet, significantly, this courseware won't be part of an online degree program; rather, it will merely be a resource for anyone who wants to peruse MIT's course-related materials (readings, syllabus, lecture notes, etc.). If you want an MIT education, you'll still have to buy a plane ticket to Boston. A university that views itself first and foremost as a bricks-and-mortar, degree-granting institution training teenagers and 20-somethings will never take seriously the opportunity to use the Internet for the on-demand education of mid-career adults. But if the august professors define their institution by its competencies (curriculum development and knowledge transfer) and its assets (a respected brand name), rather than by its current business model (in-person instruction), the opportunity seems a bit less eccentric. If poor and under-resourced newcomers grab new markets, it is because incumbents so often imprison themselves within an excessively narrow business concept.

Virgin spans industries as diverse as air travel, packaged holidays, mobile phone retailing, banking and radio broadcasting. Says Virgin's Gordon McCallum, head of business development, "There is no assumption about what business Virgin should be in or shouldn't be in." Yet Virgin will enter an industry only if it believes it can (a) challenge existing rules, (b) give customers a better deal, (c) be more entertaining and more fun, and (d) put a thumb in the eye of complacent incumbents. Says McCallum, "The culture is one of why not, rather than why."

Like Virgin, Disney owns a brand that transcends any particular business. Judson Green, chairman of Disney Attractions, doesn't define his business as "theme parks" but as "three-dimensional entertainment." Disney's success with cruise ships, Broadway shows, mini-theme parks and a host of other ventures evinces an elastic business definition. An elastic business definition helps to reduce the protectionist instincts of executives worried about cannibalization. At GE Capital, the senior executives who run the company's major business spend as much as 50 percent of their time looking for opportunities outside the boundaries of the business they're managing. Every business leader is assumed to be a business development officer for the entire company. Is that how divisional vice presidents feel in your company? Is that how you feel? Parochialism is one of innovation's most deadly enemies. It's not only the CEO who needs an elastic definition of business boundaries—so does every single employee.

To drive this point home, former GE chairman and CEO Jack Welch asked GE's business heads to redefine their markets so that each business has less than a 10 percent share of its market. After spending years driving home the message that a business needs to be number one or two in its industry to survive, GE's famed leader had to remind his divisional executives of the obverse truth that only companies with expansive business boundaries will grow faster than their competitors. In a similar way, Schwab's employees don't see their company as the undisputed leader in discount brokerage, but as having captured only about 1 percent of the accumulated savings of American investors.

An elastic business concept isn't a license for ill-conceived diversification. Entering a business where one's competencies don't count for much is a recipe for a big write-off. Disney's Judson Green notes, "You can look back over time at everything Disney has done and put it into two buckets: the stuff that leverages the Disney brand and the stuff that isn't really related to the Disney franchise. We haven't done very well in the latter stuff." In the absence of a clear plan for leveraging competencies and assets, an elastic business definition is an accident waiting to happen.

In enlarging its mission from package delivery to enabling global commerce, UPS substantially expanded its potential market, yet stayed true to the company's roots and capabilities. UPS demonstrates that it's possible to expand your horizons without forgetting where you come from. So start asking your colleagues, Who are we? Where does our opportunity horizon begin and end? What do we currently regard as "out of scope"? Get a few people together and start redefining your company in terms of what it knows and what it owns, rather than what it does. This will help you stitch some elastic into your company's sense of self.

DESIGN RULE #3: A CAUSE, NOT A BUSINESS

Gray-haired revolutionaries draw much of their strength from their allegiance to a cause that goes beyond growth and profits—a cause that goes beyond themselves, a cause that is truly noble. Listen to what they say:

Charles Schwab: Around here, we think we're curing cancer.
Virgin Atlantic: Our business is about creating memorable moments for our customers.
UPS: We had a sense that we were given something, and we had to make it better.

Without a transcendent purpose, without a deep sense of responsibility, individuals will lack the courage to behave like revolutionaries. Gray-haired revolutionaries must periodically shed their skin. Every time they abandon a decaying strategy or jettison an out-of-date belief, they leave a bit of themselves behind. The most unsettling thing about the process of renewal is the need to write off one's own depreciating intellectual capital. To a great extent, an individual's worth in an organization is determined by what he or she knows. Business concept innovation changes the price tag on every bit of knowledge in the firm. Some knowledge becomes more valuable, and other knowledge less so.

Perhaps even more distressing is that business concept innovation often undercuts the value of an individual's accumulated social capital. Think, for example, of an insurance company exec who's spent years schmoozing with brokers and agents. Countless boozy dinners, boondoggles in Hawaii with star agents, a few hundred rounds of golf—and now you're going to tell this person that, in some brave new world, the traditional insurance broker may be a handicap rather than an asset? Good luck. It's hard enough to write off some of what we know; it's even harder to watch social relationships fray under the strain of a radical new strategy.

Any individual poised between a familiar but tattered business model and a lustrous but untested new idea is bound to ask a few questions: Will my skills and my relationships be as valuable in this new world as they were in the old? How much will I be asked to unlearn? How much effort will it take for me to adapt myself to a new order of things? These are genuine, heartfelt questions. And, for the most part, they can't be answered in advance. As one wag once remarked about his ever-cautious colleagues: Few of them would have sailed with Columbus. The courage to leave some of oneself behind and strike off for parts unknown comes not from some banal assurance that "change is good" but from a devotion to a wholly worthwhile cause.

Where did Schwab get the courage to preemptively migrate its business model to the Web, knowing that the move would force it to slash prices by up to 60 percent and more? Think about how your company would react if it were faced with this kind of decision. (We know how Merrill Lynch reacted. It denied, denied, denied, then debated, debated, debated, and, finally, decided.) In most companies there would be months, perhaps years, of savage debate. Factions would form, positions would harden. The specter of cannibalization would roam the hallways, striking fear into fainthearted executives. All this was avoided at Schwab for a single, simple reason—online trading was the right thing to do for customers.

When asked to describe the cause that imbues his colleagues with their revolutionary fervor, David Pottruck, president and co-CEO of Charles Schwab, says this: "We are the guardians of our customers' financial dreams." Think about that. When was the last time a bank teller looked like the guardian of your financial dreams? It's not surprising that Schwab regularly turns itself inside out on behalf of customers. After all, how many companies do you know that list "empathy" as one of their core values?

Sometimes a "cause" is nothing more than a genuine desire to make a very special difference in the lives of customers. The commitment of Cemex to improve the housing of the world's poor is such a cause. It led a group of Cemex executives to spend a year in one of the poorest regions of Mexico, in order to better understand how they might help impoverished Mexicans improve their housing.

However mundane a company's products or services, they must be infused with a sense of transcendent purpose. This can't be a thin coating of sickly sweet sentiment; instead, it must come from the part of every human being that yearns to make the world a bit better off. Roy Disney, Disney's vice chairman, knows why his company is in business: "You go talk to anyone who works in the parks, and they're all moved by the chance to make a difference in people's lives. We all feel very much the same. You do a good movie and you watch people walk out of the theatre with more hope in their lives. I get letters every once in a while from folks who just say, 'Thanks for what you have done in my life.'" When a company loses this sense of calling, when employees look at their leaders and see unshackled greed or commercial instincts that are not ennobled by any higher purpose, it also loses a good share of the righteous courage which is so essential for innovation.

For most of the industrial age, employees were valued only for their muscle power. Henry Ford is reputed to have once asked, "Why is it that whenever I ask for a pair of hands, a brain comes attached?" Henry wanted robots, but they hadn't yet been invented. Today, we celebrate our enlightenment. We live in the "knowledge" economy. We want employees to bring their brains to work. Yet if we rob them of the chance to feel they are working on something that really matters, are we really so enlightened? Brainpower versus muscle power, neurons versus tendons—is that really such a big leap forward? Is that what distinguishes us from machines—our slightly more advanced cognitive abilities? **What we need is not an economy of hands or heads, but an economy of hearts. Every employee should feel that he or she is contributing to something that will actually make a genuine and positive difference in the lives of customers and colleagues.** For too many employees, the return on emotional equity is close to zero. They have nothing to commit to other than the success of their own career. Why is it that the very essence of our humanity, our desire to reach beyond ourselves, to touch others, to do something that matters, to leave the world just a little bit better, is so often denied at work? After all, most people devote more of their waking hours to work than to home, family, community, and faith combined. To succeed in the age of revolution, a company must give its members a reason to bring all of their humanity to work. Viktor Frankl, the great Austrian psychiatrist, said it well: "For success, like happiness, cannot be pursued; it must ensue ... as the unintended side-effect of one's personal dedication to a cause greater than oneself."[5]

So ask yourself, What are you actually working for? What kind of difference would you like to make? Who will thank you, I mean really thank you, if you succeed? Do you have a calling, or do you just have a job?

DESIGN RULE #4: NEW VOICES

If senior management wants revolutionary strategies, it must learn to listen to revolutionary voices. Ian Schrager and super-chic urban hotels (Ian Schrager Hotels), Julian Metcalfe, Sinclair Beecham and fast food (Pret A Manger), Jeff Bezos and retailing (Amazon.com), Pierre Omidyar and auctions (eBay), Dietrich Mateschitz and energy drinks

(Red Bull), Phil Knight and athletic wear (Nike)—none of these industry revolutionaries started out as industry insiders. More often than not, industries get reinvented by outsiders—by newcomers free from the prejudices of industry veterans. Yet in most companies strategy is the preserve of the old guard. Strategy conversations have the same ten people talking to the same ten people year after year. No wonder the strategies that emerge are dull as dishwater.

What, after all, do the top 20 or 30 executives in a company have to learn from each other? They've been talking at each other for years—their positions are well rehearsed, they can finish each other's sentences. What is required is not a cohort of wise elders or a bevy of planners, but a taproot sunk deep into the organization. The Information Technology Strategy Committee at UPS was comprised of next-generation leaders who ultimately involved 1,000 managers in a cross-company dialogue about potential new opportunities. The postmerger integration (PMI) teams at Cemex paid particular attention to the views of frustrated activists in the middle ranks of acquired companies.

Put simply, without new voices in the strategy conversation, the chance of coming up with a rule-breaking strategy is nil. There are revolutionaries in your company. But all too often there is no process that lets them be heard. They are isolated and impotent, disconnected from others who share their passions. Their voices are muffled by layers of cautious bureaucrats. They are taught to conform rather than to challenge. And too many senior executives secretly long for a more compliant organization rather than a more vociferous one.

Maybe you think I'm being too hard on top management. Consider this: A disaffected employee in one of America's largest companies recently showed me a simple chart that had been distributed throughout the firm as part of a major cultural change program. He pointed out the fact that only "senior executives" were accountable for "creating strategy." Not a word about thinking strategically appeared in the performance criteria for "managers" and "associates." With a single chart, the company managed to disenfranchise 99.9 percent of its employees, relieving them of any responsibility for business concept innovation and of any involvement in their own future. Ironically, the company expects executives to be "open to learning," unless, of course, it involves a suggestion for a new strategy or business concept. You may wince at this example, but don't kid yourself: This is the reality in all too many companies.

For a company to become or remain the author of industry revolution, top management must give a disproportionate share of voice to three constituencies that are typically underrepresented in conversations about destiny and direction.

LET YOUTH BE HEARD

The first constituency is young people or, more accurately, those with a youthful perspective. There are 30–year–olds who qualify as "old fogies" and 70–year–olds who are still living in the future. On average, though, young people live closer to the future than those who have more history than future. It is ironic that **THE VERY GROUP WITH THE BIGGEST EMOTIONAL STAKE IN THE FUTURE—YOUNG PEOPLE—IS TYPICALLY MOST LIKELY TO BE PREVENTED FROM CONTRIBUTING TO THE PROCESS OF STRATEGY CREATION.**

While at Siemens Nixdorf, Gerhard Schulmeyer instituted a process of "reverse mentoring" where 20–somethings got the chance to teach senior executives a thing or two about the future. A few years ago Anheuser–Busch set up a "shadow" management committee whose members were a couple of decades younger than the executives on the "real" management committee. The youngsters get to second–guess their elders on key decisions—from acquisitions to ad campaigns. What's more, they are given their own reporting channel to the board. If you want to get close to the future, listen to someone who's already living there.

LISTEN TO THE PERIPHERY

A second constituency that deserves a larger share of voice is those near the geographic edges of the organization. The capacity for radical innovation increases proportionately with each kilometer you move away from HQ. The highly successful reverse–PMI team that unlocked $100 million of wealth within Cemex's Mexican operations brought together 45 employees drawn from Spain, Venezuela, Colombia and other far–flung subsidiaries. Less encumbered by tradition and less respectful of corporate shibboleths, this group found opportunities that were invisible to home country executives.

For an American company, the periphery might be India or Singapore or even the West Coast. For a Japanese company, it might be the UK or the United States. In the late 1990s, pretty much everyone at the top of GM would have pointed to Brazil as the most innovative place in the GM empire. At the periphery, people typically have fewer resources. They are forced to be more creative. They are less easily "controlled." Orthodoxy doesn't hold the same sway it does inside the corporate heartland. Freethinkers on the periphery understand well the rationale traditionally offered by rebels in the Chinese hinterland—the emperor is far away and the hills are high. But again, in many companies, the periphery has a scant share of voice in the strategy-making process.

The third constituency is the newcomers. Particularly useful are newcomers who have arrived from other industries or who have so far managed to escape the stultifying effect of corporate training. **Again, they deserve a disproportionate share of voice in any conversation about business innovation.** Perhaps your company has looked outside for senior executives with fresh, new perspectives. But how systematically has it sought out the advice of newcomers at all levels who've not yet succumbed to the creeping death of orthodoxy?

It is ironic that companies so often pretend to celebrate "diversity" while systematically stamping it out. The kind of diversity that really counts is not gender diversity or racial diversity or ethnic diversity. It is, instead, a diversity of thinking. An organization that mimics the United Nations in its diversity is of little practical use if corporate training, "best practices," "alignment" and "focus" have destroyed intellectual diversity. In many companies, what could be a rainbow is instead monotonously monochromatic. Here's a benchmark: The next time someone in your organization convenes a meeting on "strategy" or "innovation," make sure that 50 percent of those who attend have never been asked to attend such a meeting before. Load the meeting with young people, newcomers and those from the far-flung edges of the company. Do this, and you'll quadruple the chances of coming up with truly revolutionary business concepts.

DESIGN RULE #5: A MARKET FOR INNOVATION

When it comes to innovation, most companies are more like hierarchies than they are like markets—they are more like the old Soviet Union than they are like the New York Stock Exchange. Yet history has shown again and again that markets almost always outperform hierarchies when it comes to getting the right resources behind the right opportunities at the right times. Oh sure, markets sometimes suffer from the kind of mass hysteria that fueled the Internet boom, but on average the collective intelligence of a market beats the smarts of any single person. If innovation is going to flourish in large companies—if new ideas are going to compete with the old on an equal footing, if resources are going to flow quickly and fluidly to the best new opportunities—then companies are going to have to become more like markets and less like hierarchies.

Despite the collapse of the Internet bubble, Silicon Valley has a unique track record of creating new business models and new wealth—in fact, over the past 50 years, no other region on the planet has done these two things quite as successfully as Silicon Valley. It's not surprising, then, that Silicon Valley is, in essence, three tight-coupled markets: a market for ideas, a market for capital and a market for talent. If, decade after decade, Silicon Valley has managed to create new industries, new companies and new wealth, it's not because the Valley is filled with brilliant visionaries. And if your company has consistently failed to create new billion-dollar businesses it's not because it's filled with witless drones. In Silicon Valley, ideas, capital and talent swirl in a frenetic entrepreneurial dance, melding into whatever combinations are most likely to generate new wealth. In most large companies, by contrast, ideas, capital and talent are inert and indolent. They don't move unless someone orders them to move. Where Silicon Valley is a vibrant market, the average big company is a centrally planned economy. It's no wonder that many Silicon Valley entrepreneurs are corporate exiles. Throughout its history, **Silicon Valley has been a refugee camp for revolutionaries who couldn't get a hearing elsewhere.**

If an established company wants to recreate the same kind of vibrant entrepreneurial spirit that pervades Silicon Valley, it must do more than establish a venture fund or a new business incubator. It must create an innovation marketplace that spans the entire company and is accessible to every potential innovator.

A MARKET FOR IDEAS

An average-sized venture-capital firm in Silicon Valley gets as many as five thousand unsolicited business plans a year. How many unsolicited business plans does a senior vice president in your company get every year? Five? Ten? Zero? There's not much chance of catching the next wave when your corner of the ocean is as placid as a bathtub. So what's the difference between Silicon Valley and your company?

For starters, everyone in Silicon Valley understands that radical new ideas are the only way to create new wealth. Until employees believe that rule-breaking ideas are the surest way to wealth creation, both for their companies and themselves, the market for ideas will remain as barren as a Soviet supermarket in the Brezhnev era.

There's another difference between Silicon Valley and the corporate hierarchy. In most companies, the marketplace for ideas is a monopsony—there's only one buyer. There's only one place to pitch a new idea—up the chain of command—and all it takes is one *nyet* to kill it. In the Valley, there's no one person who can say no to a new idea. It's rare to find a successful start-up whose initial business plan wasn't rejected by several venture capitalists before finding a sponsor.

What's more, in Silicon Valley there's no prejudice about who is capable of giving birth to an innovative idea and who's not. Silicon Valley is a meritocracy. It matters not a whit how old you are, what academic degrees you've earned, where you've worked before, or whether you wear denim or Armani. All that matters is the quality of your thinking and the power of your vision. In the Valley, no one assumes that the next great thing will come from a senior vice president running the last great thing. This is yet another reason the marketplace for ideas is more vibrant in Silicon Valley than in most companies.

Ailsa Petchey was a young flight attendant at Virgin Atlantic Airways. This unlikely entrepreneur got her brain wave when she was helping a friend plan a wedding. Like most brides-to-be, her friend was overwhelmed by a seemingly endless list of to-dos: find the church and a reception hall, arrange the catering, hire the limousine, pick out a dress, outfit the bridesmaids, choose the flowers, plan the honeymoon, send out the invitations and on and on. Suddenly Ailsa was struck by an idea—why not offer brides-to-be a kind of one-stop wedding planning service? Petchey took her idea to Sir Richard Branson, who encouraged her to go for it. The result: a 10,500-square-foot bridal emporium, which is Britain's largest, and an array of bridal coordinators who will help arrange everything for the big day. The name of the new business? Virgin Bride, of course. Could this happen in your company—could a 20-something first-line employee buttonhole the chairman and get permission to start a new business?

A MARKET FOR CAPITAL

Does this sound like the way capital budgeting works in your company?

Virgin: In terms of new projects, we're not in the business of calculating hurdle rates. We don't have hurdle rates. The questions we ask are, Is it sustainable? Is it innovative? Can we make money? If the answer is yes, we'll go into a business. If you think something's off the page as an opportunity, there's no point in saying it's two times off the page.

Cemex: Our people don't always expect to see an iron-clad business case. If the project is exciting, our folks will fund it. But when they do fund a project, they follow through very carefully—month-by-month.

So called "angel" investors often provide seed money to companies with a business concept that is not yet well enough developed to attract venture capital funding. Angel funding can range from a few tens of thousands of dollars up to half a million or so. Angel investors are often successful entrepreneurs who are eager to make ground floor investments in companies that just might be the next big thing. Angel investors are not financially stupid people, but they don't think like CFOs. While both may be in the business of funding projects, the market for capital in Silicon Valley isn't anything like the market for capital in large companies. The first difference is access. How easy is it for someone seven levels down in a large company to get a few hundred thousand dollars to develop a new idea? Whether the sum is $100,000 or $10,000,000, the investment hurdles usually appear insurmountable to someone far removed from top management.

Historically, roughly two-thirds of Silicon Valley start-ups received their initial funding from angels. Angels typically band together to fund new companies. The average angel puts in around $50,000, and the average first-round investment for a start-up is something less than $500,000. That's a rounding error in the annual report of a medium-sized company. Yet how easy would it be for an ardent entrepreneur in your company to find ten angels willing to invest $50,000 each?

Creative ideas seldom make it through traditional financial screens. If financial projections can't be supported with reams of analysis, top management takes a pass. But does it really make sense to set the same hurdles for a small investment in a new experiment as for a large and irreversible investment in an existing business? Why should it be so difficult for someone with an unconventional idea to get the funding needed to build a prototype, design a little market trial or merely flesh out a business case—particularly when the sum involved is peanuts?

The market for capital works differently in Silicon Valley. Talk to

Steve Jurvetson, who funded Hotmail and is one of the Valley's hottest young VCs. Ask him how he evaluates a potential business idea, and this is what he'll tell you:

> The first thing I ask is, Who will care? What kind of difference will this make? Basically, How high is up? I want to fund things that have just about unlimited upside. The second thing I ask is, How will this snowball? How will you scale this thing? What's the mechanism that drives increasing returns? Can it spread like a virus? Finally, I want to know how committed the person is. I never invest in someone who says they're going to do something; I invest in people who say they're already doing something and just want the funding to drive it forward. Passion counts for more than experience.

A VC has a very different notion of what constitutes a business plan than the typical CFO. Again, listen to Jurvetson:

> The business plan is not a contract in the way a budget is. It's a story. It's a story about an opportunity, about the migration path, and how you're going to create and capture value.
>
> I never use Excel at work. I never run the numbers or build financial models. I know the forecast is a delusional view of reality. I basically ignore this. Typically, there are no IRR forecasts or EVA calculations. But I spend a lot of time thinking about how big the thing could be.

The point is this: In most companies the goal of capital budgeting is to make sure the firm never, ever makes a bet–the–business investment that fails to deliver an acceptable return. But in attempting to guarantee that there's never an unexpected downside, the typical capital-budgeting process places an absolute ceiling on the upside.

Venture capitalists start with a very different set of expectations about success and failure. Out of 5,000 ideas, a five–partner VC firm may invest in ten, which it views as a portfolio of options. Out of ten, five are likely to be total write–offs, three will be modest successes, one will double the initial investment and one will return 50 to 100 times the investment. **The goal is to make sure you have a big winner, not to make sure there are no losers.**

In most large companies someone with a vision of a cool new business model, or a dramatically reconfigured business model, has to go to the defenders of the status quo to get funding. All too often the guy running the old thing has veto power over the new thing. To understand the problem this creates, imagine that every innovator in Silicon Valley had to go to Bill Gates for funding. Pretty soon everyone in the Valley would be working to extend the Windows franchise. ICQ instant messaging, Java, the PalmPilot and dozens of other innovations might never have come to market.

A VC doesn't ask how one venture plays off against the success of another. Nobody asks, Is this new venture consistent with our existing strategy? Now, consistency is a virtue, but in a world where the life span of the average business concept is longer than a butterfly's but shorter than a dog's, a company has to be willing to consider a few opportunities that are inconsistent with its current strategy. One of those opportunities might just turn out to be a whole lot more attractive than what you're already working on. But how will you ever know unless you're willing to create a market for capital that puts a bit of cash behind the unorthodox?

A MARKET FOR TALENT

Every Silicon Valley CEO knows that if you don't give your very best people truly exhilarating work—and a potential upside—they'll start turning in their badges.

The market for talent works with a brutal efficiency in Silicon Valley. In the early 1990s, companies such as Apple and Silicon Graphics hemorrhaged talent, while up-and-comers like Cisco and Yahoo! were magnets for the cerebrally gifted. As these companies faltered, they lost talent to a new wave of start-ups. In old economy companies, employees are still viewed as something akin to indentured servants. Divisional vice presidents think they own their key people. And if those people work in South Bend, St. Louis, Des Moines, Nashville or a hundred other cities that don't have the kind of superheated economy that exists in Silicon Valley, they may not find it so easy to jump ship. But that's no reason to chain ambitious and creative employees to the deck of a slowly sinking business model.

In too many companies there's a sense of entitlement among divisional vice presidents and business heads. "Hey, we make all the money; we ought to have the best people," they'll say. But the marginal value a talented employee adds to a business running on autopilot is often a fraction of the value that individual could add to a breakthrough project just getting started. Why not create an internal market for talent where divisional vice presidents, project leaders and others can bid for the best talent? A market for talent is more than a list of job openings. ***Employees have to believe that the best way***

to win big is to be part of a team doing something new.
That means providing incentives for employees who are willing to take
a "risk" on something out of the ordinary. It means celebrating every
courageous employee who abandons the security of a well–defined job
for the chance to work on a new project or business.

The last bastion of Soviet–style central planning can be found in Fortune 500 companies—it's called resource allocation. Big companies are
not markets, they're hierarchies. The guys at the top decide where the
money goes. Unconventional ideas are forced to make a tortuous climb
up the corporate pyramid. If an idea manages to survive the gauntlet of
skeptical vice presidents, senior vice presidents, and executive vice
presidents, some distant CEO finally decides whether or not to invest.

In contrast, Silicon Valley is based on resource attraction. If an idea
has merit, it will attract resources in the form of venture capital and talent. If it doesn't, it won't. There's no CEO of Silicon Valley. There's no giant brain making global allocation decisions. Resource allocation is
well suited to investments in existing businesses. After all, the guys at
the top built the business, and they're well placed to make judgments
about investments aimed at perpetuating existing business models. But
management veterans are not usually the best ones to judge the merits
of investing in entirely new business models or making radical changes
to existing models.

It's not that top–down resource allocation has no place in companies. It does. But it can't be the only game in town. If the goal is to
create new wealth, something much more spontaneous and less cir-
cumscribed is required—something much more like resource attraction. For this reason every company must become an amalgam of
disciplined resource allocation and impromptu resource attraction.
Can it be done? Yep.

Royal Dutch/Shell, the Anglo–Dutch oil giant headquartered more
than 6,000 miles from Silicon Valley, is seldom mistaken for a lithe and
nimble upstart. Shell's globe–trotting managers are famously disciplined, diligent and methodical; they don't come across as wild–eyed
dreamers. But a band of renegades, led by Tim Warren, the director of
research and technical services in Shell's largest division, Exploration
and Production, has been intent on changing all this. Warren and his
team have been working hard to free up the flow of ideas, capital and
talent—to make E&P an innovation–friendly zone. Their initial success
suggests that it is possible to imbue a global giant with the kind of
damn–the–conventions ethos that permeates Silicon Valley.

By late 1996, it had become apparent to Warren and some of his colleagues that E&P was unlikely to meet its earnings targets without

radical new innovation. Looking to stir up some new thinking, Warren had encouraged his people to devote up to 10 percent of their time to "nonlinear" ideas, but the results were less than he'd hoped for. His frustration was the genesis for an entirely new approach to innovation, one both simple and slightly deviant. He gave a small panel of free-thinking employees the authority to allocate $20 million to game-changing ideas submitted by their peers. Anyone could submit an idea, and the panel would decide which deserved funding. Proposals would be accepted from anywhere across Shell.

The GameChanger process, as it came to be known, went live in November 1996. At first, the availability of venture funding failed to yield an avalanche of new ideas. Even bright and creative employees long accustomed to working on well-defined technical problems found it difficult to think revolutionary thoughts. Hoping to kick start the process, the GameChanger panel enlisted the help of a team of consultants from Strategos who designed a three-day "Innovation Lab" to help employees develop rule-busting ideas. Seventy-two enthusiastic would-be entrepreneurs showed up for the initial lab, a much larger group than the panel had anticipated. Many were individuals no one would have suspected of harboring entrepreneurial impulses.

In the Innovation Lab, the budding revolutionaries were encouraged to learn from radical innovations from outside the energy business. They were taught how to identify and challenge industry conventions, how to anticipate and exploit discontinuities of all kinds, and how to leverage Shell's competencies and assets in novel ways. Groups of eight attendees were then seated at round tables in front of networked laptop computers and encouraged to put their new thinking skills to work. Slowly at first, then in a rush, new ideas began to flow through the network. Some ideas attracted a flurry of support from the group; others remained orphans. By the end of the second day, a portfolio of 240 ideas had been generated. Some were for entirely new businesses, and many more were for new approaches within existing businesses.

The attendees then agreed on a set of screening criteria to determine which of the ideas deserved a portion of the seed money. Twelve ideas were nominated for funding, and a volunteer army of supporters coalesced around each one. The nascent venture teams were invited to attend an "Action Lab." Here the teams were taught how to scope out the boundaries of an opportunity, identify potential partnerships, enumerate sources of competitive advantage and identify the broad financial implications. Next, they were coached in developing 100-day action plans: low-cost, low-risk ways of testing the ideas. Finally, each team presented its story to a "venture board" consisting of the GameChanger panel, a sampling of senior managers and representatives from Shell Technology Ventures—a unit that funds projects that don't fall under the purview of Shell's operating units.

Since the completion of the labs, the GameChanger panel has been working hard to institutionalize the internal entrepreneurial process. It meets weekly to discuss new submissions—320 were received in the first two years of the panel's existence, many through Shell's intranet. An employee with a promising idea is invited to give a ten-minute pitch to the GameChanger panel, followed by a 15-minute Q&A session. If the members agree that the idea has real potential, the employee is invited to a second round of discussions with a broader group of company experts whose knowledge or support may be important to the success of the proposed venture. Before rejecting an idea, the panel looks carefully at what Shell would stand to lose if the opportunity turned out to be all its sponsors claim. Ideas that get a green light often receive funding—on average, $100,000, but sometimes as much as $600,000—within eight or ten days. Those that don't pass muster enter a database accessible to anyone who would like to compare a new idea with earlier submissions.

Some months later, each project goes through a proof-of-concept review in which the team has to show that its plan is indeed workable and deserves further funding. This review typically marks the end of the formal GameChanger process, although the panel will often help successful ventures find a permanent home inside Shell. About a quarter of the efforts that get funded ultimately come to reside in an operating unit or in one of Shell's various growth initiatives; others get carried forward as R&D projects, and still others are written off as interesting, but unproductive experiments. Of Shell's five-largest growth initiatives in early 1999, four had their genesis in the GameChanger process. Perhaps even more important, the GameChanger process has helped convince Shell's top management that entrepreneurial passion lurks everywhere and that you really can bring Silicon Valley inside.

In Silicon Valley, ideas, talent and capital are concentrated in a small geographic area. There is seldom more than one or two degrees of separation between any given entrepreneur, VC or brilliant engineer. Given the tightly knit social fabric of Silicon Valley, it's not hard for ideas, capital and talent to find each other. This is much less true for a global company like Shell. Ideas, capital and talent are often separated by geographical and organizational distance. Hence the need for something like the GameChanger process that can serve as a magnet for new ideas, and as a central switching node for capital and talent.

Building a marketplace for innovation may sound a bit daunting, not to mention unconventional. So think of it this way, you've already turned your company inside out for ERP and CRM—projects aimed at only incremental improvements—wouldn't the potential pay-off for creating a marketplace for innovation be at least as big? Shell thinks so—and if Shell can do it, so can your company.

DESIGN RULE #6: LOW-RISK EXPERIMENTATION

Being a revolutionary doesn't mean being a big risk taker:

UPS: We have [new] subsidiaries. They are nimble, entrepreneurial, innovative, quick. We tell them to try new things and fail small and fast. That is what our subsidiaries do.
GE Capital: We go for things where the barriers to entry are small. You won't find us doing many mega-mergers. We do hundreds of acquisitions. But it's very unusual for us to do a big transaction. Big transactions bring you big risks. Have you timed the market right? Are you buying a business because the other guy thinks it's the right time to get out?
Virgin: We're very adept at managing the downside. We usually take someone else's skills and someone else's money.

There is an implicit assumption in many companies that it is less risky to be incremental than to be revolutionary. Many believe that it is best to let a foolhardy competitor take the risk of testing a new business concept, that the safe bet is to be a fast follower. There are others, a minority in most companies, who will argue that to capture new markets a company must be bold. They will argue that if you're not first off the blocks, you will never win the race to tomorrow's riches. "We need more risk takers around here" is an oft-heard plea in companies that have missed exciting new markets.

Yet there is a false dichotomy here. The choice is not between being a cautious follower on one hand and a rash risk taker on the other. Neither of these approaches is likely to pay off in the age of revolution. For example, Motorola got caught behind Nokia in the move to digital phones and paid a heavy price for its ambling pace. The company learned that you can't play catch-up with a competitor that moves at light speed. On the other hand, Motorola took a huge gamble with its participation in Iridium, the satellite-based communication business, and was ultimately forced into a big write-off when expectations about the rate of customer adoption turned out to be wildly overoptimistic. It is possible, though, to find a way between these two extremes. Gray-haired revolutionaries are prudent and bold, careful and quick.

Again, the venture capital community provides a useful analogy. Venture capitalists are risk takers, but they're not big risk takers. AT&T buying into the cable TV industry, Monsanto spending billions on seed companies, Sony betting a billion on a new video game chip—these are big risks. Indeed, in the five years through 2000, companies in the S&P 500 took more than $220 billion in extraordinary charges against earnings. This is nearly four times as much as all the venture capital raised in Silicon Valley over the same time period (which, of course, was the greatest VC spending boom in history). By contrast, extraordinary gains amounted to only about $60 billion. So no one can argue that big companies are unwilling to take big risks—on poorly conceived acquisitions and bold but highly uncertain mega–opportunities.

Historically, venture capitalists have not been big risk takers. (They got a bit carried away by all that dot–com nonsense.) VCs look for opportunities that don't need a lot of cash to get started. The initial investment in Hotmail was $300,000; the company was sold to Microsoft for something north of $400 million. Historically, Silicon Valley was fueled by nifty new ideas, not zillions of greenbacks. VCs worked hard to enforce a culture of frugality in the companies they backed. And because they were intimately involved in those companies—helping to appoint the management team, sitting on the board, plotting strategy with the owners—they were well positioned to know when to double their bets and when to cut and run. Compared to VCs, the average CFO is a spendthrift. Yet VCs also know that speed is everything. They have no tolerance for talking about doing, for getting ready to get ready. They know that the only way you resolve the inevitable uncertainty around new opportunities is to actually dangle something in front of customers and see if they bite.

VCs live by Virgin's motto of "Screw it, let's do it." Indeed, Virgin has shuttered more businesses than most companies have ever created. Virgin has an exit plan for every business it enters—one that minimizes the potential damage to the Virgin brand. This kind of forward planning doesn't evince any lack of commitment to new opportunities, it simply recognizes that what is true for Silicon Valley is also true for Virgin: Most start–ups will fail (though Virgin claims a better track record than the average VC fund).

There is an important mind–set here: Most new ventures will fail. Do people in your company understand this? A VC could have five or six failures in ten starts and still be a hero. Could anyone survive that kind of ratio in your company? What matters less than the success rate is the number of new experiments you get started. It is perverse that in many companies billion-dollar commitments to moribund businesses can be thought of as "safe," while Lilliputian experiments are viewed as risky. Risk is the product of investment multiplied by the probability of failure. A $100,000 experiment with an 80 percent chance of failing is substantially less risky than a $100 million investment with a 1 percent chance of failure. Assuming no residual value for either project in the event of failure, the expected downside for the "risky" venture is $80,000 ($100,000 × 80%) and $1 million ($100 million × 1%) for the "sure thing." Yet which would be quicker to win funding in your company? Most companies fail to grasp this simple arithmetic. If they did, they'd be doing fewer big mergers, for example, and would instead be spawning dozens upon dozens of radical low-cost, low-risk experiments.

It is important to **make a distinction between project risk and portfolio risk.** The risk that any single new experiment fails may be high—say, 80 percent. Yet in a portfolio of ten such experiments, each with a one-in-ten chance of success, the likelihood is that one of them will pay off. And while the best possible rate of return on large, incremental investments is typically modest, the same is not true of small investments in radical new business concepts or in ideas that can reinvigorate an otherwise moribund business concept. VCs look for opportunities with enormous upside potential, on the order of 10:1, 100:1, or even 1,000:1. If most of the ventures in a portfolio have this kind of upside potential, the "expected value" of the portfolio can be substantial, even though each project is far more likely to fail than succeed. A prudent investor would not want to invest in any single project but would be delighted to invest in the entire portfolio. Again, many companies fail to grasp this simple portfolio logic. This is why most companies don't have dozens upon dozens of new-rule experiments bubbling away. But to find a breathtaking breakout opportunity, every company must build a portfolio of business concept experiments.

By the way, if you treat the person who just blew a 20-percent "sure thing" the same way you treat the guy or gal who just blew a 99-percent "sure thing," you're going to end up with a company full of timid little mice. The person who is managing a highly speculative project in a portfolio of such projects is almost expected to fail. But the gal who has an incremental project in a long-established business should never fail. Yet again, this distinction is seldom made. It's a bit like treating the person who fails to get a hole-in-one on a 300-yard, par-4 golf hole the same way you treat the person who just missed a two-foot putt. Do this, and you'll end up with a company full of two-foot putters—nervous souls who will congregate in "safe" businesses. And there's not a chance in the world your company will join the ranks of the wealth creators. Personal risk must be divorced from project risk. Celebrate the individual or the team that leads an expedition into the unknown.

Companies often overestimate the risk of doing something new for the simple reason that top management is too distant to make an informed assessment—too far from the voice of the customer and too far from the voice of the future. There is an important difference between actual risk and perceived risk. Actual risk is a function of irreducible uncertainty: Will the technology work? Will customers value this new service? What will they be willing to pay for it? and so on. Perceived risk is a function of ignorance. The farther you are from a hands-on, first-person understanding of the new opportunity, the greater the perceived risk. For years Detroit designed dependably boring automobiles— cars like the Chevrolet Lumina and Ford Contour. Was this because these were the only kind of cars that Americans wanted to buy or because Detroit's designers weren't in touch with the leading edge of customer demand? Cars like the Dodge Viper and the Chrysler PT Cruiser looked risky only to those who weren't in tune with trendy young buyers and wild-eyed enthusiasts. The point is simple: You can't let people who couldn't see the leading edge with a pair of binoculars make judgments about what is and isn't risky.

In the end, though, **companies don't need more risk takers; they need people who understand how to de-risk big aspirations.** There are several ways to do this. Like Virgin, you can pass off risk to strategic partners. When Virgin launched its financial services business, Virgin Money, it relied on an Australian insurance company for the majority of the initial capital and on a British bank for back-office support. Like GE Capital, you can buy small "popcorn stands," little businesses that will help you learn about bigger opportunities. Once GE understands the basics and the opportunity to reinvent the business, it pours in capital. In the early stages of any new business concept experiment, the goal is to maximize the ratio of learning over investment.

Reconnoitering a broad new opportunity is a bit like trying to shoot a game bird in a fast-flying flock. If you use a rifle, you'll almost certainly miss. A rifle is fine if the target is big and slow. If the target is small and swift, a shotgun is your only hope. Too often a company makes a single, premature bet when confronting a new and underdefined opportunity. The greater the initial uncertainty about which customers will buy, what product configuration is best, what pricing scheme will work and which distribution channels will be most effective, the greater the number of experiments that should be launched.

Many large companies feel that it is virtually a waste of time to pour scarce management talent into pint-sized experiments. After all, the thinking goes, how big would these experiments have to be in order to make an appreciable impact in a company with $10 billion, $20 billion or $50 billion in revenue? This isn't the way they think at GE Capital. To qualify as a "bubble," the name GE Capital gives to its major operating units, a business has to be able to generate $25 million in profits per year. That may sound like a lot, but it's significantly less than 1 percent of what GE Capital earns in a good year. "Popcorn stands" are even smaller. GE Capital's senior managers spend a lot of time searching for popcorn stands and trying to grow them into pre-bubble "ventures." All too often there is a 1:1 ratio between the amount of management attention a project or business receives and its current revenues. This is a misapplication of management attention, and it is a recipe for maintaining the status quo. Small things need to be nourished by top management attention. Without the fertilizer of top management interest, they will remain small things.

Inevitably, the time will come when a fledgling business needs to borrow some critical resource from somewhere else in the organization, to win some argument around channel conflict, or to double up its investments. If top management's attention has been elsewhere, it will lack the confidence to "go for it." GE Capital's ventures and popcorn stands don't languish in some isolated "new ventures division." Instead they are nurtured and guided by line executives who know that the only way to keep growing is to keep starting a lot of small experiments.

Make small bets. Make a lot of small bets. Think of your experiments as a portfolio of options. Pass off risk to your partners. Accelerate learning. Celebrate the pathfinders. This is the ethos of low-risk experimentation. And it is a critical design rule for building organizations that are consistently revolutionary.

DESIGN RULE #7: CELLULAR DIVISION

Gray-haired revolutionaries are not monoliths. They are big companies that have been divided into a large number of revolutionary cells.

A human embryo grows through a process of cell division: a single cell becomes two, then four, then eight, then sixteen and so on. Some cells become lungs, others fingernails, bones, tendons and all the other organs and structures of the body. Division and differentiation—that's the essence of growth. The same is true for organizations. **WHEN COMPANIES STOP DIVIDING AND DIFFERENTIATING, INNOVATION DIES AND GROWTH SLOWS.**

For example, when Virgin Records showed the first signs of lethargy, Sir Richard Branson took the deputy managing director, deputy sales director and deputy marketing director and made them the nucleus of a new company—in a new building. Suddenly, they were no longer deputies, they were in charge. Collectively, Virgin became the largest independent record company in the world, but nowhere, Branson claims, did it feel like a large company. Says one of Virgin's senior executives:

> We don't run an empire, we run a lot of small companies. We call it a big, small company. We want to be a substantial business with a small company feel so people can see the results of their own efforts.

Virgin's not the only believer in cellular division. The last few years have seen a record number of de-mergers, divestitures, and spin-offs. Yet much of this is too little too late. The real champions of cellular division practice a much more radical version of corporate mitosis.

Illinois Tool Works is a $6 billion company you've probably never heard of. Yet between 1994 and 1999, its earnings growth was twice that of the S&P 500. ITW is broken into nearly 400 business units, with average revenues of just $15 million each. Each unit has its own general manager, who has all the authority of a CEO—as long as the unit is outperforming the competition. When a business gets to $50 million in revenue, it is split into two or three units. For example, the company's Deltar business, which sells plastic fasteners to the auto market, took seven years to hit $2 million in sales. After being split off from the Fastex division and getting its own manufacturing facility and dedicated sales force, its revenues grew 700 percent in four years. Since then, Deltar itself has been split again and again. The original business now has 26 "children" with combined sales of $300 million. An $800 million acquisition made in 1998 was soon split up into more than 30 units. Here's what some of ITW's executive team say about the company's penchant for cellular division:

> We love competing against a big company, because their management teams don't have the same feel that our people have. It's not that we're smarter. It's that our people are only

concentrating on one small part of the market. They are like entrepreneurs—it's not an exaggeration.

We develop managers so rapidly that a person can start running a business when he is in his 20s. Some segments start out very small, perhaps $5 million to $8 million. That's a great place to try a young person. If they fail, we just pick up the pieces and move on. If they worked for another company, they would be trapped in some function. Here they get a chance to do everything.[4]

The advantages of cellular division for business concept innovation are many. First, it frees human and financial capital from the tyranny of any single business model. You've heard it said that size is the enemy of innovation. That's wrong. Size is not the issue. Orthodoxy is the issue. A business unit, whether $1 million or $10 billion in size, typically corresponds to a single business model. It is the allegiance to that business model that inhibits innovation, not the size of the business per se. Cellular division creates space for new business models.

Second, cellular division provides opportunities to nurture entrepreneurial talent. It reduces the number of stewards minding someone else's store and increases the number of entrepreneurs running their own businesses. Third, by keeping units small and focused, cellular division keeps general managers close to the voice of the customer. And fourth, by dispersing power, it undermines the ability of strong divisions to kill projects that might cannibalize their revenue streams. For example, Hewlett-Packard's decision to put its ink jet printer unit and its laser jet printer business in separate divisions helped both businesses to sidestep the cannibalization debate that so often cramps the style of new initiatives. The benefit for HP was that it became the world leader in two printing businesses.

Sure, cellular division forces companies to forgo some shared economies, but scale's not quite the advantage it used to be, and fragmentation is not quite as expensive as it used to be. Speed, flexibility, and focus have never been more important. That's why cellular division is a critical design principle for innovation. So does your company have any $1-billion-plus divisions? Give W. James Farrell, the CEO of Illinois Tool Works, a carving knife, and he'll turn it into 66 independent businesses, more or less!

DESIGN RULE #8: CONNECTIVITY

Innovation is not a private act—it is seldom the product of a single individual's intellectual brilliance. Innovation is a product of the connections between individuals and their ideas—the more connections, the greater the number of combinatorial possibilities. It is the constant interplay of ideas, perspectives, experiences and values that spawns innovation. In this sense, innovation is like great cooking—new flavors come from new and imaginative combinations of existing ingredients. For nearly 20 years, Wolfgang Puck's Chinois has been one of LA's trendiest restaurants—a place where moguls and movie stars compete for the best tables. The food at Chinois is a French–Californian–Chinese fusion of flavors that delights the senses but defies categorization. *Fusion*—that's the essence of innovation, and it depends on connections.

This is why boundary–spanning teams and projects are so important—they connect people with diverse backgrounds and skill sets and out of this mélange, new ideas arise. How many opportunities have you had in the last month to interact deeply with colleagues who work outside of your business unit or country? At Cemex, the monthly country manager meetings, the expert groups (e-groups), the PMI teams and the innovation platform teams are just a few of the ways individuals from various backgrounds and geographies get connected. Cemex's senior executives believe this rich tapestry of interaction is central to the company's ability to innovate.

Of course, what is important is not merely the connections that you make internally, but those you make externally, as well. Today, it is important to view the world as a reservoir of interesting skills, assets and ideas—all of which can be combined and recombined to create new and interesting business concepts. In developing a strategy to compete with its tough Japanese rivals, Swatch went to Lego, in Denmark, to learn how to make watches out of brightly colored plastic, and built a design center in Milan to serve as a lightning rod for the artistic talents that would ultimately make Swatch into a fashion icon. More recently, GolfPro International added GPS technology, ultrasound sensing and an LCD screen to an electrically propelled golf cart. The result is a golf cart that will follow you down the course, stop just behind you as you reach your ball, notify you of the distance to a hazard or the green and then find its way to the back of the green as you putt out. Oh, and if you jump across a stream, the InteleCady will roll to the nearest bridge and rejoin you as you walk to the next tee. Innovation is about making unexpected connections—in this case, between technologies that heretofore had never joined forces on a golf course.

Connections are just as important on the "output" side of innovation as they are on the "input" side. The value of any innovation within a company is a product of its inherent value multiplied by the speed and breadth of propagation. Ideas that stay isolated produce little economic value. What's required for propagation is more than some sterile, IT-based knowledge system. An IT system can be helpful in transferring simple, explicit knowledge, but it's not much help in creating the kind of synthetic, cross-boundary interaction that creates *new* knowledge. What is required instead are frequent face-to-face meetings where individuals are given the time and space to question, share and learn. This was the role of the Information Technology Strategy Committee at UPS, and of the innovation platform teams at Cemex. Balkanized companies, where there are few cross-unit teams, projects or working groups are not going to be very good at radical innovation. They will be even worse at propagating new ideas. New voices are important to innovation. Just as important is the ability to connect those voices in new ways.

IS YOUR COMPANY BUILT FOR INNOVATION?

Step back for a moment and reflect on the design rules for innovation—on the qualities that imbue gray-haired revolutionaries with their revolutionary fervor. Your company may pretend to be serious about innovation, but has it fully committed itself to embodying the design rules in every way, every day?

Ask yourself these questions:

- Is your company ready to pump up its aspirations to the point where anything less than radical innovation won't suffice?
- Is your company ready to throw out its definition of "served market" and define its opportunity space more broadly?
- Is your company ready to begin searching for a cause that will be so great, so totally righteous, that it will turn a bunch of apprehensive cubicle dwellers into crusaders?
- Is top management in your company ready to shut up for a while and start listening—really listening—to the young, the new hires and those at the geographic periphery?
- Is your company ready to throw open its strategy process to every great idea, no matter where it comes from?
- Is your company ready to start funding ideas from the fringe even if many of them return precisely zilch?
- Is your company ready to emancipate some of its best people so they can get to work on the new?

○ Is your company ready to start paying attention to the tiny seeds of innovation that are right now struggling to break through the topsoil?
○ Is your company ready to take on the imperialists who would rather preside over a big but slowly crumbling empire than give self-rule to eager young business builders?
○ Is your company building the cross-boundary connections, both internally and externally, that create the kind of fusion that produces truly cool new ideas?

There are dozens—probably hundreds—of ways to institutionalize the design rules that have been covered in this chapter. My goal has not been to give you a detailed implementation guide, because what works for UPS, Virgin, Cemex, GE Capital or some other gray-haired revolutionary may not work for your company. Instead, what you must do is engage your colleagues in a serious and prolonged discussion about how to put the design rules to work in your company. I don't believe it's possible to systematize innovation—there's no simple three-step process. On the other hand, I believe that you can make innovation systemic—you can bake the values and beliefs that support innovation deeply into an organization. And, with the design rules as a foundation, you can begin to create the metrics, skills and processes that will support innovation whenever and wherever it arises. It is to this capability-building agenda we turn next.

9
THE NEW INNOVATION SOLUTION

FOR ONCE, YOU ARE NOT START–
ing from behind. Yeah, there are companies that embody some of the design rules for innovation, but none of them will claim to have made innovation as ubiquitous as six sigma, cycle time, rapid customer service or any of a dozen less essential capabilities. That's the good news. The bad news is that by the time you read fawning stories in *Business Week* or *Fortune* about companies that have bolstered internal activism, baked the "design rules" into their organizations and declared radical innovation to be a core competence, it's going to be too late.

Just how long will it take your company to embrace the new innovation agenda? Are you willing to start now, long before the principles and practices of business concept innovation have been reduced to the kind of prosaic manuals of "best practice" so beloved by consultants and the bottom–quartile companies on which they feed?

Take a moment before you respond. After all, your share of the future's wealth depends on how you answer.

It took companies such as Ford, Xerox and Caterpillar a decade and more to regain the ground they lost when they fell behind their Japanese competitors in the march toward quality. This time, you're not going to get ten years to catch up. This time you're not even going to see the warning lights come on. **Industry revolutionaries— whether they have acne or gray temples—are like a missile up the tailpipe. Boom! You're irrelevant!**

SHAKING THE FOUNDATIONS

To embrace the new innovation agenda you are going to have to challenge every management tenet you inherited from the age of progress. Belief by belief and brick by brick, you must examine the philosophical foundations that undergird your convictions about leadership, wealth creation and competitiveness. Whenever you find a brick that is old and fractured, kick it out and push a new one in. By now you should have a few ideas on where to start:

Old brick: Top management is responsible for setting strategy.
New brick: Everybody can help build innovative strategies.

Old brick: Getting better, faster is the way to win.
New brick: Rule-busting innovation is the way to win.

Old brick: Information technology creates competitive advantage.
New brick: Unconventional business concepts create competitive advantage.

Old brick: Being revolutionary is high risk.
New brick: More of the same is high risk.

Old brick: We can merge our way to competitiveness.
New brick: There's no correlation between size and profitability.

Old brick: Innovation equals new products and new technology.
New brick: Innovation equals entirely new business concepts.

Old brick: Strategy is the easy part, implementation is the hard
part.
New brick: Strategy is easy only if you're content to be an
imitator.

Old brick: Change starts at the top.
New brick: Change starts with activists.

Old brick: Our real problem is execution.
New brick: Our real problem is incrementalism.

Old brick: Alignment is always a virtue.
New brick: Diversity and variety are the keys to innovation.

Old brick: Big companies can't innovate.
New brick: Big companies can become gray-haired revolutionaries.

Old brick: You can't make innovation a capability.
New brick: Oh yes, you can, but not without effort.

If you want your company to be revolution-ready, no belief can go
unexamined.

GETTING COMMITTED

You have to believe three things in order to commit your organization to building a capability for radical innovation:

○ An investment in making innovation a capability will yield huge
dividends.
○ There is a wealth of latent imagination and untapped
entrepreneurial zeal in your organization.
○ It's actually possible to make innovation a systemic capability.

THE RETURN ON INNOVATION

If you've ever worked in a company where quality has become a
religion, you know how much time and effort were devoted to institu-
tionalizing quality as a capability. Quality may be free, but building
quality as an advantage is an expensive undertaking. Yet it is univer-

sally deemed worth the effort. Given the potential payoff to industry revolution—a payoff that's reflected in the wealth creation of rule-breaking companies—I believe the case for investing in business concept innovation as a capability is at least as sound as the case for investing in quality.

If you agree, then you must also agree that many companies have been misdirecting their energies: They've been moving heaven and hell to eke out the last bit of wealth from a dying business model while largely ignoring the chance to create new wealth from new business concepts or from a radically reconceived business concepts. Maybe your company has held a few brainstorming sessions. Maybe top management has hosted a two-day conference in a bucolic resort to consider the challenges of innovation and growth. Maybe there's even a corporate incubator or skunk works tucked away in some dark corner. But if you're honest, you're going to have to admit that there is a huge disparity in the amount of energy your company has devoted to getting better and the amount of effort it has expended in getting different—in getting revolution-ready. The implicit belief seems to be that incremental improvement is backbreaking work, while nonlinear innovation is easy. This is, of course, nonsense. Building any woof-and-warp capability is difficult and expensive. But the return on an investment in innovation will beat the return on any other capability one can imagine.

REVOLUTIONARIES EVERYWHERE

Despite the lesson of Silicon Valley, where the most unlikely sorts of people have created (and sometimes lost) fortunes, there's still a prejudice in most companies that first-line employees are unlikely to be sources of wealth-creating innovation. Thirty years ago, few people believed that blue-collar workers with no more than 12 years of formal education could take responsibility for improving quality. In a few years, the notion that "ordinary" employees are the wellspring for business concept innovation will be no more remarkable than the proposition that everyone is responsible for quality. Yet unless you and your colleagues are ready right now to accept the fact that there are revolutionaries everywhere in your company, you will lose. There is no place for elitism in the age of revolution.

MAKING SERENDIPITY HAPPEN

Can something as effervescent as innovation be systemized? Again, the analogy with quality is useful. In times past, quality of the sort offered by Rolls-Royce, Tiffany or Hermès required the unerring eye and skilled hands of an artisan. Who would have believed that a Toyota could be made as reliable as a Bentley or that a Swatch could keep better time than a Rolex? Yet this was the singular contribution of the quality movement: to make what had been unique, ubiquitous. It goes without saying that eureka moments cannot be programmed in advance. Innovation will always be a mixture of serendipity, genius and sheer bloody-mindedness. **WHILE YOU CAN'T BOTTLE LIGHTNING, YOU CAN BUILD LIGHTNING RODS.** Nonlinear innovation can be legitimized, fostered, celebrated and rewarded.

To create a hotbed of business concept innovation, you have to start with the design rules. But you can't stop there. It's not enough to create a climate for radical innovation and it's not enough to venerate the activists. You must create a positive capability for business concept innovation. What follows is an agenda for anyone who would like to get a head start on building the pivotal source of competitive advantage in the age of revolution.

THE NEW INNOVATION SOLUTION

While the ten design rules and the principles of activism are parts of the innovation solution, there are other equally important components:

○ Skills
○ Metrics
○ Information technology
○ Management processes

Each of these is a critical component of the new innovation solution. Each has an essential role to play in creating a deep capability for business concept innovation (see the figure "Innovation as a Capability").

INNOVATION AS A CAPABILITY

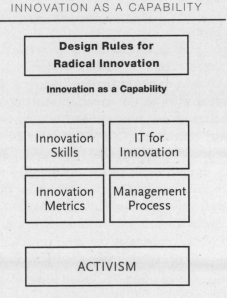

SKILLS

Your company has virtually no chance of leading the revolution if it is populated by industrial–age mind–sets. Every mind in your company must be re-tooled for the age of revolution. Training is tedious, and learning is hard work, but there's no other way to embed capability. Ask yourself these questions:

○ How many people in your company understand the role industry revolution plays in wealth creation?
○ How many know how to calculate the decay rate of current business models?
○ How many know how to identify and deconstruct industry and company orthodoxies?
○ How many are able to distill proprietary foresight out of an ocean of information on "discontinuities"?
○ How many are adept at inventing new business concepts and rein-venting old ones?
○ How many feel personally responsible for business concept innovation?
○ How many understand the principles of activism and would know how to launch a grassroots innovation campaign?
○ How many would know how to build a low–cost experiment to test a radical new idea?
○ How many are working to apply the design rules for innovation to their parts of the company?

If you didn't answer "the majority," your organization isn't yet revolution-ready. If you've read the other eight chapters in this book, you've already taken a substantial step in "re-skilling" yourself for the age of revolution, but that's not enough. To thrive in the age of revolution, companies will need thousands, not tens, of individuals who are revolution–ready. It's not enough to have little islands of capability—a few individuals here and there who are sources of nonlinear innovation. In most companies, it took systematic, cross–company training to firm-ly embed quality as a capability. The same will be true for business concept innovation. Forget all that blather in your company's mission statement about creativity and innovation. Unless it's running boot camps for industry insurgents, it's still substituting rhetoric for action. Radical innovation must become the next agenda item for every cor-porate university. So get on the phone to your HR VP or the person who runs corporate training. Tell them you have a few ideas for some curriculum changes.

Did you ever read the classic article "On the Folly of Rewarding A, While Hoping for B"?[1] There's a lesson in there for every company that wants to fuel the fires of innovation and create new wealth. Most companies have dozens of measures focused on cost, efficiency, speed and customer satisfaction—and pay people for making progress against these metrics. Yet in my experience, there are few companies that have any metrics that focus on radical innovation. If you have any doubts about this, take the following quiz:

○ How many measures do you have in your company that focus explicitly on innovation (versus optimization)?
○ How many individuals in your company could say as much about your company's innovation performance as they could say about your company's cost efficiency?
○ How many people in your company have any personal performance metrics related to innovation?
○ Does your company systematically benchmark other companies on innovation?

Most companies use a decidedly unbalanced scorecard—one that is heavily weighted toward optimization rather than innovation. Measures like RONA, ROCE, EVA and ROI often encourage managers to beat a dead horse even harder. How often have you heard an entrepreneur boasting about capital efficiency? The fact that you haven't should tell you something. It's not that industrial-age metrics are anti-innovation; it's just that they're not pro-innovation. And in a world where business concept innovation is the surest route to wealth creation, that's a fatal flaw. Without strong pro-innovation metrics, the default setting in most organizations is "more of the same."

Traditional metrics don't force a company to consider how it is performing against new and unorthodox competitors in the quest for wealth creation. What does it matter to an investor if a company is earning its cost of capital if its rivals are capturing the lion's share of new wealth in an industry? Companies need a way of measuring their relative capacity to invent new business concepts and create new wealth. One such measure is the wealth creation index, or WCI. It is currently being used by a number of companies that are eager to focus attention on the challenge of new wealth creation. The WCI lets a company determine how it has performed against a relevant set of "competitors" in creating new wealth. The process of determining your company's WCI involves two steps: defining the domain and calculating changes in the market value of your company versus the value of the entire domain.

DEFINING THE DOMAIN

The first step in calculating a company's WCI is to specify a competitive domain. I use the word "domain" rather than "industry" because measuring wealth creation within an "industry" often leads to an overly narrow definition of a company's potential opportunity horizon. The domain should include all the companies that are positioned either upstream or downstream from your own company in a vertical "value chain." It should also encompass companies that supply complementary products or services within a broader "value network." For example, an auto manufacturer would need to include the new Internet auto retailers as well as the providers of ancillary services such as body shops and oil change shops.

Further, the definition of domain should include companies that possess similar core competencies or those that satisfy the same deep customer needs. For example, Tower Records must include in its definition of domain all the new Web-based businesses where consumers can download music. An oil company should define its domain as "energy." An insurance company would define its domain as "financial services," and so on. If the definition of domain includes companies with similar competencies or serving the same broad class of needs, there is little chance of being surprised by a "disruptive technology."

CALCULATING CHANGES IN MARKET
VALUE VERSUS DOMAIN VALUE

The next step is to measure changes in a company's market value versus changes in the market value of all the companies within its domain. This lets you answer an important question: Has my company created more or less than its "fair share" of new wealth? To calculate a company's share of wealth creation, simply divide its share of total domain value at the end of a period by its share at the beginning of a period. If a company's market capitalization represented 5 percent of total domain value in Year 1, and 10 percent in Year 5, the company would have a WCI of two.

A company's market value is the net present value of its expected future net earnings—based on the collective assessment of investors. In a world of diminishing returns to incrementalism, it is unlikely that any company can dramatically grow its market capitalization in the absence of business concept innovation. Incremental efficiency programs are seldom capable of producing a step-function change in investor expectations about a company's profit potential. Aside from acquisitions and mergers, it is virtually impossible for a company to dramatically raise its market cap without inventing new profit streams.

Likewise, if a company's market value is stagnant or collapsing, it suggests a decrepit strategy. For all these reasons, changes in market cap are a reasonable proxy for strategic innovation. (Of course one must make adjustments for de-mergers and disposals, as well as for acquisitions and mergers.) Changes in a company's market capitalization relative to other companies in the same domain provide an even better proxy for strategic innovation. If a company is a division of a much larger company or privately held, one must calculate an implied market cap for that particular division using well-known valuation techniques. Don't expect to derive wealth creation measures straight out of the *Wall Street Journal*. Defining the relevant domain and establishing valuation numbers is hard work. But in my experience, the discussion engendered and the insights derived always justify the effort. When the value of the entire domain is increasing, only companies that achieve above-average growth in market cap can claim to be true strategy innovators. It is nearly tautological: In the absence of acquisitions or mergers, any company that achieves a sustained jump in its share of domain value is an industry revolutionary.

Let's take one example. The value of the nonfood retailing domain grew 6.3 times over the last decade (only U.S. companies were included in the calculation). The table "The Nonfood Retailing Domain" summarizes changes in wealth share between 1988 and 1998. Already number one in 1988, Wal-Mart continued to grow its share of wealth over the next decade. The Home Depot was another awesome wealth creator. Sears, Kmart, JCPenney and Toys "R" Us were big WCI losers. They failed to reinvent themselves or their industries.

A WCI score of less than one is a sure sign of nostalgia for an out-of-date business concept. All too often, the bonds of misplaced loyalty are severed only when the company suffers some catastrophic earnings failure. Instead of looking back over a decade and bemoaning a failure to grab new opportunities, track share-of-wealth data on an ongoing basis. A WCI that is edging lower suggests that the company is falling behind in the search for new business concepts.

The percentage of new wealth created by newcomers is a simple way of judging the susceptibility of incumbents to nonlinear innovation. Upstarts captured fully 27 percent of the new wealth in the com-

	Share of Wealth (% in 1988)	Share of Wealth (% in 1998)	Wealth Creation Index (1988–1998)
The Home Depot	1.8	13.9	7.7
Wal-Mart	20.0	28.0	1.4
Gap	1.7	4.9	2.9
Amazon.com	0.0	2.6	∞
Costco	0.0	2.4 [A]	∞
Walgreens	2.1	4.5	2.1
Sears	17.1	2.5 [B]	0.15
Kmart	7.9	1.2	0.1
JCPenney	7.3	1.8	0.2
Toys "R" Us	5.4	0.7	0.1

[A] 0.3 percent of Costco's gain reflects market cap added from Costco's 1993 $1.7 billion all-equity acquisition of Price Co.

[B] During this period Sears spun off two large holdings with a combined market value of $16.8 billion. Without these disposals, Sears' PSW would have been higher by about 2.6 percent.

Source: Standard and Poor's COMPUSTAT; Strategos calculations.

puter domain over the past ten years. In retailing, companies that didn't even exist in 1988 captured 16 percent of the new wealth created. This means that despite all their advantages, retailing incumbents surrendered $107 billion of new opportunities to agile and innovative upstarts. A caveat here: Occasionally, as we saw with high tech shares in the late 1980s, an entire sector can be overvalued. As ever, one has to be careful not to give too much weight to market values that are not supported by an underlying earnings stream. Yet because WCI is a *relative* measure, it is mostly by such bursts of irrational exuberances (or pessimism). Relatively speaking WCI still differentiates between those who are valued more from those who are valued less.

If new entrants can capture billions of dollars of new wealth in an industry without the resources and accumulated experience of an established player, imagine the possibilities if the energy and resources of an already successful company could be focused on the challenge of inventing new opportunities for new wealth creation.

Calculate your company's WCI over the past year, or two, or five. Get a discussion going over the appropriate definition of "domain." Challenge the definitions of "industry" and "served market" that prevail in your company. Ask yourself: Are these definitions broad enough? Do they blind us to nontraditional competitors? What opportunities have we missed? Then look at the companies that have created a disproportionate share of new wealth and ask, How did they define their opportunity horizon? Why did they see opportunities we didn't? What was their implicit definition of domain? How did they exploit our myopia? Answering these questions will expose the biases and beliefs that have aborted innovation in your own company.

Use the new metrics to challenge complacency. Redefine "acceptable" performance so it includes not only good stewardship but also an above-average WCI score. Look for companies that have excelled in the wealth creation sweepstakes, and use their example to reset aspirations in your own company. The distilled essence of entrepreneurial energy is the quest for new wealth. When widely discussed and understood, metrics like WCI can help you bring that energy inside your own company.

Of course, no single metric, on its own, can endow employees with imagination, make management responsive to new ideas, and bestow the courage needed to abandon comfortable orthodoxies. But be sure of this: If you don't get the metrics right, none of the other needed behaviors are likely to follow.

INFORMATION TECHNOLOGY

Intranets. E-mail. Newsgroups. Instant messaging. The fact is so obvious, it's hardly worth noting: Information technology has been dramatically changing the way organizations work. Digital communication drills through layers of bureaucracy, undermines hierarchy, makes much of middle management redundant, enables globe-spanning collaboration, unites far-flung supplier networks, makes 24/7 tech support available worldwide—and that's just for starters. Odd, then, that IT vendors and professionals have contributed so little to the cause of radical innovation. There are few companies where IT has helped to turbocharge business concept innovation.

Imagine a corporationwide IT system—an innovation network—designed to support radical innovation. Any employee with a germ of an idea, or just an urge to create, could go online and find a wealth of innovation tools—here's how you discover industry orthodoxies, here's how you build a business concept, here's how you develop a 100-day new-rules experiment, and so on. The tyro entrepreneur could toss his or her idea into a corporation-wide "Ideaspace"—essentially an online market for radical ideas. An "innovation editor" would group similar ideas together and post them on the company's intranet. Anyone visiting the site could build on the ideas submitted—"Have you thought about this?" or "Here's another way of going to market."

It would be easy to host real-time online discussions for particularly hot ideas. Ideas that attracted attention and thoughtful inputs would flower and grow, while those that didn't would wither. Individuals across the company could register their interest in working on a particular idea—"Yeah, I'd be willing to spend six months helping you get this launched," or "I'll loan you one of my team members to help you build the prototype." There could also be an internal market for funding. Anyone in the company with a budget could decide to sponsor a radical new idea. Ordinary employees might even be able to buy "options" in the nascent venture—whether in the form of phantom equity or a share of some future profit stream. A divisional vice president might say, "Okay, I'll put $100,000 in so you can take this idea to the next stage," or an individual might say, "I'll invest $5,000 for a quarter-percent of equity." Conversely, innovators could bid for talent and capital, using phantom options in return. If the new idea is a reinvention of an existing business concept, rather than an entirely new business with its own P&L, the valuation problem gets more difficult, but the providers of talent and capital might be given a share in the profit growth of an existing business. In any case, ideas that attracted talent and money would get implemented; those that didn't, wouldn't. Of course, top management could monitor the innovation marketplace and put big money and top-flight talent behind ideas that showed great promise.

To institutionalize radical innovation, companies will need to build highly efficient electronic markets for ideas, capital and talent. As they do so, it will no longer be the knowledge management function that constitutes the leading edge of corporate IT, but the innovation marketplace. Are you ready for this?

MANAGEMENT PROCESSES

Many companies have spent a decade reinventing their core business processes for efficiency. The goal has been to straighten out the kinks in the supply chain—from suppliers through incoming logistics through work-in-progress through outbound logistics and customer fulfillment. Dell Computer is the poster child for supply chain integration. To a customer, Dell Computer's delivery pipeline appears both short and slick. While supersmooth business processes are great for efficiency—Dell operates with negative working capital—they don't do squat for innovation. **In most large companies, the innovation pipeline is about as efficient as Victorian plumbing lined with Velcro.** Radical ideas get hung up in the

Byzantine complexity of the strategic planning process, the capital budgeting process, the staffing process or the product development process. Companies that have reengineered their core business processes for efficiency are now going to have to reinvent their core management processes for innovation. If supply chain integration was about minimizing the time between an order and delivery, reinventing management processes for innovation is about accelerating the payoff for radical ideas. There are several ways in which management processes are inimical to innovation. First, most of them are calendar-driven—there seems to be an implicit assumption that you can count on new opportunities to wait patiently for the arrival of the October planning round. Budgets are set on a quarterly or annual basis and, once set, are inviolable. Second, **most management processes are biased toward conservation rather than growth.** They tend to put a premium on efficiency and undervalue experimentation aimed at exploring new competitive space. Ideas for trying something new and out-of-bounds are implicitly viewed as dangerous diversions from the central task of driving down costs and building market share in the core business. I have seldom seen a management process that explicitly challenges managers to develop and test a portfolio of unconventional strategic options. In general, management processes are focused on minimizing variances rather than maximizing opportunities.

Third, most management processes take the existing business model as the point of departure. Traditional definitions of market structure, traditional ways of describing the value chain, traditional assumptions about the cost structure, traditional beliefs about where you take your profits—all these are woven into the form and substance of management processes. In ways subtle and not so subtle, management processes perpetuate the status quo. Champions of business concept innovation will, invariably, find themselves working against the grain of key management processes.

Most management processes are focused on existing customers and markets. Again, there is a subtle bias toward serving existing customers better, rather than finding entirely new types of customers. Even worse, it is the articulated needs of customers that get all the attention, rather than their unarticulated needs. Most management processes have a place to plug in the banalities produced by market research, but have no way of accommodating the highly impressionistic but infinitely more profound insights that come from experiential, out-of-bounds learning. And, of course, market share gets a lot more discussion than wealth share.

Most management processes are controlled by the defenders of the past. The senior staff who "own" corporate training, planning and capital budgeting view their role as serving the barons who run today's big businesses. Any redesign of the management process usually begins by polling the executive vice presidents. Seldom is any attention given to the needs of struggling entrepreneurs and would-be activists.

Finally, most management processes are implicitly risk averse. The burden of proof is on those who would like to change the status quo. Seldom is the risk of overinvesting in a decaying business model made explicit. In countless ways, internal revolutionaries are given the message that incrementalism is safe and radicalism is risky, when of course the reverse is more often true.

Interview successful revolutionaries in large companies, and you'll hear a familiar refrain: "I succeeded despite the system." All of them know that "the system" is there to frustrate the new, the unconventional, and the untested. Management systems are designed to enforce conformance, alignment and continuity. We would be horrified if employees said they managed to deliver quality products and services "despite the system." We should be horrified that employees have to produce innovation "in spite of the system."

So here's what you do. Identify the four or five most pervasive and powerful management processes in your company: compensation, succession planning, leadership training, strategic planning, capital budgeting, product development, whatever. For each core process, assemble a review team, comprising a diagonal slice of your company. Make sure you have a senior staff person, a VP, a couple of middle managers and a mix of successful and unsuccessful corporate rebels on each team. Ask a proven revolutionary to chair each team. Give each team one management process to redesign. Have them pull together all of the documentation used to support that process. Have them map the process across time and across the organization by asking, What are the milestones? Who gets to participate? What are the inputs? What are the outputs? What kinds of decisions does the process produce? Have them interview a couple dozen process "users." In what ways does the process hinder business concept innovation and in what ways does it foster it? Have the team go back and review the purpose behind the process—what was it originally designed to do? Is that goal still valid? Is it possible to design a process that will meet that goal without killing innovation? Ask them to review each component of the management process for any evidence that the process is any of the following: inappropriately calendar-driven; biased toward conservation and efficiency rather than experimentation and growth; too tightly intertwined with the existing business model; overfocused on existing customers and markets; controlled by and run for the benefit of those defending large, established businesses; inherently risk averse. Finally, have the team suggest ways in which each component of the process could be redesigned to make it less backward-looking and more innovation-friendly. The team will need to write a new mission statement for the process—one that explicitly includes nonlinear innovation and wealth creation.

THE WHEEL OF INNOVATION

So you're baking the design rules into your organization, you're offering succor to the activists, and you're working to make business concept innovation a systemic capability. But there's still more to do. Innovation is a dynamic process, with the following elements:

○ Heretics and novelty addicts imagine new possibilities.
○ Using the principles of business concept innovation, they design coherent business models around those ideas, or redesign existing business models.
○ They launch small-scale experiments to test the viability of their business concepts and then adapt them.

THE WHEEL OF INNOVATION

Design Rules for Radical Innovation

Innovation as a Process

Innovation as a Capability

Innovation Skills | IT for Innovation
Innovation Metrics | Management Process

IMAGINE · DESIGN · EXPERIMENT · ASSESS · SCALE

IDEAS

Activism

○ Having conducted an experiment or two or three, they assess what has been learned.
○ Depending on what has been learned, they decide whether to scale up or go through another experiment cycle.

Imagine, Design, Experiment, Assess, Scale. (By now you've spotted the helpful mnemonic.) This is the wheel of innovation, and it is the next critical component in the innovation solution (see the figure "The Wheel of Innovation").

MAKING THE WHEEL SPIN FASTER

The speed at which a company gets the wheel of innovation turning determines the amount of new wealth it creates. The first stumbling block is often an inability of potential innovators to go from the fragment of an idea to a reasonably holistic business concept design. Senior executives often tell me, "Our problem isn't a lack of ideas—we have too many ideas." But when I ask them whether they have too many truly compelling and coherent strategic options, the answer is always "no." This is why the skills needed to design a new business concept or reinvent an old one must be widely distributed. Would-be innovators must be able to do some initial quality assessment on their own ideas—is this a brainwave or a brainfart? If you can't imagine a coherent, profitable business concept supporting your idea, or if you can't imagine how your idea can profitably transform an existing business concept, send it aloft with all the other greenhouse gases.

SUCCESSIVE APPROXIMATION

Once there is a potential business concept, it must be tested experimentally, in much the same way an aeronautical engineer tests the flight characteristics of a high-performance fighter on a computer before strapping a pilot into the cockpit. Experiment, assess, adapt. Experiment, assess, adapt. The faster a company can go through this cycle, the faster it can resolve the uncertainty that inevitably surrounds a new and unconventional business concept, and the faster it can get to a viable, cash-generating business concept.

When every little new-rules experiment is scrutinized and reviewed as if it were a $100 million investment, the wheel of innovation comes to a grinding halt. **Companies are going to have to learn to run at more than one speed:** at "all deliberate speed" for big investments in capital-intensive projects where assets last for

20 years and at "light speed" for experiments in imagination–intensive opportunities. **_You can't win a Formula 1 race with a John Deere tractor._**

Listen to a couple of speed demons from our cast of gray-haired revolutionaries:

Charles Schwab: We have a learning mentality: It's better to start early and learn more than to wait around and try to get the thing perfect before you start.
GE Capital: We deal with short cycle times. We'll have a dinner, study something, and then do a transaction within weeks.

These companies understand that developing great new business concepts, or reinventing fading business concepts, is often a process of successive approximation—a succession of fast-paced experiments, each designed to test some particular aspect of a novel business concept.

CUSTOMERS AS CO-DEVELOPERS

In the age of revolution, there is simply no way to stay ahead of the innovation curve unless your customers are your co-developers. The larger the community of co-developers, the quicker problems and opportunities for improvement are identified. As Lego demonstrates, sometimes even kids can be co-developers.

The MindStorms Robotics Invention System from Danish toy manufacturer Lego lets children build and bring to life robotic machines. MindStorms kits include a microprocessor brick and an infrared connection between the microprocessor and a PC. This connection allows children to transfer instructions from the PC to the microprocessor brick and hence control the robot. Children write instructions that specify the robot's behavior by using a simplified Lego programming language.

Children have shown remarkable creativity in the design of their robots and in finding innovative uses for their robots. In fact, some of those "children" are actually college and graduate students. Regardless, recognizing that this creativity can suggest new product opportunities for Lego, the company has established several online forums, hosted on the official Lego website.[2] These open source–type communities enable MindStorms enthusiasts to share their ideas and code and help each other to overcome difficulties in programming their robots. This forum provides Lego engineers with insights into new, and unimagined, uses of the MindStorms product line—insights that can be used to generate new products and software.

Ask yourself a question: Is the development team you're using outside your company bigger than the one inside your company? If not, your wheel of innovation isn't going to spin fast enough to get you to the future first.

In the absence of bounded experiments with tightly defined learning objectives, it's all too easy for eager innovators to fall in love with a deeply flawed business concept. To kill the losers fast, you must have a short market feedback loop. While the innovation board at Cemex is willing to take a bit of a flyer on new ideas, it also insists on a month-by-month update. The focus of these frequent reviews is more than financial. It is understood that a nascent project may, at times, miss its budget numbers. The real question is whether the project's initial assumptions about customer demand, technical feasibility and business economics are being confirmed or disconfirmed. If the starting assumptions are being challenged by the reality of the market experiment, a second question arises—can we reconfigure this project or is it fatally flawed? Short-cycle feedback and dispassionate diagnosis are critical to making sure that loser projects get killed quick.

Are you getting this?

○ Be honest about what you don't know.
○ Design tight, short experiments.
○ Maximize the ratio of learning over investment.
○ Bring your customers inside the tent.
○ Love your project but kill it quick if you find unfixable flaws.

THE INNOVATION PORTFOLIO

Think of nascent business designs and early-stage experiments as options on the future. Your company's chance of creating new wealth is directly proportional to the number of ideas it fosters and the number of experiments it starts. So ask yourself, **How diverse is your company's portfolio of unconventional strategy options?** What percentage of corporate initiatives are aimed at incremental improvement, and how many are testing opportunities for business concept innovation?

The innovation portfolio is actually three distinct portfolios. First is the portfolio of ideas, of credible, but untested, new business concepts. Second is the portfolio of experiments. Ideas that have particular merit get advanced to the portfolio of experiments, where they are validated through low-cost market incursions. Third is the portfolio of new ventures. (For our purposes, the term "ventures" refers to projects that could significantly change an existing business concept as well as to projects that could spawn an entirely new business concept.) Experiments that look promising advance to venture status. Here the goal is to begin to scale up the original idea. The "imagine" and "design" phases of the innovation process fill up the first portfolio with ideas. Ideas that advance to the "experiment" and "assess" stages populate the second portfolio, and those ready to be taken to "scale" comprise the third (see the figure "The Innovation Portfolio").

While top management often views the company as a portfolio of businesses, it seldom applies the logic of portfolio investing to investments in business concept experiments. This is particularly surprising when more and more companies are setting up venture funds to invest in a portfolio of upstarts outside the company. The logic of portfolio investing is to minimize the risk of the overall portfolio by diversifying your investments. With a diversified portfolio, the risk that the entire portfolio will take a big dive is substantially less than the risk that any single stock will fall through the floor. Yet all too often, exec-

THE INNOVATION PORTFOLIO

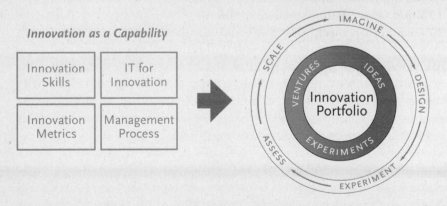

utives expect every new idea or experiment to yield a bonanza. Such an expectation will invariably make a company overconservative and will quickly drain the portfolio of ideas and the portfolio of experiments of many interesting strategic options. It is important to distinguish between the risk that a particular idea or experiment doesn't pan out and the risk that the entire innovation portfolio yields a big fat zero. A bias against anything with the slightest hint of downside ensures a company will never find anything with an amazing upside. Spectacular new opportunities seldom start out as 90 percent sure things. That's why it's important to distinguish an "idea" or an "experiment" from a venture or a fully-fledged business. Perhaps the following analogy will help. In the act of procreation, millions of sperm get "wasted." You need a lot of little swimmers to fertilize an egg. Yet we seldom bemoan the lost sperm. One huge win—a new baby—offsets millions of small failures—dead sperm. Although we can hope for a substantially better ratio of wins to losses than a prospective father, the principle is much the same: You have to be willing to tolerate a lot of small losses for the occasional gigantic win. You don't have to risk big, but you have to risk often.

While companies have long recognized the low odds of success in new product development, and have endeavored to build and fill new product pipelines in response, they haven't applied the same principle to strategy development. As a result, most companies have no process for generating a surfeit of fresh strategy ideas, nor for starting and tracking dozens of strategy experiments, and then committing to those that prove most promising. Instead of building an innovation pipeline filled with unconventional strategy options, many companies have created innovation ghettoes—incubators, new venture divisions and venture funds that are largely divorced from innovation in the core business. The assumption seems to be that it is impossible to really innovate in the core business—that the fear of cannibalization is so overpowering and the constraints of orthodoxy so absolute that the only way to innovate is to create a separate organization filled with native-born entrepreneurs. While dedicated innovation units have a purpose, they are no substitute for an innovation pipeline overflowing with ideas for revitalizing the core business.

A PORTFOLIO OF IDEAS

The portfolio of ideas is really a "portfolio of possibilities." There are hundreds of half-baked, ill-formed ideas that bump around in the heads of your colleagues. Most never get articulated. Others exist only as water cooler conversations. Few organizations have attempted to collect and manage nonlinear ideas as part of an explicit portfolio of possibilities. Fewer still actually encourage front-line employees to contribute to an innovation portfolio. So for the dozen or so ideas that actually work their way up through the usual sclerotic approval channels, there are hundreds that never escape the heads of eager but isolated entrepreneurs.

A few years back, a young woman selling sewing machines for Sears noticed a worrying trend—more and more customers were returning recently purchased sewing machines. Perplexed, she began calling her dissatisfied customers and quickly learned that many had been stymied by the sheer complexity of the feature-laden machines. Her solution was to invite these frustrated customers into the store for sewing classes. As the flood of returns began to recede, it occurred to this enterprising employee that hers might not be the only Sears store facing such a challenge. Yet to her frustration, she quickly discovered that Sears, like most companies, had no systematic way of encouraging and propagating grass roots innovation like her own.

In the absence of an explicit process for building and managing an innovation portfolio, local experiments, even when successful, are unlikely to become company-wide programs. Just as bad, small ideas, like teaching customers how to use a sewing machine, that don't get shared and discussed never get the chance to become big ideas, like developing an entire portfolio of training programs focused on everything from kitchen remodeling to assembling a home entertainment system.

This is why companies must create opportunities for the advocates of nonlinear innovation to be heard and a way of cataloging radical, innovative ideas. One can easily imagine a number of things a company might do to help fill out its portfolio of ideas.

○ Appoint several business development officers (BDOs) to serve as advisors to prospective entrepreneurs. Rather than schmoozing with investment bankers, the BDOs would get rewarded for finding and nurturing internal innovation.
○ Ask each member of the executive committee to spend a couple days every month coaching eager, young entrepreneurs drawn from the far reaches of the organization. Each member of the executive committee would be asked to sponsor at least one new idea every quarter.
○ Put an "innovation" button on your company's internal home page. Anyone who clicks on it would find a simple form that

would allow them to post their idea in a corporation-wide, virtual "Ideaspace."

Or, if you're willing to be a bit bolder, you might want to try the following. Create an internal competition for bright new ideas, perhaps offering it to every branch, region or office. Use a peer review panel to determine which projects get an initial dose of funding. Make it easy for volunteer teams to coalesce around nascent experiments by widely publicizing the list of such projects. Set up a 30-day dash where the goal is to flesh out the basic idea and design an experiment that could be used to refine and validate the original idea. At the end of the 30-day period, run the ideas through a second peer review process to decide which get to advance to the experiment stage. In my experience, this is a surer way to transform a hide-bound company than incubators, mega-deals or top-down strategic planning.

Of course, none of this obviates the need to first train people in the basics of radical innovation and successful activism.

A PORTFOLIO OF EXPERIMENTS

Ideas that have great upsides, offer the chance for increasing returns, and are sponsored by truly passionate advocates get moved into the portfolio of experiments. Ideas that fail these tests get kicked out of the portfolio or are held back for further development as ideas. The portfolio of experiments contains ideas that have been worked into reasonably coherent versions of a business concept. They are ideas that have begun to attract a constituency.

Few companies make it easy for the advocates of radical innovation to attract sponsors and team members with complementary skills. Why not, for example, let internal innovators post banner ads on the company's intranet as a way of attracting talent and resources? Moreover, most companies don't have an explicit and legitimate designation for experimental-stage businesses or for radical but underdeveloped ideas that could dramatically transform the core business.

Indeed, many large companies have a bias against small experiments. They believe you have to do something BIG to make a noticeable impact on the top line. A typical objection goes something like this: "Sure, we can start a bunch of small experiments, but you have to understand we're a $20 billion company. It takes something pretty big to make a material difference to our shareholders." This helps explain the preference for mega-mergers and bet-the-company investments. Yet the real problem is that senior management too often can't see an oak tree in an acorn. They need to consider, for a moment, the current market capitalization of eBay, Dell, The Home Depot or Southwest Airlines and then ask themselves, How big were these companies a decade or two ago? Take a walk through a forest strewn with acorns—can you pick out which ones will grow into oak trees? Neither can I. And neither can even the most vaunted CEO. In the age of revolution, the challenge isn't finding that one enormous mega-deal but planting enough acorns to raise the chances of getting an oak tree. Yeah, you can go find an oak tree, uproot it and try to replant it, but this is a difficult and risky proposition, as any CEO who's ever tried to integrate a large acquisition will tell you. It's the innovation portfolio a CEO needs to worry about, not the queue of investment bankers panting outside the door.

For every 1,000 ideas, perhaps one in ten will have enough merit to be turned into an experiment. So after you've asked yourself whether your company has a portfolio of 1,000 ideas, ask yourself if your organization has a portfolio of 100 ongoing experiments. If it doesn't, and it's a sizable organization, its future is at risk.

A portfolio of new-rules experiments should cover the discontinuities most likely to upend current business models as well as those most likely to spawn entirely new opportunities. For example, a maker of mobile phones in the late 1990s would have wanted to have a few experiments focused on the mobile telephone as a replacement for fixed-line services in large corporations. It would have focused other experiments on the cell phone as a chic fashion accessory or as a requisite in every student's backpack. Other experiments would have addressed the convergence of voice and data and the wireless phone as a way to surf the Net. Others might have explored the convergence of the phone with online games. Yet another set of experiments would have focused on using wireless technology to build a communications capability into everything from household appliances to car engines.

Capital One, an enormously successful issuer of credit cards, has taken the idea of experimentation to an extreme. George Overholser, Senior Vice President of New Business Development at Capital One, told *Esquire* magazine, "We run thirty thousand tests a year, and they all compete against each other on the basis of economic results." *Esquire's* Ted C. Fishman expands on the story:

All the big players in the credit business run tests, of course, but Capital One's mania for them is unique. The tests take almost limitless forms, each with some rejiggering of components such as interest rates, quantities of cards, fees and so-called affinity groups—like classic-rock fans. The vast majority of experiments fail, but the ones that hit, hit very big. One of the company's early innovations—allowing customers to transfer balances from one card to another—put Capital One on the map and forced the rest of the industry to play catch-up. The company is in its sixth year of showing 20 percent earnings growth per share and a 20 percent return on equity. Only ten other publicly traded U.S. companies compare.[3]

At Capital One, just about any employee can suggest a new idea. Again, listen to Overholser, "... individuals within Capital One are reporting to an idea they've created, not to their manager ... their job is not necessarily to tell their boss about it, but to find the best host for it at any given time."[4] Now, not every company can afford to conduct 30,000 experiments in a year—it's a bit easier to do a small direct mail test of a new credit card offering than it is to test a new automobile concept. Yet the principle still applies—to survive in a highly discontinuous world, every company must become capable of conducting low-cost, low-risk experiments on a broad front.
MOST EXPERIMENTS WON'T PAY OFF. BUT THIS HARDLY MEANS THEY ARE WORTHLESS. After all, your fire insurance wasn't a bad investment last year, even if your house didn't burn down. A business concept that gets killed rather than scaled up isn't a dead loss. Every experiment produces learning, which, if captured and shared, can help a company increase the odds that the next radical idea finds its mark.

A PORTFOLIO OF VENTURES

At the experimentation stage, the goal is to identify and reduce market and technology risk: Does the business concept generate sufficient customer interest? Is it technically feasible? If there's sufficient upside, and no insurmountable technical hurdles, the idea advances to the venture stage. At the venture stage learning focuses on the feasibility of the profit model and the operating model, as opposed to the business concept itself. The question is not whether the business concept will create new revenue streams, but whether they can be created economically: Can we manage the execution risk? Can we avoid the competitive risk that our innovation will be quickly imitated?

This is also the stage where one begins a serious search for strategic partners who will share risks and contribute complementary skills. There are three primary factors to consider when deciding whether to partner and how many partners to have:

- O Financial commitments: If scaling requires large, irrevocable financial commitments, partners may be needed.
- O Range of skills or assets required: If a company doesn't have all the critical skills in-house, it will need partners.
- O Size of the strategic window: If the risk of preemption is high, partners may be needed to help accelerate market penetration.

At this point, it may well be that the original sponsors have to give way to venture leaders with business-building experience. With the quality of the business concept already validated, it is the quality of the venture team that becomes critical.

This is also the stage where decisions must be made about whether to reintegrate the innovation into a line unit, set it up as a stand-alone business, license the intellectual property to another company or spin the venture off as an independent entity. At least four criteria are key to this decision:

- O The *fit* between the venture and the company's long-term strategic goals. If a venture is clearly tangential to a company's long-term aspirations, it should be spun off in order to conserve management's time for projects that are more congruent with long-term ambitions. If the venture is not spun off, it probably won't get the love and attention it needs to reach its potential.
- O The venture's *dependence on firm assets and competencies*. If a venture could benefit enormously from leveraging existing assets and competencies, it probably should not be spun off. If it is spun off, it should be given preferential access to those competencies and assets.
- O The possibility that the venture will be *a platform for other ventures*. Some ventures are ends in themselves; others are stepping-stones to other ventures. If a venture promises to open up a broad new opportunity arena, that may be a reason to keep it inside.
- O The potential for the venture to *dramatically outperform other businesses* in the portfolio. Increasingly companies are spinning off ventures that might be undervalued by Wall Street were they to be imprisoned inside a company with otherwise mediocre performance.

Clearly, some ventures will lack a tight fit with the company's long-term goals, will be only partly dependent on the company's existing assets and competencies, and won't be a gateway to a vast array of new opportunities. Hence we shouldn't be surprised if some of the ventures end up as spin-offs or licensing deals, rather than as new business units or transformation projects within existing business units.

Spinning a business off is easy—giving it sufficient independence to grow, while at the same time helping it leverage well-honed competencies, is a much more delicate balancing act. Reintegration is more subtle still. A company that embraces the new innovation agenda should expect to create, as Shell has done, dozens of game-changing ventures that need to be reintegrated into existing businesses—a radical new pricing approach here, an unconventional distribution model over there, and so on. At Cemex, most of the projects identified by the innovation platform teams were reintegrated back into the operating units. The fact that the innovation board, staffed by senior executives, continued to review the transformation projects, even once they had been reintegrated, was a powerful incentive for unit managers to make sure the projects received continued funding and access to talent.

So while high-potential ventures based on entirely new business concepts should probably be nurtured in a new business incubator, successful ventures with the power to transform the core business should be "spun up" inside those businesses. Simply, there is no single mechanism for going from a venture to a business. Most of Cemex's innovations have been spin-ups rather than spin-offs, reinforcing and reinventing Cemex's core cement business. In contrast, GE Capital's popcorn stand experiments often end up as new business units.

Let's recap. To go from a possibility to an experiment, an idea must be able to be described as a reasonably coherent business concept—with an attractive value proposition, a credible story around wealth creation potential and a clear sense of how the various components of the business concept will fit together and be mutually reinforcing. For an experiment to become a venture, it must have elicited genuine customer enthusiasm and be technically feasible (at least on a small scale). For a venture to move out of the innovation portfolio and become a business, or be spun up inside an existing business, there must be a sound profit model and evidence that the business concept can be scaled up.

Now take a detailed look at your company's various innovation portfolios. How many ideas does your company have in its innovation bank? Do you have thousands? How many rule-bashing experiments

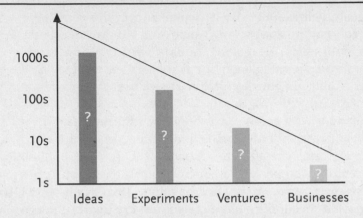

are being conducted across your company right now? Do you have hundreds? How many new ventures are being nurtured right now? Do you have dozens? And how many big new businesses are being built right now? Can you think of even one or two?

Map the size of each portfolio (see the graph "Mapping Your Innovation Portfolios"), and it will be immediately clear whether or not your company is investing in enough options on the future. Turn the diagram 90 degrees to the right, and you have a funnel. If a company hasn't learned how to fill the top of the funnel, it won't get much out the bottom. To return to our earlier analogy, you have to ask yourself, What's my company's sperm count? You don't get a terrific new business without hundreds of dumb ideas, failed experiments and aborted ventures.

GETTING YOUR TIMING RIGHT

Perhaps the most critical issue in scaling up a venture is the issue of timing—this is true whether the venture is focused on an entirely new business, or some major modification (a new channel, a dramatically altered value proposition, etc.) of an existing business. As every student of business knows, too much too soon, or too little too late can destroy an otherwise sterling opportunity.

At the height of dot–com mania, "first mover advantage" was a near-sacred mantra for VCs and entrepreneurs alike. Indeed, e–commerce zealots argued that early success would compound even more quick-ly on the Web than in the dawdling "old economy"—this due to the multiplicative impact of the "network effect." Being first to build a con-sumer brand in a new category (Amazon), invent a new business model (eBay) or achieve critical mass (what WebVan was hoping to do) were seen as sure-fire routes to Midas-like profits.

In reality, of course, first-mover advantages proved elusive. For most dot-com start-ups, being first was simply a way to lose more, faster. As a result, many pundits argued that the Net spawned *too much* innovation and that being a "fast follower" was often a better strategy than trying to lead from the front. After all, the argument goes, pioneers often end up with arrows in their backs. Big company CEOs, eager to avoid the hard work of strategic innovation, seized upon this diagnosis as justification for their instinctive fear of novelty. Suddenly, timidity was once again in fashion and incrementalism, a.k.a. "getting back to basics," was heralded as a virtue. Yet the conclusions which seem to justify these reactionary tendencies are every bit as superficial as the simple-minded adage which they challenge. Most Internet companies failed not because they were *first* movers, but because they were *dumb* movers. What companies should learn from the Internet debacle is not that being first is a dangerous form of hubris, but that being dumb seldom succeeds. When it comes to trailblazing, there are at least three ways to be a dumb mover—none of which are unique to Internet start-ups.

DUMB: MISTAKING A MARATHON FOR A SPRINT, OR VICE VERSA

Building a first-mover advantage requires impeccable timing. If a company invests faster than it learns, it will "overdrive" the opportunity and end up with an expensive and embarrassing failure. This is the fate that befell Apple's pioneering handheld computer, the Newton. Was there a potential market out there for "palm" computers? Absolutely. Could investment and marketing hype alone force the market to develop on Apple's time frame? No way. Companies that overdrive an emerging opportunity early on, often "underdrive" it later. The initial performance gap, a product of unrealistic expectations and overinvestment, produces a rapid retrenchment. In this way, overcommitment leads to undercomment. If the original vision was directionally correct, this de-commitment provides an opening for latecomers.

There is an optimally feasible market penetration curve for every emerging opportunity. This curve describes what is possible in terms of market penetration over time. Typically, the curve has an inflection point—a moment in time when all the pieces of the business model finally fall into place, when customer demand explodes, and the market takes off. The curve for videocassette recorders was long, beginning with an abortive effort by Ampex to produce a consumer video tape recorder in the mid–60s. The curve began to slope gently upward with the launch of Matsushita's VHS format in the late '70s, and it would take another seven years for VCRs to find their way into one million American homes. In contrast, the market penetration curve for Hotmail was a near vertical line, with more than 10 million users signing up in the first 18 months. Matsushita, which started working on a VCR in the 1960s, ran a marathon. Hotmail ran a sprint. The Apple Newton might have evolved into something Palm–like, but only if Apple had better paced itself by spending less, learning faster, and iterating more quickly. Apple blew the handheld opportunity not because it was the first mover, but because it was a dumb mover.

Any management team that aspires to be a first mover must ask itself, what race are we running: sprint or marathon. If you try to run a 100–yard sprint like a marathon, you'll get beat. If you try to run a marathon like a 100–yard sprint, you'll quickly keel over from exhaustion. For this reason, it is critically important to correctly estimate the general shape of the market penetration curve. To make this assessment, a number of questions have to be answered: How significant are the remaining technical hurdles? Does market take–off depend on the development of complementary products or services? Will a new infrastructure be required? Will customers need to learn new skills or adopt new behaviors? Are there high switching costs for customers? Will competing standards confuse customers and delay adoption? Does success depend on aligning the interests of diverse constituents? Are there powerful competitors who will seek to delay or derail us? If the answer to any of these questions is "yes," a company must be careful not to pour in too many resources too soon. This is going to be a marathon. (Think the wireless Internet, streaming video or industry–wide B2B hubs.) Other questions to consider include: Are the customer benefits clear and substantial? Are there potential network effects that will accelerate take–off? Are there powerful competitors who will be compelled to follow us? If the answer to these questions is yes, you'll need to sprint out of the starting blocks. (Think eBay in online auctions or BEA Systems, a pioneer in the market for application servers.)

The shape of the market penetration curve for a new product or business is largely determined by factors outside a company's direct control. All the money in the world won't force a market to develop faster if there are structural impediments that stand in the way of a quick take–off. Conversely, if a company gets behind the optimal penetration curve, all the money in the world may not let it catch up— unless, of course, the company is Microsoft and it actually *has* all the money in the world, or unless some technology discontinuity gives latecomers an opening. Staying on the optimal penetration curve is a neat trick, but it's not impossible. Intuit (Quicken), AOL and Sun Microsystems are companies that have demonstrated a great sense of timing, getting out in front on new product and service curves, but not getting *too* far out in front. There are a bunch of things a company can do to ensure it neither overdrives nor underdrives an emerging opportunity: Build an infrastructure that is easily scaleable, constantly review initial assumptions about product and business design, make sure that premium pricing and a narrow market definition doesn't create a pool of pent-up demand that can be easily drained by latecomers, move quickly to collaborate with would-be competitors, shorten the cycle time for product iterations and use outsourcing to improve flexibility. Like first-time tennis players, dumb movers have a hard time getting their swing in synch with a moving target. Smart movers have Venus Williams's perfect pace and timing.

DUMBER: OVER-PAYING
FOR MARKET SHARE

The allure of capturing a first-mover advantage often produces a spending orgy among a gaggle of look-alike competitors each intent on ramping up faster than its rivals. This is exactly what happened in many areas of e-commerce and in the race to encircle the globe with optical fiber. It's hard to be first when a horde of similarly minded competitors are making tit-for-tat investors. In such cases, it's easy to overpay for market share, particularly when investment funds are eager to come buy.

To reap a first-mover advantage, a company must buy market share at a discount, that is, it must be able to buy a big chunk of market share before its competitors figure out just how much that market share will yield in future profits. This is possible only if a company possesses a unique strategic insight—one not shared by less imaginative or more orthodox competitors. To be first, a company must start with a business idea that is truly revolutionary, as did eBay and ICQ (the instant messaging pioneer). Think of it this way. If you're the only one with a treasure map, you can easily justify the cost of the expedition to recover the hidden bounty. But if the map is widely available, and a teeming throng sets out at roughly the same time in search of the same treasure, the odds of grabbing the loot decline precipitously, and the expected value of one's reward quickly sinks below the cost of the journey. Of course this simple arithmetic was no more effective in deterring investors from backing hundreds of me–too Web–based business models than it was in dissuading otherwise sane individuals from joining the California gold rush of 1849.

The fact is, the Internet didn't produce too *much* in the way of authentic business model innovation, but too *little*. The moral is simple: If you want to profit from a first–mover advantage, you better make sure you start with an idea that is truly unique and, at least initially, unattractive to would–be competitors or protected by a wall of patents. Dumb movers swarm, smart movers take the road less traveled.

DUMBEST: BEING FIRST WITH A BUSINESS MODEL THAT'S DEAD-ON-ARRIVAL

Pets.com. Iridium. WebVan. XFL. NorthPoint. Global Crossing. Many business models are brain dead from the get–go. They breathe as long as they are hooked up to the ventilator of investor funds, but expire the moment investors swallow their grief and pull the plug. There are two fundamental flaws that can render a business model DOA: a complete misread of the customer (does she really want to order dog food online), and/or utterly unsound economics (there will never be enough petroleum geologists and arctic explorers to make satellite telephony pay). There's no advantage in being first if the destination ain't worth the trip. Of course, the pioneers will tell you that "the market wasn't ready." But this is usually nothing more than exculpatory baloney. It was the business model that "wasn't ready."

Being first is no substitute for sound business thinking, and a stupid idea that fails is hardly an indictment of the general concept of first–mover advantage. So think twice before you let someone else's idiocy lull you into believing that being first is always a peril–strewn path. Ask Andy Grove if he is glad that Intel got an early lead in microprocessors, or Herb Kelleher at Southwest Airlines (discount air travel), or Pete Kight at CheckFree (online billing and payment).

I don't believe any company should set out to be a follower, fast or otherwise. Sure, in hindsight, first movers often look dumb, but it would be imprudent to bet that they will always screw up. Indeed, when you look beyond the weirdness of the Internet bubble, and consider companies with high–quality management, deep pockets and real competencies, you find that being first pays off a surprisingly high percentage of the time. So before you bet against the first mover, you'd be wise to ask yourself: Is the first mover a slow learner? Is market penetration still in single digits and likely to stay that way for a while?

Is the rate of technology change extremely high, creating opportunities for a leap-frog strategy? Is the product or service still significantly underdeveloped? Are there a number of potential partners who are still unallied? If you can answer yes to all these questions, then you may want to keep your powder dry.

Instead of betting that your competitors are stupid, learn how to be a smart mover! Face up to the fact that a new business idea can be exhilarating and apparently compelling and yet completely wrong-headed. Don't let enthusiasm get in the way of deep thinking. If you're going to invest, make sure you're starting with a unique insight—a truly revolutionary strategy. And then work hard to keep your financial commitments in synch with the underlying pace of market development. Smart movers don't bet the company—they just learn a little bit faster, while spending a little bit less, than their competitors.

In the end, the distinction between first mover and fast follower hides more than it reveals. The goal, after all, is not to be first to market in some absolute sense, but to be first to put together the precise combination of features, value and sound business economics that unlocks a profitable new market. Sometimes this is the first mover, and sometimes it is not. But it's always the *smart* mover.

FROM RADICAL INNOVATION TO CORPORATE STRATEGY

So where does all this leave corporate strategy? Indeed, where does it leave the very concept of a "corporation"? In the age of revolution, will corporate strategy be anything more than the sum of a few dozen, or a few hundred, loosely connected experiments and ventures? Will companies be anything more than a set of bottom-up projects united by shared overhead? Will some combination of internal markets, de-verticalization, value networks, and self-organizing teams reduce the notion of a corporation to disembodied bits of intellectual property floating free in some kind of virtual innovation network? While all these things will undoubtedly make companies less monolithic, they are not going to remove the need for an overarching strategy, nor are they going to entirely do away with the benefits of size and scale.

SIZE STILL MATTERS

A lot of young entrepreneurs learned a painful lesson in the last few years: Size still matters. Sure, incumbency isn't worth as much as it used to be, but it's still worth something. The companies that survive that dot-com shakeout aren't going to be will-o'-the-wisp, thin-as-gossamer virtual companies. They are going to be companies like Cisco and Amazon.com—companies that have had their share of ups and downs, but have never lost sight of the fact that scale matters. Most Silicon Valley start-ups fail to capture the full benefits of scale and scope. These companies end up as acquisition fodder for companies that have. Mirabilis, Broadcast.com, Netscape and hundreds of other Internet start-ups have already been swallowed up. Hundreds more have simply folded.

Of course it is not size, per se, that counts. Size is the first-order derivative of profit boosters that rely on increasing returns, network effects, learning effects and economies of scale and scope. Exploit these, and a company will inevitably grow, and smaller, me-too competitors will begin disappearing out the rearview window.

A few years ago, many among the digerati were predicting the collapse of large-scale enterprises. They end wrong. **Size will always matter.** Indeed, at the end of 1999, in the midst of the dot-com craze, 32 companies accounted for half the market capitalization of the S&P 500. An oft-used analogy is the movie industry, where teams of writers, producers, directors and actors coalesce around a project and then disband when the film is completed. Yet the most enduring fact of the movie business has been the power of the big studios. They are repositories for an enormous amount of project management wisdom. Despite the occasional "duds," they are skilled story editors, and they have the global reach necessary to market films around the world. Indeed, as every European cultural minister knows, it is the studios that have given Hollywood its global hegemony in the film business. You don't hear Italian or French filmmakers complaining that their colleagues aren't creative enough; you hear them complaining that they can't match the size and scale of American studios. Of course a market of 250 million customers helps, but a market of this size is of no particular advantage unless there are economies of scale in serving such a market.

It is interesting to note that even highly fluid, project-based companies such as Bechtel, Accenture and Schlumberger are far, far more than a collection of individual projects. If that were all they were, they wouldn't be multibillion-dollar enterprises. So, yes, companies may become more like film studios, relying on free agents, raising outside funding for each new venture and creating short-lived project teams. But somewhere in this brave, new model, size and scale will still matter—because if they don't, you're back to frictionless capitalism where no one has an incentive to invest in something new. On average, companies may shrink. After all, scale and scope advantages apply to activities, not companies per se. But size will be far from irrelevant in the age of revolution.

Indeed, without scale and scope advantages, it is difficult to imagine how a company can enjoy the fruits of radical innovation. Of course when a hot start-up is sold, its founders get a big win. But this just shifts the problem of building scale and scope onto the acquirer—and if the acquirer fails at this, it will never recoup its investment (a common enough occurrence, by the way).

CONSISTENCY COUNTS

You can't build economies of scale and scope without consistency, without doing things over and over in a reasonably consistent way. You can't build difficult-to-imitate competencies without cumulative learning. In turn, it is impossible to achieve consistency and cumulativeness without a degree of coordination across projects or businesses. Consistency requires a set of mutually agreed upon rules about what is "in" and what is "out," what a company is and what it isn't. Lacking some overarching strategy, a company will have a vast greenhouse where thousands of shoots are pushing up through the soil but where few grow big enough to yield a substantial harvest. So **innovation is not the whole story, but it is the big story**—because most companies have already figured out the scale and scope thing and now need to start planting new seeds.

In the age of revolution, the challenge will be to marry radical innovation with disciplined execution—to merge the efficiency of a Toyota production line with the radical innovation of Silicon Valley, to blend diligence and curiosity. To be a gray-haired revolutionary, a company must be systematic and spontaneous, highly focused and opportunistic, brutally efficient and wildly imaginative.

Oil and water, chalk and cheese, such amalgams are impossible without a new synthesis. Notice that in making an argument for mass and scale, I haven't used words like hierarchy, control and plan. These are industrial-age words. Instead I talk about consistency, cumulativeness, boundaries and focus. Remember, the goal is "order without careful crafting." So where does this order come from? It must emerge from the stream of radical innovation that begins to flow once you make innovation a corporate-wide capability.

In any stream of ideas, some kind of deeper pattern will be evident.
The trick is to look for patterns, for consistency and cumulativeness
that will yield advantages of scale and scope across ideas, experiments
and ventures. Patterns come in many forms:

○ Allegiance to a standard, such as Microsoft's allegiance to the
  Windows operating system, which spawned, both within
  Microsoft and without, hundreds of small innovations built atop
  the Windows standard.
○ A widely shared core competence, such as UPS's competence in
  logistics, based on cumulative learning.
○ A set of values around a brand that can be applied broadly, as in
  the case of Virgin and Disney, and thereby yield economies of
  scope.
○ A common customer set that is best served in a coordinated way,
  which is the logic behind Amazon.com's creating a wide variety
  of "stores within a store" rather than making each store an entirely independent entity.

These patterns provide the logic for the corporation. They provide the
connective tissue that makes the company more than a collection of
stand-alone projects. While there is nothing new in saying that a company must be more than the sum of its parts, what is new is how the
summing up gets done. It can't start with some grand pronouncement
from on high about "what business we're in." It can't come from a
bunch of senior vice presidents working to craft a common mission
statement. It certainly shouldn't come as the panicked reaction to
demands from stock analysts for a strategy that will hold water.
Instead, it has to be filtered out of the stream of innovation that flows
from the fertile minds of individuals throughout the organization.

While senior executives can no longer be the sole source of new business concepts, it is their responsibility to look across the patchwork of
radical innovation to find the interesting—and wealth-laden—patterns.
One set of opportunities will push the company in one direction,
allowing it to build one kind of scope or scale advantage; another set
of opportunities will push the company in another direction, with
another set of potential synergies. While idea generation should be
unbounded, a company is compelled to make choices about where it
focuses its energies. Yet it is important that such choices do not rule

out the possibility of entirely "unscripted" innovation. That's why every company needs well-functioning markets for innovation that funnel resources to nascent ideas and propel them through the experimentation stage. But at some point the most promising experiments will need big injections of capital. It is here that senior management must begin to make choices about which patterns it wants to emphasize and which it wishes to de-emphasize.

Those choices must be based on an unimpeachable and clearly articulated logic—"We will create more wealth by exploiting this particular dimension of scale and relatedness than we will by exploiting some other dimension." Over time, these choices will begin to bias the innovation process. Again, it's not that top management declares some kinds of innovation to be out of bounds. Nothing is out of bounds. Instead, would-be revolutionaries come to understand that by exploiting shared assets and competencies or getting access to a big customer base, they gain scale and scope advantages that give their ideas added momentum. Of course those who want to go off in different directions can still do so, and there will be mechanisms—licensing, spin-offs and alliances—for capturing wealth out of ideas that don't fit within the emerging corporate strategy. Occasionally those out-of-bounds ideas will be so compelling and valuable that they will force the company to redefine the very essence of its strategy. This has been the case at GE, which no one regards any longer as an "industrial" company. In this sense, top management doesn't so much make strategy as find strategy.

Of course there are already deep patterns that determine what kinds of strategies people create in your company—I've called these patterns orthodoxies. But they are the patterns of precedent, not the patterns of possibility. So don't take any of what I've just said as an excuse to simply lock down your current definition of corporate strategy. Remember, corporate strategy must be distilled from a torrent of innovation. If you don't yet have a torrent of nonlinear business concepts and weird and wonderful experiments, that's where you need to start. Don't build a dam before you have a stream.

ARE YOU REVOLUTION-READY?

Is your organization ready for the age of revolution? Does it have an irrevocable commitment to building the components of the new innovation solution? Is its top management finished "making" strategy and ready to "find" it? To determine this, ask yourself these questions:

- ○ Have individuals been given the training and the tools they need to become business concept innovators?
- ○ Do the metrics in your company focus as much on innovation and wealth creation as on optimization and wealth conservation?
- ○ Does your IT system support a corporation-wide electronic marketplace for innovation?
- ○ Has your organization committed itself to systematically redesigning its core management processes to make them more innovation-friendly?
- ○ Does the "wheel of innovation" spin rapidly in your organization, or is it limited by the speed of quarterly and annual processes?
- ○ Do would-be entrepreneurs know how to design experiments around radical ideas?
- ○ Are there formal mechanisms for capturing and monitoring the learning from innovation experiments?
- ○ Does your organization get the very best talent behind the best new ideas, even when those ideas are at an early stage of development?
- ○ Is your organization explicitly managing a portfolio of ideas, a portfolio of experiments, and a portfolio of ventures?
- ○ Is your organization flexible enough to design the right kind of institutional home for promising ventures?
- ○ Are you confident that your company is in charge of the transformation agenda in its industry?

Don't despair if you answered "no" more often than "yes." There's not one company in a hundred that has fully committed itself to building the new innovation solution. What matters is what you're going to do next.
Are you ready to commit yourself to the new innovation agenda?

THE NEW INNOVATION AGENDA

Continuous improvement	*and*	Nonlinear innovation
Product and process innovation	*and*	Business concept innovation
"Releasing" wealth	*and*	Creating wealth
Serendipity	*and*	Capability
Visionaries	*and*	Activists
Hierarchies	*and*	Markets

Are you ready to start working on the new innovation solution? (See the figure "The Innovation Solution.")

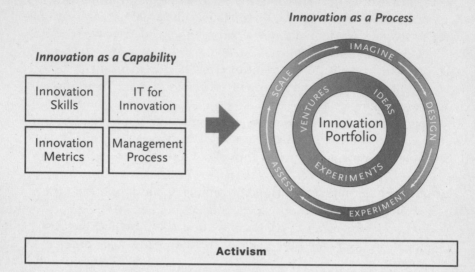

You can start now and get ahead of the curve, or wait and fight a rearguard action. What's it going to be?

ARE *YOU* A REVOLUTIONARY?

It doesn't matter whether you're the big cheese or a cubicle rat. It doesn't matter whether you fly in a Gulfstream V or ride the crosstown bus. It doesn't matter whether you command a legion of minions or only your PalmPilot. All that matters is whether you care enough to start from where you are. So ask yourself, Do you care enough about your integrity to speak the truth and challenge the little lies that jeopardize your company's future? Do you care enough about the future to argue with precedent and stick a thumb in the eye of tradition? Do you care enough about your colleagues to help them get off the treadmill of progress? Do you care so much about the magnificent difference you can make in this world that you're willing to try and change it with your bare heart? Do you care enough about finding meaning and significance in the 80 percent of your life you devote to work that you're ready to start a movement within your company? Do you care enough about the creative impulse that resides in every human breast that you're ready to help everyone be a revolutionary? Do you care enough about doing something so wonderful and unexpected for customers that you're willing to put your comfy job on the line? Go ahead, ask yourself, Do you care enough to lead the revolution?

I began this book with a simple observation—that for the first time in history our heritage is no longer our destiny. Our dreams are no longer fantasies, but possibilities. There isn't a human being who has ever lived who wouldn't want to be alive right now, at this moment so pregnant with promise. Among all your forebears, among the countless generations who had no hope of progress, among all those whose spirits were betrayed by progress, you are the one who now stands on the threshold of a new age—the age of revolution. You are blessed beyond belief. Don't falter. Don't hesitate. You were given this opportunity for a reason. Find it. Lead the revolution.

○ NOTES

1 THE END OF PROGRESS

1 Patricia Sellers, "Who's in Charge Here?" *Fortune*, 24 December 2001, 79.
2 "Competition 2000," an unpublished survey sponsored by MCI and carried out by The Gallup Organization.
3 "P&G to Slash 15,000 Jobs, Shut 10 Plants," *Wall Street Journal*, 10 June 1999.
4 "ConAgra Products," <www.conagra.com/product.html>.
5 Susan Moran, "The Candyman," *Business 2.0*, June 1999, 66–67.

2 FACING UP TO STRATEGY DECAY

1 Nikhil Deogun and Steven Lipin, "When the Big Deal Turns Bad," *Wall Street Journal*, 8 December 1999.
2 "Addicted to Mergers?" *Business Week*, 6 December 1999, 85.
3 Strategos calculations.
4 Tish Williams, "WorldCom's Big Bluffer," *Upside Today*, 14 July 1999, ,www.upside.com/texis/mvm/daily_tish?id37649f420.
5 Richard Waters, "Shape-up for long distance telecoms," *Financial Times*, 7 June 2001, 22.
6 Martin Brookes and Zaki Wahhaj, "Is the Internet Better Than Electricity," Global Economics Paper No. 49, Goldman Sachs.
7 Jolie Solomon, "When Cool Goes Cold," *Newsweek*, 30 March 1998, 37.
8 John Markoff, "Silicon Valley Accelerates to Web Speed," *International Herald Tribune*, 4 June 1996.
9 *Primetime Network Ratings and Shares*, Nielsen Media Research, 2000.
10 Bill Carter, "As Their Dominance Erodes, Networks Plan Big Changes," *New York Times*, 11 May 1978.

3 BUSINESS CONCEPT INNOVATION

1 Marianne Wilson, "Say Chic—C'est Sephora," *Chain Store Age*, July 1998, 134.
2 Neal Templin, "Electronic Kiosk Checks in Guests at More Hotels," *Wall Street Journal*, 16 February 1999.
3 "Interview: Gordon Moore, Intel," *PC Magazine*, 25 March 1997, 236.
4 United Rentals, <www.unitedrentals.com> (23 August 1999).
5 Michael A. Hiltzik, *Dealers of Lightning: Xerox PARC and the Dawn of the Computer Age* (New York: HarperBusiness, 1999).

4 BE YOUR OWN SEER

1 "Garbage In, Garbage Out," *The Economist*, 3 June 1995, 70.
2 Fara Warner and Joseph B. White, "New From Japan: Bar Stools on Wheels," *Wall Street Journal*, 25 October 1999.
3 Michael Kavanagh, "Porn Will Continue to Dominate Web Revenue," *Marketing Week*, 27 May 1999, 43.
4 These distinctions are adapted and reprinted from *European Management Journal*, volume 13, Georg von Krogh and Johan Roos, "Conversation Management," page 393, copyright 1995, with permission from Elsevier Science.

5 CORPORATE REBELS

1 Debra E. Meyerson and Maureen A. Scully, "Tempered Radicalism and the Politics of Ambivalence and Change," *Organizational Science* 6, no. 5 (September–October 1995): 585–600.
2 Robert A. Guth, "Inside Sony's Trojan Horse," *Wall Street Journal*, 25 February 2000.

6 GO AHEAD! REVOLT!

1 Saul D. Alinsky, *Rules for Radicals: A Practical Primer for Realistic Radicals* (New York: Vintage Books, 1989).
2 Mary Beth Rogers, *Cold Anger: A Story of Faith and Power Politics* (Denton, TX: University of North Texas Press, 1990), 88.

8 DESIGN RULES FOR INNOVATION

1 M. Mitchell Waldrop, *Complexity: The Emerging Science at the Edge of Order and Chaos* (New York: Simon & Schuster, 1992), 241, 242.
2 Writing for MIT's *Technology Review*, Michael Schrage was quoted in the University of Phoenix's 2001 Annual Report.
3 Viktor E. Frankl, *Man's Search for Meaning* (New York: Pocket Books, 1984), 17.
4 Tim Stevens, "Breaking Up Is Profitable Too," *Industry Week*, 21 June 1999, 28–34.

9 THE NEW INNOVATION SOLUTION

1 Steve Kerr, "On the Folly of Rewarding A, While Hoping for B," *Academy of Management Journal* 18 (December 1975): 769–783.
2 mindstorms.lego.com/forums/default.asp.
3 Ted C. Fishman, "Disruption, Subversion, Disorder, Yes!" *Esquire*, October 2000.
4 "Simulation and the Venture Capital Business," an unpublished paper by George Overholser, Josh Epstein, and Rob Axtell.

○ INDEX

Boston Scientific Corp., 108
boundaries, 73, 97–99, 221;
    pushing, 247, 257, 318;
    spanning teams, 280
BP, 42
Brady, Sarah, 155
BrainReserve, 134, 137
brand appeal, declining, 8
Branson, Sir Richard, 82, 249, 266, 278
breakeven, 116
British Telecom, 5
"broadband," vii, 109
Broadcast.com, 317
broad recommendations, 193–94
Brookes, Martin, 51, 52
Brown, John Seely, 138, 145
Brown, Linda Carol, 155
building industry, 80–81, 242–45
build-to-order model, 46, 80
Burger King, 15, 93
business concept: blind spots in, 73, 75;
    network effect and, 104
business concept innovation, x, 59–118, 286;
    alignment as enemy of, 154;
    becoming innovator and, 117–18;
    competitors and, 72;
    creating space for, 153–58;
    cyber B-school as, 65–69;
    defined, 61–65, 69–73;
    employees and, 288;
    goals of, 64–65, 69–70;
    investing in, 285–87;
    management processes and, 297–99
    systemizing, 287–88;
    unpacking business model and, 73–117;
    wheel of innovation and, 299
business definition, elastic, 256–58
business development officers (BDOs), 305
business mission, 74–75
business model(s), 73–118;
    bridge components, 73, 81–83, 91–93, 97–99;
    as built-in monopolies, 103;
    core components, 73, 74–81, 83–91, 93–97;
    creative accounting and, 41;
    dead-on-arrival, 315–16;
    decay of, 154;
    efficiency and, 74, 99;
    fit and, 74, 99, 101–2;
    four distinct, 153;
    increasing returns and, 104–6;
    Internet and, 4;
    learning effects and, 105–6;
    new, 69, 72;
    profit boosters and, 74, 99–117;

pushing boundaries of, 257–58;
    rethinking, 117–18;
    strategy convergence and, 46–47;
    strategy decay and, 36, 37;
    uniqueness and, 74, 99;
    wealth potential and, 74, 99–117
business plan, 268
business process improvement, 24–25
business schools, cyber, 65–69
business-to-business hubs and exchanges, 96
Butterfield & Butterfield, 10
buyback champs, 40
Buy.com, 100
buyers, 53

cable television companies, 47, 56, 109, 274
Cable & Wireless, 247
call centers, outsourcing, 220
Calloway, 128
Cambridge University, 103
Canadair, 10
Canavino, Jim, 162
cannibalization, 125, 200, 222, 228, 260
Canon, 62
capability, 20–24, 287–88, 290
capital: budgeting, 65, 268, 298;
    market for, 266–69;
    spending, boom in, 33
capitalism, 5
Capital One, 307
Carrefour, 96
Casey, Jim, 220
catalysts, 200
category killers, 8, 52, 127
Caterpillar, 79, 286
cause, business as, 259–61
cellular division, 278–79
cellular telephone business, 6–7, 15, 94, 170, 212, 307
cement industry, 230–47, 248
Cemex, 26, 58, 125, 211, 212, 230–47, 250, 255, 260, 262, 263, 267, 280, 281, 302, 310;
    Capital, 244;
    Dynamic Synchronization of Operations (DSO), 238;
    Key Value Creators group, 239
Centex, 35
CEOs, 12, 21, 43, 44
chain of consequences, 133–34
Chambers, John, 45
Champion, 44
change, ix–x, 45, 138, 155, 222, 287;
    abrupt, 5–7, 11–13;
    knowing what's not, 134–35;
    rates of, 126–28
Charles Schwab, 8, 26, 38, 211–12, 222–30, 250, 254, 256, 258–60, 301

Iñiguez, Gelacio, 232–33, 237–38, 242
innovation, radical, vii–xi, 5, 13–20,
    225–27, 242–46;
    button on home page, 305–6;
    capability, viii, xi, 23–24, 281–82,
        287;
    as corporate strategy, viii, 316–20;
    connectivity and, 280–81;
    contrarianism and, 122;
    creating time and space for, 247;
    design rules for, 251–82;
    expanding horizon, 64;
    growth vs., 38;
    investment in, 287;
    latent imagination in, 287;
    low-risk, 18;
    market for, 264–73, 320;
    meritocracy and, 230;
    optimization and, 24–29;
    precedent vs., 28;
    product-focused innovation vs., 62–65;
    return on, 287–88;
    seeing and being different and, 124–26;
    shaking foundations and, 286–87;
    size and, 44;
    smart vs. dumb, x;
    strategy convergence and, 48–49;
    suppliers and, 93–94;
    wheel of, 299–302. *See also* business
        concept innovation
innovation editor, 295
innovation ghettoes, 304
"Innovation Lab," 271
innovation pipeline, 296–97, 304
innovation portfolio, 302–11
innovation risk, 17
innovation solution, 283–323;
    customers and, 301–2;
    information technology, 295–96;
    innovation wheel and, 299–300;
    management processes and, 296–99;
    metrics and, 291–95; skills and, 289–90
instant messaging, 50, 54, 62, 269, 314
insurance companies, 45, 52, 57, 89–90
insurrection, 190–206;
    coalition and, 195–97;
    co-opting and neutralizing and, 199–201;
    isolate, infiltrate, integrate and, 203–5;
    manifesto and, 192–95;
    point of view and, 190–92;
    targets and moments and, 197–99;
    translator and, 201–2;
    winning small, early, and often and,
        202–3. *See also* activism; corporate
        rebels
integration, 7, 36, 203–5, 244
Intel, 51, 64, 95, 97, 103, 111, 158, 203,
    315;
    64 fund, 248–49
intellectual authority, 195

intellectual capital, 27
International Data Corporation, 147
International Paper, 44
International Space Station, 10
Internet Protocol (IP), 109–10
Internet (Web), 4–6, 52, 69, 133, 135,
    315;
    customer interface and, 83;
    IBM and, 28, 159–70, 191, 202;
    distribution model, 16;
    pioneers, 50;
    portals, 7, 107;
    Schwab and, 223, 226–30;
    start-ups, 38;
    strategy conversion and, 51–55
intranets, 27
Intuit, 314
iPhoto, 84–85
Iridium, 17, 315
isolation, 133, 203
Is the Internet Better than Electricity (Brookes
    and Wahhaj), 51–52
Itanium architecture, 248
Ives, Jonathan, 76

Jacobs, Brad, 112
Japan, 9, 37, 116, 127
Java, 269
JCPenney, 8, 19, 47, 293
jet engine industry, 90
Jobs, Steve, vii, 21
Johnson & Johnson, 108, 248
J.P. Morgan, 42
J Sainsbury plc, 96
Juran, 24
Jurvetson, Steve, 267
JVC, 64

kaizen, 13
Kasparov, Garry, 166
Kay, Alan, 125, 140–41
KB Toys, 8
Kelleher, Herb, 315
Kellogg, 53
Kelly, Florence, 155
Khrushchev, 206
Kight, Pete, 315
"killer app" models, 4, 22
King, Martin Luther, 27, 155, 195
Kmart, 7, 17, 211, 293
Knight, Phil, 262
knowledge: accumulation, 105–6;
    arbitrage, 53, 132;
    economy, 261;
    management, 13
Kodak, 7, 62
Kohl's, 19, 47
Kohnstamm, Abby, 160
Koslowski, Dennis, 45
Kovacevich, Richard, 146–47

○ ABOUT THE AUTHOR

Gary Hamel is a Founder and Chairman of Strategos, a company dedicated to helping its clients develop revolutionary strategies. He is also Visiting Professor of Strategic and International Management at London Business School.

The Economist calls Hamel "the world's reigning strategy guru." Peter Senge calls him "the most influential thinker on strategy in the Western world." As the author of a multitude of landmark business concepts, he has fundamentally changed the focus and content of strategy in many of the world's most successful companies. The *Journal of Business Strategy* recently ranked Professor Hamel as one of the top 25 business minds of the twentieth century.

His previous book, *Competing for the Future*, has been hailed by *The Economist*, the *Financial Times*, the *Washington Post*, and many other journals as one of the decade's most influential business books, and by *Business Week* as "Best Management Book of the Year." With C. K. Prahalad, Hamel has published seven articles in the *Harvard Business Review*, introducing such breakthrough concepts as strategic intent, core competence, corporate imagination, expeditionary marketing, and strategy as stretch. Hamel's more recent articles, "Strategy as Revolution" and "Bringing Silicon Valley Inside," are already on their way to becoming management classics. His articles have also been published in *Fortune*, the *Wall Street Journal*, MIT's *Sloan Management Review*, and a myriad of other journals. Hamel serves on the board of the Strategic Management Society.

Hamel has led initiatives within many of the world's leading companies. In his work he helps companies to first imagine and then create the new rules, new businesses, and new industries that will define the industrial landscape of the future.

He resides in Woodside, California.